Applications of the Unified Protocol for Transdiagnostic Treatment of Emotional Disorders

ABCT Clinical Practice Series

Series Editor

Susan W. White, Ph.D., ABPP, Associate Professor, Department of Psychology, Virginia Tech

Associate Editors

Lara J. Farrell, Ph.D., Associate Professor, School of Applied Psychology, Griffith University & Menzies Health Institute of Queensland, Australia

Matthew A. Jarrett, Ph.D., Associate Professor, Department of Psychology, University of Alabama

Jordana Muroff, Ph.D., LICSW, Associate Professor, Clinical Practice, Boston University School of Social Work

Marisol Perez, Ph.D., Associate Professor & Associate Chair, Department of Psychology, Arizona State University

Titles in the Series

Applications of the Unified Protocol for Transdiagnostic Treatment of Emotional Disorders
Edited by David H. Barlow and Todd J. Farchione

Forthcoming title in the Series

Conducting Exposure with Children and Adolescents
Stephen P. Whiteside and Thomas H. Ollendick

Applications of the Unified Protocol for Transdiagnostic Treatment of Emotional Disorders

EDITED BY

DAVID H. BARLOW

AND

TODD J. FARCHIONE

OXFORD
UNIVERSITY PRESS

Oxford University Press is a department of the University of Oxford. It furthers
the University's objective of excellence in research, scholarship, and education
by publishing worldwide. Oxford is a registered trade mark of Oxford University
Press in the UK and certain other countries.

Published in the United States of America by Oxford University Press
198 Madison Avenue, New York, NY 10016, United States of America.

Library of Congress Cataloging-in-Publication Data
Names: Barlow, David H., editor. | Farchione, Todd J., 1974– editor.
Title: Applications of the unified protocol for transdiagnostic
treatment of emotional disorders / edited by David H. Barlow, Todd Farchione.
Description: New York, NY : Oxford University Press, [2018] |
Includes bibliographical references and index.
Identifiers: LCCN 2017022824 (print) | LCCN 2017025892 (ebook) |
ISBN 9780190255558 (updf) | ISBN 9780190669713 (epub) |
ISBN 9780190255541 (alk. paper) Subjects: | MESH: Mood Disorders—therapy |
Anxiety Disorders—therapy | Affective Symptoms—therapy |
Cognitive Therapy—methods Classification: LCC RC531 (ebook) |
LCC RC531 (print) | NLM WM 171 | DDC 616.85/22—dc23
LC record available at https://lccn.loc.gov/2017022824

CONTENTS

SERIES FOREWORD

Mental health clinicians desperately want to help their clients, and they recognize the importance of implementing evidence-based treatments toward achieving this goal. In the past several years, the field of mental healthcare has seen tremendous advances in its understanding of pathology and its underlying mechanisms, as well as proliferation and refinement of scientifically informed treatment approaches. Coinciding with these advances is a heightened focus on accountability in clinical practice. Clinicians are expected to apply evidence-based approaches and to do so effectively, efficiently, and in a patient-centered, individualized way. This is no small order. For a multitude of reasons, including but not limited to client diversity, complex psychopathology (e.g., comorbidity), and barriers to care that are not under the clinician's control (e.g., adverse life circumstances that limit the client's ability to participate), delivery of evidence-based approaches can be challenging.

The *ABCT Clinical Practice Series*, which represents a collaborative effort between the Association for Behavioral and Cognitive Therapies (ABCT) and Oxford University Press, is intended to serve as an easy-to-use, highly practical collection of resources for clinicians and trainees. The series is designed to help clinicians effectively master and implement evidence-based treatment approaches. In practical terms, it represents the 'brass tacks' of implementation, including basic how-to guidance and advice on trouble-shooting common issues in clinical practice and application. As such, this series is best viewed as a complement to other series on evidence-based protocols such as the Treatments *ThatWork*™ Series and the Programs *ThatWork*™ Series. These represent seminal bridges between research and practice and have been instrumental in the dissemination of empirically supported intervention protocols and programs. The *ABCT Clinical Practice Series*, rather than focusing on specific diagnoses and their treatment, targets the practical application of therapeutic and assessment approaches. In other words, the emphasis is on the *how-to* aspects of mental health delivery.

It is my hope that clinicians and trainees find these books useful in refining their clinical skills, as enhanced comfort as well as competence in delivery of evidence-based approaches should ultimately lead to improved client outcomes. Given the emphasis on application in this series, there is relatively less emphasis on review of the underlying research base. Readers who wish to delve more deeply into the theoretical or empirical basis supporting specific approaches are encouraged to go to the original source publications cited in each chapter. When relevant, suggestions for further reading are provided.

APPLICATIONS OF THE UNIFIED PROTOCOL FOR TRANSDIAGNOSTIC TREATMENT OF EMOTIONAL DISORDERS

In this book, Barlow, Farchione, and colleagues present the application of the Unified Protocol (UP) across a range of presenting problems. It complements the detailed therapist guide and workbook (Barlow, Farchione et al., 2nd Edition, 2018). In addition to describing how the disorder can be conceptualized dimensionally as a problem related to core negative reactivity and perceived lack of control of emotion, each chapter explains how the core UP modules can be flexibly implemented for that problem or context. Every chapter also includes detailed case examples to demonstrate how the principles of the UP manifest in clinical practice.

As all clinicians are aware, comorbidity is the rule rather than the exception. Indeed, this is a primary impetus for transdiagnostic treatments such as the UP. Across the volume's chapters, which align to particular diagnoses, we see how the UP can be used by clinicians to conceptualize disorders and co-occurring conditions along common temperamental features and apply the core elements of the UP in an individualized way. The chapters are written by experienced UP clinicians, who provide a wealth of first-hand practical knowledge that helps bring the UP, an evidence-based protocol with a great deal of research to support its efficacy, to life.

Susan W. White, Ph.D., ABPP
Series Editor

This book focuses on clinical applications of the Unified Protocol for Transdiagnostic Treatment of Emotional Disorders (UP). It may be helpful at the outset to say what this book is *not*. First, it is not simply another in-depth description of the UP. An updated and revised therapist guide for utilizing the UP, along with a detailed, step-by-step workbook for patients containing all the necessary elements of the UP will be published shortly (Barlow, Farchione, et al., 2018; Barlow, Sauer-Zavala, et al., 2018). In addition, the book is not focused on an in-depth description of the theoretical and conceptual basis of the UP with accompanying research findings, although those topics are touched upon in various chapters when appropriate. Rather, the focus of this book is on providing detailed practical advice on applications of the UP in a variety of cases, including very complex comorbid cases, along with typical roadblocks that a clinician might encounter in the course of treatment and troubleshooting strategies.

Some readers, when first coming across the table of contents for this book, may be puzzled by the focus on existing categorical DSM diagnoses (or classes of diagnoses), such as major depressive disorder (MDD), bipolar disorder, and eating disorders. After all, we are presenting a transdiagnostic assessment and treatment approach focused on core common therapeutic elements applicable to all disorders of emotion, so why put it in the context of specific disorders? But once again, the point of this book is to explicate how it is possible to conceptualize these varied emotional disorders, most often with accompanying comorbidities, from a common framework focusing on shared temperamental characteristics, which then leads to the application of five core transdiagnostic elements across the full range of these disorders. Therefore, the steps in this treatment approach are presented in some detail for each disorder, beginning with explanations of the therapeutic rationale to the patient, as well as the application of each of the core modules or elements.

The central premise of developing this transdiagnostic treatment is to make life easier for clinicians on the front line, who are faced with treating patients presenting with a wide variety of emotional disorders, such as social anxiety disorder, depression, and panic disorder, most of which, up until now, have had their own evidence-based, single-diagnosis protocols, many of them differing considerably from each other. Few clinicians become even aware of all the protocols available, let alone become proficient in their application. It has been the experience of clinicians who have mastered the core transdiagnostic elements of the UP that this is pretty much all they need to address these disorders.

This book begins with a chapter outlining the development of the UP over the preceding decades, a description of the elements of the protocol, and some of the research supporting the effectiveness of the protocol at this point in time, including a recent large clinical trial sponsored by the National Institute of Mental Health (NIMH), showing that the UP is at least as good as individual, single-diagnosis protocols for the major anxiety disorders (Barlow et al., in press). This is followed by an important chapter covering transdiagnostic assessment and case formulation that takes a step-by-step approach to educating patients on the nature of emotions and how their own clinical problems relate to dysregulated functional mechanisms in their emotional life. This is followed by a series of 11 chapters covering specific disorders or classes of disorders with which we now have had experience, including bipolar disorder (Chapter 6), emotional disorders connected with alcohol use disorders (Chapter 8), borderline personality disorder (BPD), which we conceptualize as the most severe of all emotional disorders (Chapter 12), and other major disorders. The last several chapters of the book deal with complex clinical presentations (which, of course, are more the norm than the exception on the front lines of clinical practice). In many cases, these presentations may include other dysregulated emotional targets such as shame, guilt, or embarrassment. Next comes an all-important chapter on group treatment applications. Administration in groups may be an emerging strength of the UP since the common transdiagnostic therapeutic elements of the UP allow one to form heterogeneous groups of individuals with emotional disorders (anxiety, depression, etc.), thereby increasing efficiency in clinics. Also, a chapter on cross-cultural applications reflects our growing experience with the UP in very different cultural contexts across the world, including the victims of the long civil war in Colombia and recent applications of the UP developed in Japan. Finally, we conclude with a chapter on future directions of the use of the UP, including some of our nascent efforts in the area of employing these principles to prevent emotional disorders.

We sincerely hope that clinicians struggling with the welter of emotional problems presented to them every day that often don't fit neatly into any categorical DSM diagnoses will find the specific case-study elements of this book helpful in their day-to-day practice. As experience with the UP broadens and deepens, more varied applications will be forthcoming, and we would be delighted to hear from clinicians on their own experiences with this protocol as they unfold.

Todd J. Farchione
David H. Barlow

ABOUT THE EDITORS

David H. Barlow, Ph.D.
David H. Barlow is Professor of Psychology and Psychiatry Emeritus and Founder of the Center for Anxiety and Related Disorders at Boston University. He has published over 600 articles and chapters and over 80 books and clinical manuals mostly in the area of the nature and treatment of emotional disorders. His books and manuals have been translated in over 20 languages, including Arabic, Chinese, Hindi, Japanese and Russian. He is the recipient of numerous awards, including honorary degrees from the University of Vermont and William James College, and the two highest awards in psychology, the Distinguished Scientific Award for Applications of Psychology from the American Psychological Association and James McKeen Cattell Fellow Award from the Association for Psychological Science honoring individuals for their lifetime of significant intellectual achievements in applied psychological research. He was a member of the DSM-IV Task Force of the American Psychiatric Association, and his research has been continually funded by the National Institutes of Health for over 45 years.

Todd J. Farchione, Ph.D.
Todd J. Farchione is Research Associate Professor in the Department of Psychological and Brain Sciences at Boston University (BU). He received his Ph.D. from the University of California, Los Angeles in 2001. He completed his predoctoral internship training at the VA West Los Angeles Medical Center and a postdoctoral fellowship at the UCLA Neuropsychiatric Institute and Hospital. For nearly fifteen years, Dr. Farchione has been a member of the clinical research group at the Center for Anxiety and Related Disorders at BU (CARD), where he has collaborated on several federally funded research studies on the nature, assessment, and treatment of anxiety, mood, and related disorders. His research focuses on understanding emotion regulation processes, identifying mechanisms of change in treatment, and on developing and disseminating new preventative measures and improved treatments for emotional disorders.

CONTRIBUTORS

Amantia A. Ametaj, M.A.
Department of Psychological and
Brain Sciences, Center for Anxiety and
Related Disorders, Boston University,
Boston, Massachusetts

Obianujunwa Anakwenze, B.A.
Department of Psychological and
Brain Sciences, Center for Anxiety and
Related Disorders, Boston University,
Boston, Massachusetts

David H. Barlow, Ph.D.
Department of Psychological and
Brain Sciences, Center for Anxiety and
Related Disorders, Boston University,
Boston, Massachusetts

Kate H. Bentley, M.A.
Massachusetts General Hospital/
Harvard Medical School, Boston,
Massachusetts

Emily E. Bernstein, M.A.
Department of Psychology, Harvard
University, Cambridge, Massachusetts

Hannah Boettcher, M.A.
Department of Psychological and
Brain Sciences, Center for Anxiety and
Related Disorders, Boston University,
Boston, Massachusetts

Christina L. Boisseau, Ph.D.
Department of Psychiatry and
Human Behavior, Warren Alpert
Medical School of Brown University,
Providence, Rhode Island

James F. Boswell, Ph.D.
Department of Psychology, University
at Albany, State University of
New York, Albany, New York

Matteo Bugatti, M.A.
Department of Psychology, University
at Albany, State University of
New York, Albany, New York

Jacqueline R. Bullis, Ph.D.
Division of Depression and Anxiety
Disorder, McLean Hospital/
Harvard Medical School, Belmont,
Massachusetts

Clair Cassiello-Robbins, M.A.
Department of Psychological and
Brain Sciences, Center for Anxiety and
Related Disorders, Boston University,
Boston, Massachusetts

Laren R. Conklin, Ph.D.
Department of Behavioral Health,
Chalmers P. Wylie VA Ambulatory
Care Center, Columbus, Ohio

Thilo Deckersbach, Ph.D.
Massachusetts General Hospital/
Harvard Medical School, Boston,
Massachusetts

Steven Dufour, B.A.
Massachusetts General Hospital/
Harvard Medical School, Boston,
Massachusetts

Kristen K. Ellard, Ph.D.
Massachusetts General Hospital/
Harvard Medical School, Boston,
Massachusetts

Todd J. Farchione, Ph.D.
Department of Psychological and
Brain Sciences, Center for Anxiety and
Related Disorders, Boston University,
Boston, Massachusetts

Matthew W. Gallagher, Ph.D.
Department of Psychology, Texas
Institute for Measurement Evaluation
and Statistics, University of Houston,
Houston, Texas

Tracie M. Goodness, Ph.D.
Department of Psychological and
Brain Sciences, Center for Anxiety and
Related Disorders, Boston University,
Boston, Massachusetts

Masaya Ito, Ph.D.
National Center for Cognitive
Behavior Therapy and Research,
National Center of Neurology and
Psychiatry, Tokyo, Japan

Katherine A. Kennedy, B.S.
Department of Psychology, Fordham
University, the Bronx, New York

Heather Murray Latin, Ph.D.
Department of Psychological and
Brain Sciences, Center for Anxiety and
Related Disorders, Boston University,
Boston, Massachusetts

Andrew A. Nierenberg, M.D.
Massachusetts General Hospital/
Harvard Medical School, Boston,
Massachusetts

Jennifer M. Oswald, Ph.D.
Department of Psychology, University
at Albany, State University of
New York, Albany, New York

Laura A. Payne, Ph.D.
Department of Pediatrics, Pediatric
Pain and Palliative Care Program,
David Geffen School of Medicine at
UCLA, Los Angeles, California

SriRamya Potluri, B.A.
Department of Psychological and
Brain Sciences, Center for Anxiety and
Related Disorders, Boston University,
Boston, Massachusetts

Michel Rattner-Castro, M.A.
Department of Psychology, Universidad
de Los Andes, Bogota, Colombia

Shannon Sauer-Zavala, Ph.D.
Department of Psychological and
Brain Sciences, Center for Anxiety and
Related Disorders, Boston University,
Boston, Massachusetts

Johanna Thompson-Hollands, Ph.D.
Department of Psychiatry, Boston
University School of Medicine,
Boston, Massachusetts

Stephanie Vento, B.S.
Department of Psychological and
Brain Sciences, Center for Anxiety and
Related Disorders, Boston University,
Boston, Massachusetts

Katelyn M. E. Williams, M.A.
Department of Psychological and
Brain Sciences, Center for Anxiety and
Related Disorders, Boston University,
Boston, Massachusetts

Julianne G. Wilner, B.A.
Department of Psychological and
Brain Sciences, Center for Anxiety and
Related Disorders, Boston University,
Boston, Massachusetts

Nina Wong Sarver, Ph.D.
Department of Pediatrics, University
of Mississippi Medical Center, Jackson,
Mississippi

Applications of the Unified Protocol for Transdiagnostic Treatment of Emotional Disorders

The Unified Protocol
for Transdiagnostic Treatment
of Emotional Disorders

An Introduction

KATHERINE A. KENNEDY AND DAVID H. BARLOW ■

The development of the Unified Protocol for Transdiagnostic Treatment of Emotional Disorders (UP) had its origins in a book published nearly three decades ago, *Anxiety and Its Disorders* (Barlow, 1988). In a chapter entitled "The Process of Fear and Anxiety Reduction: Affective Therapy," the author made an attempt to outline a coherent and consistent therapeutic approach to the full range of emotional disorders based on emotion theory. Among the transdiagnostic targets for change described there were the *action tendencies* associated with strong emotions, phenomena that we now refer to as *emotion-driven behaviors*. Other core targets included a pervasive sense of uncontrollability over life stressors (now considered research team to be part of the core temperament of neuroticism itself), and negative attentional biases, including a focus on internal, affective, and self-evaluative schemata.

Those ideas were put aside for over a decade while we focused on further developing and evaluating single-diagnosis treatments, such as treatments for panic disorder in large clinical trials (e.g., Barlow, Gorman, Shear, & Woods, 2000). In 2004, we revived this focus on targeting shared features of emotional disorders with the publication of an article called "Toward a Unified Treatment for Emotional Disorders" (Barlow, Allen, & Choate, 2004). At that time, recognizing the plethora of treatment manuals developed for each individual anxiety, mood, and related disorder reflecting DSM-IV categories, we returned to the approach first articulated in 1988: attempting to identify a common set of principles of change that could apply to all these disorders.

At the same time, research on the classification and nature of emotional disorders conducted with our colleague Tim Brown underscored the fact that fundamental temperamental aspects underlying anxiety, mood, and related disorders seemed more central to the nature of these disorders than did the symptom presentations that were the defining features in DSM-IV and DSM-5 systems (Brown & Barlow, 2009). This led in turn to a greater focus on the underlying temperament of neuroticism and other related traits, such as extraversion or positive affect, as well as the beginnings of conceptualizations of treating these temperaments directly rather than focusing on disorder-specific symptoms. The protocol that eventually emerged, as detailed next, consists of five core therapeutic procedures thought to be *transdiagnostic*, or widely applicable to all disorders of emotion. The remainder of this chapter is devoted to explaining the rationale for this approach and providing a description of the UP as it now exists. Subsequent chapters in this book focus on illustrating applications of the UP to diverse disorders of emotion.

RATIONALE FOR A UNIFIED APPROACH

In recent years, differing strands of research have come together to provide a strong rationale for creating a unified transdiagnostic approach to disorders of emotion. Commonalities among the emotional disorders have become increasingly apparent, including high rates of comorbidity, a similar responsiveness to treatment among comorbid disorders, and the presence of a common neurobiological syndrome. In addition, a hierarchical structure of emotional disorders has emerged, with a focus on core dimensions of temperament. In other words, the same traits and tendencies appear to leave individuals vulnerable to experiencing a wide variety of mental health problems, such as panic attacks, intrusive thoughts, posttraumatic stress, worry, and depression. Recently, we have developed an understanding of one reason why emotional disorders have so much in common: they appear to be maintained by similar functional processes, such as marked negative reactions to intense emotional experiences. We now elaborate briefly on each of these different strands of research.

Commonalities Among Disorders of Emotion

Since the turn of the century, research has begun to highlight commonalities among disorders of emotion (Barlow, 2002; Brown, 2007; Brown & Barlow, 2009). Specifically, high rates of comorbidity, broad treatment responses across comorbid emotional disorders, and common neurobiological mechanisms serve as examples of how emotional disorders are more similar than different. At the diagnostic level, overlap among emotional disorders is demonstrated by high rates of current and lifetime comorbidity (e.g., Allen et al., 2010; Brown, Campbell, Lehman, Grisham, & Mancill, 2001; Kessler et al., 1996; Roy-Byrne, Craske, & Stein, 2006; Tsao, Mystkowski, Zucker, & Craske, 2002, 2005). For example, results from a study of 1,127 patients at the Center for Anxiety and Related Disorders (CARD) at Boston University indicated that 55% of patients with a principal anxiety disorder had at least one additional anxiety or depressive disorder at the time of assessment (Brown et al., 2001). When including lifetime diagnoses, this rate increases to 76%. Further, 60% of patients diagnosed with panic disorder with or without agoraphobia (PDA) utilizing DSM-III-R or DSM-IV diagnoses met the criteria for an additional anxiety or mood disorder, or both—a statistic that increases to 77% when considering lifetime diagnoses. Diagnoses with the highest overall comorbidity were posttraumatic stress disorder (PTSD), major depressive disorder (MDD), dysthymia (DYS), and generalized anxiety disorder (GAD). Especially strong comorbid patterns were found between social phobia (SOC) and mood disorders, PDA and PTSD, and PTSD and mood disorders. Furthermore, Merikangas, Zhang, and Aveneoli (2003) studied nearly 500 people for 15 years and found that relatively few people suffer from a single mood or anxiety disorder.

Second, psychological treatments for a single disorder often generate improvements in comorbid anxiety or mood disorders not specifically targeted during treatment (Allen et al., 2010; Borkovec, Abel, & Newman, 1995; Brown, Antony, & Barlow, 1995; Tsao, Lewin, & Craske, 1998; Tsao et al., 2002). Brown et al. (1995) examined the course of comorbid diagnoses in patients receiving cognitive-behavioral treatment specifically for PDA and found that overall comorbidity significantly declined from pretreatment to posttreatment (from 40% to 17%). To take another example, a wide range of emotional disorders [e.g., MDD, obsessive-compulsive disorder (OCD), PDA] respond analogously to antidepressant medications (Gorman, 2007). These findings could mean that individual treatments coincidentally target symptoms from more than one disorder, or that treatments for single diagnoses target the core underlying features of all emotional disorders, at least to some extent.

Third, research from affective neuroscience has suggested that disorders of emotion share neurobiological mechanisms. For example, increased negative emotionality among people with anxiety and related disorders is associated with hyperexcitability of limbic structures and limited inhibitory control by cortical structures (Etkin & Wager, 2007; Mayberg et al., 1999; Porto et al., 2009; Shin & Liberzon, 2010). Specifically, increased "bottom-up" processing, along with dysregulated cortical inhibition of amygdala responses, has been indicated in studies of GAD (Etkin, Prater, Hoeft, Menon, & Schatzberg, 2010; Hoehn-Saric, Schlund, & Wong, 2004; Paulesu et al., 2010), SOC (Lorberbaum et al., 2004; Phan, Fitzgerald, Nathan, & Tancer, 2006; Tillfors, Furmark, Marteinsdottir, & Fredrikson, 2002), specific phobias (Paquette et al., 2003; Straube, Mentzel, & Miltner, 2006), PTSD (Shin et al., 2005), and depression (Holmes et al., 2012). Individuals with high levels of neuroticism also have been found to have this relatively uninhibited amygdala overactivation (Keightley et al., 2003).

Hierarchical Structure of Emotional Disorders

Research on latent dimensional features of emotional disorders has revealed a hierarchical structure based on two core dimensions of temperament: neuroticism and extraversion (Barlow, 2002). *Extraversion* broadly refers to having a positive outlook on the world, including an energetic and social disposition. In contrast, neuroticism describes a tendency to develop frequent, intense negative emotions associated with a sense of uncontrollability (the perception of inadequate coping) in response to stress. Extraversion also has been called *positive affect* or *behavioral activation*, while constructs isomorphic with neuroticism include *negative affect, behavioral inhibition*, and *trait anxiety*. Neuroticism and extraversion have been identified for their key roles in explaining the onset, overlap, and maintenance of anxiety and mood disorders (Brown, 2007; Brown & Barlow, 2009; Brown, Chorpita, & Barlow, 1998; Gershuny & Sher, 1998; Griffith et al., 2010).

The study of neuroticism has been ongoing for decades, with many researchers referring to traits similar to neuroticism (as well as extraversion) in their work (Eysenck & Eysenck, 1975; Gray, 1982; Kagan, 1989, 1994; McCrae & Costa, 1987; Tellegen, 1985; Watson & Clark, 1993). Prominent personality conceptions, such as the Big Three and Big Five (see McCrae & Costa, 1987; Tellegen 1985) reference these dimensions of personality. Gray's (1982) conceptions of the behavioral inhibition system and behavioral activation system seem to correspond to varying intensities of neuroticism and extraversion (e.g., high levels of behavioral inhibition relate to high levels of neuroticism). While Gray's fight-flight system corresponds with the emotion of fear (panic), Clark and Watson (1991) proposed their tripartite theory based on two core dimensions: neuroticism/negative emotionality and extraversion/positive emotionality (Clark, 2005; Clark, Watson, & Mineka, 1994; Watson, 2005).

In order to understand these concepts more clearly, researchers have been using latent variable modeling to examine their role in anxiety and mood disorders (Brown et al., 1998; Chorpita, Albano, & Barlow, 1998; Clark, 2005; Clark & Watson, 1991; Watson, 2005). Brown and colleagues (1998) confirmed a hierarchical structure for emotional disorders, in which neuroticism and extraversion were higher-order factors with significant paths from neuroticism to GAD, SOC, PDA, OCD, and MDD. Notably, low positive affect is associated with significant paths to MDD and SOC. In addition, Rosellini, Lawrence, Meyer, and Brown (2010) found that agoraphobia (AG) is also related to low extraversion, separating it from panic disorder.

Several other research groups have replicated these findings (e.g., Griffith et al., 2010; Kessler et al., 2011). Results from a large study of adolescents, using self-report and peer-report measures, identified neuroticism as a common factor in lifetime diagnoses of mood and anxiety disorders (Griffith et al., 2010). Although specific symptoms defining each diagnostic category of anxiety and mood disorders cannot be wholly collapsed into higher-order temperamental dimensions, based on these data, we have concluded that similarities among disorders of emotion outweigh differences.

Negative Reactions to Emotional Experience

Individuals with an emotional disorder, as opposed to their healthy peers, have higher levels of negative affect/neuroticism (Brown & Barlow, 2009) and express a greater frequency of negative emotions (Campbell-Sills, Barlow, Brown, & Hofman, 2006; Mennin, Heimberg, Turk, & Fresco, 2005). Importantly, however, they also react more negatively to their own emotional experiences (Barlow, 1991; Barlow et al., 2011; Campbell-Sills et al., 2006; Brown & Barlow, 2009), have greater difficulty accepting their emotions (McLaughlin, Mennin, & Farach, 2007; Tull & Roemer, 2007; Weiss et al., 2012), and are more intolerant of their negative emotions (Roemer, Salters, Raffa, & Orsillo, 2005). As a result, many individuals with emotional disorders attempt to downregulate these negative emotional experiences (Aldao, Nolen-Hoeksema, & Schweizer, 2010; Baker, Holloway, Thomas, Thomas, & Owens, 2004).

This negative reactivity to emotional experience is shaped by how individuals process emotions as they occur (Sauer & Baer, 2009; Sauer-Zavala et al., 2012). For example, in early models of PDA where this functional relationship was first noticed, after a person experiences a panic attack, physical symptoms associated with the attack (e.g., shortness of breath) signal anxiety focused on what will happen next (e.g., fainting; another panic attack), which further exacerbates the somatic and cognitive symptoms (Barlow, 1988; Clark, 1986). Since panic attacks in individuals without PDA do not cue similar emotional reactions (and therefore are called *non-clinical panic attacks*) (Bouton, Mineka, & Barlow, 2001), the negative emotional reaction to panic in people with PDA is more important to generating PDA than the panic attacks themselves.

Negative interpretations of emotions that intensify an emotional experience are not unique to PDA and are prevalent in other anxiety and mood disorders. For instance, Rachman and de Silva (1978) found that patients with OCD and control participants had similar intrusive negative thoughts under stress, but only patients with OCD reacted with intense distress and anxiety to these emotionally salient thoughts. To take another example, when individuals with GAD encounter potentially stressful situations, they may try to downregulate their emotions by worrying (an intense verbal-linguistic process activating brain structures that dampen affect) or checking, unlike individuals without GAD (Newman & Llera, 2011). Differences among emotional disorders (i.e., different presenting symptoms in PDA, OCD, and SOC) may be determined by specific early learning experiences (Barlow, Ellard, Sauer-Zavala, Bullis, & Carl, 2014); however, the core psychopathological mechanism or functional relationship consists of negative reactions and subsequent efforts to downregulate emotional experiences.

Associated Constructs Reflecting
This Functional Relationship

Research has identified several transdiagnostic constructs associated with the development and maintenance of emotional disorders, which collectively describe a propensity to find emotional experiences aversive (Barlow, Sauer-Zavala, Carl, Bullis, & Ellard, 2014). They include experiential avoidance, anxiety sensitivity, deficits in mindfulness, and negative appraisals and attributions reflecting the neurotic sense of uncontrollability (see *Figure 1.1*).

Experiential avoidance is the urge to escape or avoid uncomfortable internal experiences such as thoughts, memories, or emotions (Hayes, Wilson, Gifford, Follette, & Strosahl, 1996). Studies have shown that individuals with anxiety and depressive disorders have high levels of self-reported experiential avoidance (Begotka, Woods, & Wetterneck, 2004; Berking, Neacsiu, Comtois, & Linehan, 2009; Kashdan, Breen, Afram, & Terhar, 2010; Shahar & Herr, 2011). Lee, Orsillo, Roemer, and Allen (2010) found that after accounting for variance related to frequency of negative affect, experiential avoidance predicts GAD symptoms. Also noteworthy is that this construct mediates the association between neuroticism and PTSD (Maack, Tull, & Gratz, 2012; Pickett, Lodis, Parkhill, & Orcutt, 2012). Recent research found that the relationship between experiencing negative emotions and major depressive symptoms is partially mediated by avoidant coping in individuals high in experiential avoidance (Cheavens & Heiy, 2011). Individuals with emotional disorders use several forms of avoidant coping strategies, including emotion suppression and rumination. *Emotion suppression* is a strategy where individuals try to eliminate negative, unwanted, emotion-provoking experiences. However, these emotions often end up returning with greater intensity, resulting in an increase in negative affect (Abramowitz, Tolin, & Street, 2001; Rassin,

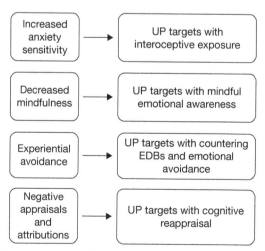

Figure 1.1 Associated constructs reflecting negative reactivity and perceptions of lack of control of intense emotion.

Muris, Schmidt, & Merkelbach, 2000; Wegner, Schneider, Carter, & White, 1987). Individuals with emotional disorders, including depression, GAD, OCD, and PTSD, demonstrate high levels of emotion suppression (Purdon, 1999).

Rumination is another cognitive strategy where individuals repetitively fixate on negative moods and their possible causes, meanings, and consequences (Nolen-Hoeksema, 1991). Rumination has been shown to intensify negative affect, leading to more rumination about increased negative mood; this process often continues until individuals engage in an avoidant behavior (e.g., reassurance seeking, substance use, or self-harm) to divert their attention (Selby, Anestis, & Joiner, 2008). This cycle is also negatively reinforced, as it temporarily protects individuals from more distressing concerns (Lyubomirsky & Nolen-Hoeksema, 1995; Lyubomirsky, Tucker, Caldwell, & Berg, 1999). Use of this strategy seems to be consistent across emotional disorders and predicts increases in anxiety and depressive symptoms (Aldao et al., 2010; Butler & Nolen-Hoeksema, 1994; Calmes & Roberts, 2007; Hong, 2007; Nolen-Hoeksema, 2000; Nolen-Hoeksema, Larson, & Grayson, 1999; O'Connor, O'Connor, & Marshall, 2007; Sarin, Abela, & Auerbach, 2005; Segerstrom, Tsao, Alden, & Craske, 2000).

Another transdiagnostic construct that has been identified as a factor in the development of emotional disorders is *anxiety sensitivity (AS)*, which refers to the tendency to believe that symptoms of anxiety and fear will have negative consequences (Reiss, 1991). This construct specifically looks at an individual's unique response to an emotional experience as it occurs, aside from the duration or severity of the emotion itself. Although anxiety sensitivity has primarily been studied in the context of PDA (e.g., Maller & Reiss, 1992; Plehn & Peterson, 2002; Rassovsky, Kushner, Schwarze, & Wangensteen, 2000), research has shown that it also is associated with other anxiety and depressive disorders (Boswell et al., 2013; Naragon-Gainey, 2010; Taylor, 1999; Boettcher, Brake, & Barlow, 2016).

Interestingly, it has been found that anxiety sensitivity transdiagnostically predicts the onset of anxiety and depressive disorders beyond the propensity to experience anxiety (Maller & Reiss, 1992; Schmidt, Keough, Timpano, & Richey, 2008). Reduction in anxiety sensitivity during treatment predicts patient recovery (Gallagher et al., 2013). Furthermore, anxiety sensitivity predicts symptoms of mood and anxiety disorders with even greater incremental validity than neuroticism (Collimore, McCabe, Carelton, & Asmundson, 2008; Cox, Enns, Walker, Kjernisted, & Pidlubny, 2001; Kotov, Watson, Robles, & Schmidt, 2007; Norton et al., 1997; Reardon & Williams, 2007). This supports the proposition that how an individual relates to negative emotions is just as much of a determinant of the development of an emotional disorder as the duration or severity of negative affect. For this reason, we are currently working on expanding the construct of AS to emotion sensitivity generally.

A deficit in mindfulness is another feature of emotional disorders; *Mindfulness* refers to being aware and accepting of one's experience, including emotions in the present moment, no matter how unpleasant the experience (Cheavens et al., 2005; Hayes et al., 1996; Kabat-Zinn, 1982). Deficits in mindfulness are also transdiagnostic occurring across emotional disorders (Baer, Smith, Hopkins, Kritemeyer, &

Toney, 2006; Brown & Ryan, 2003; Cash & Whittingham, 2010; Rasmussen & Pidgeon, 2011). A recent study found that after a laboratory stressor, individuals with higher levels of mindfulness reported fewer feelings of anxiety and lower cortisol response than those with lower levels of mindfulness (Brown, Weinstein, & Creswell, 2011). Moreover, the frequency with which individuals use mindfulness while responding to negative emotions predicts psychopathology more than the inherent tendency to experience negative emotions (Segal, Williams, & Teasdale, 2002; Sauer & Baer, 2009). Similar to experiential avoidance and anxiety sensitivity, these results support the importance of focusing on an individual's reactions to negative emotions as they occur.

Finally, since Beck's pioneering work from the 1970s (e.g., Beck, 1976), we have recognized that all disorders of emotion are associated with pessimistic, negative, and, most important, very rigid and automatic attributions and appraisals of persons (including oneself) and situations. As noted earlier, although these negative interpretations and appraisals were first noticed in the context of depression, they are prevalent across the anxiety and mood disorders.

DIMENSIONAL DIAGNOSES AND ASSESSMENT

Beginning with DSM-III and continuing in DSM-IV and DSM-5, there has been an ever-increasing splitting of mental disorder diagnoses into more narrowly defined categories. Based on these categories of anxiety, depressive, somatoform, and related disorders, specific pharmacological and psychological treatments emerged (Barlow et al., 1984), requiring specific treatment protocols for each diagnosis, which constituted the independent variable. Researchers then validated these protocols empirically in clinical trials, and the process of delineating the treatment in the form of a manual in order to create an operationally defined independent variable began with the study of psychodynamic treatments (Strupp, 1973). This process of research resulted in numerous individual efficacious treatment protocols that clinicians needed to master to treat patients presenting with symptoms pertaining to specific disorders (e.g., GAD, OCD, and MDD).

Although this splitting approach produced high rates of diagnostic reliability, this has occurred almost certainly at the expense of validity, in that the current system may be overemphasizing categories that are trivial variations of underlying temperament. In this conceptualization of nosology, a quantitative approach using structural equation modeling would optimally examine emotional disorders without the constraint of DSM-5 categories. A more dimensional classification of emotional disorders constructed in this way would eliminate issues of comorbidity while representing significant characteristics of these disorders.

Recently, we have proposed such an approach (Brown & Barlow, 2009). This dimensional approach, when fully developed, should provide a more complete picture of a patient's clinical presentation than a categorical approach consisting of multiple comorbid diagnoses. In this system, a profile for each patient is created consisting of several constructs, including temperaments of neuroticism, extraversion (referred to as *behavioral activation/positive affectivity*), avoidance, mood, and autonomic arousal (as in panic attacks and flashbacks), as well as a dimensional assessment of severity on several specific foci of anxiety (e.g., intrusive cognitions, social evaluation, and trauma experience). Scores on neuroticism reflect the frequency, intensity, and distress associated with negative emotions, perceptions about uncertain future experiences, and low self-efficacy regarding the ability to cope with these emotions. Low levels of extraversion/positive affect are associated with MDD, SOC, and AG, while high levels are associated with euthymic states of bipolar and cyclothymic disorders.

A recently developed measure, the Multidimensional Emotional Disorder Inventory (MEDI), assesses these vulnerabilities and characteristics of emotional disorders. This measure is currently under validation, but recent research has indicated that it may be a reliable and valid method for assessing emotional disorder dimensions (Rosellini, 2013; Rosellini, Boettcher, Brown, & Barlow, 2015). For instance, while using this measure, patients with PTSD might present with high levels of neuroticism and a preoccupation with past trauma and autonomic arousal (flashbacks), but their profile might also reflect some degree of social evaluation concerns and intrusive ego dystonic thoughts unrelated to trauma. Given high rates of comorbidity among emotional disorders, the MEDI will be especially useful for assessing patients with clinical or subclinical comorbid disorders, since previously discarded information on these disorders could be integrated into treatment plans. More information on dimensional diagnoses and assessment will be provided in Chapter 2.

DEVELOPMENT OF THE UNIFIED PROTOCOL

The UP was first published in manual form as a patient workbook and therapist guide in 2011 (Barlow, Ellard, et al., 2011; Barlow, Farchione, et al., 2011), and has recently been revised (Barlow, D. H., Sauer-Zavala, S., Farchione, T. J., Latin, H., Ellard, K. K.,...& Cassiello-Robbins, 2018; Barlow, D. H., Farchione, T. J., Sauer-Zavala, S., Latin, H., Ellard, K. K., Bullis, J. R., . . . Cassiello-Robbins, C. (2018). The goal of the UP is to help patients understand and recognize their emotions and respond to their uncomfortable negative emotions in more adaptive ways. Changing these maladaptive responses can lessen the intensity and frequency of uncomfortable emotions. The UP consists of five core treatment modules and three additional modules intended to be covered in 12–18 one-on-one weekly treatment sessions lasting 50 to 60 minutes each, with flexibility in the number of sessions per module. The clinician can decide to hold last few sessions every week or every other week, depending on the patient's progress. If the patient is doing well, holding final sessions every other week could allow the patient to consolidate gains; on the other hand if the patient is having difficulty using treatment concepts, then weekly reinforcement might be more beneficial. The five core modules (3–7) correspond with transdiagnostic constructs reflecting functional

---

Box 1.1

UP MODULES AND SUGGESTED SESSION LENGTHS

Module 1: Setting Goals and Maintaining Motivation *(1 session)*
Module 2: Understanding Emotions *(1–2 sessions)*
Module 3: Mindful Emotion Awareness *(1–2 sessions)*
Module 4: Cognitive Flexibility *(1–2 sessions)*
Module 5: Countering Emotional Behaviors *(1–2 sessions)*
Module 6: Understanding and Confronting Physical Sensations *(1 session)*
Module 7: Emotion Exposures *(4–6 sessions)*
Module 8: Recognizing Accomplishments and Looking to the Future
  (1 session)

Core modules are in bold.

---

relationships in emotional disorders described earlier (see *Box 1.1*). In the following section, we will briefly review each module.

Module 1: Setting Goals and Maintaining Motivation

This first treatment module uses motivational interviewing principles and techniques (MI; Miller & Rollnick, 2013) to increase patients' readiness and motivation for change by developing awareness that they have the ability to effect change in themselves. We include MI due to recent research revealing that this approach may enhance treatment gains for anxiety disorders (Westra, Arkowitz, & Dozois, 2009; Westra & Dozois, 2006). The therapist targets motivation by using a decisional balance exercise and a treatment goal–setting exercise. In the decisional balance exercise, patients discuss with the therapist the advantages and disadvantages of changing versus staying the same. During the treatment goal–setting exercise, patients talk about areas that they would most like to change. These exercises are used to identify potential obstacles to change and concrete goals during treatment. This module helps prepare patients for learning as they progress through the core modules; principles in this module can be revisited at any point during treatment to enhance treatment engagement.

Module 2: Understanding Emotions

This module, which is typically covered in one to two sessions and could either precede or follow the motivational enhancement module, provides patients with psychoeducation about the function and development of emotions. In addition to discussing the function of anxiety, the UP covers many other emotions, including anger, sadness, and fear. During this module, the therapist explains cognitive, physiological, and behavioral components of emotions and the interaction of these components. Patients should begin to understand that their emotions serve a functional and adaptive role of providing information about the environment and guiding appropriate action.

The therapist then provides an example of the three-component model of emotions (cognitions, behaviors, and physiological sensations), using experiences from the patient's life to improve understanding. The therapist and patient work together to identify how the patient's emotions correspond to the model. This model is used as a framework for looking closely at the patient's emotions during treatment as each component interacts with the other components and contributes to the overall experience. Patients develop a greater awareness for their own patterns of emotional responding and associated triggers through careful monitoring of their responses to emotional experiences.

In order to facilitate careful monitoring of emotions, the UP uses the acronym ARC to describe the sequence of events around emotions. Emotions are always triggered by an event, situation, or experience known as an *antecedent* (the A in the ARC), which can occur immediately or several days (or even longer) before experiencing an emotion. Often, there are multiple antecedents, and they may include recent and distal events. One's *response* to the emotional experience (the R of ARC) corresponds to all cognitions, somatic sensations, and behaviors from the three-component model. Finally, short- and long-term outcomes of emotional responding are referred to as *consequences*, or the C. During this explanation, the therapist will clearly work through an example with the patient.

Negative reinforcement serves as an illustration of how this cycle of emotions is maintained. The therapist describes how escape or any form of avoidance during an emotional episode (a consequence) perpetuates the anxiety and distress associated with the emotional experience since it reduces the emotion in the short term (i.e., by avoiding it), but fails to teach the patient that she or he can manage the emotions and that they will naturally run their course. This process is key for the patient to benefit from the emotion exposures covered in future modules.

Module 3: Mindful Emotion Awareness

This is the first of the core modules, and it is typically covered in one to two treatment sessions. The goal of this module is for patients to learn and begin using an objective, present-focused, nonjudgmental perspective of their emotions. Often, patients report that their emotions happen spontaneously, are confusing, and seem out of their control; this module will help patients recognize the interaction between their thoughts, feelings, and behaviors during an emotional experience. The therapist will review *primary emotions*, or the first emotional responses to a situation or memory, as well as *reactions* to primary emotions that tend to be negative and not present-focused. The teaching of these concepts occurs in sessions during specific examples of emotionally arousing experiences tailored to individual patients.

Specifically, reactions to emotions tend to be subjective, judgmental, and negative; for instance, worrying that anxiety will preclude meeting one's obligations in the future. Since these reactions are typically not based on information from the present, they can block positive information regarding the nature of the emotional response. At this point, patients' understanding of their emotions should be sufficient to utilize the strategies covered in subsequent modules.

Module 4: Cognitive Flexibility

The primary purpose of this module, typically covered in one or two sessions, is to encourage flexible thinking using principles originated by Beck (1975) and modified in our setting over the decades (e.g., Barlow & Craske, 1988). In it, the therapist helps patients understand how they misinterpret situations and that their appraisals influence their emotional reactions. Automatic appraisals happen quickly, while in the moment, and are most often negative. *Core* automatic appraisals are more generalizable cognitions that patients have about themselves, such as "I am a disappointment," and they may shape many emotional responses. Automatic appraisals force patients to exclude other, potentially more appropriate perspectives on a situation. These thoughts are considered "thinking traps" if patients are unable to view the situation in another way. Two thinking traps common to all emotional disorders (and the only two that are taught in the UP, reflecting our longstanding approach) are *probability overestimation,* or the tendency to assume that a negative outcome is very likely to occur, and *catastrophizing,* or thinking that the outcome will be disastrous. Each patient is taught to identify these biases and encouraged to be more flexible by using reappraisal strategies in a standard cognitive therapy approach.

Module 5: Countering Emotional Behaviors

This module is typically administered over one to two sessions. Emotion avoidance strategies are behaviors where patients attempt to avoid or suppress intense emotional experiences. The role of emotion avoidance is discussed since these strategies prevent patients from fully experiencing emotion in a situation. That is, avoidance maintains the initial high anxiety and distress levels since patients are unable to let the emotion repair naturally. In addition, extinction of anxiety and distress in response to the intense emotion is prevented since adequate exposure resulting in the disconfirmation of negative expectancies cannot occur. Finally, patients are unable to learn more adaptive emotion regulation strategies. Patients should provide examples of their own avoidance strategies and how those continue the cycle of their negative emotions.

The therapist introduces three main types of emotion avoidance: subtle behavioral avoidance, cognitive avoidance, and the use of safety signals. Subtle behavioral avoidance strategies correspond to a number of behaviors, depending on the disorder. For instance, someone with OCD may avoid touching the sink or toilet to avoid feeling contaminated. Similarly, avoiding caffeine and controlling breathing are forms of subtle behavioral avoidance in PDA. It is important to do a functional analysis to determine which behaviors serve to reduce or negate emotional experiences or are functionally related in some way. The second type of strategy, cognitive avoidance, includes distraction, checking lists, and reviewing previous events. Worry and rumination may also serve as strategies to avoid emotions, since the individual would be focusing on future events instead of the present (Borkovec, 1994). Worrying prevents experiencing emotions to the fullest because patients are preparing for something negative that might happen in the future (Borkovec, Hazlett-Stevens, & Diaz, 1999). Finally, safety signals include objects that individuals carry in order to feel comfortable or reduce arousal in potentially emotional situations. Individuals have been known to carry actual medicine, empty medication bottles, and even supposedly "lucky" objects with them. These strategies are harmful because they perpetuate the cycle of negative reinforcement.

In addition to identifying and modifying emotion avoidance, this module concentrates on identifying and altering *emotion-driven behaviors (EDBs)*. The UP coined the term *EDB* to describe behavioral responses to emotions termed "action tendencies" in the emotion science literature (Barlow, 1988). *Action tendencies* are universal, evolutionary, favored behaviors motivated and driven by the emotional state to achieve a desired goal that is often associated with survival itself. There are adaptive and maladaptive EDBs—for instance, an adaptive EDB could be a fear-driven escape from a situation where there is a direct threat to one's safety (i.e., escaping a burning building). However, an EDB is maladaptive if there is no clear threat present (i.e., a false alarm), but the emotion and behavior occur anyway. EDBs are maintained through negative reinforcement since the function of EDBs is to reduce negative emotion intensity in the short term; thus, EDBs maintain the cycle of emotions. It is helpful if patients can discuss examples of EDBs from their own experiences. Two strategies that the patient should engage in to address emotional avoidance and EDBs are experiencing emotions and situations that they are currently avoiding, and developing and using behaviors that are more appropriate than and different from maladaptive EDBs.

Module 6: Understanding and Confronting Physical Sensations

This module typically lasts one session and aims to increase patients' awareness and tolerance of somatic sensations as an integral part of emotional experiences. After demonstration by the therapist, patients will engage in interoceptive exposure (IE) exercises to elicit somatic sensations typically experienced during times of emotional distress and begin to strengthen their understanding of how somatic sensations contribute to emotional experiences (e.g., shortness of breath, heart palpitations, or dizziness). Examples of standard IE exercises include hyperventilating, spinning, and running in place, representing common strategies to provoke physical sensation in the respiratory, vestibular, and cardiovascular systems. Many other strategies are covered in subsequent chapters of this book. After the patient completes each IE exercise, he or she is asked to rate the intensity, distress, and similarity to somatic sensations typically experienced during an intense emotional reaction. The patient then will complete the most relevant exercises several times a day over the next week and prior to the next therapy session. Associated distress should decrease with repeated exposure, and as the patient disconfirms the expectation that somatic sensations are dangerous.

Module 7: Emotion Exposures

This final core module emphasizes the practice of treatment concepts through in-session and out-of-session exposures to emotion experiences uniquely created by the therapist to address the individual patient's symptoms (this module typically lasts four to six sessions). Emotion exposures should involve actual situations, events, or activities that trigger strong levels of previously avoided emotion, but the focus is on provoking the emotion, not the situation itself. Examples include giving a public speech, riding an elevator, imagining a past emotional event (often appropriate for PTSD or GAD), leaving the bathroom without washing one's hands, or watching a sad movie clip (for MDD). Interoceptive cues identified in the last module are integrated into the exercises. Emotion exposures serve to replace interpretations about the dangerousness of situations with more adaptive appraisals, reverse emotion avoidance, modify EDBs, and, most important, extinguish anxious reactions to intense emotional experiences. As the patient engages in in-session emotion exposures, the therapist should note the use of any avoidance strategies or EDBs, of which the patient may not be aware, and help the patient with any negative automatic appraisals by finding appropriate reappraisals. Some patients will also benefit from continuing IEs to develop greater tolerance of uncomfortable somatic sensations.

Module 8: Recognizing Accomplishments and Looking to the Future

In the final treatment session, an overview of major treatment concepts and the patient's progress is reviewed. If applicable, reasons for lack of improvement or shortcomings of treatment goals are discussed, including diagnostic error, lack of participation, lack of understanding of principles, and unrealistic treatment goals. Due to the inevitability of future stressors and potential symptoms, specific strategies for preserving and extending treatment gains are discussed.

Early Results and Current Clinical Trial

The UP has received preliminary support for its efficacy in treating emotional disorders from several studies, including a small randomized control trial (N = 37). In this experiment, the UP was found to be an efficacious treatment for a range of anxiety disorders compared to a wait-list control group (Farchione et al., 2012; Ellard, Fairholme, Boisseau, Farchione, & Barlow, 2010) with patients continuing to improve even 18 months after treatment (Bullis, Fortune, Farchione, & Barlow, 2014).

Based on these promising results, we recently completed a five-year, large, National Institute of Mental Health (NIMH)–sponsored randomized controlled equivalence trial (N = 223) comparing the UP with four efficacious single-disorder treatment protocols (SDPs) for principal diagnoses of GAD, SOC, OCD, or PDA and a wait-list control group. Results posttreatment and at a six-month follow-up indicate clear differences among all treatment groups and the control group, with the UP at least as efficacious as SDPs at both time points. Importantly, significantly fewer patients dropped out of the UP than the SDPs (Barlow et al., in press).

We have also studied the UP's ability to change dimensions of temperament in the scope of the randomized control trial mentioned previously (Carl, Gallagher, Sauer-Zavala, Bentley, & Barlow, 2014). The results revealed that the UP, compared to the wait-list group, produced small to moderate effects from pretreatment to posttreatment for both neuroticism and extraversion. Significantly, these changes in temperament are related to improvements in functional impairment and quality of life (Carl et al., 2014). These results underscore the potential importance of factoring in changes in temperament when considering treatment outcome.

Furthermore, based on the relative advantages of group treatment to individual treatment (e.g., ability to treat more patients, reduced stigma associated with seeking treatment, and patients learn from other group members), we have studied the efficacy of the UP delivered in a group format, which happens to be where the protocol originated (Barlow et al., 2004). Results indicated moderate to strong effects on anxiety and depressive symptoms, functional impairment, quality of life, and emotion regulation skills, along with good acceptability and overall satisfaction ratings from patients, all of which were roughly equivalent to individual administration (Bullis et al., 2015). Additional applications include a clinical trial administering the UP to emotional disorders in patients with a substance abuse diagnosis (Ciraulo et al., 2013). The results indicated the efficacy of the UP on anxiety and related substance use measures. Other applications are detailed in subsequent chapters of this book.

Role of Positive Affect

While the modules described in this chapter target negative affect and neuroticism, research on intervention strategies targeting positive affect or extraversion is also beginning to appear. Individuals with anxiety and mood disorders are less likely to maintain and more likely to minimize positive emotions. A recent study in our lab found that an augmented intervention for enhancing positive emotion, delivered in four sessions following a standard course of cognitive behavioral therapy (CBT) for anxiety and depressive disorders, was effective in improving positive emotion regulation skills for approximately 55% of participants (Carl & Barlow, submitted). Patients benefited from improvements in anxiety and depressive symptoms, positive and negative emotion, and quality of life.

In addition, Mata and colleagues (2012) found that directly after a session of moderate exercise, participants with MDD and control participants evidenced increases in positive affect. Interestingly, depressed participants, in comparison to healthy controls, reported greater increases in positive affect with longer and more intense physical activity. Furthermore, research from animal laboratories has found that exercise increases neurogenesis in the hippocampus, a possible mechanism of action in the successful combination of psychological treatment with exercise (Speisman, Kumar, Rani, Foster, & Omerod, 2012).

CONCLUSION

In summary, due to overlap among emotional disorders, common treatment response, and a common neurobiological syndrome, emotional disorders have more similarities than differences, suggesting the appropriateness of one treatment approach. The UP purports to treat the common temperament underlying all emotional disorders, neuroticism, which is a tendency to experience frequent, intense negative emotions and to react with anxiety and distress to these emotional experiences. The five core modules of the UP utilize mindful emotional awareness, increasing cognitive flexibility, countering emotion-driven behaviors (action tendencies), increasing awareness of emotionally salient somatic sensations, and emotion exposure to target negative emotionality and associated distress aversion, the putative driving mechanism of emotional disorders.

The following chapters will delve into specific case presentations and applications of the UP. Chapter 2 will cover the transdiagnostic assessment and case formulation needed to identify underlying traits and associated symptoms needing treatment. Chapters 3 through 13 discuss specific clinical applications of the UP to diverse disorders of emotion and patterns of comorbidity, in order to illustrate the wide range of cases in which the UP is appropriate. Chapter 14 focuses on complicated clinical presentations that can benefit from targeting comorbid diagnoses. Chapter 15 highlights advantages of using the UP in a group setting. Cross-cultural applications, which are relevant for addressing the need for transdiagnostic treatment in other countries, are discussed in Chapter 16, followed by a discussion of future directions in prevention, dissemination, and implementation in Chapter 17.

2

Transdiagnostic Assessment and Case Formulation

Rationale and Application with the Unified Protocol

HANNAH BOETTCHER AND LAREN R. CONKLIN ■

Assessment and case formulation are among the most important tasks facing researchers and clinicians hoping to develop or administer effective treatments. A functional understanding of individual psychopathology—that is, an understanding of the processes that develop, maintain, and exacerbate psychopathology—provides a foundation for case conceptualization and the creation and personalization of evidence-based intervention. It is unsurprising, then, that there is no shortage of views in the field about how best to go about assessing and conceptualizing cases. Prominent in this discussion are strong arguments for the merits and demerits of our most ubiquitous classification system, the largely categorical DSM-5.

Clinicians and researchers are increasingly torn between the advantages of this categorical classification (e.g., efficiency and communicability) and the growing appreciation for the dimensional nature of psychopathology (e.g., Maser et al., 2009; Brown & Barlow, 2009; Rosellini, Boettcher, Brown, & Barlow, 2015). Coupled with the necessity of taking into account the unique processes maintaining and exacerbating each patient's difficulties, it is clear that assessment and case formulation can be far from straightforward.

The purpose of this chapter is to present a practical, flexible framework for these tasks. We begin by discussing ways in which the current categorical DSM approach to classification could be improved, followed by our perspective on why transdiagnostic approaches are a promising alternative. Next, we provide instructions for assessing and conceptualizing transdiagnostic processes using the Unified Protocol for Transdiagnostic Treatment of Emotional Disorders (UP), and we close by highlighting a new direction in transdiagnostic classification: a novel transdiagnostic assessment tool that was developed at our clinic, the Center for Anxiety and Related Disorders at Boston University (CARD).

CLASSIFYING MENTAL DISORDERS: ROOM FOR IMPROVEMENT?

We start our discussion with classification (i.e., assignment of diagnostic labels) because in most settings, the approach taken to classification dictates not only the approach taken to initial assessment, but also subsequent case formulation and assessment of treatment outcomes. In any discussion of classification, it is important first to acknowledge the advantages of a categorical system like that used by the DSM-5 and earlier versions. Categorical classification is a useful and necessary part of both research and clinical practice.

Studies show that emotional disorder diagnoses exhibit good reliability using both DSM-IV and DSM-5 criteria (Brown, Campbell, Lehman, Grisham, & Mancill, 2001; Brown, Di Nardo, Lehman, & Campbell, 2001; American Psychological Association, 2013), likely as a result of clearly defined sets of symptoms and clinical severity cutoffs. Categorical classification also establishes a common language among scientists and provides guidelines for clinicians searching for appropriate interventions. Treatment outcome research depends upon clearly defined sample characteristics, and categorical classification can facilitate the selection of evidence-based treatments from the literature. Categorical diagnosis, in some cases, can also offer patients useful labels for their difficulties, which may promote better understanding of their mental health struggles and facilitate self-advocacy for good care. Finally, insurance companies utilize a categorical diagnostic system in determining coverage for mental health services—without a diagnosis, patients can experience more limited access to affordable, quality care.

Coexisting with these strengths, purely categorical classification nevertheless has several major disadvantages, particularly for the study and treatment of emotional disorders. These disadvantages have been explored in detail previously (Brown & Barlow, 2009; Rosellini et al., 2015) and we return to them here, as they have informed our efforts to develop improved systems of classification, assessment, case conceptualization, and treatment.

First, categorical classification overemphasizes differences between diagnoses that have many shared features, as researchers have demonstrated. As described in Chapter 1, this problem is exemplified by high rates of comorbidity among emotional disorders. In a large study of DSM-IV emotional disorders at our clinic, 81% of patients met criteria for more than one current or lifetime Axis I disorder (Brown, Campbell, et al., 2001). Troublingly, statistics such as these are vulnerable to significant variability based on DSM diagnostic rules. For example, the use of the hierarchical rule in which generalized anxiety disorder (GAD) is not assigned when it occurs within the course of a depressive disorder (American Psychiatric Association, 2013) causes the comorbidity of GAD and persistent depressive disorder (DSM-IV dysthymic disorder) to drop from 90% to just 5%, obscuring important information about anxiety in depressed patients (Brown, Campbell, et al., 2001).

DSM-5 exacerbated this issue by introducing a variety of new diagnoses and further splitting emotional disorders into additional categories (for a review, see Rosellini et al., 2015). As an example, the previously unified DSM-IV anxiety disorders are now split into three categories: DSM-5 anxiety disorders, trauma- and stressor-related disorders, and obsessive-compulsive and related disorders. Many disorders are newly counted in these categories due to being moved from other sections of the DSM (e.g., separation anxiety disorder, trichotillomania, and body dysmorphic disorder). There are also several new emotional disorders in DSM-5, such as hoarding disorder (previously considered a subtype of OCD), premenstrual dysphoric disorder, and disruptive mood dysregulation disorder. As the number of functionally similar emotional disorders grows, it is inevitable that high comorbidity rates will continue to be present.

Categorical classification also can inadvertently downplay subthreshold symptoms, which may independently benefit from intervention or make significant contributions to the maintenance or exacerbation of another diagnosis. For example, a patient with OCD who avoids touching surfaces in public could experience additional distress from subthreshold symptoms of social anxiety that lead her to be overly concerned that others will judge her for her OCD-related behaviors. Symptoms that do not make the diagnostic cut risk being insufficiently addressed in case conceptualization, or else not clearly communicated across providers.

In the domain of emotional disorders specifically, our current diagnostic system is also ill suited to detecting some examples of emotion dysregulation that may be central to some patients' difficulties. While there are a number of diagnoses related to the experience of intense, frequent anxiety or sadness, other emotions, like anger and shame, are often present in patients with emotional disorders and may be a source of significant distress and impairment, but they are not adequately captured in DSM diagnoses. Although the former is central to intermittent explosive disorder, that diagnosis is constrained by a highly specific and behavioral definition (i.e., destructive outbursts) that captures just one of many other possible manifestations of anger (e.g., being easily provoked to anger, excessively critical, or intolerant of situations that require patience). While anger and shame are both acknowledged as possible features of posttraumatic stress disorder (PTSD), this is also too narrow a domain to capture the many ways in which shame may be problematic (e.g., shame about one's appearance contributing to social anxiety or disordered eating, or shame about perceived incompetence leading to avoidance of tasks that carry the risk of failure). Next, we discuss the ways in which a flexible transdiagnostic framework for case conceptualization need not be limited to the disordered emotions that receive the greatest coverage in DSM diagnoses, or the ways in which problems with anger, guilt, embarrassment, and shame can be maintained by the very same processes that perpetuate difficulties with fear, anxiety, and sadness. In summary, there is substantial room for improvement in current approaches to assessment and case formulation of emotional disorders.

ADVANTAGES OF A TRANSDIAGNOSTIC APPROACH

Fortunately, it has been our experience that incorporating a transdiagnostic perspective to case conceptualization offers several promising benefits. Focusing on common features of psychopathology that transcend diagnostic boundaries allows clinicians to appreciate etiology and maintenance factors contributing to an individual's difficulties, regardless of whether these problems fit solely within one diagnosis or across diagnostic categories. This in turn yields targets for interventions that are efficient and easily personalized. For example, we have found that a transdiagnostic approach to case formulation often reveals important processes that might not be captured by traditional categorical assessment.

A transdiagnostic approach is well suited to understanding functional connections between symptoms that span more than one DSM disorder. For example, a therapist seeing a patient with principal OCD and subclinical social anxiety might help him plan an exposure where he introduces himself to his new coworkers and shakes their hands to increase his tolerance of both social anxiety and contamination fears. A transdiagnostic framework also illuminates the role of processes such as guilt, anger, and shame, which, as described previously, often contribute to psychopathology despite falling outside traditional diagnostic categories. For instance, an individual may find feelings of anger and fear (in the form of panic) to be frequent and intense, and may similarly engage in strategies to avoid experiencing either emotion. When assessed from a categorical diagnosis perspective (i.e., using DSM-5 diagnostic categories), one might identify and classify fear-related emotional distress and diagnose the individual with panic disorder, but miss a similar presentation of anger in terms of the distress, impairment, and associated avoidance that it causes.

We have found transdiagnostic case conceptualization to be less overwhelming for both therapists and patients, who can conceptualize heterogeneous difficulties as growing from the same basic processes rather than mentally switching among multiple diagnostic labels. This may help patients reduce their self-judgment about being diagnosed with two, three, or more comorbid diagnoses, and it also alleviates the burden of choosing which disorder to focus on first, as features of all emotional disorders may be addressed simultaneously.

Perhaps most important, we have found that a transdiagnostic approach allows us to see commonalities among patients' experiences that may superficially appear quite different. We notice, for example, that just as an agoraphobic patient avoids taking the bus when worried about a panic attack, a depressed patient avoids attending social events when worried about not enjoying herself sufficiently—the behaviors function the same and serve as the patients' way of trying to reduce their distress. Patients can engage in catastrophic thinking about the consequences of getting frustrated at a spouse or giving a speech in a class, and they can experience judgmental reactions to the whole range of emotional experiences. By emphasizing the similarities within and between diagnoses, and even nondiagnosable concerns (e.g., experiencing frequent guilt without depressive symptoms or a trauma-related disorder), we are able to provide patients with a more parsimonious explanation of their difficulties and provide a course of treatment designed to assist them with their range of presenting difficulties.

In addition, a transdiagnostic approach can help identify important differences within a diagnostic category that may seem similar on the surface. For instance, one individual with an alcohol use disorder may exhibit symptoms consistent with an emotional disorder, such as frequently experiencing negative emotions and attempting to avoid emotional experiences through consuming alcohol. For these individuals, their alcohol use may function similarly to avoidant reactions commonly found in other emotional disorders, and as you will see in Chapter 8, can be treated similar to other emotional disorders. On the other hand, an individual with an alcohol use disorder who consumes alcohol in problematic and interfering ways due to a maladaptive interest in promoting enjoyment (not avoidance) or is consuming alcohol primarily due to physiological addiction may not be experiencing difficulties consistent with an emotional disorder, and other forms of treatment (e.g., motivational interviewing or medical detoxification) may be more appropriate.

Finally, a transdiagnostic approach is flexible and widely applicable to diverse patients while remaining sensitive to their needs, making it ideal both for novice clinicians and for those faced with complex emotional disorder presentations. For instance, an individual may meet criteria for multiple disorders, such as major depressive disorder (MDD), social anxiety disorder, and alcohol use disorder, and the therapist may identify that the patient is experiencing a series of problems that share similar underlying vulnerabilities, such as frequent negative emotions and aversive reactions to those emotions. Based on this finding, the therapist can construct a more efficient course of treatment that targets those shared vulnerabilities that may manifest themselves in seemingly different ways.

It is important to note that even as we recognize the importance of a transdiagnostic approach to case conceptualization, we simultaneously acknowledge the benefits of categorical diagnosis. As mentioned previously, categorical labels are often essential for communication among researchers, clinicians, consumers, and third-party payers. From empirical research to treatment manuals, our field is organized around a categorical system. For this reason, we do not recommend doing away with categorical diagnosis entirely. Indeed, our treatment still begins with a semistructured clinical interview and assignment of DSM-5 diagnoses. We consider transdiagnostic case conceptualization to have a unique and adjunctive purpose: better understanding the functional mechanisms maintaining a patient's difficulties in order to plan the most effective and efficient treatment.

In the remainder of this chapter, we will describe the method of assessment and case conceptualization within the transdiagnostic framework of the UP. At the end of this chapter, we discuss in greater detail one compelling alternative to the current classification system.

ASSESSMENT AND CASE CONCEPTUALIZATION
USING THE UNIFIED PROTOCOL

As was outlined in Chapter 1 of this book, the UP was developed to treat emotional disorders, which are a broad category of disorders that share common underlying characteristics, such as (a) the experience of frequent, intense negative emotions, (b) aversive reactions to these emotional experiences, and (c) efforts to change or control emotions through avoidance, suppression, or escape. Thus, to begin case conceptualization within this framework and to assess whether the UP is appropriate for a particular patient, it is important to identify the extent to which the patient is experiencing characteristics consistent with an emotional disorder.

We have found it helpful to first describe to patients the characteristics of an emotional disorder, followed by a collaborative exploration of the degree to which these features are reflected in their own experiences. Here is an example conversation we may have to describe the concept of an emotional disorder to patients:

> Prior to when this treatment [the UP] was developed, clinicians and researchers noticed that, more often than not, people presented for help with multiple areas of difficulty. So, for instance, someone reporting difficulties with anxiety might also be struggling with depression. We also noticed it was not uncommon for folks treated for one disorder to experience another disorder at a later point in time. For instance, someone treated for social anxiety may come back for treatment again if they lost their job and fell into a deep depression as a result. On the flip side, they also noticed that some patients getting treated for one problem actually experienced some improvement in their other problems too!
>
> Researchers wanted to understand why it was that mental health difficulties that appeared different commonly cooccurred, and why addressing one area of difficulty sometime helped with other areas as well. They collected lots of data about symptoms of different psychological problems and found that these disorders, at their core, were very similar—they all shared several common characteristics. We refer to this similar group of disorders as emotional disorders.
>
> One underlying characteristic is that people at risk for emotional disorders experience emotions more strongly, intensely, and frequently than the average person. This characteristic exists on a spectrum—some people are low on this characteristic, others are higher. Some people at one end of the spectrum seem like they are not fazed by anything—everything just rolls off their back. And then there are people at the other end of the spectrum, who are just more affected by things, are more emotional, or take longer to calm back down. Where would you put yourself on the continuum?
>
> Let me tell you about another characteristic that's important to emotional disorders. Even more important than experiencing more frequent or intense emotions is having a negative reaction to those emotions when they occur. Responses like "This is really bad," or "I shouldn't be feeling this way" make the

ebbs and flows of our emotional life more scary or distressing, and we can start to be hard on ourselves for feeling the way we feel, making things even worse. Does any of that resonate with you?

What maintains problems like this is the tendency to engage in avoidant coping, which means trying hard to dampen or escape emotions rather than tolerating and accepting them. Examples of avoidant coping can include withdrawing from others when you feel sad, leaving a party when you feel anxious or uncomfortable, procrastinating on a task that might stress you out, or just not making eye contact during a serious conversation with a boss. The Unified Protocol was developed to address these underlying vulnerabilities: intense, frequent emotional experiences, aversive reactions to emotions, and efforts to avoid or dampen them. The focus of the UP is targeting those vulnerabilities—changing the way we process and respond to our emotional experiences.

Following this introduction to emotional disorders and the UP, we will cover each component of an emotional disorder. First, we will discuss the subjective intensity and perceived frequency of each of the patient's uncomfortable or unwanted emotions. We endeavor to assess not only the emotions consistent with the presenting disorders (e.g., anxiety, for someone presenting with an anxiety disorder), but also the full range of subjectively negative emotional experiences: anxiety, sadness, anger, fear, guilt, embarrassment, and shame, as well as any other emotions experienced as uncomfortable by the patient, such as pride. We ask about the frequency of these emotions, how intense they find them, how long they last, and how often they believe that their emotions are stronger than the context of the particular situation may call for (e.g., getting very sad upon experiencing a small setback).

We then assess the extent to which patients find their emotional experiences to be aversive, unwanted, and "bad." We ask how bothersome not only overall emotional experiences are for them, but also specific emotional components, such as how aversive they find certain thoughts or physical sensations associated with those emotions. For instance, an individual with OCD may find her intrusive thoughts to be particularly upsetting, whereas an individual with panic disorder may be particularly distressed by heart palpitations or tightness in his chest that he experiences when anxious or during a panic attack.

Throughout treatment, we stay vigilant for statements that patients make that are judgmental of their emotional experiences or of themselves for experiencing their emotions as they do. These statements can be particularly salient markers of aversion to emotional experiences. Judgments of emotional experiences or of themselves, as mentioned previously, may include "This is really bad," "I shouldn't be feeling this way," "This means I'm out of control," or "I'm just being stupid (for feeling this way)."

While patients may initially focus on situations that they find aversive, the goal is to identify the emotional experience associated with that situation and assess the extent to which the patient finds that emotional experience aversive. For instance, a person may say that he finds parties to be aversive, but the anxiety that he experiences when at a party may actually be the part that is most aversive. For example, avoidance of sex after a sexual trauma may reflect aversion to the sense of fear and vulnerability associated with sexual situations, not opposition to sex itself (Barlow, Farchione, et al., in press).

It is also important to be able to distinguish when a patient is *not* experiencing an aversive reaction to emotions, even strong ones. Patients who acknowledge their emotional experiences, express tolerance of their feelings, understand that their negative emotions will fade eventually, and provide appropriate contextualization of their emotions would not be considered to be having an aversive reaction to their emotional experiences. Sample statements may include "It makes sense that I would feel anxious before a test," or "I have been having a stressful time lately, so I know it will take longer for me to relax after a long day."

In addition to assessing aversive reactions to negative emotions, it is helpful to identify any aversion to positive emotional experiences. This is often more subtle, in that patients do not frequently identify this as a presenting concern (with the focus instead being on distressing negative emotions). Nevertheless, for some patients, aversion to certain positive emotions is relevant to integrate into the case conceptualization. For some individuals, experiencing happiness can trigger concern that their situation or mood will change for the worse ("waiting for the other shoe to drop," so to speak), or that they do not deserve to feel happy for various reasons. Feeling hopeful or optimistic may increase fear that their hopes will be crushed. Feelings of love or affection for another person may increase fear of abandonment or other loss of that relationship. Feeling relaxed and peaceful may increase concern that one is forgetting something or letting one's guard down irresponsibly.

Table 2.1 presents examples of ways in which patients might describe the aversive reactions to emotions typically seen in emotional disorders.

When discussing aversive reactions to emotions with patients, it can be useful to help them identify ways that their aversion to uncomfortable emotions can make emotional experiences even more intense or impairing to their lives. Clinicians can ask patients to describe what happens when they evaluate their emotions negatively in an effort to arrive at a collaborative understanding of the perpetuating effects of aversion. For example, feeling scared about the health consequences of heart palpitations may cause the heart to beat even faster. Highlighting this snowball effect illustrates the rationale for targeting the vulnerability of emotion aversion with the UP.

Next, it is important to assess for the presence of avoidant coping strategies. As described in the Therapist Guide to the UP (Barlow, Farchione, et al., in press), this includes any strategy whose primary function it is to minimize the degree that a patient comes into contact with or remains in contact with an unwanted emotion. Just as we allude to in the description of emotional disorder vulnerabilities presented to patients, such strategies may include the following: (a) overt situational avoidance (e.g., declining to take the bus due to agoraphobia or shake hands due to contamination-based OCD); (b) overt escape (e.g., excusing oneself

Table 2.1. EXAMPLES OF AVERSIVE REACTIONS
TO EMOTIONAL EXPERIENCES

EMOTIONAL EVENT	AVERSIVE REACTIONS	ASSOCIATED DISORDER
Heart racing when stepping onto a crowded train	"If my heart beats any faster I'm going to have to get off the train"	Panic disorder
	"I'm weak for having panic attacks and not overcoming this fear by now"	
Intrusive thought about harming newborn daughter	"Only a monster would think of something like that"	Obsessive-compulsive disorder
	"I'm a horrible parent"	
	"I can never tell my husband this"	
Jitters before giving a speech	"Everyone will be able to tell I'm nervous"	Social anxiety disorder
	"I'll never get promoted if I can't hold it together for a simple presentation"	
Excitement after a first date	"I shouldn't get my hopes up, it probably won't work out anyway"	
Remembering an embarrassing moment	"If that ever happens again I'll just die of humiliation"	
	"Just thinking about that makes me cringe"	
Waking up with a low mood	"This is going to ruin my day"	Depressive disorders
	"I have no major problems, I'm so ungrateful to feel this way"	
	"I hate not feeling 100%"	
Anxiety before a test	"If I keep worrying, I'll never be able to concentrate and will get a bad grade"	Generalized anxiety disorder
	"Why am I such a worrywart about trivial things?"	
Worry that plane will crash	"I'm such an idiot, everyone knows plane crashes are rare"	Specific phobia*
	"I shouldn't think about it, I might jinx us"	

(continued)

Table 2.1. CONTINUED

EMOTIONAL EVENT	AVERSIVE REACTIONS	ASSOCIATED DISORDER
Concern that partner may end relationship	"I couldn't survive alone"	Borderline personality disorder
Anger when dog breaks something	"Even a moron could tell it was an accident, why can't I chill out?"	
Pride after getting cast in a play	"It's lame to be excited about such a small role"	Any emotional disorder
Sadness after a breakup	"I'll never love again"	
	"I can't handle feeling this horrible"	

NOTE: We do not consider all specific phobias to be emotional disorders necessarily; rather, they should be designated as such only if they involve frequent, intense experiences of negative emotion, aversive reactions to these emotions, and avoidant coping.

from a meeting when feeling socially anxious); (c) subtle behavioral avoidance (e.g., rushing through a stressful task or restricting use of caffeine), (d) cognitive avoidance (e.g., distracting oneself or attempting to engage in thought suppression), or (e) use of safety signals (e.g., only going out with one's spouse or carrying medication at all times).

Of course, it is not necessary or recommended to describe all these variations on avoidant coping during case formulation at the first session; instead, we mention them here to draw readers' attention to the diversity of strategies that fall under this umbrella. Often the most salient example of avoidant coping, which is sufficient for illustrating this vulnerability to patients, is overt situational avoidance or escape. Note that avoidant coping, like aversion, may be directed at a single component of an unwanted emotion, such as a thought (e.g., avoiding religious material for fear that it might trigger blasphemous intrusive thoughts) or a physical sensation (e.g., avoiding walking up the stairs quickly due to anxiety about elevated heart rate). Table 2.2 provides examples of avoidant coping.

When assessing features of emotional disorders, it is important to consider the ways in which a patient's sociocultural context may affect her presentation. As we discuss in Chapter, 16 a patient's cultural background may influence the way he describes and reacts to strong emotions. For example, somatic complaints are often more prominent in Latino individuals' understanding of anxiety compared to European Americans (e.g., Varela et al., 2004). Cultural considerations are also important when evaluating the extent to which certain behaviors are adaptive. For example, many patients with social anxiety find it difficult to be assertive, and they may engage in exposure tasks that challenge them to be assertive. On the

Table 2.2. EXAMPLES OF EMOTION AVOIDANCE

Emotion/Emotional Event	Avoidance
Anxiety related to worry	Perfectionistic behavior
	Procrastinate on tasks that will bring up stress
	Avoid things with possible negative outcomes (e.g., checking bank statements)
	Call relatives excessively to check on safety
	Plan excessively for upcoming events
Anxiety related to social situations	Avoid eye contact
	Decline plans with coworkers
	Leave party early
	Avoid participating in meetings or classes
	Refrain from offering opinions
Fear of panic sensations	Take benzodiazepine medication
	Avoid caffeine
	Avoid strenuous exercise
	Carry water at all times
Fear of feeling unable to escape	Only go to the grocery store at off-peak times
	Get off the subway when feeling uncomfortable
	Sit near the exit at movie theaters
	Drive on back roads to avoid getting stuck on highways
	Take the stairs instead of elevators
	Carry reading material to distract from a trapped feeling
Anxiety/shame related to weight or body shape	Delete photographs of self from social media
	Wear baggy clothing
	Restrict calorie intake
	Exercise excessively
	Purge
Anxiety related to abandonment concerns	Text or call partner excessively to check whereabouts
	End relationship preemptively
	Accuse partner of wanting to end the relationship (reassurance-seeking)
	Threaten suicide in the event of a breakup
Sadness	Take a nap
	Watch TV
	Binge-eat
	Drink alcohol
	Engage in self-harm (or attempt suicide)
Anger	Avoid expressing disagreement or asking others to change their behavior
	Leave the room when a touchy subject comes up

(continued)

Table 2.2. CONTINUED

Emotion/Emotional Event	Avoidance
	Refuse to watch the news with friends who have different political views
	Drink alcohol before visiting irritating in-laws
Guilt	Blame another person for a negative outcome
	Change the subject when reminded of a guilty act
Embarrassment	Avoid someone after making a mistake
	Change the subject when a topic of embarrassment comes up

other hand, patients whose cultures have strong collectivist values may also act in ways that European Americans would not consider to be assertive, which could be independent of social anxiety or exacerbate existing social anxiety. Factors such as these may influence the behavioral responses or "alternative actions" that are most effective for a given patient within their cultural context. Chapter 16 discusses cultural adaptations of the UP in greater detail.

Importantly, assessment should not end after the initial session. Rather, there are a variety of opportunities to continue evaluation of neurotic traits at later stages of treatment, which at times may be necessary as well as convenient. Some patients, for example, may lack the insight to report adequately on their reactions to emotions until they have received further psychoeducation and practiced monitoring their emotional experiences. In these cases, and indeed in all cases, we encourage the therapist to be aware of additional points at which transdiagnostic assessment and case formulation can occur.

The first opportunity for further assessment occurs with the introduction of the three-component model and ARC of emotions in Module 2, in which the patient begins to practice identifying the thoughts, physical feelings, and behaviors that comprise their emotional experiences, as well as the antecedents and consequences of those emotions (see Chapter 1). Here, look for thoughts reflecting judgment of, aversion to, or catastrophizing of emotions. This may include stand-alone cognitions (e.g., "I hate that I'm not enjoying this"), or interpretations of other components of emotion (e.g., in response to an elevated heart rate, "This means I'm going to have a nervous breakdown!"). Also, look for behaviors that may be examples of avoidant coping (e.g., "Took a nap," "Procrastinated"). When discussing the ARC of emotions, notice and point out to the patient any emotional responses that provide immediate relief from uncomfortable emotions (i.e., short-term consequence, such as feeling calmer after canceling an interview), particularly those that lead to more negative emotions in the long term (e.g., feeling guilty for not pursuing a new job).

The session on mindful emotion awareness (Module 3) is another opportunity to identify aversion to emotions because this module asks patients to observe and gently disengage from judgmental thoughts during emotional experiences. Similarly, the module on cognitive flexibility (Module 4) involves noticing thinking habits in which the patient overestimates the probability of a negative outcome (e.g., "I'll definitely have a panic attack if I get on an airplane") or underestimates her ability to cope with a negative outcome (e.g., "If I have a panic attack, I'll die of heart failure"), both of which may be signs of negative beliefs about emotions.

Module 5, later in the treatment, asks patients to explicitly identify examples of avoidant emotional behaviors. Specifically, patients identify ways in which certain emotional behaviors may at times contribute to maintaining negative emotions in the long term (e.g., escaping an anxiety-provoking situation). Furthermore, the therapist can continue identifying examples of aversion and avoidance when monitoring the patient's progress through exposures at the end of treatment.

In addition to ongoing assessment of functional processes via the UP modules, we recommend ongoing weekly assessment of anxiety and depressive symptoms. We use the Overall Anxiety Severity and Impairment Scale (OASIS; see Norman, Hami Cissell, Means-Christensen, & Stein, 2006) and Overall Depression Severity and Interference Scale (ODSIS; see Bentley, Gallagher, Carl, & Barlow, 2014). Both are brief, five-item, self-report questionnaires assessing the intensity and interference of anxiety or depression over the previous week, and we graph scores on these measures over time as a basic indicator of treatment progress. At the onset of treatment, it is often helpful to show patients the progress record example in the workbook, in order to highlight the general anticipated downward trajectory and normalize the presence of fluctuations in symptoms across time. The ODSIS and OASIS are not diagnosis-specific, and they have the unique advantage of capturing general difficulties that a given patient considers noteworthy, as opposed to asking about more specific symptoms that may not match the patient's experiences.

Box 2.1 is reproduced from our Therapist Guide (Barlow, Farchione, et al., in press) and presents examples of questions to assist in identifying features of emotional disorders. These questions are designed such that if individuals answer in the affirmative, the clinician then would ask additional questions to clarify further.

FROM ASSESSMENT TO TREATMENT PLANNING

After completing initial assessment of emotional disorder processes, the next step is to translate this information into a personalized approach to treatment. Here, it is important to keep in mind that all the skills in the UP are designed to be used in the service of cultivating a more willing and accepting attitude toward uncomfortable emotions and to reduce maladaptive emotion regulation strategies. As you proceed through the treatment, look for opportunities to highlight and target aversive reactions to emotions and efforts to cope using avoidance. For example, you might notice and point out judgmental qualities of a

Box 2.1

EXAMPLES OF QUESTIONS TO ASSIST IN IDENTIFYING FEATURES
OF EMOTIONAL DISORDERS

To assess for experiences of negative emotion that are *frequent or intense:*

> Does it seem like you feel sad/anxious/frustrated more than other people?
> Is it hard for you to stop thinking about things that upset, anger, or
>   embarrass you?
> Do you consider yourself a worrier?
> Do you have trouble controlling your temper?
> Have other people observed that your emotions seem more intense than
>   others in response to situations?
> Does it take you longer than other people to calm down when you
>   get upset?
> Does it seem like you feel things more intensely than other people?

To assess for *negative reactions to or beliefs about unwanted emotions:*

> Do you beat yourself up for feeling certain ways, like giving yourself a hard
>   time for getting upset about something?
> Do you get frustrated thinking that your emotions are irrational?
> When you start to feel nervous, do you often worry that it's going to escalate
>   into even more anxiety?
> When you start to feel down, do you feel like it's going to ruin your
>   whole day?
> Do you sometimes wish you could get rid of negative emotions altogether?
> Are there parts of your thoughts/feelings/symptoms that scare you?
> Do your emotions feel uncontrollable at times?

To assess for *avoidant efforts to control or change emotions:*

> Do you tend to avoid or put off doing things that make you anxious?
> Do you tend to avoid situations where you think you'll be uncomfortable?
> Do you avoid doing things when you're in a bad mood or feeling down?
> Do you try not to think about the things that make you upset?
> Do you sometimes cope with uncomfortable emotions by distracting
>   yourself?
> Are there things you wish you could do, but don't because you're concerned
>   about feeling a strong emotion like anxiety, sadness, or frustration?
> Do you try to do things to get rid of your negative emotions?
> Do you try to do things to prevent yourself from feeling certain emotions?

patient's report of her overall mood or her response to an event in the past week. Alternatively, you may notice and discourage avoidance of uncomfortable emotions, even outside the context of exposure (e.g., rushing through the retelling of a shameful experience).

Also consider the ways in which a patient's particular strengths and weaknesses may affect the delivery of treatment, as the protocol allows for therapists to select the number of sessions dedicated to each module. For example, a patient who struggles a great deal with self-judgment (e.g., a patient whose social anxiety is worsened by negative thoughts about his own performance in social situations) may benefit from additional practice of mindful, nonjudgmental emotion awareness. In contrast, for a patient whose avoidance of important tasks is most interfering (e.g., a patient's job is in jeopardy due to avoidance of speaking in group meetings), it may be beneficial to move through early skills with greater speed for the purpose of arriving at behavioral change and emotion exposure practice more quickly. Initial case conceptualization would allow a therapist to outline the patient's potential treatment targets and estimated duration of treatment.

We provide a worksheet to facilitate case conceptualization within the UP model at the end of this chapter, along with an example of the completed worksheet. We suggest using the worksheet in conjunction with the steps given here as a guideline for transdiagnostic assessment and case formulation. As with any case formulation, this worksheet should be updated as additional relevant information is obtained during the course of treatment.

1. *Presenting Problems.* Begin by enumerating the problems for which the patient is seeking treatment.
2. *Strong Uncomfortable Emotions.* Assess the patient's experiences of emotions he or she finds distressing to determine whether these experiences seem excessive in frequency and/or intensity, considering questions from Table 3.
3. *Aversive Reactions to Emotional Experiences.* Assess aversive reactions to unwanted emotions, considering Table 1 for examples and questions from Table 3.
4. *Avoidant Coping.* Assess avoidant efforts to cope with unwanted emotions, considering Table 2 and questions from Table 3. Consider overt situational avoidance, subtle behavioral avoidance, cognitive avoidance, and safety signals, recording examples of each.
5. *Focus and Application of Core Modules.* Review the three parts of emotional disorders that you have just identified: strong uncomfortable emotions, aversive reactions to emotions, and avoidant coping. Consider how the skills of each of the core modules can be applied to each element to suit your patient's unique needs and experiences. Use the bottom of the worksheet to record ideas for each module, updating this section as you progress in treatment.

A New Direction: Transdiagnostic Classification Using the Multidimensional Emotional Disorder Inventory (MEDI)

INTRODUCTION

We have just outlined one approach to assessment and case formulation that is flexible, personalized, and sensitive to vulnerabilities common to emotional disorders. As the benefits of a transdiagnostic approach to treatment planning are increasingly examined, it is important to consider another domain in which a transdiagnostic approach may be advantageous: diagnostic classification.

In addition to the limitations of categorical diagnosis discussed previously, taxometric research suggests that many disorders are best modeled as dimensional constructs instead of dichotomous categories. This includes social anxiety disorder, GAD, MDD, PTSD, and somatic symptom disorders (Kollman, Brown, Liverant, & Hofmann, 2006; Ruscio, Borkovec, & Ruscio, 2001; Ruscio & Ruscio, 2002; Ruscio, Ruscio, & Keane, 2002; Jasper, Hiller, Rist, Bailer, & Witthöft, 2012). Furthermore, the cooccurrence of emotional disorders is often explained by higher-order temperamental factors (Brown & Barlow, 2009). For example, the comorbidity of social anxiety disorder and depressive disorders is partially accounted for by the shared feature of low positive affect, and the increased risk for panic disorder among individuals with PTSD may be explained by elevated autonomic arousal in both conditions.

A PROFILE-BASED CLASSIFICATION APPROACH

As described in Chapter 1, colleagues at our research and treatment center have developed the MEDI, a novel approach to emotional disorder assessment that blends the benefits of categorical classification with the advantages of a flexible dimensional approach (Rosellini, 2013; Rosellini & Brown, 2014; Rosellini et al., 2015). The MEDI is a self-report questionnaire that assesses the dimensional vulnerabilities and characteristics of emotional disorder pathology that transcend diagnostic boundaries (e.g., somatic concerns, intrusive cognitions, or depressed mood), yielding an idiographic pattern of T-score elevations. Then, this pattern of elevations can be classified into one of several profile types or classes, reflecting the principal difficulties experienced by an individual with those elevations. For example, an individual showing elevations in depressed mood and social-evaluative concerns, as well as reductions in positive affect, would be grouped in the Social-Depressed class, whereas another individual whose principal elevation was related to intrusive cognitions with smaller elevations in depressed mood and general neurotic temperament would be classified as Obsessed-Worried.

This profile classification approach demonstrates strong convergent validity with DSM diagnostic categories (i.e., diagnosis strongly predicts membership in our phenotypic classes; Rosellini & Brown, 2014). Moreover, our approach adds incremental utility to the current diagnostic system by predicting unique variance in disorder outcomes above and beyond DSM diagnostic status (Rosellini & Brown, 2014), suggesting that such an approach may practically improve upon existing tools. Next is an example of a MEDI score profile for an individual treated with the UP at our clinic.

Using the MEDI: A Case Example

Candace was a female patient in her early 30s who presented to CARD seeking treatment for impairment related to avoidance of social situations and travel. Upon further assessment, she was able to describe that her anxiety was intense enough in a number of situations that it led her to change her daily routine to accommodate avoidance and reduce the likelihood of experiencing anxiety. She reported experiencing panic attacks but indicated that they were infrequent (an estimated two to three full panic attacks in the last six months) due to her efforts to avoid doing things or entering situations where she would feel anxious. She described avoidance of unfamiliar social situations, restaurants, movie theaters, driving, hiking in remote places, and air travel. She also indicated immense concern about being perceived negatively by others and described significant anxiety and avoidance related to giving presentations at work, attending parties, and having conversations with unfamiliar people.

On the basis of her presenting symptoms, Candace received three DSM-5 diagnoses: panic disorder, agoraphobia, and social anxiety disorder. What was not captured in her diagnostic profile was her report of experiencing attenuated pleasure from experiences for as long as she could remember (which she noted was consistent with her family's general affect, but inconsistent in comparison to friends), as well as feelings of boredom in her life that were more recent as a result of the restriction in her activities due to avoidance. She was assessed for a mood disorder, but she did not meet criteria as she was not experiencing significant anhedonia, denied depressive symptoms, and was not experiencing associated symptoms related to a mood disorder diagnosis. In her interpersonal interactions, however, her mood often appeared relatively flat, which was consistent with her description of her internal state.

As seen in Figure 2.1, the MEDI profile for Candace is consistent with her DSM-5 diagnoses. While Candace's social anxiety was judged by her assessor to be less severe than the panic disorder and agoraphobia, her highest elevation was on the Social Concerns dimension, which she rated on average as between "very" and "extremely" characteristic of her. This is likely related to her endorsement that she feels anxious and avoids social situations both for reasons related to her agoraphobia and for fear of panicking when feeling trapped by social convention, but also because it relates to her fear of being judged. Thus, in some ways, the severity of this dimension was split between two diagnoses.

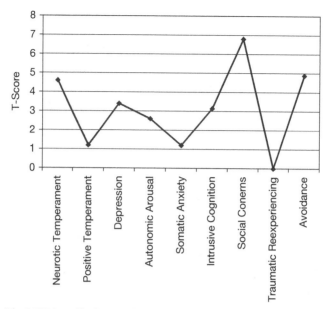

Figure 2.1 The MEDI profile for Candace.

The predominance of her avoidance, as discussed in her interview and as seen as the elevation on the corresponding MEDI dimension, was clear, as she indicated that avoidance behaviors were, on average, rated between "somewhat" and "very" characteristic of her. In addition, the elevation on neurotic temperament and her very low scores on positive temperament (which the MEDI captured and her DSM-5 diagnoses could not) suggest a predisposition to experiencing emotional disorders. Low positive affectivity is related to social anxiety disorder and MDD in particular (Brown, Chorpita, & Barlow, 1998; Rosellini et al., 2010), the latter of which, notably, she developed midway through treatment after her relationship with her husband ended. Due to the transdiagnostic nature of the UP, she and her therapist were able to seamlessly place a greater emphasis on feelings of sadness in treatment, while still working on helping her face situations related to her anxiety.

Testing and refinement of the MEDI is ongoing, as our colleagues continue to collect both cross-sectional and longitudinal data on MEDI profiles in large samples of treatment-seeking individuals. As the use of this instrument becomes more widespread, it promises to provide clinicians with a powerful, unprecedented tool for classification that leads naturally to transdiagnostic treatment planning.

SUMMARY

In this chapter, we have focused on presenting a model for transdiagnostic assessment and case formulation using the UP. In evaluating both categorical and dimensional approaches to assessment, it is critical not to lose sight of our purpose as researchers and clinicians: to achieve an understanding of psychopathology—on the group and individual levels—that leads to effective treatment. While we continue to recognize the value and current necessity of categorical classification, we believe that a functional approach to psychopathology, assessment, and treatment is supported and warranted.

Our functional model of emotional disorders emphasizes the neurotic traits that we have observed to be central in the etiology and maintenance of these disorders. This flexible transdiagnostic framework allows clinicians to determine the ways in which patients' relationship with their emotions is driving their difficulties, which in turn illuminates the degree to which treatment with the UP is appropriate.

In later chapters of this book, you will learn about applications of the UP treatment to patients with a varied range of symptom presentations, ranging from substance use disorders to personality disorders to insomnia. For each, consider the ways in which the patient's experience displays the neurotic traits discussed at the beginning of this book—frequent, intense experiences of unwanted emotion that is experienced as aversive and managed through avoidant coping. Notice, also, how these traits are assessed and incorporated into personalized treatment planning within the UP framework. We hope that the commonalities found across diverse applications of this treatment will be highlighted in the discussion that follows, just as, in clinical practice, they have been impressed upon us.

WORKSHEET 2.A CASE CONCEPTUALIZATION
WITH THE UP: EXAMPLE

UP Case Formulation   Patient: _____

PRESENTING PROBLEMS:

STRONG UNCOMFORTABLE
EMOTIONS:

AVERSIVE REACTIONS:

AVOIDANT COPING

SITUATIONAL AVOIDANCE/ESCAPE:

SUBTLE BEHAVIORAL AVOIDANCE:

COGNITIVE AVOIDANCE:

SAFETY SIGNALS:

TREATMENT PLAN: FOCUS / APPLICATION OF CORE MODULES

MODULE 3:

MODULE 4:

MODULE 5:

MODULE 6:

MODULE 7:

UP Case Formulation   Patient: _____

PRESENTING PROBLEMS:

- Trouble finishing work assignments on time
- "Overthinking" interactions with coworkers
- Anxiety when presenting at meetings
- Unhappy with social circle

STRONG UNCOMFORTABLE EMOTIONS:

- Anxiety about interactions, work

- Fear of embarrassment when presenting

- Sadness about lack of friends

AVERSIVE REACTIONS:

- "Can't get anything done when I'm stressed at work"

- Fearful of blushing

- "It's stupid to feel bad because it's my fault I don't have friends"

AVOIDANT COPING

SITUATIONAL AVOIDANCE/ESCAPE: Turn down opportunity to lead meeting, leave work event early, reluctant to reach out to old friends

SUBTLE BEHAVIORAL AVOIDANCE: Procrastinate on work assignments, poor eye contact when talking to coworkers, rush through presentations

COGNITIVE AVOIDANCE: Start watching TV when think about being lonely, take a nap to avoid thinking about upcoming presentation

SAFETY SIGNALS: Only socializes with sister present

TREATMENT PLAN: FOCUS / APPLICATION OF CORE MODULES

MODULE 3: Practice nonjudgment about having few friends, anchor in the present when worried about work at home

MODULE 4: Decatastrophize making a mistake at work, reframe likelihood of being rejected by old friends

MODULE 5: Practice alternative actions (e.g. talk slowly when presenting)

MODULE 6: Exposure to blushing (pinching cheeks, drinking hot beverage, wearing heavy coat) - later combine this with public speaking exposure

MODULE 7: Emotion exposures: Call old friend, give speech at work, start work assignment immediately

3

The Unified Protocol
for Anxiety Disorders

LAREN R. CONKLIN, TODD J. FARCHIONE,
AND STEVEN DUFOUR ■

INTRODUCTION

Of any cluster of illnesses outlined in the *Diagnostic and Statistical Manual of Mental Disorders* (5th ed.; DSM-5; American Psychiatric Association, 2013), none is more prevalent, likely to serve as a comorbid diagnosis, or costly in the United States than anxiety disorders (Kessler, Chiu, Demler, & Walters, 2005). Recognized as 11 diagnoses in the DSM-5, anxiety disorders are characterized by different degrees of heightened emotional reactions to real or perceived danger, excessive worry about the future, and the resulting cautious or avoidant behavior. Anxiety in its many presentations has become relatively well treated following approximately 60 years of research and clinical advances in the treatment of anxiety disorders (Barlow et al., 2004). Much of the focus during the decades of research into developing effective psychotherapies for these disorders has been related to the question of how best to treat individual conditions, such as social anxiety disorder (formerly known as *social phobia*) or generalized anxiety disorder (GAD; e.g., Clark et al., 2006; Dugas et al., 2003). As a result, many evidence-based treatments for anxiety disorders, particularly those that are behavioral or cognitive-behavioral in nature, have been disseminated as manualized treatments specific to individual diagnoses (e.g., Antony, Craske, & Barlow, 2006).

While there is some evidence to suggest that nontargeted comorbid conditions can show improvement in cognitive-behavioral, single-diagnosis protocols (Borkovec, Abel, & Newman, 1995; Brown, Antony, & Barlow, 1995; Tsao, Lewin, & Craske, 1998), possibly due to similar treatment components being efficacious for a variety of anxiety disorders, the emphasis on developing and researching treatments for single anxiety disorders has carried with it a notable downside for practicing therapists—namely, what to do when a patient presents with more than one diagnosis. Therapists who want to use evidence-based treatments can feel like they are "stuck between a rock and a hard place" when they are working with with these patients. They can choose an evidence-based protocol for one diagnosis and try to fit in the nontargeted anxiety disorder by using examples or supplementary treatment components, risking the patients feeling like some of their problems are getting short shrift. Alternatively, therapists can sequentially apply one single-diagnosis protocol after another, significantly increasing the length of treatment and potentially creating redundancy in content, given the similarities across treatment protocols. Otherwise, therapists may decide to eschew a protocol-based approach entirely, opting instead to try to string together evidence-based components to treat more than one disorder at once. This option may increase the burden on a therapist and lead to a loss of efficacy as the therapist strays from administering a specific empirically supported protocol with fidelity.

Thus, the Unified Protocol for the Transdiagnostic Treatment of Emotional Disorders (UP; Barlow et al., 2018), with its intentional ability to target comorbidity in a manualized treatment, is an approach that can be especially helpful for therapists who want to use an evidence-based treatment, prefer the structure of a manualized protocol, and value the benefits that a workbook can bring to patients in terms of fostering additional understanding from sessions and promoting the review of skills during and after treatment.

CLINICAL CASE EXAMPLES

The following two case examples will be used to illustrate the application of the UP for the treatment of anxiety disorders. Both patients met criteria for more than one DSM-5 anxiety disorder diagnosis.

"Kevin," a married Caucasian man in his 40s, was diagnosed with coprincipal panic disorder and agoraphobia, both with therapist-rendered clinical severity ratings (CSRs) of 5 on a scale ranging from 0 (no symptoms) to 8 (extremely severe symptoms) following administration of the Anxiety Disorders Interview Schedule (ADIS) for the DSM-5 (Brown & Barlow, 2014). In addition, he met criteria for a specific phobia of flying (CSR = 4). He endorsed having panic attacks several times a month and had difficulty riding in elevators, going places without his anxiolytic medication, traveling on the subway, and driving long distances, over bridges, and through tunnels. In response to his fear of flying, Kevin would avoid traveling by plane if he could, and when he did have to travel by plane, he would take only direct flights, even at significantly higher cost. He would also choose flight times he thought would be associated with less turbulence, which he perceived would make it safer. Kevin also would extensively research unfamiliar places (e.g., hotels or restaurants) before visiting for the first time to reduce his uncertainty about his ability to cope with new environments. This research would include looking up whether there were elevators that he would have to travel in (versus being able to take stairs) and how easily he could leave the building if he panicked. While anxiety was the most frequent negative emotion that he experienced, he also indicated that he was bothered by regular irritability and anger, notably in interactions with his wife and children. In session, he was observed to be a friendly, outgoing individual who used humor regularly, even when discussing distressing topics.

The second clinical case is "Susan," a college student in her 20s who was in a stable, committed relationship. At her intake appointment, she was diagnosed with GAD (CSR = 5) and social anxiety disorder (CSR = 4). She endorsed a moderate level of worry about her day-to-day activities, schoolwork, future career, and her relationship with others, which led her to avoid some activities, overprepare for others, and seek reassurance from her boyfriend. She also endorsed significant apprehension about social activities, such as speaking in public, calling people she did not know well, meeting strangers, and disagreeing with people with whom she was not well acquainted.

Susan knew that her desired career in the creative arts field was competitive and required her to "put herself out there" and advocate for her ideas and proposed projects. She worried that she would not be able to excel enough in school, have enough projects in her portfolio to be competitive, or be able to face required social situations (like job interviews or project pitches) with the necessary frequency and skill to succeed. In her personal relationships, she was often anxious about being judged by those closest to her. For instance, she was regularly concerned that her boyfriend or friends would blame her if any part of a planned outing did not go well or if she was not adequately social and outgoing. Her anxiety led her to overprepare for social events or, alternatively, avoid them completely, sometimes cancelling at the last minute. She wished that she felt more capable of hosting parties and confident attending ones to which she was invited. While she did not meet criteria for a depressive disorder, Susan also endorsed a low mood that often mirrored her anxiety fluctuations—that is, on weeks where she felt more worried and overwhelmed, she would also feel more down and more judgmental of herself. In session, she was observed to be well spoken and personable, although she was frequently tired from her worrying and from how much she pushed herself to complete schoolwork.

On the surface, the primary symptoms of these clinical cases appear to be quite different. Kevin is avoiding situations that may cause him to have a panic attack or from which escape may be difficult, such as flying. Susan, on the other hand, is the prototypic worrier, who seeks reassurance from others, is intolerant of uncertainty, and attempts to gain control over an environment that she views as intimidating, demanding, and difficult to manage. Certainly, using DSM-5 criteria, these cases would be conceptualized as diagnostically distinct, which would likely have an impact on how these cases are treated clinically. However, there are also consistencies across these cases that should be considered—common underlying factors that may account for the surface-level differences in symptom presentation. Specifically, one can see that both individuals are experiencing frequent, intense emotions and are reacting to their emotional experiences in aversive and maladaptive ways.

SETTING GOALS AND MAINTAINING MOTIVATION

Individuals bothered by frequent, intense experiences of anxiety can initially present as quite motivated to make changes in treatment because their experiences are so aversive to them, and they can often identify the negative consequences of their short-term efforts to avoid experiencing anxiety. During Module 1, when the decisional balance activity is conducted to assess the patients' motivation and possible ambivalence about treatment (see chapter 1 for a more detailed description), many individuals can easily identify the pros/benefits of making changes, such as being able to relax and experience greater life enjoyment, make more friends, or reduce destructive avoidance and procrastination. They also tend to easily identify the cons/costs of staying the same, such as continuing to be stressed or lonely. What is often more challenging for patients is to identify the cons/costs of making changes and the pros/benefits of staying the same. The reasons for identifying these elements are less intuitive to patients—it makes more sense for them to identify why they want to change and accomplish through treatment, as opposed to the costs of doing so and the benefits of not making changes in treatment.

It is helpful to describe that while identifying motivating factors is beneficial, identifying what might get in the way of making changes can also be important. The UP, while a time-limited treatment, is also long enough for initial motivation to waver. When motivation wavers, the cons of making changes can loom larger. Treatment requires time, money, and effort that could be devoted to other pursuits. If patients are fully engaging in treatment, they are likely going to be feeling (and learning to tolerate) uncomfortable emotions. While patients are not comfortable, per se, with their current experiences, their symptoms and behaviors are familiar to them, and change can feel unknown and intimidating. Further, implementing change over the course of treatment and beyond (after treatment has been completed) requires sustained commitment to practicing treatment skills and consistent application in one's daily life. This requires a considerable amount of effort on a patient's part.

Kevin identified two cons of making changes in treatment. The first was that "change is scary," and the second was that he did not want his "hopes dashed" by achieving a less-than-desired level of symptom reduction with treatment. In using the UP extensively, we have found both of these cons to be common among patients presenting with anxiety disorders. His identified benefit of staying the same was that he "knew what to expect" from his anxiety and related avoidance behaviors. He further elaborated that avoiding things such as tunnels and flying made him feel less anxious, despite being frustrated by his limitations. His identified benefits to making changes in treatment were related to being able to relax more and be a better father, which for him outweighed the benefits of staying the same.

Other individuals with predominant anxiety will present with greater ambivalence regarding change. For instance, individuals whose worry compels them to engage in perfectionistic tendencies or be overly cautious may say that they believe that their behaviors protect them, or that they would not be as successful if anxiety were less of a driving force in their lives. Susan began treatment with a habit of meticulously thinking through and planning each day because she worried that if she did not do so, she would not be sufficiently productive and would be overwhelmed. This created some ambivalence for her at the start of treatment, but Susan was motivated to make changes in her life because she was aware of the additional strain that her worries were placing on her on top of her already stressful school schedule.

When the cons/costs of making changes in treatment and pros/benefits of staying the same have been identified, it is helpful to take time to problem-solve in advance how the patient might respond to them in order to reduce the likelihood that the costs will create a barrier to treatment. One response may involve having patients read their completed decisional balance worksheets to remind them of the benefits of making changes. In cases of ambivalence due to focusing on the positives of worry and anxiety, it can be helpful to highlight that the goal of treatment is *not* to eliminate anxiety. Instead, it is to ensure that patients can use anxiety and other negative emotions in useful ways, such as providing useful information about the immediate situation and motivating them to engage in adaptive behaviors that are most consistent with their goals.

The second component of Module 1 is the delineation of treatment goals. This section is completed with the help of a treatment goal worksheet, which walks patients through outlining their goals, determining ways of making the goals more concrete, and generating a small list of steps that could help them work toward each goal. We have found that patients often benefit from therapist facilitation when selecting treatment goals and identifying concrete steps that could help them make progress toward their goals.

It can be challenging for patients to understand how to set goals that are neither too broad nor too narrow, as well as to create goals that encompass their main areas of difficulty. For instance, Kevin set three goals: (a) reduce his avoidance of situations; (b) have greater spontaneity and be more "carefree" in his decisions (i.e., think less about potential consequences and/or refrain from planning things extensively before doing them); and (c) have an easier time flying.

The first of these is an example of a broader goal, as it encompassed a greater variety of behaviors. In making this goal more concrete, he specified that he wanted to reduce avoidance so that he could ride in more elevators, take routes that involved driving in tunnels or over longer distances, and be able to travel on the subway. To reach this broader goal, he generated ideas of steps that he could take that spanned a few activities, including taking an elevator to the top of a tall building and driving a particular highway that had several tunnels.

In contrast, his third goal, related to flying, started out more specific and (one might argue) could have fallen under his first goal. In his case, given how much fear he had specifically around flying and the avoidance and safety behaviors that he had built up around this activity, it made more sense to separate out this particular goal to help him better understand the steps that he could take to work toward achieving his goal. Some of the steps that he generated included talking to people about flying, reading about turbulence, taking a short flight, and taking a trip with a connecting flight without his anxiolytic medication. When starting to discuss goals with patients, it can be helpful to start drafting ideas of goals on a blank piece of paper first so that you can help them decide which goals might be able to be collapsed because they are related, or which might benefit from being a separate goal.

UNDERSTANDING EMOTIONS

Module 2 begins with a conversation with the patient regarding the adaptive nature of different emotions, including anxiety. Some individuals experience anxiety so frequently and intensely that they have difficulty moving away from a goal of "getting rid" of this emotion and toward an understanding of how their emotions can inform them about situations and motivate action. The emotion of anxiety, for instance, communicates to us that we perceive the possibility of a negative outcome (a future "threat," so to speak) and motivates behaviors designed to reduce the likelihood of such an outcome. The use of the word *perceive* is key here, as it is when describing the other emotions, as it allows for the role that our interpretations of situations play in our perception, as well as the objective facts of the situation.

Following this introduction, the therapist can discuss common examples where anxiety arises and can actually motivate helpful actions. For instance, prior to a big test or job interview, many people experience some level of anxiety. It makes sense that they would feel this way if the outcome is important to them (e.g., doing well on the test or getting the job), and they do not want the more negative, less desired outcomes to occur (e.g., getting a low grade on the test or not getting the job). The adaptive function of anxiety helps individuals focus on preventing the negative outcomes and motivate them in the face of other competing demands. Thus, anxiety can motivate a person to sit down and prepare for the test or interview even in the face of other desired activities, such as watching a movie. When anxiety is too low, it can be difficult to focus on and engage in adaptive, goal-directed behaviors that ultimately could prevent a negative outcome from occurring. Similarly, if anxiety is very high, it might serve as its own distraction, and people may be motivated to avoid actions that would be helpful for obtaining the desired outcome. Patients can often understand why it is helpful to have some level of anxiety in those situations, which can help underscore the point that the goal of the UP is not to eliminate feelings of anxiety (or any other feelings), but instead to help people better tolerate their emotions and respond to them in appropriate ways.

Emotions are, in a manner of speaking, our bodies' way of alerting us that something may be important to pay attention and respond to. With the emotion of anxiety specifically, it is helpful for the individual to first determine what they perceive the future threat to be. In Kevin's case, his anxiety was triggered by a concern that he would experience a panic attack in various situations and be unable to obtain relief or help. In Susan's case, one area in which her anxiety arose was when she perceived that she could jeopardize her career aspirations by not performing well enough in school or not making enough connections in her field to be a success.

When patients start tracking the three components of their emotional experiences (thoughts, physical sensations, and behaviors), those with anxiety regularly include questions as their thoughts. For instance, in Susan's first set of three component model worksheets, she included multiple questions, such as "Have I done enough work?" and "Is my boyfriend ignoring me?" It is helpful to encourage patients to start writing down the implicit answers to the questions that are most related to the emotion that they are feeling in the moment because questions are not typically very distressing in and of themselves. Instead, emotional intensity often comes from certain answers they are focusing on and possibly assuming are true. For Susan, she felt anxious in response to both questions because she was thinking, "I haven't done enough work" and "My boyfriend is ignoring me." Were she focusing on different implicit answers to whether she had done enough work ("Yes, of course I have") or whether her boyfriend was ignoring her ("No, he's just distracted today"), her initial questions would not have been particularly distressing. Identifying the implicit answers to questions when working on three-component worksheets is also important in setting the stage for later cognitive flexibility in Module 4, as it can be difficult to apply the challenging questions to thoughts that are still in the form of questions.

Following the three-component worksheets, patients start identifying the antecedents and consequences of their emotional reactions. When patients begin doing this, it can be challenging to identify more than just the obvious antecedent to an emotional reaction, such as attending a party (anxious) or getting in a fight with a partner (angry). We encourage patients to try to identify other possible antecedents that may be contributing to or making them more vulnerable to experiencing strong emotions in a given situation; for instance, having a stressful day at work or not getting enough sleep the night before attending a party may contribute to feelings of anxiety when trying to socialize and meet new people there.

Having a goal for patients to try to identify at least one additional antecedent other than the most clearly identified antecedent can help them start to put their emotional reactions more in context. Many patients find this process helpful in alleviating some of the distress that they are experiencing over their emotional reactions. Kevin, for instance, noted that having an appreciation for the antecedents of his anxiety and fear helped challenge the belief that his panic attacks occurred "for no reason," and he found it helpful to observe that he had a tendency to "overreact" with stronger anxiety or anger to situations when he was already stressed from events earlier that day or week. With respect to consequences for anxious individuals, helping them to identify short- and long-term consequences of avoidance can be useful in helping them understand why avoidance is so compelling (it eases uncomfortable feelings, sometimes immediately), but also why it contributes to maintaining problems over time (e.g., it becomes harder to face things the more they are avoided).

MINDFUL EMOTION AWARENESS

When teaching mindful emotion awareness (i.e., present-focused, nonjudgmental awareness of emotional experiences), it is helpful to remember that for some individuals, the exercises within this module will serve as an early interoceptive exposure. Turning their attention to how they are feeling in the present moment can increase anxiety temporarily for some, as one form of emotion avoidance is to distract from the physical sensations that they experience. Alternatively, it is quite common for individuals to report that the exercises increase feelings of relaxation, particularly the present-focused, nonjudgmental awareness exercise. This is not what this treatment component is intended to do, and it may, in fact, convey the wrong message to patients regarding their anxiety.

Completing all exercises in session allows the therapist to help patients identify their initial responses and provide an opportunity for corrective feedback or working through any emotional obstacles that may arise. In the case of experiencing anxiety during the exercises, it is helpful to explain to patients that it makes sense that they would feel this way if they find their physical sensations to be threatening (due to their interpretations of what they might mean). Over time, the sense of threat can start to subside if, during the mindfulness exercises, they practice willingly and nonjudgmentally observing their physical sensations instead of trying to distract their attention from them, trying to push the feelings away, or judging them as bad. In cases where patients express feelings of relaxation, we describe to them that while they can feel calm during mindfulness exercises, the determinant of whether they have acquired mindfulness skills is the extent to which they can notice the components of their emotional experiences (thoughts, feelings, and behaviors or behavioral urges) in the moment and can do so nonjudgmentally.

For the mood induction exercises, it is recommended that the therapist and patient generate examples of songs that provoke various emotional states, including songs that provoke feelings of anxiety or tension. Patients sometimes can have an easier time generating examples that may elicit sad or pensive feelings (for instance, Susan selected "My Funny Valentine," and Kevin selected "Blackbird") than songs that have more of an anxious or tense tone. Two examples of songs that we have encountered that can provoke a more anxious mood are "Directions," by Miles Davis, and "Circus Galop," by Marc-André Hamelin.

It can be helpful to clarify that the goal of the music mood induction exercises in the UP is to use the music to learn to observe emotions and the three components of emotions in a present-focused and nonjudgmental way, not as a calming exercise or to practice being mindful of the music itself. In this way, the emotion induction exercises are an early example of an emotion exposure (albeit in a more neutral context), particularly for those individuals who are especially distressed by their emotions. Susan, for instance, found that the mindfulness exercises helped her notice her emotional distress and increase her acceptance of when negative emotions were present, which led to a reduction of her judgment of herself for experiencing them and, relatedly, her low mood.

COGNITIVE FLEXIBILITY

Following the content and skills covered in previous modules that have helped patients gain a better awareness of their emotional experiences, the next three modules of treatment focus on each component of an emotional experience and help patients learn skills to adaptively respond to and better tolerate their emotional experiences. In this module, patients develop an awareness of how they tend to interpret situations automatically, how these interpretations influence their overall emotional state, and how they respond to the situation behaviorally. The UP targets two thinking traps that are common in emotional disorders, especially in anxiety: overestimation of the probability of negative events occurring and catastrophizing the consequences of those negative events should they occur. The exercises in this module help patients identify the thinking traps and promote flexibility by practicing answering targeted questions to help identify alternative thoughts.

Some patients, Susan included, initially express concern that they will not be able to differentiate between adaptive cognitive processes and their maladaptive worry process. In such cases, we discuss a few distinctions between the two. In the UP, adaptive cognitive processing is intentional, mindful, deliberate, and (at least initially) a structured activity where they identify possible thinking traps and ask specific questions to help generate alternative appraisals. Worry, particularly for individuals with GAD, often feels uncontrolled and repetitive and is motivated by the desire to avoid greater emotional upset, either by distracting from more upsetting thoughts (Borkovec, Alcaine, & Behar, 2004) or by trying to prevent the feared outcome, which is perceived to be more distressing than the worry process itself (Newman & Llera, 2011).

Maladaptive worry is difficult to resolve and often revolves around the question "What if this unwanted thing happens?" The product of cognitive flexibility, on the other hand, is a determination of what interpretations of a situation are realistic and what ways of coping would be most helpful, which then are used to move on from a situation or take appropriate action. For instance, Susan indicated that she was able to tell the difference between her repetitive, "what if" thinking that she used to reduce uncomfortable anxiety in uncertain situations and when she engaged in cognitive flexibility, in part because the cognitive flexibility felt less pressured, making her better able to set aside a topic of concern when she engaged in this process in comparison to her process of worry. Further, some patients (particularly those prone to worry) may report using the cognitive skill in the UP to manage their anxiety, but in fact they are engaging in cognitive avoidance, which is addressed more explicitly later in the treatment protocol. We see this illustrated in the following clinical vignette between Susan and her therapist:

SUSAN: *I feel like I'm already using cognitive flexibility to some extent.*

THERAPIST: *You may be. Perhaps you could tell me more.*

SUSAN: *Well . . . when I get really upset about something, I just try to tell myself that everything is fine, and that I shouldn't really be worrying about it.*

THERAPIST: *You try to reassure yourself that things are okay.*

SUSAN: *Yeah, that's right. It's like a little mantra. I just keep telling myself that everything's fine, and that everything will be okay.*

THERAPIST: *Do you find that it works?*

SUSAN: *Sometimes, but usually it doesn't make me feel better for too long. I guess I don't really believe what I'm saying to myself.*

Susan believes that she is engaging in cognitive flexibility because she is trying to adopt a belief that is the polar opposite of her worry. But here, we can see that while the self-reassuring statements function to reduce her anxiety temporarily, the soothing effect fades quickly, and her anxiety and worry return. Some patients will seek reassurance from others in a similar fashion. In both cases, the behavior constitutes avoidance of negative affect.

An additional strategy that is included in the cognitive flexibility module is the downward arrow exercise, which helps patients identify more "core" negative appraisals. This exercise can be especially helpful in instances when the intensity of the patient's emotional response does not seem to match up well with the content of his or her thoughts. In Kevin's case, he completed a downward arrow exercise following a conversation with his wife where he interpreted that she was not listening to him, which led to significant distress. He described feeling anxious and angry, which resulted in him accusing his wife of never listening to him. His reaction to the situation contributed to a drawn-out argument with his wife. Kevin wanted to explore what it was about this situation that made him so upset, so he completed a downward arrow exercise and brought it in to discuss as part of his homework:

KEVIN: *The thought that came up was "She isn't listening to me." That upset me, but it was like a switch went off. One minute I'm having a conversation with my wife, and then I'm all pissed off at her. It was like a trip-wire.*

THERAPIST: *The emotion really ramped up quickly. Zero to sixty.*

KEVIN: *Definitely. After we had the argument and I had some time to think about it later, I really couldn't understand why I got so upset.*

THERAPIST: *It sounds like you noticed how intense your emotions were and you decided to take a close look at what you were thinking. I'm really glad you took some time to complete the downward arrow exercise. Let's review what you wrote. You noted that you had the thought "She's not listening to me." I see you put that at the top of the worksheet.*

KEVIN: *I did. I then asked the different questions on the worksheet, like what it would mean to me if that thought were true. If she wasn't listening to me,*

*I thought it meant she was disinterested in what I was saying . . . that it
wasn't important. I just felt like she didn't care.*

THERAPIST: *That certainly cuts a little deeper. And if that were true?*

KEVIN: *I don't know exactly. I guess I worry that deep down maybe she doesn't
really love me . . . that I'm not good enough for her. That's what I ended up
writing down.*

In asking successive questions related to what it would mean to him if the
thought were true and why it mattered to him, Kevin realized that his core appraisals were that he believed his wife did not care about him and, by extension, that
he was not a worthwhile person to be married to. He realized that this thought
contributed to worry about their marriage (which he cared about greatly) and
caused him to be overly watchful in conversations with his wife for signs that she
may not really love him. Through this example, challenging questions were used
to examine the extent to which he was overestimating the likelihood that this core
appraisal was true.

COUNTERING EMOTIONAL BEHAVIORS

In this module, the focus shifts from thoughts to identifying unhelpful and maladaptive behaviors that are contributing to continued anxiety and distress. This
module includes emotion avoidance and emotion-driven behaviors (EDBs), which
are behaviors that follow and are a result of the emotion experienced. Emotion
avoidance refers to strategies that are used to avoid experiencing strong emotions
or to prevent emotions from being as intense. It can include overt behaviors where
a person fully avoids a situation (e.g., not going to a movie theater if you expect it
to be crowded), as well as less obvious forms of avoidance.

Four kinds of emotion avoidance discussed in this module include overt avoidance, subtle behavioral avoidance, cognitive avoidance, and the use of safety
signals. Sometimes subtle behavioral and cognitive avoidance can be difficult to
identify, but it can be assisted by a few questions to explore patients' responses
for potential avoidance strategies. For example, for subtle behavioral and cognitive avoidance, respectively, the therapist can ask, "What kinds of things do you
do when faced with an anxiety-provoking situation to make yourself feel more
comfortable?" and "When you're in an anxious situation, what do you do to get
your mind off of what is making you feel that strongly?" To identify the use of
safety signals, questions such as "If you left these things at home accidentally, what
would lead you to feel anxious and question your ability to cope with situations?"
or "Are there people for whom you would really feel anxious doing something
without bringing them along or being able to call them?" can help identify objects
and people that are being used to engage in emotion avoidance.

Returning to our clinical examples can show the diversity present in the manifestation of emotion avoidance. Susan identified her subtle behavioral avoidance strategies as making lists prior to starting something, letting others go first

into places by holding the door so that she would minimize being the "center of attention" once inside, and checking the time repeatedly to ensure that she is never late. She identified distracting herself from her anxiety by watching television and using her iPad, reading books, and checking social media repeatedly as forms of cognitive avoidance. Also, as noted previously, she would reassure herself that "everything is okay" or seek reassurance from others. She also noted that her boyfriend was a safety signal for her, as well as carrying books and her phone in her backpack at all times so that she can distract herself if she feels anxious.

It is important to note that sometimes the same behavior can be adaptive in some situations but not others. For instance, with Susan, completing homework in a timely manner was generally adaptive and important to doing well in school, but at times, she would work on homework to avoid doing something social or to distract herself from her worries. By discussing the function of this behavior at different times, Susan was able to recognize that even a healthy behavior, such as being productive, could be used as an avoidance strategy.

In our experience, this type of discussion can occur for a variety of behaviors, such as relaxation techniques, mantras, worry stones, drinking lots of water, getting plenty of rest, and avoiding caffeine. For each behavior, it is helpful to examine whether (or at what times) the patient is using that behavior as a way to avoid experiencing negative emotions because they are so intolerable. For instance, Kevin identified making jokes in situations as a frequently occurring form of subtle behavioral avoidance, listening to music while driving as a form of cognitive avoidance, and carrying his anxiety medication with him as his primary safety signal. Once identified, these forms of emotion avoidance can be targeted during the emotion exposure module.

This module also focuses on identifying and changing maladaptive EDBs. By this point in treatment, most patients are able to identify the EDBs that are problematic for them, like escaping a situation where they feel anxious, because earlier modules have incorporated the identification of EDBs into their practices (e.g., the three-component model of emotions worksheet). In this module, the task moves from identifying EDBs and understanding their short- and long-term consequences to taking steps to change them by responding with alternative actions that are determined to be more adaptive.

For homework, patients can choose behaviors that they want to change in addition to making an effort to select at least one EDB to change in a day. Kevin, for instance, felt anxious about his job and wanted to drink; instead, he developed a plan to work on some tasks that he was stressed about. On a different day, he noticed a desire to yell at his children when he was frustrated with them, but instead he tried to be "mindful of the chaos" and calmly explained why they needed to be quieter. For her part, Susan noticed a few instances where she wanted to respond to her anxiety by overplanning for social gatherings, but she refrained from doing so. As a result, she reported experiencing more anticipatory distress; however, she also found the experiences to be more positive overall, as she was spending less time attending to what she described as "unimportant details."

UNDERSTANDING AND CONFRONTING PHYSICAL SENSATIONS

This module contains similar interoceptive exposure exercises to those contained within treatment protocols for panic disorder, as, typically, the sensations that patients struggling with anxiety experience as distressing can be captured with these exercises as well. The goal of this module is to help patients better tolerate physical sensations associated with intense emotions such as anxiety and fear so that they are less likely to engage in maladaptive behaviors to avoid, distract, or suppress their emotions.

Therapists who are introducing this module are encouraged to discuss with patients what physical sensations associated with their emotions they find most distressing. Some of these sensations may already be clear from earlier modules, where physical sensations are discussed and tracked as part of emotional experiences. As part of this session, the therapist introduces patients to each of the standard interoceptive exercises and then has the patients note the level of distress and similarity of sensations to those that are associated with their distressing emotions. It is helpful to then discuss with patients whether there are any sensations that they find distressing that are not captured by the standard exercises, and brainstorm with them the kinds of exercises that would bring on these sensations. For instance, hot and cold sensations with panic can be brought about by standing in front of a heater and holding ice cubes, pressure in the chest can be simulated by lying on the floor and stacking some books on the chest, and tightness in the throat can be brought about by tying a scarf around the neck or wearing a turtleneck sweater.

For Kevin and Susan, each completed the full list of interoceptive exercises in session to learn how to do the interoceptives correctly, identified their responses to each exercise, and determined which exercises were associated with more than mild distress. For Kevin, the interoceptives that he practiced for homework were hyperventilation, spinning, running, and breathing through a thin straw. Similarly, Susan's list contained hyperventilation, spinning, tensing, and straw breathing. Both patients practiced two exercises daily for a few repetitions each time.

For Kevin, his highest distress and similarity to his panic symptoms came from hyperventilation, starting at an 8/8 in distress (the first edition of the workbook used a scale of 0, no distress, to 8, extreme distress) and ending at a 5/8 on his sixth day of practice. For Susan, her highest distress and similarity to her anxiety symptoms were similar for hyperventilation and straw breathing, both starting at 7/8. Her distress related to hyperventilation reduced after three days of practice to a 3/8, and her distress related to straw breathing was reduced to a 3/8 on her second day of practice.

EMOTION EXPOSURES

The emotion exposure module is the longest in the UP, typically lasting anywhere from four to six sessions. In this module, patients use the skills that they have learned in earlier modules to gradually and repeatedly face emotion-provoking situations. For those with primary anxiety disorders, patients are most likely to include situations that provoke anxiety and fear on their hierarchies, though certainly other emotional experiences, such as feelings of embarrassment (common to social anxiety) or tolerating positive feelings of relaxation (common in those with GAD), also can be included. Through emotion exposures, patients learn that they can cope with distressing emotions and that they can respond effectively to challenging situations. They also gain evidence that helps them further challenge their thoughts related to the chance of negative outcomes occurring or their predictions that they cannot cope with a negative outcome should it occur. While a reduction of anxiety or fear is a common occurrence with emotion exposures, this is not the main goal or a primary indicator of success with exposure exercises, unlike other exposure therapies for anxiety disorders.

Susan's exposure hierarchy highlights how emotion exposures can easily include exposures from more than one diagnostic category. Her list included exposures related to her GAD diagnosis, such as not completing a list or agenda and taking a day/weekend off from schoolwork, interspersed with exposures related to her social anxiety, including hosting a party, making small talk with strangers, and public speaking. Kevin's hierarchy included exposures related to his panic disorder and agoraphobia, such as meeting with clients, driving through a long tunnel, and taking an elevator up a tall building by himself. Furthermore, Kevin's hierarchy also included exposures to help him tolerate difficult emotional experiences not related to his primary diagnoses, such as having serious conversations (without humor or defensiveness), playing golf (related to concerns of embarrassing himself), or calling clients (which he related to low self-esteem).

Susan and Kevin both selected about three different situations each week for their emotion exposure practices and completed their hierarchies over four sessions. While all of Kevin's emotion exposures occurred outside of session, Susan completed a few public speaking exposures in session using a small audience of graduate students and volunteers at the Center for Anxiety and Related Disorders (CARD). When it is possible to practice emotion exposures in session, it is helpful to see whether patients are fully engaging in the exposure exercises and to provide feedback if any emotion avoidance strategies are observed.

RECOGNIZING ACCOMPLISHMENTS AND LOOKING TO THE FUTURE

Module 8 is the final session of the UP, and it focuses on summarizing treatment and relapse prevention. In this session, the patient and therapist discuss progress in treatment, review the skills learned, develop a plan to maintain ongoing skills practice, and generate ideas of longer-term goals and steps for completing them.

By the end of treatment, Susan had gained greater confidence in her ability to present her ideas to groups and cope with the anticipatory anxiety. She also learned that she did not need to overprepare for classes, and facing social situations helped her see that she enjoyed socializing much more when she was able to be present-focused and reduce her self-judgments. After 16 sessions, she no longer met criteria for GAD (CSR = 3) or social anxiety disorder (CSR = 2).

Kevin completed 12 sessions, as is typical for an individual with a principal diagnosis of panic disorder. He experienced increased tolerance of anxiety symptoms, felt more confident facing situations related to his agoraphobia (e.g., elevators), and, toward the end of treatment, was no longer experiencing panic attacks. He also experienced less irritability and anger and developed a greater closeness with his wife after he had some serious conversations with her about their relationship and spent time with her doing fun activities. He saw that, despite his initial nervousness that things related to his wife would not go well, he was able to cope with his anxiety and experience success through productive, nondefensive conversations and mindfulness of the fun activities they did. His CSRs for his panic disorder, agoraphobia, and flying phobia were all reduced to 1 at his post-treatment assessment.

CONCLUSION

In this chapter, we illustrated the application of the UP for two patients presenting with different comorbid anxiety disorders. Differences existed between these cases, most notably at the symptom level, though due to the focus of the UP, the underlying psychopathological processes were addressed in a similar manner. Both patients had difficulty maintaining nonjudgmental awareness of their emotional experiences, frequently experienced negative and anxious thoughts, and tended to engage in maladaptive patterns of behavioral avoidance.

In targeting these underlying processes, both patients experienced significant improvements during the course of treatment. These results were entirely consistent with results from clinical trials examining the efficacy of this protocol for anxiety disorders (Ellard, Fairholme, Boisseau, Farchione, & Barlow, 2010; Farchione et al., 2012; Barlow et al., in press). Long-term follow-up data were not available on these two patients, but based on existing research (Farchione et al., 2012; Bullis, Fortune, Farchione, & Barlow, 2014), maintenance of treatment gains is expected.

4

The Unified Protocol
for Obsessive-Compulsive
and Related Disorders

JOHANNA THOMPSON-HOLLANDS ■

NEUROTICISM IN OCD

Although the presence of obsessions (i.e., intrusive, persistent thoughts or images) is a hallmark of obsessive-compulsive disorder (OCD), research since the late 1970s has shown that intrusive, nonsensical thoughts are actually widespread among the nonclinical population (Freeston, Ladouceur, Thibodeau, & Gagnon, 1991; Rachman & de Silva, 1978; Salkovskis & Harrison, 1984). Furthermore, the distinction between obsessions and the sorts of distressing and future-oriented cognitive activity that characterizes other disorders is often not immediately clear (Comer, Kendall, Franklin, Hudson, & Pimentel, 2004). Worry, a construct central to generalized anxiety disorder (GAD) but present across the anxiety disorders, also has an intrusive quality; although diagnosticians may attempt to distinguish obsessions from worry based upon features such as frequency, duration, or meta-cognitive beliefs (Coles, Mennin, & Heimberg, 2001), this may be difficult to do. In addition, worry (and rumination, in the case of depression) may be self-initiated and result in some feelings of relief if individuals experience these activities as helping them to prepare for or understand a bad outcome, further muddying the distinction between mental compulsions and other types of maladaptive thought processes.

Given the evidence that some level of intrusive thoughts is normative, as well as the difficulty in precisely separating OCD processes from those of other psychological disorders, interest has been aroused as to whether overarching personality factors such as neuroticism might explain the presence of prob-lematic levels of obsessions and compulsions in particular individuals. The negative cognitive style present in neuroticism, combined with specific learning experiences (Barlow, Ellard, Sauer-Zavala, Bullis, & Carl, 2014), may contribute to maladaptive reactions to otherwise normal intrusive thoughts. Indeed, patients with OCD have higher scores on self-report measures of neuroticism than healthy controls (Rector, Hood, Richter, & Michael Bagby, 2002; Samuels et al., 2000; Wu, Clark, & Watson, 2006). Neuroticism has also emerged as a significant predictor of whether nonclinical individuals are classified as high or low in obsessive-compulsive (OC) symptoms, with better predictive ability than other personality dimensions such as extraversion, psychoticism, and sensitivity to punishment or reward (Fullana et al., 2004; Scarrabelotti, Duck, & Dickerson, 1995).

In the fifth edition of the *Diagnostic and Statistical Manual of Mental Disorders* (DSM-5; American Psychiatric Association, 2013), OCD and "obsessive compulsive-related disorders (OCRDs)," a broader range of disorders that includes body dysmorphic disorder (BDD), trichotillomania, and skin-picking, has been split off from the anxiety disorders category (for a discussion of the category of OCRDs and their phenomenology/similarities, see Phillips et al., 2010).

The non-OCD disorders in this category are less well studied, and thus less is known about the contribution of neuroticism in these cases. Nonetheless, all these disorders are characterized by strong negative reactions to an emotional experience, such as a judgment about one's body or an urge to pull out a "not right" hair. These reactions are deemed intolerable by the patients, and they respond with deliberate, maladaptive emotional avoidance (i.e., compulsive behavior). They may state that they "can't stand" not to engage in such behaviors, or that they fear that they will go crazy if they do not follow through with the compulsion. This determined rejection of their emotional experience is thus the target of treatment with the Unified Protocol for Transdiagnostic Treatment of Emotional Disorders (UP). Regardless of the content of the obsessions or the form of the compulsions, patients are taught a new way of relating to their internal reactions and learn that their feelings can be tolerated.

OVERVIEW

"Luke" was a 25-year-old, never-married, Caucasian man, working full time as an elementary school teacher. He lived with his girlfriend of three years. His extended family lived nearby, and he remained quite close to them. Luke presented for treatment at a specialty clinic focusing on the treatment of anxiety and related disorders. During his initial assessment using the Anxiety Disorders Interview Schedule (ADIS) for DSM-IV (Di Nardo, Brown, & Barlow, 1994), Luke was diagnosed with OCD and began 16 sessions of treatment in accordance with the Unified Protocol for Transdiagnostic Treatment of Emotional Disorders (UP; Barlow et al., 2018).

CASE FORMULATION

Luke's most frequent and interfering obsessions concerned fears of something terrible happening to people that he cared about. These thoughts were most distressing to him when they occurred during what he considered to be a transition period; examples of transitions were actions such as crossing a threshold from one room to the next, moving from one activity to another, or touching a new object. If Luke were to have a "wrong" thought (e.g., the image of his mother being treated for cancer) during any of these transitions, he felt a strong urge to redo the action or transition until it "felt right." Feeling "right" meant performing the action or transition while having an opposing "good" thought ("My mother does *not* have cancer"), and often the action needed to be repeated three times or in multiples of three.

Luke believed that having a negative thought during a transition would "seal" that thought and make it more likely to occur [an example of thought-action fusion (TAF; Shafran & Rachman, 2004)]. This belief resulted in so much discomfort for Luke that he was driven to perform a compulsion ("undoing the negative outcome," in his mind) in order to reduce his own distress. The compulsions came up regularly throughout the day; for instance, when getting dressed in the morning, Luke would need to take his pants off and put them back on several times, and brushing his teeth would take up to 10 minutes because he felt compelled to stop on a "good" thought. He struggled with using light switches, walking through doorways, and getting up from a chair. He attempted to mask his OCD around other people by feigning forgetfulness or clumsiness, but he was often late because of his time-consuming rituals.

Luke sometimes would try to minimize the interference of the compulsions, such as by deciding ahead of time that he would limit himself to only three repetitions of a given action, but in practice, he often became stuck in his compulsive behaviors because the guilt associated with not performing them to completion (i.e., "feeling right") was so intense. In those moments, he would have the thought, "If you can't take the time to undo this, you are saying you don't care if [the bad outcome] happens." He was thus overwhelmed by feelings of both fear (of the bad outcome) and guilt (for not caring enough about his family); performing a compulsion temporarily addressed both emotions, but the cycle always resumed.

A secondary area of concern for Luke centered on fears of contamination. Again, the fear was related to harming others, either by allowing them to come into contact with contaminants (bacteria, allergens) or by Luke contracting an illness that would then hurt other people. Because Luke worked with young children, he was frequently exposed to common illnesses like colds and conjunctivitis. He found this aspect of his job to be very distressing and noted that he used avoidance to decrease contact with potential germs. Although his school encouraged a multimodal approach to learning, with frequent use of physical objects as learning aids, he had difficulty using these tools when children were showing signs of illness and would instead use paper worksheets. He also reported using antibacterial wipes and cleansing lotions much more frequently than other teachers did, as well as constantly monitoring his students for signs of illness. In times of very high stress, he would make excuses not to work with the children directly, leaving his coworkers to teach his classes.

In addition to worrying about becoming contaminated by others, Luke worried about inadvertently contaminating others. He was anxious about spreading allergens, particularly peanuts, to the children at school. Luke did not have any allergies to nuts, but he reported that he virtually never consumed them and was often distressed when he needed to eat in an environment where cross-contamination seemed likely (e.g., a cafeteria). He worried that he would get particles of peanuts on his hand, transfer those to a doorknob, and then a child with a nut allergy would touch the doorknob and go into anaphylactic shock. Similarly, Luke was unable to prepare meat at home because of fears that he would undercook it or not clean his work surface sufficiently and therefore would give someone food poisoning.

Luke attempted to manage many of his negative emotions via avoidance. He did not like to speak about possible bad outcomes that could befall those he was close to, and often would whisper when describing his specific fears. He struggled to say certain words or sentences aloud ("My dog could die"). He used physical barriers, such as gloves or the sleeve of his shirt, to avoid feelings of contamination. In this way, Luke prevented himself from feeling the uncomfortable increase in anxiety that would accompany doing or saying upsetting things; however, this also reinforced his belief that such feelings were unbearable.

Importantly, Luke's girlfriend was highly attuned to his OCD and engaged in substantial accommodation (Calvocoressi et al., 1995, 1999) of his symptoms. For instance, she always took responsibility for cooking any meat that they consumed at home, and she performed virtually all kitchen-related cleaning. This was a practical, time-saving strategy because Luke's anxiety caused him to be overly meticulous in cleaning this potentially contamination-laden area of the house, but it also reinforced his avoidance and prevented him from learning to tolerate his distress.

TREATMENT

Luke had sought previous treatment for his OCD during college but described this as fairly unstructured. His sessions had mostly focused on any immediate stressors that had arisen during the week. His therapist had suggested to Luke that he should "try something different" instead of engaging in his usual compulsions, but they had never formally discussed exposures or developed a hierarchy.

Luke was eager to begin a more systematic form of treatment with the UP; he appreciated that the clinician had an outline for what was to be accomplished in each session, and that there were specific forms and exercises to help hold him accountable. He recognized that his avoidance was problematic, and he already forced himself to engage in some activities despite his distress. Luke knew that allowing himself to do only what was comfortable would result in an ever-narrowing repertoire of behavior. In this respect, the UP treatment approach made sense to him.

Setting Goals and Maintaining Motivation

The session began with setting concrete treatment goals. The first overarching goal that Luke identified was to eliminate the need to redo actions throughout the day: "It would be so great to just put on a pair of shoes one time and leave the house like that." Together, Luke and the clinician broke this goal down into the following steps:

1. Delay the repeated action for five minutes.
2. Decrease the number of repetitions (e.g., if he felt the urge to redo the action six times, limit himself to three).
3. Deliberately repeat the action incorrectly (e.g., if he felt the urge to tap the table with his left hand, tap it with his right hand instead).
4. Notice the urge to repeat, but do not do anything.
5. Repeat the action while thinking a so-called "bad" thought.

Luke's second goal of not reacting to fears of contamination was similarly broken down into the following steps:

1. Purposely avoid monitoring which pencil is used by a student with a cold.
2. Only use antibacterial hand cleanser twice per day, at the beginning and end of the school day.
3. Use a public restroom without using any physical barriers (e.g., a shirtsleeve) to touch surfaces.
4. Clean his kitchen in a nonexcessive, nonritualized manner.
5. Deliberately touch a "contaminated" item and resist washing for several hours afterward.

Despite Luke's early acceptance of the treatment model, several important concerns were highlighted when he completed the Decisional Balance Worksheet. Luke's main motivations for seeking treatment were to spend less time on rituals, become a better boyfriend and teacher, and reduce the physical impact of stress on his body. He felt embarrassed about his compulsions and disliked that he was so controlled by what he knew to be irrational fears.

When asked about the costs or drawbacks of initiating treatment now, he mentioned losing a sense of security. Luke had always been an anxious child, and when he "discovered" compulsions in his early adolescence, it felt like he had found a magical solution to his discomfort. Even though he recognized that his compulsions were now imprisoning him as much as his anxiety ever had, he still felt uncertain about voluntarily giving up the only bit of (short-term) control he had ever had over his emotions. Furthermore, he worried that even if he were successful in reducing or eliminating compulsions, his anxiety would merely find a new target. Luke and the clinician talked about the issue of symptom substitution, which has long been disproven (Tryon, 2008). They also discussed that compulsions give a powerful illusion of being able to control anxiety, but Luke's own experience showed that this was not actually the case.

Understanding Emotions

After a more detailed presentation of the rationale for treatment and the three-component model, Luke began completing the Following Your ARC form daily. He was consistent with his monitoring but required some help in distinguishing thoughts from feelings. On his early sheets, Luke would write "Feel like I need to do the right thing by repeating the action" in the column intended for feelings; the clinician explained that the Feelings column was intended for physical feelings only, and that the sentence would be better phrased as the thought "I need to do the right thing by repeating the action" (and placed in the appropriate column).

After some discussion to clarify his experience, it was determined that Luke's "just not right" and contamination sensations should be considered as physical feelings, and Luke recorded them as such. He described the physical aspect of a "just not right" feeling as agitation or restlessness; the physical feeling connected with contamination was a tingling sensation. Regarding his thoughts in these situations, Luke struggled at first to identify any specific fear at all during these "just not right" moments. He would simply experience a strong sense of discomfort and then perform a simple compulsion (like tapping a door frame until it "felt right"). These episodes felt different from some of Luke's other compulsions because he wasn't responding to a particular image or feared thought; the clinician encouraged Luke to identify what he worried would happen if he didn't perform a compulsion in these moments.

Rather than a specific negative consequence to other people, Luke noticed that in these more diffuse anxious moments, he worried about being able to tolerate his own experience. He would think, "I'm worried that the discomfort will just keep building on itself and ruin my whole day" or "What if I get so anxious that I 'snap' mentally?" Once he was able to identify these thoughts, he could monitor them in the usual manner. Luke's fears of infinitely increasing discomfort were a theme that was challenged when he began engaging in emotional exposures; he was able to experience his distress peaking and then slowly reducing over minutes or hours. The urges and distress associated with his "just not right" obsessions were particularly short-lived, in contrast to Luke's predictions.

Luke was very adept at identifying the negative long-term consequences of his compulsions. He noted that the compulsions wasted his time and energy, that he felt embarrassed and disappointed in himself for giving in to them, and that his girlfriend was unfairly burdened with more than her share of household tasks. During the review of his ARC forms, the clinician was careful also to emphasize the short-term consequence of the compulsions (namely, a reduction in anxiety). Luke could acknowledge that even though his compulsions were not rational, he felt momentary relief from distress when he engaged in them. Highlighting this critical piece of the cycle was important in order to reduce Luke's negative self-judgments about his compulsive behavior. In addition, the clinician noted that by consistently engaging in the compulsions, Luke never had the opportunity to test whether his distress would in fact continue to increase to intolerable levels if he did not ritualize. The short-term anxiety reduction was both highly compelling and self-perpetuating.

Mindful Emotion Awareness

Luke was able to understand the goals and rationale of mindful awareness, but he found the practice exercises difficult. Focusing on his breath made him immediately aware that the start and end of each breath was another transition point, and he felt the urge to extend each breath so that it could end on a "good" thought. Immediately after becoming aware of this urge, Luke had a corresponding wave of self-judgment about his inability to relax during the exercise. He felt angry with himself for wanting to engage in compulsions even during a therapeutic exercise.

The clinician assured him that this difficulty was to be expected; his compulsions were present in every other context of his life, so it was only natural that they would come up during mindfulness practice. In fact, the presence of anxiety and corresponding urges to engage in emotion-driven behaviors (EDBs) is part of the purpose of the mindfulness exercise. Luke would be able to objectively notice the development of the distress and the urge to ritualize, and practice letting go of the negative thoughts about his experience. The clinician encouraged Luke to be aware of his desire to change his breathing but to keep breathing naturally throughout the exercise; in this way, the mindfulness also became an early emotional exposure for him.

Cognitive Flexibility

The cognitive flexibility module can be challenging for patients with OCD because they are asked to focus on "second-order" thoughts rather than on their intrusive obsessions. Much research has been conducted regarding the metacognitive beliefs that OCD patients hold regarding their intrusive thoughts, as well as the ways in which intrusive thoughts can be categorized (e.g., overimportance of thoughts, overestimation of danger, intolerance of uncertainty, etc.) (Obsessive Compulsive Cognitions Working Group, 1997).

In Luke's case, this focus meant that reappraisal did not focus on the thought "I am going to become sick/contaminated" or the image of his sister getting in a car accident, but rather on what it meant that he had these thoughts (and what it would mean to *not* act on them). The following are examples of some of Luke's interpretations of his OCD thoughts and how he and the clinician worked to challenge them:

- *This thought is meaningful/predictive of the future/powerful* (TAF)—Luke and the clinician discussed the fact that thoughts cannot predict the future or cause future events, especially not events that are completely outside of one's behavioral control (e.g., a relative getting cancer). These appraisals were conceptualized as a form of jumping to conclusions.
- *It is my responsibility to act on this thought*—The clinician worked with Luke to challenge the idea of whether it was his duty to somehow protect everyone from every possible bad outcome, and the impossibility of this supposed duty. These appraisals were seen as a form of catastrophizing.
- *It is selfish not to perform the compulsion*—This thought implied that there was no cost to Luke's compulsions. Together, the clinician and Luke examined the impact of the OCD behaviors on him, and also whether performing an irrational compulsion truly reflected how much he loved or valued the person in question. These appraisals were a form of catastrophizing.
- *If I don't get rid of this "just not right" feeling, it will make me go crazy/I can't handle the feeling*—The clinician reviewed that strong emotions do not make people "go crazy"; together, they discussed times in the past when Luke had tolerated (or been forced to tolerate) very uncomfortable feelings and managed well. These appraisals were a form of jumping to conclusions.

It can be difficult for both patients and therapists to remain focused on such higher-level appraisals of obsessions, particularly when the obsessions are quite irrational. However, reappraisal can quickly be derailed by targeting the obsessions themselves, rather than the meaning of the obsessional experience. Luke made a great deal of progress, solidifying his willingness to approach exposures, when he addressed the meaning that he was attaching to his intrusive thoughts and considered the evidence.

Countering Emotional Behaviors

Like most anxious patients, Luke was adept at using emotion avoidance. He most commonly engaged in subtle behavioral avoidance: constantly using barriers (a shirtsleeve or gloves) to prevent contamination, maintaining separate caches of teaching supplies for himself and his students, deliberately planning chores around the house so as to "do his part" without having to enter or touch especially difficult rooms, and other behaviors. Cognitive avoidance was more rare, although he did endorse playing video games when he felt too tired to engage in compulsions, especially mental rituals. No specific safety signals were identified.

Luke's EDBs were primarily his compulsions, but he also engaged in reassurance seeking in response to his anxiety. He would directly ask his girlfriend to reassure him around fears of contamination, and he also subtly sought reassurance by calling family members "just to say hi" after having an anxious thought about them.

The requirement that Luke monitor his EDBs and avoidance was somewhat challenging because of the sheer number of examples throughout the day. He experienced urges to ritualize any time that he was aware of transitioning from one place or activity to another, making it unrealistic for him to monitor every instance of resisting (or engaging in) compulsive behavior. Instead, he and the clinician developed the following guidelines: First, Luke should write down a *minimum* of one example per day; second, he should always write down any instance when he truly struggled with engaging in EDBs/avoidance—the instances when he was ultimately able to resist the behavior were important successes to note, as well as the times when he was not able to stop himself from engaging in the compulsions, were clues to remaining challenges that could be more directly targeted with exposures.

Monitoring emotional behaviors allowed Luke to experience a new level of awareness of how often these symptoms were coming up for him on a daily basis. During this portion of treatment, he struggled the most with resisting his contamination obsessions, "because those really could happen." The clinician reminded him that the target for reappraising these fears was not whether the obsession (getting sick from germs) was true or not, but what it would mean if he ignored that thought; he identified this second-order thought as "I'm 100% responsible for making sure that others don't get sick." He also endorsed the fear that "the distress won't go away and the contamination will ruin everything." The clinician reiterated that the goal wasn't for the distress to go away, but to practice tolerating the distress and learning that it wouldn't in fact ruin his day.

Understanding and Confronting Physical Sensations

During Luke's course of treatment, one session and one week of homework was devoted to the module on interoceptive sensations. Luke tested several interoceptive exercises (spinning, running in place, hyperventilating, and straw breathing). Straw breathing was the most effective at replicating his anxious physical response, as he endorsed significant lightheadedness when his anxiety was at its peak. In order to attempt to mimic the sensations that he associated with contamination obsessions, the clinician asked Luke to cross his arms and rub his palms briskly against the fabric of his long-sleeved shirt. This created a tingling feeling in his hands that was similar to his feeling of contamination. He practiced each of these exercises daily for one week and reported a decrease in his anxiety related to the sensations.

Emotion Exposures

For patients with OCD, the exposure hierarchy often includes specific thoughts that are avoided, in addition to traditional behavioral exposures. If patients have high levels of TAF, they will need to practice deliberately thinking about negative things that could happen in the world without compensating with mental rituals. Luke's exposure hierarchy included behavioral tasks such as leaving his office at work without going back multiple times, using a pen that a sick child had touched, touching surfaces in a public restroom without washing his hands, and so on. However, the cognitive items were some of the most difficult, such as deliberately having thoughts about bad things happening to his family and girlfriend; the hierarchy also included lower-intensity items, such as thinking about bad things happening to a stranger. Other relatively easier items for Luke included performing certain movements or daily routines "out of order," meaning not in groups of three or not in the usual pattern (e.g., right to left rather than his preferred left to right). Luke started with these routine-based exposures as homework assignments; this allowed him to achieve a few early, relatively easy successes. He was less likely to avoid these types of exposures because the perceived consequences were lower (his own discomfort rather than harm befalling his family).

When arranging emotion exposures for Luke, it was important to discuss the parameters ahead of time, particularly the length of time during which he was expected to refrain from engaging in his compulsions. Of course, the most ideal situation was for him not to engage in compulsive behavior at all, such as never undoing an upsetting thought. However, exposures around contamination required firm guidelines for the minimum amount of time that he was to resist before washing. Initially, this was on the order of a few hours, and the contamination was limited to his hands; as treatment progressed, Luke was encouraged to contaminate not only his entire body (by touching his hair, face, etc.), but also to spread the contamination to valued items that were difficult or impossible to wash (such as his laptop or a pair of suede shoes).

As is the case when performing any exposure exercises with patients, the clinician needed to be alert to Luke's attempts at emotion avoidance. Early in the exposure work, Luke needed to be reminded gently to grasp a public restroom handle with his entire hand, rather than just touching it with his fingertips. Fortunately, by this point in the treatment, Luke was fairly committed to the treatment rationale and would frequently "confess" when he had engaged in a ritual or act of avoidance; this is especially critical in the case of mental rituals, when the clinician cannot directly observe the behavior.

The final exposure sessions focused on deliberate images of harm to Luke's family. Although he had already had success with exposures to thinking about bad things happening to a stranger, similar thoughts about his family were still extremely anxiety provoking for Luke. In exploring his fears prior to conducting the first exposure of this type, he stated that he still felt that there was a 30% chance that having such thoughts would lead to real-life harm. The clinician worked with

Luke to explore his second-order thoughts about the images ("Thinking these things means that I don't care about protecting my family"), and he was able to reappraise these worries.

Luke was asked to close his eyes and vividly imagine a scenario in which his girlfriend began experiencing mysterious physical symptoms, was diagnosed with cancer, and subsequently died. The clinician asked Luke to describe the story out loud in the session; this allowed her to track the story and encourage Luke to linger on elements that appeared to be the most anxiety provoking for him. Speaking aloud also helped to keep Luke focused on the content of the exposure (increasing present focus) and further heightened his anxiety because saying the thoughts out loud made them feel more real and therefore dangerous.

As with many of Luke's exposures, the period of time immediately following the "active" portion of the exposure was also critical. Following about 15 minutes of imagining his girlfriend's death from cancer, Luke was asked to sit for a further 15 minutes and reflect on having deliberately brought on these terrible thoughts. Because his feelings of responsibility were such a strong factor in his fears, it was important that Luke expose himself to this feeling of having done something that he could not "take back." Similarly, the clinician always asked Luke to generate the specific content for the imaginal exposures, rather than providing the suggestions herself, to increase his feelings of culpability.

Luke and the clinician discussed that the goal of these imaginal exposures was not for him to feel happy or unconcerned at the thought of his family members suffering. Rather, the intent was to reduce his extreme distress around the experience of having these thoughts and to stop actively pushing them away or countering them.

Recognizing Accomplishments and Looking to the Future

As is common in time-limited treatments, Luke was anxious about terminating. He worried that he was "not done." The final session of treatment was spent reviewing his progress, particularly everyday changes that he had noticed since he began the treatment. He was able to recognize that several of his old habits (e.g., using a napkin to provide a barrier when picking up a salt shaker at a restaurant) felt like they existed in the distant past, rather than just four months previously.

To highlight the changes in his behavior and emotional experience, the clinician provided a copy of his original hierarchy with the old ratings of anxiety and avoidance erased; she asked Luke to rerate each item, and the new ratings were compared against the old. This exercise was enhanced Luke's confidence in his progress. Furthermore, we were able to highlight that the categories of obsessions on the hierarchy that showed the most change were those that had been targeted in exposures; the few items that had not yet been challenged showed less improvement. This reinforced to Luke the power of the exposure exercises and increased his motivation to continue addressing any remaining problem areas on his own.

ASSESSMENT DATA

Diagnoses on the ADIS are assigned a clinical severity rating (CSR) of 0-8; CSRs of 4 or higher are considered to be at a clinical level (i.e., meeting the diagnostic threshold for that disorder). At the beginning of treatment, an independent evaluator diagnosed Luke with OCD at a CSR of 6; this decreased to a CSR of 5 at week 8, and further dropped to a 4 and a 2 at weeks 12 and 16, respectively. By the end of treatment, Luke no longer met diagnostic criteria for OCD. His scores on the Yale-Brown Obsessive-Compulsive Scale, second edition (Y-BOCS-II; Storch et al., 2010) showed a similar pattern, with a baseline total of 31 and a final total of 20 at posttreatment, which nevertheless remains above the clinical cutoff of 14 (Fisher & Wells, 2005).

Notably, the decrease in Luke's Y-BOCS-II score was almost entirely due to reductions in the performance of and interference from compulsions; while the obsessions subscale total moved from 14 to 12 over the course of his treatment, the compulsions subscale total dropped from 17 to 8 over that time period. At posttreatment, Luke was continuing to experience frequent and moderately upsetting obsessions, but he was having substantial success in resisting the compulsive behavior and reporting minimal distress when he did so.

Luke's self-report scores indicated that his improvement was not limited to OCD symptoms. He also completed general measures of anxiety and depression weekly (the Overall Anxiety Symptoms and Interference Scale (OASIS; Campbell-Sills et al., 2009) and the Overall Depression Symptoms and Interference Scale (ODSIS; Bentley, Gallagher, Carl, & Barlow, 2014); his OASIS score decreased from 10 to 4 over the course of treatment, and his ODSIS score decreased from 6 to 2.

In addition to these global measures, Luke was periodically asked to complete measures of hypothesized mediators of treatment outcome. One such measure was the Southampton Mindfulness Questionnaire (SMQ; Chadwick et al., 2008). The SMQ measures an individual's ability to observe and accept their emotional reactions nonjudgmentally, and to let those reactions pass; scores range from 0–96. Luke's baseline score on the SMQ was a 6, indicating very minimal mindfulness. However by session 8, following several weeks of practice observing his emotions, Luke's SMQ total jumped to 59. The score continued to increase during the second half of our work, reaching a high of 76 at posttreatment. This impressive growth in his ability and willingness to react mindfully to his experiences likely contributed to Luke's success in treatment; his frequent use of these tools reflects his understanding of and confidence in the model of emotional dysfunction presented in the UP.

Luke also completed measures of temperament during his course of treatment. At baseline, his scores on the Negative Affect and Positive Affect subscales of the Positive and Negative Affective Scales (PANAS-X; Watson & Clark, 1994) were 41 and 33, respectively. At posttreatment, his level of positive affect had improved slightly (to 43) and his level of negative affect/neuroticism had decreased substantially (to 18). These changes are consistent with previous data from a clinical trial of the UP that demonstrated measurable effects on temperament (Carl, Gallagher, Sauer-Zavala, Bentley, & Barlow, 2014).

TREATMENT CHALLENGES

When working with patients with OCD, clinicians must be careful not to inadvertently supplant the patient's original compulsions with new compulsions. For example, at the beginning of treatment, Luke reported that he showered in a very ritualized manner; he always washed his body parts in the same order, and had a particular pattern of applying the soap and washing for a specific amount of time. He reported that it was anxiety provoking to consider washing in another manner, but he also stated that he had been using this pattern for so long that he did not know *how* to shower in a non-OCD way. He asked for guidance about precisely how long he should be spending in the shower and whether any particular pattern of washing was acceptable. After some discussion in session, it became clear to Luke that his questions amounted to reassurance seeking from the therapist about the true "right way" to shower.

This issue of the therapist providing expert advice in OCD treatment must be managed carefully. In Luke's case, the therapist encouraged using his anxiety as a guide as to what behaviors he should move *toward*. He was instructed to set a firm time limit on the shower, to make the overall process more functional, and furthermore, to wash in a pattern that felt mildly unbalanced or otherwise "not just right." Luke brainstormed several possible "not just right" scenarios in session, such as washing in a random order, washing more thoroughly on one side of his body than the other, or leaving a small patch of soap on his body when rinsing off. Anything that left the shower experience feeling incomplete was a good option.

The role of Luke's girlfriend in accommodating his OCD symptoms was another challenge that was addressed throughout treatment. Not only is family accommodation in OCD associated with increased symptomatology and decreased functioning (Amir, Freshman, & Foa, 2000; Calvocoressi et al., 1999; Stewart et al., 2008), but both cross-sectional and longitudinal studies have shown that higher accommodation is related to worse treatment outcomes (Amir et al., 2000; Merlo, Lehmkuhl, Geffken, & Storch, 2009), making this a particularly crucial issue for us to manage.

Luke relied heavily on his girlfriend in his day-to-day life, particularly early in treatment. He was less likely to get "stuck" in rituals if she was around because she would gently encourage him to move on; her comments reassured Luke because he felt that now the responsibility for any bad outcome would transfer to her. She also independently took on many tasks around the house that were highly anxiety provoking for Luke. These accommodating behaviors were highlighted in treatment as examples of emotional avoidance.

Luke regularly shared information about his treatment sessions with his girlfriend; he was able to educate her regarding the treatment model and his goals to begin challenging himself by facing his feared emotions. His girlfriend in turn began to find ways to provide reinforcement for his noncompulsive behavior without engaging in verbal reassurance (e.g., saying "I really appreciate your help with cleaning the kitchen—I know that's hard for you!" rather than reassuring him that he would not get sick or that he was doing a good enough job and there were no germs left behind). Both she and Luke were highly satisfied with and motivated by his progress as he continued through treatment, which facilitated continued reductions in her accommodation. It is possible that future iterations of the UP will include an optional component to address family accommodation; specific attention to accommodation has been shown to enhance treatment outcomes in OCD (Thompson-Hollands, Abramovitch, Tompson, & Barlow, 2015; Thompson-Hollands, Edson, Tompson, & Comer, 2014), and accommodation is a transdiagnostic phenomenon (Lebowitz et al., 2013; Thompson-Hollands, Kerns, Pincus, & Comer, 2014). It is prudent for clinicians to assess for the role of family behaviors in maintaining an emotional disorder and to address those behaviors as they would any other emotion avoidance strategy.

CONCLUSION

Luke's case is an example of a very successful course of UP treatment for OCD. Luke understood and was committed to the treatment model early in the process; he was able to tolerate significant distress in order to reach the top of his exposure hierarchy, and he experienced notable improvement in symptom measures (both general and specific), as well as functioning. The treatment contained challenges, but these difficulties were ultimately overcome, with very positive results.

Although OCRDs are no longer classified among the anxiety disorders in the DSM-5 (American Psychiatric Association, 2013), the current case demonstrates that the UP does not require special modifications to be applied successfully to these disorders. The UP formulation can be readily applied to any pathology involving distressing emotions and deliberate efforts to reduce or avoid that distress. A consistent focus on the rationale for the various treatment elements will facilitate a successful outcome for both patient and clinician.

5

The Unified Protocol for Major Depressive Disorder

JAMES F. BOSWELL, LAREN R. CONKLIN,
JENNIFER M. OSWALD, AND MATTEO BUGATTI ■

INTRODUCTION

Major depressive disorder (MDD) is often a chronic, debilitating condition that waxes and wanes over time but seldom disappears (Judd, 2012). The median lifetime number of major depressive episodes is four to seven; in one large sample, 25% of individuals experienced six or more episodes (Angst, 2009; Kessler & Wang, 2009). For those who do not meet the established criteria for MDD, even mild symptoms of depression are clinically relevant, impactful, and costly at the individual and societal levels (Horwath, Johnson, Klerman, & Weissman, 1994). In addition, MDD and other unipolar depressive disorders demonstrate a high level of comorbidity with anxiety disorders. Approximately 76% of those diagnosed with MDD have at least one comorbid disorder (Kessler et al., 2005), and in a large outpatient sample, 50.6% of individuals with MDD had a comorbid anxiety disorder, with social anxiety disorder being the most common (Fava et al., 2000).

The high degree of observed comorbidity and overlapping variance among depressive and anxiety disorders has led several investigators to conclude that these disorders represent phenotypic variations of the same "general neurotic syndrome" (Andrews, 1990, 1996; Tyrer, 1989). Multiple studies support this conclusion (e.g., Barlow, 2000; Barlow, Allen, & Choate, 2004). For example, Brown and colleagues (Brown, Chorpita, & Barlow, 1998; Brown, 2007) have provided support for a hierarchical structure of emotional disorders, with higher-order temperament constructs accounting for significant covariation among traditional DSM anxiety and depressive disorder constructs. Consistent with the anxiety disorders, MDD has been associated with high levels of negative affect (Clark & Watson, 1991) and behavioral inhibition. Similar to social anxiety disorder, MDD has been associated with low levels of positive affect and behavioral activation (Brown, 2007). As described elsewhere (e.g., Barlow, Ellard, Sauer-Zavala, Bullis, & Carl, 2014), such patterns are in keeping with traditional conceptualizations of neuroticism (Eysenck, 1967, 1981).

TREATMENT IMPLICATIONS

Depression, similar to other emotional disorders, is characterized by inherited temperamental patterns that comprise neuroticism; in particular, a predisposition to experience more frequent and intense negative affect and a high degree of negative reactivity to such affect. Although in MDD, the content may be distinguished from anxious themes (e.g., past loss versus future threat), there are similar psychological processes of inadequate coping and rigid cognitive styles. Key principles from evidence-based MDD treatment approaches have been incorporated into the core modules of the Unified Protocol for Transdiagnostic Treatment of Emotional Disorders (UP), including psychoeducation regarding the nature of emotions and the interactions among cognitions, emotions, and behaviors; practicing objective monitoring; facilitating cognitive flexibility; reducing emotion avoidance and replacing emotion-driven behaviors (EDBs) with more adaptive alternative actions (e.g., behavioral activation); and the extinction of the conditioned associations between reactive distress and emotional experience (through exposure and behavioral experiments). In the sections that follow, we provide a clinical example using the UP with an individual with primary MDD. Starting with the background and case conceptualization, we will outline each module with a description of how that module is utilized generally for those with depressive symptoms (threshold or subclinical) and describe its use specifically through the clinical case example. During the description of the clinical example, we begin to note how this individual experiences frequent, negative emotions, as well as his aversive, maladaptive reactions to these emotions.

CLINICAL EXAMPLE

John was a 20-year-old, single, European-American male. He presented to the Center for Anxiety and Related Disorders (CARD) at the urging of his parents. John initially completed a clinical assessment that involved self-report measures and administration of the Anxiety Disorders Interview Schedule for DSM-IV (Lifetime Version, ADIS-IV-L; Di Nardo, Brown, & Barlow, 1994). Based on this assessment, he was given a principal diagnosis (most severe and interfering) of MDD, with a clinical severity rating (CSR) of 6, on a scale from 0 to 8, with 8 being most severe and interfering); and secondary diagnoses of panic disorder (CSR = 4) and alcohol abuse (CSR = 4).

During the initial intake, John's mood appeared depressed, and his affect was flat. He had difficulty maintaining eye contact, was slow to respond verbally, and

his responses were rather brief. Despite this, John was able to communicate a relatively clear self-narrative of his problems. He reported growing up in a financially
well-off family, having many friends, and endorsed only infrequent, brief periods
of anxiety or low mood prior to when his current difficulties began. He was active
in a number of school sports, yet was most gifted at baseball. He strongly identified with being an athlete and was offered a scholarship to play baseball, which
was his dream. Unfortunately, this was the point at which things took a turn for
the worse.

By his own admission, John reported "completely blowing my chance." He
described being caught off guard by the level of rigor and competition on his
college team. Rather than work or train harder, he reported developing a negative attitude toward his coach and teammates. In addition, he struggled to keep
up with his coursework. Rather than seek assistance or attempt to improve his
study habits, he reported "drinking more [alcohol] and missing more classes."
Consequently, John was placed on academic probation after his first semester,
further compromising his standing on the baseball team. Rather than accept
assistance, John described "pulling away and blaming others," shutting himself
off from his teammates and friends. In addition, he began experiencing panic
attacks and insomnia. Subsequently, John was academically dismissed after failing
to meet minimum GPA requirements for the second consecutive semester.

This was a devastating blow for John. He returned home to live with his parents and began working part time for his father. When he was not working, he
reported sitting alone all day in his parents' basement, either watching television
or "staring at the wall." During the previous summer months, he had isolated
himself from several of his friends who were back from college for the summer. During the fall, he became more depressed as he thought of his friends
back at school, progressing "on schedule" with their lives. John reported being
uncertain if he would return to college. However, his parents had become more
concerned and expressed frustration with the option of continuing to support
him financially without a plan. At the beginning of treatment, John received total
scores that were well into the clinical range on the Overall Depression Severity
and Impairment (ODSIS; Bentley, Gallagher, Carl, & Barlow, 2014) and Overall
Anxiety Severity and Impairment (OASIS; Norman, Cissell, Means-Christensen,
& Stein, 2006) scales (see Table 5.1). In addition, he received scores that were well
into the clinical range on the Emotion Regulation Questionnaire (ERQ; Gross
& John, 2003), Southampton Mindfulness Questionnaire (SMQ; Chadwick
et al., 2008), and the emotion suppression subscale of the Multidimensional
Experiential Avoidance Questionnaire (MEAQ; Gamez, Chmielewski, Kotov,
Ruggero, & Watson, 2011).

Case Formulation

John's initial case formulation could be summarized by two factors: (a) significant
negative reactivity to frequent negative internal experiences, and (b) maladaptive

Table 5.1. BASELINE AND POSTTREATMENT DESCRIPTIVE DATA, RELIABLE AND
CLINICALLY SIGNIFICANT CHANGE

	Baseline	Post	R.CI	Cutoff Score
OASIS	13	6	3.32	≥ 7
ODSIS	15	7	3.42	≥ 8
SMQ	29	58	18.66	≤ 37
ERQ-R	12	30	8.23	≤ 28
MEAQ D/S	20	15	8.11	≥ 25

NOTE: ODSIS = Overall Depression Severity and Impairment Scale; OASIS = Overall
Anxiety Severity and Impairment Scale; SMQ = Southamptom Mindfulness
Questionnaire; ERQ-R = Emotion Regulation Questionnaire-Reappraisal scale;
MEAQ D/S = Multidimensional Experiential Avoidance Questionnaire-Distraction/
Suppression scale. RCI = Reliable change index. Cutoff score = score differentiating
clinical from nonclinical samples.

and inflexible emotion regulation strategies. He may have, in reality, lived a version of a "charmed life," as he initially described, but potential vulnerabilities
for emotional disorders also could be identified. For example, according to his
descriptions, his parents were quite anxious and perfectionistic, and his brother
was reportedly experiencing social anxiety and problems with low mood. It is
possible that the earlier life stressors that John experienced failed to activate a
level of negative emotion that persistently overwhelmed his coping resources.
Based on the history provided, he had always excelled in the area that he valued
most: athletics. This provided consistent positive reinforcement.

  In addition, John's history and demeanor indicated that he may not have been
fully aware of or willing to acknowledge or engage with strong negative emotions; common coping strategies included dismissing the perceived source or
cause of distress, externalizing responsibility, and/or engaging in additional
physical activity to manage stress and provide additional opportunities to bolster his positive feelings about himself. Starting college was a significant source
of stress, and there was a need to perform well on both the athletic field and in
the classroom to keep his scholarship. It is not surprising, therefore, that the
overall level of expectable stress that was triggered by such a major life transition, coupled with no longer being a big fish in a small pond, activated a level
and persistence of negative emotion to which John had hitherto never been
exposed. Furthermore, athletics had always been his primary outlet for positive
reinforcement, as well as a method of stress management, yet this had become
one of the primary contexts for his negative emotion. With the loss of his primary coping mechanism, he started to engage in significant behavioral and cognitive emotion avoidance that only served to exacerbate his difficulties. After
being dismissed from school and returning to his parents' home, he continued
to engage in various forms of emotion avoidance and EDBs (e.g., socially isolating, sleeping, and no longer engaging in physical activity). These behaviors and

associated negative and judgment-laden cognitions maintained and strengthened his depressed mood and anxiety, which contributed to an increased sense
of hopelessness.

Treatment

Treatment with the UP begins with psychoeducation regarding the nature of emotions, neuroticism, and experiential avoidance. For individuals with MDD, it is
helpful to highlight and emphasize the adaptive nature of sadness—essentially,
that it informs us that we perceive ourselves to be experiencing an uncontrollable
setback or loss of some kind. In turn, this can prompt us to withdraw temporarily to mourn and process the loss or consider ways of resolving the setback, if
possible.

In our experience, patients can struggle with understanding why sadness is
adaptive, not simply a painful, undesired emotion. When initially asked how sadness is adaptive, a number of our patients state, "Without sadness, there can be
no happiness," but this explanation falls flat for them (as it should). People can
identify and appreciate happiness as opposed to a euthymic mood, as happiness or
joy is adaptive for its own reasons—it helps us know what experiences to continue
to seek out or identify experiences that we value. When individuals have difficulty understanding how sadness can communicate important information about
a situation, it can be helpful to use examples to demonstrate this concept. For
instance, the therapist could say, "Let's imagine that you work at a job for several
years and are downsized. What would it tell you if you felt sad about this situation
versus, in comparison, that you did not feel sad about your job ending? Next, let's
imagine that you realize you have not been in as close contact with a friend over
the last year. What would it tell you if you felt sad about this realization versus if
you did not feel sad?"

With continued discussion, patients can observe how sadness can fit the context of a situation (i.e., the emotion makes sense in the face of a setback or loss),
can inform them of things that are important to them and the next steps that they
might take. As an example, if a patient felt sad about growing distant from a friend,
that might prompt them to get in touch with that person again and rekindle the
friendship. Nevertheless, it can be helpful to empathize with how difficult it is for
some patients to recognize the adaptive nature of sadness; the adaptive function
of any emotion may be unclear when it is clouded by secondary emotional reactions and other forms of disrupted processing.

Even with a healthy dose of empathy, it is important to watch for signs that
the patient may find this rationale to be invalidating (e.g., the patient perceives
that the therapist does not understand the depth of her depression). At this
early stage of the treatment, it is inadvisable for the therapist to strong-arm the
patient into agreement. Rather, it can be useful to acknowledge that one might
not yet fully understand the patient's experience and that it will be important

to work together on the problem and to weigh objectively what does and does not fit.

The setting of goals and discussion of motivation that occurs at the beginning of treatment can be particularly important for those with MDD or anyone with notable depressive symptoms, as generating and maintaining adequate motivation for treatment when depressed can be a challenge (Arkowitz & Burke, 2008; Olfson, Marcus, Tedeschi, & Wan, 2006). Discussing ways of increasing motivation and generating potential solutions for times of particularly low motivation can be helpful, such as placing the decisional balance sheet (with the pros of making changes) in a location where it can be reviewed regularly. In the same vein, working closely with the patient to set clear treatment goals may be necessary if the patient has been depressed for long enough that he has lost perspective on what goals may be important and meaningful for him to pursue beyond the goal of simply feeling better.

In John's case, information about the adaptive nature of emotions was integrated with the previously described case formulation based on his assessment information (e.g., history, presenting concerns). He reported finding information about emotional disorders and the adaptive nature of emotions credible. Specifically, he endorsed that the model appeared logical and the working formulation was a reasonably accurate representation of his experience. Subsequently, time was spent assessing motivation for change and treatment engagement.

Importantly, John expressed a high degree of motivation to change. He expressed agreement with the formulation that his depression and anxiety were a function of his responses to his environment and own internal experience. Interestingly, the key elements of the offered formulation were derived from transdiagnostic cognitive behavioral therapy (CBT) principles. In taking a transdiagnostic approach, the therapist does not throw out specific terms or labels (e.g., MDD); rather, less emphasis is placed on manifest symptom labels. Although somewhat anecdotal, our experience has been that patients view this more descriptive, functional focus favorably. In line with this, we have found that patients find the UP credible and report positive outcome expectations following introduction of the model (Thompson-Hollands, Bentley, Gallagher, Boswell, & Barlow, 2014).

Nevertheless, this was John's first experience with mental health treatment, and he did express some ambivalence regarding the likelihood that treatment of any kind would be helpful. This exemplified the hopelessness that he was experiencing. The therapist helped him further articulate the nature of his ambivalence and empathized with the part of him that felt hopeless for the future. Ultimately, the therapist decided to move forward with Module 2 for the following reasons: (a) despite his understandable ambivalence, John appeared sufficiently motivated for treatment, and he acknowledged that treatment could be helpful; (b) his coping style and treatment expectations were action-oriented; and (c) the early introduction of specific coping skills could yield some initial benefit that might increase hope and enhance further engagement (Hayes et al., 2007; Ilardi & Craighead, 1994).

UNDERSTANDING EMOTIONS

Adaptive emotion regulation involves objective monitoring and labeling of emotions, as well as distinguishing between primary and secondary emotions (Greenberg, 2008). For individuals with predominant depression, care should be taken to help patients identify all three components of their emotional experience, as physical sensations associated with sadness and anhedonia, while often present, can be less easily identifiable than thoughts and behaviors. In addition, although certain emotions such as sadness and guilt may predominate in depressed individuals, we encourage patients to practice identifying the full range of basic emotions. For example, given that low positive affect is a common characteristic of MDD, this underscores the importance of raising awareness of both the experience of positive emotions, if and when they are felt, and one's reaction to positive emotions (e.g., does the individual automatically discount this experience or judge herself for not experiencing it as strongly as she used to?).

John was taught how to identify the core components of his emotional experience (i.e., thoughts, physical sensations/feelings, and behaviors) using the three-component model, as well as identifying the antecedents and consequences of his emotional responses. The following is an abbreviated exchange from an early session:

THERAPIST: *Can you think of a recent example when you experienced a strong emotion?*

JOHN: *Well . . . I cried yesterday, so I guess I was sad.*

THERAPIST: *Would you mind telling me more about that?*

JOHN: *This is really stupid . . . I found out that my brother got a big promotion at work . . . On the one hand, I should be happy for him, but I couldn't stop thinking about how good things are for him and how much of a loser I am, I guess . . .*

THERAPIST: *So you hear this news, and you feel . . .*

JOHN: *Actually, maybe anxious first . . . heart started to race a little and thinking to myself, "How am I going to measure up?" . . . Then I just got real depressed and started to tear up a little . . .*

THERAPIST: *Tell me if I'm on the wrong track, but it sounds like your answer to "How am I going to measure up?" was that you* aren't *ever going to measure up . . .*

JOHN: *Right . . . and then I got really down.*

THERAPIST: *What else did you notice?*

JOHN: *Umm . . . I was thinking that I am not good enough and that this will never change . . . I shut myself up in my room and drank a couple of beers to try and quiet my head and sleep . . . I, uh . . . also called in sick to work yesterday morning.*

During this discussion, the therapist recorded the sequence and content of events on a whiteboard. After identifying the components of John's anxiety and sadness, the therapist further investigated his behaviors and the short- and long-term consequences of his emotional response. Specifically, the therapist explored the consequences of John's avoidance and emotion-driven withdrawal behavior. Together, they identified that while John's isolation may provide short-term relief from a world that feels overwhelming, it undermines his ability to engage in activities and be productive. John's feeling of sadness appeared to stem from his perceived loss of status and his potential to lead a meaningful adult life; his related shame emanated from a sense that this lack of meaningful engagement in the world was a symptom of an inherently flawed self. Consequently, his natural tendency to withdraw and disengage in response to strong negative emotion only served to reinforce his beliefs ("See, I really am a loser and this is hopeless."). The therapist wondered aloud if John could brainstorm alternative actions that might lead to different consequences. For example, would his experience of shame be as intense had he decided to work the day before despite feeling down?

Mindful Emotion Awareness

As is the case with anxiety disorders, individuals with depression experience deficits in mindful awareness of their emotions and experiences, particularly with respect to nonjudgmental awareness and allowing oneself to notice emotions without triggering a repetitive negative thinking process such as rumination (Desrosiers, Klemanski, & Nolen-Hoeksema, 2013). Mindfulness-based therapies are increasingly being examined for MDD, and a meta-analysis indicated similar efficacy for the treatment of mood and anxiety disorders (Hofmann, Sawyer, Witt, & Oh, 2010). The research is consistent with our observations that individuals experiencing depressive symptoms are often quite judgmental of their emotional experiences and the impairment that it has caused them socially and in activities of daily living, leading to secondary emotions of shame, guilt, and hopelessness. Thus, the inclusion of mindful emotion awareness practices can be beneficial both for reducing the frequency of secondary emotions and starting the process of increasing tolerance to negative emotions. In addition, the increase in awareness of how emotions are unfolding in the present moment can be beneficial for responding more adaptively in the moment when alternative action skills receive more attention in later modules.

Returning to our case example, at this point in treatment, John was several sessions in, and there were small signs that he was making progress. His anxiety appeared to be improving, as evidenced by decreasing scores on the OASIS, and he demonstrated compliance with treatment tasks both within and between sessions. John was naïve to psychotherapy and his internal experience at the beginning of treatment, and the combination of early psychoeducation and self-monitoring seemed to foster meaningful self-awareness and increased motivation to engage in therapy. Unlike his anxiety, his depressive symptoms were relatively unchanged. In an effort to improve his mood and provide additional opportunities for self-monitoring practice, John was encouraged to slowly increase his physical and social activity levels. In the context of this discussion, he reported experiencing difficulty remaining present-focused and that various triggers (e.g., being asked about his future plans) would lead him to ruminate excessively:

THERAPIST: *Can you think back to your senior year of high school, and recall what it was like when people asked you [about your future plans] then?*

JOHN: *I guess I would be excited. I was pumped about college and playing lacrosse. It was something to be proud of . . . unlike my current situation.*

THERAPIST: *The contrast is notable from an emotion perspective. The question now almost automatically evokes a very different response.*

JOHN: *I think a lot of people in my situation would respond the same. Not a lot to brag about.*

THERAPIST: *Maybe. Given the circumstances, sadness may be a reasonable emotional response . . . but it isn't that simple.*

JOHN: *Because I get stuck?*

THERAPIST: *I think that's a good way of putting it. This is the distinction we're trying to make between primary and secondary emotional reactions, right? It's more what you're doing with that sadness in that moment that drives the problem, maybe . . . I'm not going to tell you "You shouldn't feel sad." But that response is possibly becoming overlearned . . . and we . . . need to somehow break it up . . .*

To learn more about John's unfolding emotional responses in such moments, the therapist asked him to participate in a mindful mood induction exercise. John was asked to select the stimulus, and he chose to listen to the song "Let Down" by the band Radiohead. The therapist instructed John to pay attention to the components of his emotions as they unfold, and most important, to his responses to his emotions. Although certainly a matter of interpretation, the lyrics imply a mundane work commuter who fantasizes about growing wings and attempting to fly, only to be crushed into the ground ("hysterical and useless"). John began to cry during the song and remained visibly upset. The session continued:

THERAPIST: *Are you stuck?*

JOHN: *I can't stop thinking about how much I blew it . . . and I don't know how to make it right . . . such a disappointment . . .*

THERAPIST: *Disappointment. What does that feel like?*

JOHN: *Punch in the stomach . . . worthless . . . want to crawl away and disappear . . .*

THERAPIST: *Because you disappointed . . .?*

JOHN: *Myself . . . I'm a disappointment . . . to me and everyone else . . .*

THERAPIST: *Because you blew it . . . that's the mantra. "I blew it."*

The degree of John's pain produced a "sinking" feeling in the therapist, yet it also facilitated a feeling of closeness. Initially, the therapist sat with him and attempted to offer space for him to process his experience. The therapist then wondered aloud if disappearing was a fair punishment for "blowing it." In addition, the therapist pointed out that John had been essentially doing just that—disappearing from the world—and also expressed his belief that John will eventually reappear/reintegrate himself with fresh eyes and a new plan for the future.

This discussion and exercise illustrated several important elements of John's emotional experience. For example, his secondary emotional reaction was self-focused and colored by intense shame, and perhaps anger. In addition to being ruminative, his language was extremely self-punitive. Subsequently, John continued to practice mindful emotion awareness while paying particular attention to shifts into ruminative processing and secondary reactions of shame and hopelessness. Initially, he struggled with how to understand the role of shame because although it often indicated a secondary response, it is also a natural emotion that was central to his subjective experience. He reported finding the encouragement to adopt an open and curious stance toward his experience of shame helpful.

Cognitive Flexibility

The UP also integrates cognitive interventions that are commonly included in CBT protocols for depression and anxiety (Beck, Rush, Shaw, & Emery, 1987; Craske & Barlow, 2007). The emotion-focused framework of the UP results in a particular emphasis on: (a) rigid, automatic thoughts that are embedded in emotional experiences; (b) the idea that beliefs and negative automatic thoughts, although potentially maladaptive, often make sense when considered in relation to the emotion being experienced (e.g., hopeless thoughts when sad); and (c) cognitive change is maximized when meaningful affective experience is evoked (so-called hot cognitions; Teasdale & Barnard, 1993).

The UP emphasizes two core "thinking traps": overestimating the likelihood that a negative event will occur and overestimating the consequences of negative events if they were to happen (in combination with underestimating one's ability to cope). For individuals with depression, these thinking traps may look like overestimating the likelihood of negative outcomes of situations ("I probably won't get that job I interviewed for"), overestimating the likelihood that they will experience no pleasure or interest in activities, and underestimating their ability to cope with feeling down or less interested in things while they are working on their recovery (e.g. "I can't handle it if I'm depressed for another week!" or "It will be awful if I'm depressed when I visit my family for Thanksgiving"). Individuals with depression often engage in jumping to conclusions (a variant of overestimation) and come to negative conclusions about situations (e.g., thinking "I'm a loser" if they cannot work themselves up to studying for a test).

The same challenging questions for overestimation work well for these kind of thoughts, although we recommend additionally completing the downward arrow task in the workbook to identify what predictions might follow from the negative conclusions that they draw. For example, upon completing the downward arrow related to the automatic appraisal "I'm a loser," the patient and therapist may uncover that the patient is particularly upset in response to this thought because she believes that being a "loser" will mean that she will never achieve anything positive in life, which is almost certainly an overestimation of that outcome.

In John's case, he gravitated toward the concept of "thinking traps" because this captured his cognitive-affective experience ("When I'm feeling depressed, I just get caught in this negative loop . . . I need to be able to take a step back and realize when I'm in the trap."). Here, the therapist works with John to elicit relevant appraisals and practice flexibility:

> JOHN: *My older brother asked me to do this relay race for some charity. He's helping put it all together. I don't want to do it. I'm out of shape, and he'll just get annoyed with me.*
>
> THERAPIST: *How so?*
>
> JOHN: *I'll hold the team back. He wouldn't say it, but I know he'd be pissed.*
>
> THERAPIST: *Can we slow down and examine that thought? Can you break it down for me?*
>
> JOHN: *I guess it makes me anxious. Maybe I'm jumping to the conclusion that I'll be the weak link . . . I guess I'm also catastrophizing that— assuming that happens, of course—that I guess he'll get angry at me. That makes me kind of depressed . . . maybe ashamed . . . it all makes me not want to do it.*
>
> THERAPIST: *This is really impressive work, John. You connected some common emotions with potential traps. It seems like a behavioral urge to avoid is a common thread.*

The therapist asked John to close his eyes and anchor himself to his breathing. He was then asked to imagine himself standing at the finish line of the race with his brother. First, he was instructed to imagine that his brother was staring at him blankly, and to reflect on his anticipated emotional response. He was then instructed to do the same, but this time to imagine that his brother was visibly upset about something. In both scenarios, John described a negative emotional experience and anticipated a critical response from this brother. He agreed that this was further evidence of rigid responding ("That's the trap"). The therapist then asked John to reflect on the meaning of this trap:

> THERAPIST: *Your brother is angry because . . .*
>
> JOHN: *Not good enough.*
>
> THERAPIST: *Not good enough . . . not fast enough equals not good enough . . .*
>
> JOHN: *Yes . . . but that doesn't seem fair . . .*
>
> THERAPIST: *I agree, but that doesn't seem to stop you from going there.*
>
> JOHN: *No. I blow it up. I don't want to do that anymore . . . but it's hard.*

THERAPIST: *On the one hand, you have high standards and have found a lot of meaning in being physically dominant . . . on the other hand, maybe you've been holding on too tight . . . maybe you've been defining yourself, your own self-worth too narrowly.*

As homework, the therapist asked John to identify other "worth = X" statements that ring true for him, and to record his emotional response to each one. In addition, he asked John to identify other potential sources of meaning and personal virtues that he prizes. The intent of this was to (a) address rigidity in his core beliefs regarding self and (b) prepare for subsequent treatment modules targeting reduction of emotion avoidance and promoting alternative action tendencies.

Countering Emotional Behaviors

The UP integrates CBT strategies (e.g., behavioral experiments) that are designed to counter patterns of emotion avoidance and maladaptive EDBs. Considerable research has demonstrated that individuals with MDD develop patterns of behavioral avoidance and social withdrawal (Hopko, Lejuez, Ruggiero, & Eifert, 2003). The UP model proposes that such behaviors can be conceptualized as maladaptive emotion regulation tendencies that ultimately maintain and strengthen depression, anxiety, and further avoidance of aversive internal and external stimuli (Ferster, 1973). Interestingly, depending on the specific contingencies, rumination and social withdrawal (as well as substance use) can function as either emotion avoidance or EDBs. For example, John would fail to follow through with social invitations, which would function as negative reinforcement (escaping potential discomfort that might be triggered by interacting with peers). He also would prematurely escape from social situations when anxiety, sadness, or shame would be triggered (e.g., someone asks him about college).

It is important to note that John's depressive behaviors were also likely maintained by positive reinforcement. For example, he received sympathy from his parents and was supported by them financially. John himself identified these factors while discussing the pros and cons of both changing and staying the same during his initial sessions. In fact, his parents' changing attitudes toward his behavior did play a role in his decision to seek treatment.

John and the therapist worked together to identify the most notable patterns of avoidance and EDBs. Many approach behaviors are incompatible with depressive behaviors. He was able to identify the following targets: (a) reducing his use of alcohol, (b) exercising daily, (c) following through with social invitations, and (d) contacting his school to begin developing a readmission plan. John reported being more motivated to return to regular exercise after verbally committing to participate on his brother's relay team.

In addition to "avoiding avoidance" of social situations, he was instructed to practice noticing if/when he shifted into a ruminative process, and to practice mindful awareness using anchoring and three-point check strategies. In practice, avoiding avoidance represents a relatively complex set of skills. In order to remain behaviorally and cognitively engaged in social interactions, for example, John was being asked to (a) objectively reflect upon his emotional responses in the here and now, (b) analyze the function of his responses in relation to overlearned behavioral tendencies, (c) consider reappraisal and behavioral alternatives, and (d) choose an alternative action that is more consistent with his long-term goals and values.

Emotion Exposures

Exposure interventions are typically associated with disorders characterized by fear and anxiety. The UP model offers a conceptual and empirically based foundation for broadening the use of exposure strategies in psychological treatments. Specifically, neuroticism is targeted by facilitating tolerance and eventual extinction of distress in response to strong emotions and associated maladaptive emotion regulation (e.g., behavioral and cognitive avoidance). The treatment of primary MDD does not require any modification to this proposition because any and all emotions are potentially relevant, and specific emotion regulation strategies that have been traditionally associated with MDD in the literature, such as rumination, have been empirically demonstrated to be transdiagnostic (McLaughlin & Nolen-Hoeksema, 2011).

This is not to say that no symptoms or processes (e.g., neurobiological) are unique to MDD, but many such symptoms and processes represent manifest variations of the same underlying etiological and/or maintenance factors (Barlow et al., 2004). It stands to reason, therefore, that emotion-focused exposure interventions can be applied to MDD following similar principles to those that are applied in other problem areas. In fact, previous research (e.g., Boswell, Anderson, & Barlow, 2014; Grosse Holtforth et al., 2011; Hayes et al., 2007) has demonstrated that exposure strategies can be effectively integrated with cognitive therapy for depression. In addition, similar principles of change can be found in mindfulness and acceptance-based approaches (e.g., Roemer & Orsillo, 2009).

INTEROCEPTIVE EXPOSURE

Interoceptive exposure (IE) was originally developed for the treatment of panic disorder (Barlow, Craske, & Cerny, 1989; Klosko, Barlow, Tassinari, & Cerny, 1990), and designed to target fearful responding and sensitivity toward physical sensations associated with anxiety and fear. The conceptual and empirical literature, however, supports IE as a transdiagnostically relevant intervention strategy that can be cohesively and effectively integrated into CBT-oriented treatments for diverse emotional disorders (Boswell et al., 2013; Boswell, Anderson, & Anderson, 2015).

In depression, a subset of the diagnostic criteria relates to distressing physical experiences and functioning, such as fatigue, low energy, psychomotor retardation or agitation, and appetite and sleep disturbances. In addition, anxiety sensitivity has demonstrated unique and meaningful relationships with MDD and depressive symptoms that are not captured by the comorbidity with anxiety disorders (Naragon-Gainey, 2010). Furthermore, all basic emotions, including sadness and the so-called moral emotions like shame and guilt, have a physical component (Barlow, 2002). For instance, sadness-specific physical sensations can include feeling heavy, tired, throat tightness or a lump in the throat, or pain in the chest. It can be challenging for a depressed individual to tolerate these feelings and experience them nonjudgmentally, especially while choosing to engage in activities that they believe are adaptive, such as spending time with friends or engaging in work tasks.

When applied transdiagnostically, targeted, idiographic IE strategies aim to extinguish sensation-associated subjective distress, increase interoceptive tolerance, and increase adaptive behavioral responses in the presence of interoceptive activation (e.g., going to work despite experiencing fatigue and a subjective need for sleep). Examples of interoceptive exercises that can help individuals with MDD better tolerate the physical symptoms specific to sadness include lying down with books on the chest or arms to simulate feelings of heaviness or, similarly, wearing ankle weights during activities; engaging in exercise and then completing daily activities to tolerate feelings of fatigue; or swallowing several times in succession to experience a tightness or lump in the throat.

For John, although he was experiencing frequent panic attacks when he presented for treatment, he also often identified and recorded physical sensations in the context of sadness and shame. His examples included a heavy chest, shortness of breath, and feeling weighed down. Consistent with established IE procedures (Barlow, Farchione, et al., 2018; Barlow, Sauer-Zavala, et al., 2017; Craske & Barlow, 2007), the therapist worked with John to develop a hierarchy of specific exercises and real-world activities that serve to elicit relevant sensations and promote tolerance and extinction of distress. Specific exercises included hyperventilation, narrow straw breathing, and lying down with heavy books on the chest. Real-world activities included increasing the intensity of his exercise and wearing ankle weights (borrowed from the therapist) around the house and while at work.

John was asked to practice these interoceptive activation strategies repeatedly throughout the week. In addition, he continued to work on the aforementioned emotion approach and alternative action goals. The following example illustrates how these strategies ideally become integrated over time. John reported experiencing fatigue, as well as significant anxiety and associated physical symptoms, prior to and during his conversation with his school's admissions office. Rather than avoid making the phone call, cutting it short, or distracting himself, he reported "leaning into" the sensations and staying on the phone call until all his questions were addressed. He reported being somewhat surprised by how quickly his distress diminished over the course of the call, and he reported feeling proud of himself for fully completing this important task. In addition, he was able to recognize that anxiety was a natural and expectable response in this circumstance, given the importance of this phone call.

EMOTION EXPOSURES

The emotion-focused exposure module of the UP can serve multiple purposes. When applied sequentially, it is likely that earlier modules serve similar therapeutic functions, such as increasing emotion tolerance and promoting more adaptive emotion regulation strategies. Interoceptive and situational exposures provide an opportunity to fully integrate and build on previously taught skills, as well as enhance the generalizability of new learning. Consistent with the recommendations of Craske, Treanor, Conway, Zbozinek, and Verliet (2014) for optimizing exposure therapy, rather than focusing on a narrowly defined content area in a very gradual fashion, patients are encouraged to work through diverse, emotionally salient, and meaningful contexts in the absence of avoidance. For MDD specifically, emotion exposures often include engaging in valued activities when experiencing (or predicting) sadness or anhedonia, such as socializing with others or completing work or school tasks. As low motivation is often a barrier to initiating an emotion exposure activity, patients can be encouraged to notice and tolerate the feelings that they experience prior to getting started with the activity as an important part of the emotion exposure experience.

Indicators of successful emotion exposure activities include whether patients were able to complete the activity mindfully and nonjudgmentally without engaging in emotion avoidance or EDBs, whether they were open to experiencing and tolerating negative affect during the activity, and whether they were able to cope with any negative (or undesired) outcomes. For individuals with more severe depression and related avoidance, simply choosing to engage in situational exposure is a major accomplishment. In our experience, it is important to verbally reinforce any such approach behavior and exercise patience when difficulties arise during the exposure process, such as problems with maintaining mindful emotion awareness throughout the activity.

John's main emotion exposure hierarchy can be found in Figure 5.1, though it was used as a rough guide and other relevant exposures were added when indicated. Throughout a given week, he engaged in therapy-informed activities that would be conceptualized as emotion exposures, yet several of these were not specifically identified in session or on this list.

For example, John identified attending one of his old college baseball team's games as the most distressing situation/likely avoided situation. In previous months, the idea of this triggered sufficient anxiety to prompt alcohol use. John anticipated that this situation would elicit a strong, yet complex, emotional response involving anxiety, panic, sadness, shame, and anger. He reported recognizing the importance of this because ultimately, if he did return to his former college, there was a possibility that he would not play baseball, yet still be exposed to various reminders of it. Without the knowledge or assistance of the therapist, however, John decided to join a group of friends who had planned to play tennis, even though he had little experience with the sport and anticipated struggling significantly.

Typically, falling short in an athletic endeavor in front of his peers would trigger anxiety, sadness, shame, and anger; consequently, John viewed this as a good

Do Not Avoid	Hesitate To Enter But Rarely Avoid	Sometimes Avoid	Usually Avoid	Always Avoid
0		**5**		**10**
No Distress	Slight Distress	Definite Distress	Strong Distress	Extreme Distress

	Description	Avoid	Distress
1 **WORST**	Go to old team's baseball game	10	10
2	Visit friend at college	10	10
3	Write letter to admissions committee	9	9
4	Take course at community college	8	9
5	Participate in relay race	7	7
6	Play in recreational hockey league	7	7
7	Spend time with older brother	6	7
8	Ask woman out on a date	6	5

Figure 5.1 Emotion exposure hierarchy.

emotion exposure opportunity and an adaptive alternative action to sitting alone in his parents' basement. John reported experiencing each of these emotions at various points because, by his report, his play was "awful." However, he refrained from engaging in avoidance and less adaptive EDBs (anger outbursts). In addition, he was able to join his friends in seeing the humor in the situation, and subsequently, he joined them for lunch, which likely would not have occurred had he stayed home.

In many ways, this functioned as a corrective emotional experience for John (Hayes, Beck, & Yasinski, 2012): "It didn't matter to them that I sucked. I saw [my doubles partner] getting irritated sometimes, but that came and went . . . I don't have to be perfect . . . I can just be, you know . . . Life is good when I'm not so wrapped up in bullshit."

A similar learning experience took place when John addressed a specific hierarchy item. Although he reported that a part of him wanted to "back out" of his brother's relay race, he followed through with this commitment:

JOHN: *I was nervous because the distance and wanting our team to do good . . . maybe even win. I was about five miles into my first leg, and I felt a pop in my hamstring . . . it seized up and felt like it was on fire. I had to stop running.*

THERAPIST: *I'm sorry to hear that . . . Do you remember experiencing anything besides pain?*

JOHN: *I just felt really bad. I guess disappointed and some shame when my mind was not focused on my leg . . . I felt like I let everyone down a little bit . . .*

THERAPIST: *Did that continue? What happened next?*

JOHN: *Honestly, my mind would go back to a negative place [from] time to time . . . but I also made a conscious effort to stay in the moment. I was like "It's not all about you. This sucks, but you should support your teammates who are working hard . . . maybe my leg will loosen up and I can get back out there at some point."*

THERAPIST: *That's really impressive and shows real flexibility and responsiveness. You recognized and even accepted the disappointment, but also made a choice to stay present-focused and follow through with what was most important about the situation in front of you . . .*

John was able to run a few more miles for his team, but at a relatively slow pace, and he ultimately completed approximately half the anticipated distance. He reported that his older brother was concerned about his injury and expressed his appreciation for John's willingness to participate and stay engaged with the team after his leg injury. Hypothetically, had he internally retreated and "shut down" in response to his injury, his brother and teammates might have responded differently. In reality, his initial pain and observable disappointment elicited sympathy and support in the short term, and his subsequent flexibility (refocusing attention on the present moment and supporting his peers) elicited additional affiliative behavior from others and a subjective sense of connectedness.

POSTTREATMENT

John was seen for 15 sessions of individual psychotherapy. At the end of treatment, John no longer met criteria for MDD, panic disorder, or substance abuse. Throughout treatment, he evidenced gradual improvement in his mental status. John's posttreatment questionnaire scores can be found in Table 5.1. By the end of treatment, John had evidenced reliable change on the calculated reliable change indices (RCIs; Jacobson & Truax, 1991) for depression, anxiety, reappraisal and mindfulness capacity, and emotion suppression. Finally, John enrolled in a community college course and was on track to return to a four-year college.

CONCLUSION

First and foremost, the UP is a comprehensive integration of CBT principles and strategies that seamlessly targets both depression and the constellation of emotional disorders within a coherent theoretical framework. From the perspective of clinical training and practice, this reduces the potential burden of integrating multiple protocols.

We offer the following recommendations for future work involving the UP for MDD and other depressive disorders. Although preliminary research has demonstrated improvements in symptoms and functioning for individuals with depressive disorders who are treated with the UP (Boswell et al., 2014; Boswell & Bugatti, 2016; Boswell, Farchione, Ellard, & Barlow, 2012), more research is needed to examine the efficacy and effectiveness of the UP for principal MDD. However, rather than devote extensive time and resources to conducting traditional comparative efficacy trials, we believe that this research and clinical observation should focus on (a) the optimal sequencing of UP modules for a given patient, (b) common and unique change mechanisms in the UP and alternative treatments, and (c) the interpersonal functions of emotions and its relevance to transdiagnostic CBT for depression. We end this chapter by briefly addressing two of these areas in more detail.

Our first recommendation related to sequencing interventions is not specific to MDD and is motivated by the perceived importance of personalized medicine. Existing empirically supported treatments for MDD, such as cognitive therapy (Beck, Rush, Shaw, & Emery, 1987) and behavioral activation (Lejuez, Hopko, & Hopko, 2001), upon which many UP strategies were derived, introduce their respective core skills relatively early in treatment. It is important to note, however, that initial psychoeducation and monitoring are common across these treatments. In addition, there is mounting evidence that early attention to patient motivation and resistance enhances the efficacy of CBT (Westra, Constantino, & Antony, 2015).

In the absence of empirical scrutiny, we cannot conclude that an earlier introduction of modules focused on cognitive flexibility and behavioral activation skills is necessarily indicated for all depressed patients. However, it may be required for some patients. The case of interest in this chapter, for example, appeared to experience a relatively greater magnitude of change in the second half of treatment. In response to this, an alternative strategy is to preserve the structure of the UP while integrating behavioral activation earlier in treatment as a way of providing practice for early skills. For some patients who are sufficiently inactive that their lives are not providing sufficient material for, say, self-monitoring practices or mindful emotion awareness exercises, this strategy may be appropriate. As an example, one might encourage a patient to make plans with a friend and complete a three-component model related to her experiences or make dinner for herself while practicing present-focusing, nonjudgmental awareness.

Finally, we believe that the UP can be thought of as both transdiagnostic and transtheoretical (Boswell, 2013). While being grounded in a CBT framework, the UP is emotion-focused and shares many theoretical (and even technical) commonalities with emotion-focused therapy (Greenberg & Watson, 2005). A less obvious point of convergence with interpersonal psychotherapy (IPT) is an appreciation for both the intrapersonal and interpersonal functions of emotions. Both maladaptive and adaptive reactivity to, and regulation of, emotions frequently took place within an interpersonal context for the case of interest in this chapter. We believe that the UP model offers a promising pathway for integrating the interpersonal in CBT through its focus on emotion. This is fertile ground for future empirical work.

6

The Unified Protocol for Bipolar and Comorbid Disorders

KRISTEN K. ELLARD, EMILY E. BERNSTEIN,
ANDREW A. NIERENBERG, AND THILO DECKERSBACH ∎

INTRODUCTION

Bipolar disorder is a chronic, severe mental illness affecting approximately 4.5% of Americans (Merikangas et al., 2007). It is defined by the occurrence of manic or hypomanic episodes, which consist of abnormally and persistently high or irritable mood, often accompanied by inflated self-esteem or grandiosity, decreased need for sleep, pressured speech, racing thoughts or flight of ideas, increased goal-directed activity, psychomotor agitation, and excessive involvement in risky, pleasurable activities. However, bipolar disorder is also characterized by episodes of prolonged and often severe depression, and it is frequently accompanied by anxiety, substance dependence, and personality disturbances such as extreme affective lability.

Over 95% of patients with bipolar disorder have at least one other lifetime cooccurring psychiatric disorder (Merikangas et al., 2007), most commonly anxiety disorders, with up to 90% of all individuals with bipolar disorder having a lifetime diagnosis of at least one anxiety disorder and one-third of patients meeting criteria for a current comorbid anxiety disorder at a given time (Goldberg & Fawcett, 2012; Merikangas et al., 2007; Simon et al., 2004). Further, this comorbidity exacerbates the severity and course of the disorder and is related to worse functioning and treatment outcomes (El-Mallakh & Hollifield, 2008; Krishnan, 2005; Otto et al., 2006; Simon et al., 2004). Thus, the reality of bipolar disorder, and by extension the treatment of bipolar disorder, extend beyond traditionally emphasized mood episodes.

As with many of the other disorders featured in this volume, the complex diagnostic picture of bipolar disorder and the accompanying high rates of comorbidity may be partially explained by the construct of neuroticism. *Neuroticism* describes the broad tendency to experience negative emotions in response to stress and to perceive the world in a negative, threatening, and vulnerable way. As described throughout these chapters, neuroticism is strongly associated with risk and maintenance of affective disorders, including bipolar disorder (e.g., Barlow, Sauer-Zavala, Carl, Bullis, & Ellard, 2014).

However, research on the role of neuroticism in risk and the course of illness for bipolar disorder specifically is limited. This may be in part due to the historical taxonomy of mental disorders, which characterized "manic-depression" as a distinct category from "neurosis," the former comprised of what we now call the bipolar mood disorders and the latter comprised of unipolar depression and anxiety disorders. But recent studies show that individuals diagnosed with bipolar disorder score significantly higher on measures of neuroticism than the general population, even after parceling out the effects of related sociodemographic factors and symptoms of depression and anxiety (although these differences may be driven by the minority of patients with extreme levels of neuroticism; Jylhä et al., 2010).

Prospective studies have differed on whether premorbid neuroticism can distinguish healthy controls from patients who will go on to develop bipolar disorder (Hecht, Genzwürker, Helle, & van Calker, 2005). Further, although patients with a family history of any mood disorder tend to show higher neuroticism than patients without this history (Antypa & Serretti, 2014), family studies of bipolar disorder have thus far failed to find elevated incidences of neuroticism in healthy first-degree relatives of patients with bipolar disorder, unlike those with major depressive disorder (MDD; Maier, Minges, Lichtermann, Franke, & Gansicke, 1995). Still, connecting neuroticism to bipolar disorder remains compelling in light of affective and behavioral instability, which are definitional features of both neuroticism and bipolar disorder (Murray, Goldstone, & Cunningham, 2007).

Although high trait neuroticism may or may not diagnostically predict the development of bipolar disorder, research does converge on its link to worse course of illness. Levels of neuroticism reliably show strong positive associations with symptom severity and negative associations with psychotherapy and pharmacologic treatment outcomes in bipolar disorder. More specifically, studies consistently find neuroticism to be associated with more severe bipolar illness overall, as well as more severe depressive and anxious symptoms, consistent with findings in other mood and anxiety disorders. Whereas neuroticism has been found to predict the onset, relapse, and worsening of depressive episodes and symptoms, the specific connection between neuroticism and mania warrants further exploration, as studies have found a direct relationship between the two, no relationship between the two, an association mediated by depression, and a relationship dependent on the rare combination of concurrently high extraversion (Barnett et al., 2011; Jabben et al., 2012; Lozano & Johnson, 2001).

In addition to direct associations with worse mood symptoms, higher trait neuroticism in bipolar disorder has been associated with other significant markers of illness burden, including greater mood lability and intensity, lower self-confidence, greater likelihood of new onset suicidality, and worse quality of life, social functioning, and sleep quality (Bauer & Wisniewski, 2006; Brieger, Röttig, Röttig, Marneros, & Priebe, 2007; Carpenter, Clarkin, Isman, & Patten, 1999; McKinnon, Cusi, & MacQueen, 2013; Pope, Dudley, & Scott, 2007; Saunders, 2013; Stringer et al., 2014; Watson & Naragon-Gainey, 2014). Not only can these symptoms precipitate or exacerbate manic and depressive mood, they also can independently worsen daily life, overall functioning, and likelihood of remission or recovery. Even more basically, neuroticism seems integral to the impaired regulatory processes evident in bipolar and related comorbid disorders. These patterns can be mutually reinforcing and could underlie much of the affective dysregulation evident in this disorder.

Emotion Dysregulation in Bipolar Disorder

Affective dysregulation, or difficulty managing emotional experiences in an adaptive way, in many ways is at the center of the bipolar diagnosis, and it may be the product of the underlying trait neuroticism reviewed previously (Hafeman et al., 2014). Emotion dysregulation is a persistent feature of bipolar illness and strong predictor of functional impairment for patients (Rowland et al., 2013). In addition to perpetuating emotional distress and lability, difficulties with emotional regulation are associated with worsened neuropsychological deficits (e.g., behavioral slowing, poor working memory, impaired executive control), more frequent mood episodes, and worse course of illness (Green, Cahill, & Malhi, 2007; Kanske, Heissler, Schönfelder, & Wessa, 2013).

Further, it has been postulated that difficulties in regulating emotions underlie the chronic course of the illness (Johnson, Gruber, & Eisner, 2007; Phillips & Vieta, 2007; Wolkenstein, Zwick, Hautzinger, & Joormann, 2014). Individuals at high risk for bipolar disorder have shown deficits in emotion regulation and reactivity similar to those found in patients themselves, identifying emotion dysregulation as a potential vulnerability factor for bipolar disorder (Heissler, Kanske, Schönfelder, & Wessa, 2014; Kanske, Heissler, Schönfelder, Forneck, & Wessa, 2013).

Even during periods of perceived euthymia, individuals with bipolar disorder exhibit greater emotional reactivity and intensity for both positive and negative emotions (Gruber, Kogan, Mennin, & Murray, 2013; Gruber, Purcell, Perna, & Mikels, 2013; Van Rheenen & Rossell, 2013). Minor indications of potential threat or reward, for example, have been shown to disproportionately influence self-esteem and vulnerability for mood depressions and elevations (Van Rheenen & Rossell, 2013; Urosević et al., 2010). Habitually intense emotional experiences further correlate with worse subjective psychosocial functioning in this population (Hoertnagl et al., 2011). Such emotionality has been attributed to neurotic temperament, which predisposes people to hypervigilance for emotional content, biased interpretations of events and experiences, and decreased likelihood of shifting attention away from stressors.

This sensitivity and heightened affect intensity is further complicated by how individuals with bipolar disorder respond to and cope with their emotions. Patients tend to report investing more time and effort in trying to regulate their emotions than others. Research consistently shows that depressed, manic, and remitted patients alike engage maladaptive coping strategies more frequently compared to nonpsychiatric populations—namely, rumination and suppression (Gruber, Harvey, & Gross, 2012; Thomas, Knowles, Tai, & Bentall, 2007; Van der Gucht, Morriss, Lancaster, Kinderman, & Bentall, 2009; Wolkenstein, Zwick, Hautzinger, & Joormann, 2014). Compared to nonpsychiatric individuals, patients with bipolar disorder show deficits in dampening emotional responses, inhibiting impulsivity, and differentiating emotions, often relying upon strategies like rumination and catastrophizing that inadvertently worsen distress (Van Rheenen, Murray, & Rossell, 2015).

Although much of the research on emotion dysregulation focuses on the regulation of negative emotions, individuals with bipolar disorder show deficits in the regulation of both negative *and* positive emotions. The few existing studies on dysregulation of positive emotion show that bipolar patients tend to exhibit heightened approach responses (e.g., liking and wanting), more persistent mood elevation, and more rumination in response to positive or rewarding stimuli (Gruber et al., 2013). In addition, suppression or negative appraisals of positive emotions prospectively predict more manic and depressive symptoms in this population (Gilbert, Nolen-Hoeksema, & Gruber, 2013).

Application of the Unified Protocol for Bipolar Disorder

Given the extensive link in bipolar disorder to neuroticism, affect lability, emotion dysregulation, and comorbidity, this population may be particularly suited to benefit from the Unified Protocol for Transdiagnostic Treatment of Emotional Disorders (UP). The UP treatment approach directly targets transdiagnostic deficits in adaptive emotional processes rather than individual disorders. Therefore, complex bipolar cases, which are more common than not, can be more effectively and efficiently addressed in one combined intervention, such as the UP. Further, the UP has a direct and explicit focus on teaching adaptive emotion regulation skills, and thus directly meets a paramount need in this population.

Learning effective coping skills can have enormous implications for patient health; how patients respond to their affective states, more than the affective states themselves, influences course of illness and is even associated with medication adherence in bipolar disorder (Fletcher, Parker, & Manicavasagar, 2013). Effectively employing strategies like reappraisal has been found to reduce state emotional reactivity across multiple domains for individuals with bipolar disorder, including subjective ratings of positive and negative affect, behavioral expressions of emotion, and physiological response (e.g., skin conductance; Gruber, Hay, & Gross, 2014). By incorporating lessons from the treatment of anxiety, behavioral disorders, and depression, and highlighting common underlying cognitive and affective processes, the UP seeks to fill important gaps in the usual treatments for this difficult-to-treat disorder.

Given the success of the UP in treating a full range of anxiety and unipolar mood disorders, it has recently been adapted to serve patients with comorbid anxiety and bipolar disorder and was tested in a pilot feasibility acceptability trial compared to pharmacotherapy treatment as usual. Results showed high rates of client satisfaction with treatment, average to above average homework compliance, treatment-related decreases in anxiety and depression symptoms and functional impairment, and increases in emotion regulation skills (Ellard et al., 2016). Overall, the results from this pilot trial were promising, suggesting the UP may be a feasible and viable treatment option for this population.

In the following section, we will present an illustrative example of the application of the UP for the treatment of an individual with Bipolar I disorder and comorbid anxiety, adjunctive to pharmacotherapy.

CASE PRESENTATION

Sophia is a 43-year old, white Hispanic female who was interested in trying cognitive behavioral therapy (CBT) to help her manage her anxiety and depression symptoms. Sophia had been diagnosed with Bipolar I disorder following a severe mixed episode with psychotic features. Before this episode, she had been fairly high functioning. She was a divorced mother with two teenage girls and had held a high-level corporate position in a fast-paced marketing firm. Following her self-described "mental breakdown," she was forced to go on disability and lost her position with the firm.

Since that time, Sophia's mood symptoms had been stabilized through pharmacotherapy (lamotrigine, 300 mg; luoxetine, 40 mg; quetiapine, 400 mg). At the time of intake, she had returned to work and had successfully maintained a full-time position as an associate in a marketing firm for a little over a year. However, despite making significant strides toward stabilization, she still struggled with ongoing depressive mood episodes, frequently accompanied by intense feelings of hopelessness and despair, and occasionally suicidal ideation. She had begun experiencing panic attacks and was avoiding situations like crowds, public transportation, or any situation in which she felt she could not quickly escape.

In addition, she struggled with severe social anxiety, which she felt was threatening her progress at work. She was terrified of meetings for fear she would be asked to give her opinion, which others would reject, or that others would view her as incompetent. She was particularly fearful of being "found out"—that her coworkers would view her as less capable if they knew of her bipolar illness. She found herself proofreading and rereading her emails several times before sending in order to make sure they were perfect and error free, which slowed her productivity considerably. She also described living in constant fear that she will lose control, say the wrong thing, or otherwise behave in a manner suggesting that she is crazy or out of control.

Upon intake, Sophia was assessed using a combination of clinician-administered measures of anxiety and mood symptoms and self-report measures related to emotion regulation and emotion processing (See Table 6.1). In addition to her bipolar I diagnosis, Sophia met DSM-IV-TR (American Psychological Association, 2000) criteria for panic disorder, social phobia, and generalized anxiety disorder (GAD), as assessed by the Structured Clinical Interview for DSM-IV (SCID-IV; First, Spitzer, Gibbon, & Williams, 1997). She endorsed moderate levels of anxiety and depression symptoms, as measured by the Hamilton Anxiety (HAM-A; Hamilton, 1959) and Hamilton Depression Rating Scales (HAM-D; Hamilton, 1960). She denied any current symptoms of mania or hypomania, as assessed by the SCID-IV and Young Mania Rating Scale (YMRS; Young, Biggs, Ziegler, & Meyer, 1978). She endorsed high levels of anxiety sensitivity (assessed through the Anxiety Sensitivity Index; Reiss, Peterson, Gursky, & McNally, 1986), difficulties with emotion regulation (assessed through the Difficulties with Emotion Regulation Scale; Gratz & Roemer, 2004), and fear of emotions (assessed through the Affective Control Scale; Williams, Chambless, & Ahrens, 1997).

In Sophia's case, although she has been diagnosed with Bipolar I disorder, she predominately experiences low mood and only occasionally experiences mild hypomanic symptoms. She had not had another full manic episode since

Table 6.1. PRETREATMENT AND POSTTREATMENT
SCORES ON PRIMARY OUTCOME MEASURES

Assessment	Pretreatment	Posttreatment
HAM-A	16	6
HAM-D	12	4
YMRS	1	0
LIFE-RIFT	16	11
NEO-N	37	28
ASI	40	11
ACS	6	4
DERS	4	2

NOTE: HAM-A = Hamilton Anxiety Rating Scale (range 0–56; Hamilton, 1959). HAM-D = Hamilton Depression Rating Scale (range 0–23; Hamilton, 1960). YMRS = Young Mania Rating Scale (range 0–60; Young et al., 1978). LIFE-RIFT = Longitudinal Range of Impaired Functioning Tool (range 0–16; Leon et al., 1999). NEO-N = NEO Neuroticism subscale (range (0–48; Costa & McCrae, 1992). ASI = Anxiety Sensitivity Index (range 0 = 64; Reiss et al., 1986). ACS = Affective Control Scale (range 1–7; Williams et al., 1997). DERS = Difficulties in Emotion Regulation Scale (range = 1–5; Gratz & Roemer, 2004) beginning treatment with mood stabilizers. This is quite common for patients with bipolar disorder, particularly those who are followed closely with medication management by a psychiatrist. Whereas hypomanic symptoms may still occur, manic symptoms can often be well managed with medication. However, depressive symptoms often continue to be a problem, and anxiety symptoms are frequently the source of the greatest day-to-day distress. In the following sections, we will discuss each of the UP treatment modules and how they were applied to Sophia's case. Where applicable, we will also note how the treatment concepts and skills can apply to an individual experiencing manic or hypomanic symptoms, as well as areas of specific relevance to a bipolar disorder patient population in general.

Module 1: Setting Goals and Maintaining Motivation

As discussed previously in Chapter 1, the primary aim of Module 1 of the UP is to articulate specific treatment goals and to identify and address up front any ambivalence toward engaging in the treatment. These two aims can be particularly helpful for patients struggling with bipolar disorder in the following ways: First, individuals like Sophia who carry a diagnosis of bipolar disorder often feel overwhelmed by the burden of their disorder. Sophia described struggling to "survive" her bipolar diagnosis, focusing primarily on just getting by and keeping destructive episodes at bay. She articulated this sense even though she had not experienced a severe manic episode in over three years. Helping bipolar patients articulate treatment goals beyond simply managing mood episodes can be quite powerful, allowing the focus to shift from just getting by to living a better life, envisioning concrete ways in which their individual quality of life could be improved. Second, actively weighing the pros and cons of treatment through the decisional balance exercise allows patients to shift their thinking from a dichotomous outcome of success or failure, instead allowing them to see ambivalence as a normal part of the process of change. In addition, it suggests a choice to either accept the status quo or to take active steps toward improved well-being.

Sophia listed spending time with friends, spending more time with her children, and "being OK alone" as three concrete goals for treatment. For the first, this would mean addressing much of her social anxiety, focused on potential rejection by others because of her bipolar illness. She had isolated herself and had not kept in contact with friends since her severe episode three years ago, for fear of what they might think of her. Reconnecting with friends and regaining a social life thus was a primary treatment goal. This would also mean addressing her panic symptoms, which were preventing her from going to social events like concerts or movies.

Relating to her second treatment goal, spending more time with her children, Sophia described spending many nights and weekends catching up on work that she had been unable to finish in a timely manner due to her anxiety related to doing things perfectly, which she felt she needed to do in order to avoid rejection or ostracism. A particular fear was that her coworkers would "discover" that she is no longer capable of doing high-level work. Thus, addressing her fears related to rejection by her professional peers and her subsequent perfectionistic behaviors were listed as concrete steps toward freeing up more time to spend with her kids.

Sophia's third treatment goal, "being OK alone" was an especially important one for her. She described, on the one hand, isolating herself from others for fear of rejection, but on the other hand feeling extremely anxious when she was "alone with her thoughts," fearing that she would lose control or "go crazy." This meant that she was rarely at peace with herself and often felt unsafe when she was alone due to her fear of losing control. Thus, another primary treatment goal was to address Sophia's fears about losing control and helping her to relearn safety around being alone. Articulating treatment goals in this way allowed Sophia to see that she deserved to live a life that included attention to her well-being, not just the management of her illness.

Next, by exploring both the pros and cons of engaging in treatment through the Decisional Balance Form, Sophia was able to normalize her own feelings of ambivalence and hesitation about treatment. Specifically, through this exercise, she was able to articulate both a desire to better manage anxiety and depression symptoms and a fear of what it might mean to face her anxiety and depression. In particular, whereas she was able to see how her patterns of avoidance were interfering in her overall well-being and ability to meet some of her goals, she was also very hesitant to give up these behaviors.

The Decisional Balance Form helped Sophia to see this not as an either-or issue, but instead, both as a desire to engage in treatment and a hesitance to give up avoidance strategies that she has developed to manage her anxiety and bipolar mood symptoms can exist side by side. Further, using the decisional balance exercise in this way helped Sophia to see that, should she have days where engaging in the treatment exercises or homework feels difficult, this does not mean that she is failing at her treatment. Instead, both a desire to change and a fear of change are present and part of her, so the greater pull toward one or the other does not necessarily mean that the other is no longer true. This discussion helps patients like Sophia to see hesitation or faltering not as a treatment failure, but as part of the process of change.

Module 2: Understanding Emotions

As mentioned in Chapter 1, the primary aim of Module 2 is to introduce the adaptive nature and function of emotions. As has been well established, individuals struggling with anxiety and mood disorders tend to view emotions as aversive and tend to focus on negative emotions. A common stated goal for treatment is to escape or eliminate negative emotions. This is perhaps especially poignant for patients struggling with bipolar mood disorders. These patients often experience intense emotions, and these emotions may lead to destructive behaviors or fuel a sense of being out of control.

For patients struggling with bipolar disorder, the experience of strong emotions often becomes associated with negative events or consequences. An important message in this module, therefore, is the idea that not only do emotions serve an evolutionarily adaptive function, but they also can be broken down into component parts that allow room for altering and influencing their overall intensity. By making the distinction between automatically elicited emotions and maladaptive reactions to these emotions, patients begin to see that, whereas they may not be able to "turn off" their emotions (nor would they want to), they can make changes that can reduce the aversiveness of emotional experiences, allowing them some control over their own well-being. This can be a particularly powerful message for a population that often feels stigmatized by their illness and powerless to affect meaningful change in their lives.

For Sophia, anxiety had come to symbolize impending catastrophe, and particularly a fear that she might "again lose control, go crazy, and lose everything." Sadness or disappointment signaled hopelessness, failure, and an intense fear of falling into a severe depression. Positive emotions often were followed by anxiety and the fear of becoming disinhibited and "doing something I might regret." Thus, for Sophia, both negative and positive emotions were viewed as potentially aversive and something she struggled to contain, rather than as anything useful or adaptive. Given this relationship to her emotions, Sophia initially found it difficult to accept that negative emotions like anxiety, fear, or sadness had any positive function at all. However, by using concrete examples from her own experiences (e.g., fear being triggered by a near-miss rear-end accident while driving), she was able to see how even her emotional experiences could serve a helpful purpose.

A particularly helpful discussion for Sophia centered on the distinction between automatic emotions and reactions to these emotions. Specifically, automatic emotions were described as those that are triggered by some sort of stimulus (either external or internal) without conscious deliberation or effort. The ability to generate emotions quickly and automatically was explained as an evolved capacity that serves to protect us and promote our survival. For example, wasting time thinking about the color or model of an automobile that is heading straight for us before deciding that we should be afraid and jump out of the way would not be an adaptive response. The fact that we can generate a fear response and jump out of the way without having to think about it betters our chance of survival.

To do away with all negative emotions could actually put us in harm's way. Further, we have discussed how automatic emotional experiences are usually followed by reactions to emotions, and these reactions are where we can affect change. Thus, whereas we are somewhat powerless to change our automatic emotional responses, we can change how we respond to these experiences. Finally, we detailed how strong emotions become paired and associated with certain experiences, contexts, perceptions, and behaviors. The adaptive purpose of this innate ability is again stressed—by making these quick associations, we gain a "blueprint" of our world so that we don't have to relearn "this means that" over and over every day. However, these associations are helpful only if they fit the current context, and they are maladaptive when tied only to past experiences. Thus, identifying maladaptive patterns of responding that are learned over time and updating these associations to fit the current context is a main focus of treatment.

Using this as a framework, we explored some of Sophia's recent emotional experiences, using the three-component model of emotion worksheets to map out her experience, starting from what had triggered the emotional experience and then identifying the first emotion that she can remember that was elicited by that trigger and what thoughts, feelings, and behaviors came next. We initially focused on identifying the first emotion she could recall and then evaluated what adaptive function that emotion might have been trying to serve. After that, we evaluated her response to that initial emotion, identifying where the experience may have gone from something adaptive and useful to something aversive and unhelpful:

> THERAPIST: *Can you think of a time in the past week you felt especially anxious?*
>
> SOPHIA: *Well, yes. A couple of days ago, we had a team meeting at work, and at one point, I felt almost paralyzed by anxiety. I was so anxious about it ahead of time, too. I did end up going, but sitting in that meeting was unbearable.*
>
> THERAPIST: *If we were to map out this experience, what would you say was the trigger for your anxiety at that time?*
>
> SOPHIA: *I think mainly I was nervous I was going to be called on to give my opinion! I was afraid of coming across incompetent, or that they would think I didn't know what I was doing.*
>
> THERAPIST: *This might be hard, because it can be hard to remember* exactly *what we were feeling in a given moment in the past, but can you take a guess as to what the first emotion was you felt in that room?*
>
> SOPHIA: *I guess anxiety.*
>
> THERAPIST: *Can you remember how that felt physically? Was your heart racing? Were your hands shaking?*
>
> SOPHIA: *My heart was definitely racing! Not sure if my hands were shaky, but I know my checks got hot, and I felt sort of nauseous.*
>
> THERAPIST: *So let's say hypothetically that the first emotion that was triggered when you sat down at that meeting was anxiety. What was your reaction to that experience of anxiety?*
>
> SOPHIA: *Well, when I feel anxious like that, I just feel incompetent and like everyone is watching me.*
>
> THERAPIST: *Do you think that anxiety was serving any sort of a purpose in that moment? Do you think that very first experience of anxiety in that situation had any sort of function?*
>
> SOPHIA: *I don't think so; it just made me feel like completely* not *calm.*
>
> THERAPIST: *Let's think about it this way—remember when we spoke of the adaptive function of emotions? What were some of the functions we talked about anxiety having for us?*
>
> SOPHIA: *You mean like alerting us to danger?*
>
> THERAPIST: *Present danger, or potential danger?*

SOPHIA: *Potential danger, I guess . . . oh, I remember, anxiety helps us prepare?*

THERAPIST: *Exactly! Anxiety signals us to prepare for some future event that may or may not be threatening to us, so that we can be better prepared for that threat. It's as if our brain says, "Wait, pay attention to this thing, it might mean something important!" What do you think your anxiety might have been alerting you to in this case?*

SOPHIA: *That the meeting might go bad?*

THERAPIST: *If anxiety's purpose is to alert us to prepare, how would you prepare against a meeting "going bad"?*

SOPHIA: *Prepare ahead of time what I'm going to say?*

THERAPIST: *Exactly! Your anxiety in this situation isn't signaling a clear and present danger, it is signaling that whatever this situation is that you are in, it is important to you, therefore you should be prepared. In this sense, there is nothing "bad" or maladaptive about feeling anxiety at the meeting; it's just your body and mind helping you to prepare so that you can be your best. The truth is, the initial emotion like anxiety is rarely the culprit, it is all the things we do and say in response to these emotions that become maladaptive.*

In this introductory phase of treatment, it is typical for patients to have difficulty seeing their emotions serving any adaptive function at all, as was the case for Sophia. However, after discussing possible functions that her anxiety may have been serving in that context, Sophia suggested that perhaps her anxiety was simply alerting her to the need for her to prepare a response. In this sense, at least initially, the anxiety was not necessarily a bad thing; rather, it served as a signal to alert her to something that was about to happen that was important to her, so she could prepare accordingly.

Next, we examined what followed this initial experience of anxiety. We identified several negative and catastrophic thoughts, centered on themes of embarrassment, failure, or potential ostracism by her peers, and discussed how these thoughts served to increase her anxiety. We also identified physiological sensations, such as increased heart rate, sweaty palms, and faint nausea—all symptoms associated with the evolutionarily adaptive fight-or-flight system.

We saw that for Sophia, these sensations came on quickly and intensely and added to the perception of danger or impending doom. We discussed these sensations as evolutionarily ancient automatic responses that are also intended to help Sophia, which may simply be coming on stronger than the situation calls for (e.g., since she isn't under attack and her life is not being threatened, she does not need to fight or flee). By going through one of Sophia's emotional experiences in this deliberate way, she was able to see how her experience quickly went from something adaptive to something maladaptive, and this helped to normalize the experience of anxiety. This process of identifying adaptive versus maladaptive aspects of her experience was emphasized as the main focus of treatment, and learning new adaptive responses to emotions as the primary goal for change.

The homework for this module focuses on monitoring and recording emotional experiences. An additional modification for bipolar patients is the inclusion of mood monitoring (see Figure 6.1). Specifically, patients are asked to monitor mood levels (low mood, normal mood, high mood), hours of sleep per night, medications taken and amounts, levels of anxiety, and levels of irritability. Mood monitoring helps patients anticipate extremes in mood by recognizing triggers for elevated or depressed mood (i.e., changes in sleep patterns, missed medication). Mood monitoring in this way is incredibly helpful toward identifying typical maladaptive patterns of behaviors, and it also can be an excellent speaking point from which to anchor future sessions.

Module 3: Mindful Emotion Awareness

For some bipolar patients, staying in contact with their emotions during the nonjudgmental, present-focused awareness exercises in Module 3 can be somewhat distressing at first. Some patients feel so overwhelmed by their emotions that they have become accustomed to keeping their emotions at bay, and some express concern that staying in contact with their emotions will make them feel worse. For many, emotions are something to be feared, as they can become associated with spiraling out of control. However, modeling acceptance, guiding patients through brief exercises, and highlighting safety within the current context of the therapy office can foster greater willingness to engage in these exercises. In addition, by reinforcing the goal of these exercises—to increase awareness of thoughts, feelings, and behaviors so that the patient and therapist can work together toward adaptive change—the focus is shifted toward the patients gaining a better understanding of themselves, empowering them toward positive changes rather than feeling powerless about their emotional experiences. Emphasizing the benefits of continued practice, as opposed to an expectation of immediate mastery, can also be helpful toward increasing compliance with practice.

For Sophia, she struggled initially with completing the exercises, both in and outside of session. When doing the mindfulness exercise in session, she noted that simply observing rather than doing something initially felt foreign and made her nervous. At home, practice was also difficult, as being "alone with her thoughts" aroused a fear of losing control. A turning point came when practicing present-focused awareness with music. Sophia chose a piece that elicited strong emotions in her, and an intense emotional experience ensued. Using music helped to more concretely demonstrate objective observance of her experience by illustrating how a stimulus (music) can elicit all components of emotions (e.g., memories and thoughts, visceral responses, and specific behaviors) and help to solidify the function of present-focused awareness. In addition, having the opportunity to experience strong emotions in a supportive, nonjudgmental environment had a significant impact on Sophia, aiding her own sense of compassion for herself and her experiences.

	Days	1	2	3	4	5	6	7	8	9	10	11	12	13	14	15	16	17	18	19	20	21	22	23	24	25	26	27	28	29	30	31
Elevated	Severe																															
	Moderate																															
	Mild																															
Normal	Normal																															
Depressed	Mild																															
	Moderate																															
	Severe																															
Anxiety	0 = None / 1 = Mild / 2 = Moderate / 0 = Severe																															
Irritability																																
Hours Slept																																
Medications																																

Name _____ Month _____ Year _____

Figure 6.1 Sample daily mood monitoring chart.
Adapted from Janssen Pharmaceutica (2009) Psychiatry 24 × 7.com. Beam Mood Chart. https://www.schizophrenia24x7.com/

Because engaging in objective awareness of emotions can be a new experience for patients, it is important to encourage ongoing practice and consolidation of this skill. By and large, even though this experience can be initially off-putting, it can foster a greater sense of power and control and can reinforce the possibility that individuals can affect real change in their own lives. In addition, by demonstrating early success in session, which often feels like a safer environment than being out in the world, the therapist can work with patients to gradually increase their practice on their own at home.

However, some patients may still be hesitant about or resistant to more formal mindfulness practice. The "Anchoring in the Present" exercise can help build a sense of mastery or connection to this skill without more formal practice, serving as an introduction to mindful awareness. Anchoring in the Present teaches patients to simply notice a sound, sight, smell, or tactile sensation in the moment and notice their focus shift to the present. Although not intended to be a replacement for more formal mindfulness practice, this exercise is less cumbersome and can be done at any time and in any place. It is often an effective way to get a patient who is initially resistant to mindfulness to experience the effects of mindful, present-focused attention, and it can serve as a bridge to more formal practice.

Module 4: Cognitive Flexibility

For many individuals struggling with bipolar disorder, a history of repeated, severe mood episodes can have a profound impact on their beliefs about themselves, their relationships with others, and their ability to have a normal healthy life. Often, depressive or manic episodes have left profound destruction in their wake, frequently causing ruptures in relationships with family, friends, and coworkers. As such, many individuals describe feeling tainted by these episodes and the behaviors they may have fueled, such as excessively risky, sexual, or self-destructive acts. Many describe a belief that they must subsequently contain themselves as tightly as possible, exercising strict control over themselves so as not to experience subsequent episodes that could potentially cause further damage to their lives. Many also subsequently live in fear of any intense emotional experience. However, this rigidity and fear interfere with their ability to lead happy and fulfilling lives. Further, in the midst of this struggle, they must continue to manage ongoing periods of elevated or depressed mood.

The core beliefs that are formed out of these experiences, such as being a failure, being "tainted" in some way, or being unworthy of love, ironically serve to intensify and worsen subsequent mood and anxiety symptoms, creating a vicious cycle. Addressing recurrent, maladaptive automatic thoughts associated with emotional experiences, both positive and negative, as well as core beliefs that have developed over time, is thus an important aim of Module 4.

Module 4 proved to be one of the more profound modules for Sophia to go through. Using the three-component model of emotions, we were able to identify recurrent themes in Sophia's negative interpretations of her experiences. Specifically, we were able to identify several profound misconceptions and beliefs that she held about herself, including being a "misfit" worthy of rejection, being unworthy of love and admiration, and needing to maintain her composure at all costs. These themes came up repeatedly and were tightly associated with the experience of both anxiety and low mood. Most profoundly, through a process of identifying automatic thoughts associated with emotions she experienced in her daily life, we were able to uncover how deeply affected she was by her past severe manic and psychotic episode. For example, one automatic thought that she identified, which permeated much of how she interacted with friends and coworkers, was that she would "never be the same" after her psychotic break. She viewed herself as having been a powerful, competent, and successful person prior to this episode, but that she had lost this person completely after her "breakdown."

Using one of the core skills of Module 4, we applied the "downward arrow" technique to uncover Sophia's core beliefs underlying this appraisal. Going one layer down, she identified the thought "I feel different. My whole life and lifestyle has changed," to which we posed the question, "What's so bad about that?" This line of questioning can be very powerful—by suggesting that someone else could make the exact statement "I feel different . . .," and for them it could mean something positive, Sophia was able to see that there were other core beliefs underlying this statement that made it feel painful.

Using the downward arrow technique, she identified additional thoughts that underlie her sense of being different, such as "My friends and coworkers will no longer want to spend time with me; I am no longer the person I used to be; I will be alone." These core beliefs were connected to additional automatic thoughts, such as "Everything that has happened to me is my fault; I could have prevented all of my breakdowns; I deserve to lose everyone and everything because of these breakdowns; I am worthless." By breaking down Sophia's automatic thoughts using current examples of emotional experiences, we were able to uncover these very painful core beliefs and to demonstrate how these beliefs were influencing the intensity of her negative emotions. Further, once we identified what lay at the core of these maladaptive automatic appraisals, we could begin to challenge and question these interpretations using cognitive reappraisal skills and to compare their usefulness when they were initially formed to their usefulness now, in the present context.

After monitoring and recording automatic thoughts such as those given here, we were able to map out a typical scenario in which Sophia struggled with negative emotions, to see how these automatic thoughts were influencing the intensity of those experiences. For example, a main trigger of anxiety for her was replying to her manager's emails. Using the three-component model of emotion, we first discussed the function that the initial emotion of anxiety might be serving. In this case, Sophia was able to recognize her anxiety as simply alerting her to something that was important to her (i.e., making a good impression on her boss so as to keep her job), and which was motivating her to prepare (i.e., put some thought into her response so that her boss could see that she is doing a good job). At this point, her experience of emotion was adaptive—her anxiety was motivating her to prepare for something that is important.

Next, we identified what thoughts followed this initial triggering of anxiety. Sophia recalled thoughts such as "What if he thinks I don't know what I'm talking about?" "What if he thinks I am incompetent?" or "He's going to see I am actually a fraud and don't know what I'm doing." We discussed how each of these thoughts increased the intensity of her anxiety, which in turn increased the catastrophic nature of her thoughts. In this way, we were able to illustrate and demonstrate how tightly paired the experience of anxiety and the perception of worthlessness, failure, and rejection had become. Instead of being interpreted as something helpful and useful (e.g., signaling the need to prepare), her anxiety had come to mean failure and rejection. (We also noted behaviors that were triggered by this experience, which we cover in more detail in the next module.)

Using cognitive reappraisal skills, we were able to explore each of these automatic thoughts, providing examples for and against each of these perceptions in order to evaluate their accuracy as they pertain to the present context. For example, her core belief of being perceived as incompetent was in direct opposition to her position and trajectory at her current job. She had been hired based upon her merits and had succeeded in being quickly promoted. Further, her boss gave her opinion great weight when making major decisions for the company.

The goal at this stage is to increase awareness of these automatic associations between certain emotional experiences and certain patterns of thoughts, perceptions, and memories, and to point out any inconsistencies with the present context. In the second half of treatment, the work is focused on building new, more adaptive associations that better align with the current context and allow more adaptive interpretations of emotions.

As noted previously, in Sophia's case, her thoughts were focused primarily on negative, anxiety-driven themes. However, identifying automatic thoughts associated with elevated or manic states is also important. For some patients, particularly those who are more rapid-cycling, monitoring automatic thoughts associated with both low and elevated mood states can be extremely helpful. By reviewing a record of automatic thoughts and core beliefs that are active in one state (low mood) while experiencing the opposite state (elevated mood), patients are able to see how powerful an influence their moment-to-moment emotional experiences have on their perceptions of themselves and the world.

The goal is to identify these thought patterns using present-moment awareness skills learned in Module 3, and to begin to evaluate these thought patterns in the context of the present moment. Patients can ask themselves, "Would this still feel true if I were in another mood state?" And, most important, patients can use present-moment observation and this line of questioning to evaluate the most adaptive and helpful response given the current context, a point to which we return in the next module.

Module 5: Countering Emotional Behaviors

In Module 5, the emphasis is on understanding the connection between triggered emotions and behaviors. This is another important module for bipolar patients. Often, individuals with bipolar disorder engage in risky or self-destructive behaviors that are directly linked to intense emotions. For example, intense feelings of anxiety and depression can drive individuals to extreme avoidance behaviors, such as isolation, withdrawal, and even self-injurious or suicidal behaviors. Intense feelings of euphoria or elation can drive individuals to extreme approach behaviors, such as risky sexual encounters, excessive spending, or reckless behavior. Understanding the tight link between emotions and automatic modes of behavior, therefore, is crucial in this population.

For Sophia, some of her maladaptive behaviors were easily identifiable. For example, she was avoiding movie theaters, crowded places, and situations that she did not feel she could easily escape in response to panic symptoms. Again, using the three-component model, we were able to draw connections between paniclike physiological sensations, catastrophic automatic appraisals of these sensations, and her avoidance behaviors. Some other behaviors were less apparent and came only after close monitoring of her emotional experiences. For example, after increasing her awareness of times when she felt uncomfortable emotions, she noted that she regularly experienced anxiety when she first came home from work to an empty house.

After exploring this scenario further, we identified several emotion-driven and avoidance behaviors. Specifically, she had developed a strategy of quickly turning on the television after coming home, which we identified was a method to avoid anxiety triggered by silence. We also identified a pattern of tidying and cleaning, which was done with some urgency and at the expense of relaxing at the end of a busy day. Sophia also connected this with her anxiety about being alone—cleaning gave her a sense of control over her environment and helped reduce her anxiety. However, we discussed this behavior as motivated not from a desire for a clean home, but rather as a strategy to avoid feeling anxious, and at the cost of resting after a long day. Therefore, this was illustrative of a maladaptive avoidance behavior. Specific strategies for countering these behaviors were addressed as part of Sophia's emotion exposures, which we discuss in Module 7.

Ironically, addressing avoidance behaviors can be much easier than addressing approach behaviors in this patient population. It is much more difficult for patients to identify approach behaviors as something maladaptive than it is for withdrawal behaviors. Therefore, it is important when addressing maladaptive approach behaviors to help patients identify whether the behavior can be considered beneficial to their overall well-being or if there are any potential negative consequences to the behavior. One method for drawing this distinction is to ask patients to consider whether they might choose to engage in the same behavior if they were feeling more neutral or calm, or even experiencing a low mood.

Using a similar line of questioning as presented in Module 4, patients can ask themselves, "Would I feel as strongly about this situation, or would this still seem like the right thing to do if I were calm, or even if I were depressed?" and "Is this the most adaptive and helpful action I can take right now?" This can help them to differentiate between an action taken simply because the level of arousal and emotional intensity fuels a sense of urgency rather than because it is the right action to take.

For example, one patient who felt quite passionate about matters relating to social justice felt a sense of urgency to bring a particular injustice at work to his boss's attention. He had experienced similar scenarios in the past, and had in fact been fired after deliberately going against his boss's orders in one situation, in which he stormed into a manager's office to "give him a piece of my mind." In reviewing these past situations, he recalled feeling so "fired up" about the issue in the moment that there seemed no other course of action except to act right away. This, of course, had negative consequences—not only was he unable to effectively communicate his concerns related to the injustice that he had identified, but he ended up insulting his boss and getting fired in the process.

By reviewing his emotional state surrounding these incidents, he recalled feeling an overwhelming sense of purpose, even euphoria. These are very positive feelings, and the motivation to control them or contain them can be very low. However, in this case, we first discussed what messages his emotions were sending him, which we identified as positive emotions associated with a sense of urgency toward approach and accompanying expansive thoughts. We then evaluated the current context in which that emotional experience was occurring, which was during work, at a job that was valuable to him both for his paycheck and for the work itself, in an environment where there are certain social rules around acceptable ways to interact, such as showing respect for his boss and managers.

Having all these pieces of information in front of him, we then asked what would have been the best way to proceed in the past, and what might be the best way to proceed now. We decided that the social injustice issue was worth discussing with his boss. However, the way in which the message was delivered, as well as the sense of urgency behind its deliverance, could cause the situation to go from something adaptive and helpful to something maladaptive and potentially even self-destructive. In this case, his exaggerated euphoric response was more intense than what he needed to get his ultimate message across to his boss. We agreed he would still bring the issue to his boss, but that he would wait to do so until his mood had stabilized and he felt calmer.

By taking a sort of "mindful time-out," getting better at recognizing the associations between certain feeling states, ways of thinking, and subsequent urges to act, bipolar patients become better at evaluating what might be the most adaptive response given a certain situation, and this logic applies to both intense negative emotions and intense positive emotions. Of particular help in breaking patterns of emotion-driven behaviors (EDBs) is the use of the UP "Anchoring in the Present" exercise (taking a deep breath, turning attention to sensory environmental stimuli such as a sound, and doing a "three-point check" of thoughts, feelings, and behaviors). This strategy can be used to help break patterns of automatic responding not only in the case of euphoria or mania, but also in response to anxiety, fear, or even depression.

The key purpose of this skill is to interrupt ongoing, automatic patterns of behavior, allow attention to shift to the current situation, and allow an awareness of automatic associations between specific emotions and thoughts, physiological sensations, and behaviors. For example, Sophia found this skill helpful when coming home and practicing sitting alone. As her anxiety increased, by taking a deep breath and anchoring her awareness to a sound in the room (such as the ticking of a clock), she was better able to recognize her catastrophic thoughts as just thoughts and her urge to escape to be inconsistent with evidence that she was in that moment safe in her home. After practicing the "Anchoring in the Present" exercise and consolidating this skill, patients can use this as a powerful method for quickly interrupting cycles of EDBs, countering impulsivity and avoidance, and ultimately selecting more adaptive behavioral responses.

Module 6: Understanding and Confronting Physical Sensations

Increasing the awareness of the contribution of physiological sensations to emotional experiences is an especially critical point for bipolar patients. The difference in physiological context between a depressive state and a manic state is notable—the thoughts and behaviors accompanying a depressed state, with physiological sensations of heaviness and lethargy, are quite different than the thoughts and behaviors that accompany a manic state, with high arousal and sensations of agitation or elation.

Thus, increasing patients' awareness of the visceral context in which their emotional experience is taking place at any given moment aids in the evaluation of the validity or adaptiveness of accompanying thoughts and behaviors. Notably, by making the connection between certain behaviors and visceral, physiological contexts, physiological sensations can become very important cues for specific behaviors or thought patterns. As patients get better at recognizing their physiological state, this becomes an easily accessible heuristic for evaluating the adaptiveness of their current responses to emotions.

For example, someone might wake up one day and begin to ruminate about his perceived failures. He might then decide to call in sick and stay in bed. By better recognizing that physiological sensations of heaviness and lethargy are often associated with catastrophic, guilty, or hopeless thoughts, the patient can ask himself, "Are these hopeless thoughts here because my situation is actually hopeless, or does it just *feel* more hopeless in this moment because I am also feeling heavy and tired?" Understanding the visceral context in which thoughts, feelings, and behaviors are taking place thus becomes very important for ultimately evaluating and selecting adaptive versus maladaptive responses.

Interoceptive exercises in this module are no different than those that might be used for anxiety or unipolar depressed patients. For Sophia, much of her distress was triggered by anxiety and panic-related sensations. Thus, traditional interoceptive exposure (IE) exercises, such as breathing through a thin straw, were used to demonstrate and consolidate skills. In many ways, the straw-breathing exercise ended up to be the most powerful one, leading to some extraordinary breakthroughs for Sophia. This exercise can be a very effective way to demonstrate the interplay between physiological sensations, thoughts, and behaviors. Specifically, the fear response that is generated can be understood as a normal adaptive response to a shift in oxygen supply—when the brain detects this shift, it elicits a fear response as an alert. If the thoughts and perceptions generated in response to this alert are of a further alarming nature (i.e., "I can't breathe!"), then the fear response intensifies. If the person is gripping the chair, holding on for dear life, this behavioral response is also compatible with fear, therefore reinforcing the validity of the fear response and increasing it further. Thus, the straw-breathing exercise can be a concrete way to demonstrate the interaction of thoughts, feelings, and behaviors in the intensity of emotions.

Although the straw-breathing exercise was very aversive for Sophia at first, by repeating the exercise several times in session, helping Sophia to identify and label her responses and connect these responses directly to the intensity she was experiencing, and making small adjustments each time (i.e., having her sit back in a relaxed posture, having her keep her eyes open, and encouraging nonjudgmental and curious awareness of thoughts and feelings), she was able to slowly increase the length of time she completed the exercise. This was immediately validating for Sophia, and increased her confidence in her ability to tolerate her anxiety.

Sophia continued to practice straw breathing on her own at home and completed additional IEs, including hyperventilating to induce derealization and spinning in circles to induce dizziness and stomach discomfort. In addition, she paid close attention to and noted physical sensations that she was feeling during emotional experiences throughout her day-to-day life. Through these exercises, Sophia was able to not only recognize the relationship between physiological sensations and emotional states, but also to better tolerate physiological sensations associated with anxiety and depression.

Module 7: Emotion Exposures

As with any other patient population, the consolidation of treatment skills ultimately comes together through collaboratively designed emotion exposures. For Sophia, we created an emotion exposure hierarchy based on recurring themes that had arisen through treatment, as well as by revisiting the treatment goals that she had explicated at the start of treatment. As such, we designed exposures focused on in vivo exposures to confined or enclosed spaces to address her fear of panic attacks; asserting herself at work by participating in meetings and proofreading emails only once, to address her fear of rejection at work; reconnecting with old friends; and spending time alone.

In vivo exposures to target Sophia's fear of panic attacks included going to a haunted house with her daughters, riding in the middle seat in a taxi, and sitting in the middle of a row at a movie theater. In addition, Sophia continued to practice interoceptive awareness exercises, which helped her to recognize physiological sensations signaled by false versus true alarms during in vivo exposures. Several exposures were designed to help address her fear of rejection at work, such as contributing at least one opinion during staff meetings, reading through email drafts only once before sending, and returning phone calls right away. In essence, designing exposures around these scenarios for patients diagnosed with bipolar disorder is no different from how one might address any other individual's anxiety and avoidance.

To address the remaining issues on Sophia's hierarchy (namely, fears about spending time alone or reconnecting with old friends), we revisited some of Sophia's core beliefs surrounding these two situations. Both of these fears were influenced by the negative perception that she held about her most severe manic and psychotic episode, and in particular what this episode said about her as a person and what it meant for her going forward. In order to explore these themes, her first emotion exposure consisted of writing the story of her "breakdown" and reading this account aloud in session. This was a very challenging exercise for Sophia, as she had tried to put this episode out of her mind. However, it was apparent that even though she was trying not to think about it, this event was interfering in her ability to maintain close relationships with people from her past and was causing her to be afraid to be alone with her own thoughts. Sophia brought her account into session and reread the account aloud three times, each time allowing herself to experience more of the emotions that the account elicited. We then went back through her account and identified any cognitive distortions, thinking traps, or maladaptive core beliefs. We worked to revise her narrative accordingly, replacing cognitive distortions with other possible interpretations.

For example, Sophia had been fixated on a moral account of her breakdown. In other words, she had attributed her episode to a lack of strength or moral character on her part, rather than other biological or psychological factors such as stress that could have triggered her mania. She also had made assumptions about "people who go crazy" as being distinct from people who can be smart, successful, or viable members of society. By addressing these ideas in detail using examples, Sophia was able to see her episode not as a moral flaw that has caused her to no longer be considered a successful person, but rather an illness that occurred following a "perfect storm" of factors (stress at home and at work, lack of sleep, and substance abuse) that triggered a manic episode, and that the person she was prior to this episode—successful, confident, worthy—is the same person she still is.

Using examples from her current life, Sophia was able to articulate many instances of being not only competent, but also very successful, at her job and in her personal life. She was also able to recognize that the work that she has put into her own treatment to help keep her mood stable and to better manage anxiety, depression, and hypomanic symptoms has been both hard work and admirable work—not concepts that might be used to describe someone who is "worthless."

Using this renewed understanding of her illness as a framework, we next addressed Sophia's fear of being alone. This consisted of graded exercises that she performed immediately upon coming home from work. She had identified a pattern, which included turning on the TV before even taking her coat off in order to fill the silence, immediately cleaning and arranging the house, and then busying herself with her kids, making dinner, or performing any other chores that needed to be done. We discussed the adaptive versus maladaptive aspects of this routine. Specifically, turning the TV on was labeled maladaptive, as it was being used to avoid anxiety triggered by silence. By filling this silence, Sophia has been unable to learn that she can tolerate silence without something terrible occurring. Cleaning and arranging the house, attending to the children, and making dinner are all adaptive activities of housekeeping, if considered in the right context. Here, however, Sophia was *using* chores as a way to avoid quiet downtime with herself. So long as she kept busy, she wouldn't have to worry about her mind wandering into thoughts that she did not want to have. Thus, doing chores immediately after work was also identified as being maladaptive.

For the exposures, we started with avoiding turning on the TV when she came in the door. Next, instead of cleaning, Sophia sat quietly on her couch and practiced mindful breathing. She started with 5-minute periods of mindful sitting, with a goal of reaching 20 minutes of mindful sitting within five days. Her specific instructions were to observe and notice any thoughts, feelings/sensations, or behaviors (including urges to get up and move around) that arose during that time. Sophia was also encouraged to set a timer, but to keep it out of view so as to avoid "clock watching."

Sophia found this exercise very aversive at first. She found herself thinking about negative events from her past, both the severe episode and other negative events. This was followed by "a barrage of negative thoughts," nondelusional voices that would tell her how bad she was, how she was a fool to think that she would be able to function normally or keep her job, or how she is no longer the same person, and when people find out, they will reject her. Using skills learned throughout treatment, we were able to systematically process these early exposures and begin to make adjustments.

For example, Sophia used present-focused awareness to observe the connection between physiological sensations of anxiety and these negative thoughts. Her revised objective interpretation was as follows: "Being alone is something new I am not used to, which triggers anxiety. As soon as I feel anxiety, my mind starts hitting me with all of these negative thoughts. These thoughts are associated with old feelings of anxiety, but right now I am just sitting in my house. I have a good job, my children are well, I am healthy, I am OK, it is OK for me to sit quietly in the moment." In this way, she was able to recognize the emotion that she was feeling, situate that emotion within the current context (e.g., anxiety triggered by something new or unusual, but not necessarily dangerous), observe the associated thoughts and feelings that arise when she feels anxiety, recognize that those fears do not have anything to do with the current context, use cognitive reappraisal skills to generate alternate meanings and interpretations, and shift her focus back to the task at hand. Sophia repeated this exercise every day for two weeks, charting the intensity of the anxiety that she felt, recording any automatic appraisals or EDBs that arose, noting physiological sensations and how they shifted over time, and recording how long she was able to complete the assignment each time.

Completing this exposure exercise was very powerful for Sophia, as it allowed her to make the distinction between negative memories of her past severe mood episodes and the reality of where she is at in her life today, using concrete examples from her day-to-day life. In essence, the evidence from her current life suggested a relatively high-functioning individual who has shown courage, strength, and perseverance toward regaining stability and health, and who is serving as a positive role model for her children—a self-image that was quite different than the one painted by her maladaptive and outdated core beliefs.

Using the insight gained from these exposure exercises, Sophia was able to approach some of the other situations that she had avoided, such as reconnecting with old friends. One of the biggest sources of anxiety was having to talk about her recent past and struggles with old friends, for fear they would view her struggles as weaknesses or a sign of a flawed moral character. By capitalizing on the new interpretations that she was able to generate during her mindful sitting exposures, she used this knowledge to help complete graded exposures with friends, starting with inviting a friend to coffee and practicing engaging mindfully in the conversation, followed by sharing information about herself with her friend.

Sophia was surprised to see that the reactions she got from old friends were not what she had predicted they would be; instead, her friends expressed gratitude that she was finally opening up to them and letting them back into her life. Importantly, Sophia noted that some of her friends were not as accepting of her story, but she was able to recognize this as indicative of others' comfort level with her struggles rather than as a commentary on her self-worth. In addition, Sophia was able to combine exposures targeting panic fears and fears of social rejection by going to the movies and sitting in the center aisle, sitting in the middle of the seat during a taxi ride, and attending a concert with friends. At the conclusion of treatment, Sophia brainstormed several additional exposures such as these to continue consolidating her skills.

CONCLUSION

Treatment for bipolar disorder traditionally focuses on maintaining mood stability and preventing episode relapse. However, given the paramount role of
neuroticism and subsequent emotional lability and dysregulation in functional
impairment in these disorders, directly targeting emotion-related processing and
teaching patients adaptive emotion regulation skills may be crucial elements for
these patients to regain a sense of autonomy and control and greater hope for
improvement in well-being. Further, due to the high rates of comorbidity in these
disorders, utilizing treatments such as the UP, which is able to target transdiagnostic processes, are important.

In this chapter, we illustrated the application of the UP for a case of Bipolar
I disorder and comorbid panic disorder, social phobia, and GAD. Although many
aspects of the treatment were challenging and did not come easy, Sophia made
great progress throughout treatment. In her case, persistence with the concepts,
compliance with homework, and a willingness to engage in treatment all contributed greatly to her treatment gains.

This case illustrates the ways in which the UP treatment components can
be applicable to patients with bipolar disorder. However, there are still challenges to be acknowledged. First, engaging in this treatment requires a level of
stability in order to support regular weekly attendance for sessions, the consolidation of treatment concepts from one session to the next, and successful engagement in homework practice. Individuals with bipolar disorder often
have chaotic, disorganized, or otherwise stressful lives that can interfere with
consolidation of treatment concepts between sessions. This can become apparent through weekly review of homework and concepts covered in the previous
weeks' sessions.

Thus, extra support or measures to promote stability between sessions should
be considered, such as developing a plan for when and where to complete
homework assignments, using phone alarms and other reminders to complete
homework, or enlisting the help of supportive others (friends, family members). Further, patients who are rapid-cycling or experiencing severe mood
episodes may have greater difficulty engaging in the heavily didactic portions
of treatment. The UP introduces many new concepts that patients may have
never encountered, or that represent a somewhat radical departure from what
has been learned over a lifetime (e.g., that strong emotions can be a good thing,
providing important information for survival, rather than being something to
be feared or contained). Many of these skills take repeated practice in order to
acquire them, so early "buy-in" to treatment is important. Therapists should
be mindful of ways to maximize early treatment gains in order to encourage motivation for continued practice of skills, and they should be willing to
spend additional time on treatment modules so as to aid in consolidation of
skills.

As the case of Sophia illustrates, the UP can be a particularly helpful and viable treatment for individuals with bipolar disorder. She made notable gains over the course of 18 sessions of the UP, showing significant decreases in anxiety and mood symptoms, as well as reductions in anxiety sensitivity, increases in emotion regulation skills, and decreases in fear of emotions (see Table 6.1).

Research is ongoing to investigate ways to continue to improve access to the UP for even the most severe bipolar patients, such as consolidating early didactic sessions into two-day intensive introductions to treatment concepts, or augmenting the UP with other strategies to strengthen baseline emotion regulation skills, such as the use of neuromodulation. Overall, the UP may be a promising approach for the treatment of affect lability, emotion dysregulation, and comorbidity that are paramount barriers to wellness in bipolar disorder, offering a potentially method for improving the well-being of these patients.

7

The Unified Protocol
for Posttraumatic Stress Disorder

MATTHEW W. GALLAGHER ■

The majority of individuals will experience at least one traumatic event during the course of their lives (Kilpatrick et al., 2013). Fortunately, people are typically very resilient in the aftermath of trauma, but estimates of lifetime prevalence indicate that as many as 8% of adults will develop posttraumatic stress disorder (PTSD) following a traumatic event (Kessler et al., 2005; Kilpatrick et al., 2013). PTSD is associated with high levels of functional impairment (Holowka & Marx, 2011), has a dramatic impact on quality of life in the aftermath of trauma (Schnurr, Lunney, Bovin, & Marx, 2009), and increases the risk of attempting and completing suicide (Gradus et al., 2010). PTSD, therefore, represents a significant public health concern.

It also has been shown to be associated with very high levels of comorbid mood and anxiety disorders. Research with both civilian (e.g., Kessler et al., 2005) and veteran/military (Miller, Fogler, Wolf, Kaloupek, & Keane, 2008) samples has demonstrated that comorbidity is the norm rather than the exception in individuals with PTSD. One recent study indicated that the modal number of current and lifetime comorbid emotional disorders in individuals with PTSD was two and three, respectively (Gallagher & Brown, 2015). Therefore, transdiagnostic treatments that intentionally target the underlying features of emotional disorders that underlie comorbidity represent an important future direction in the treatment of PTSD.

Current Treatments for PTSD

There are currently multiple protocols that have been extensively studied and demonstrated to be efficacious treatments for PTSD, with cognitive-behavioral treatment protocols generally being found to have the greatest efficacy (Watts et al., 2013). The two most widely studied current treatments for PTSD are Cognitive Processing Therapy (CPT) and Prolonged Exposure (PE) therapy. CPT is a more cognitively focused treatment that uses cognitive strategies to target "stuck points" that develop and maintain symptoms of PTSD in the aftermath of trauma. CPT has been shown to be efficacious for both civilian (Resick, Nishith, Weaver, Astin, & Feuer, 2002) and military trauma (Resick et al., 2015), with promising evidence that the benefits of CPT persist for as long as five years post-treatment (Resick, Williams, Suvak, Monson, & Gradus, 2012). PE primarily uses imaginal and in vivo exposure activities to target PTSD symptoms, but it also has significant empirical support (Powers, Halpern, Ferenschak, Gillihan, & Foa, 2010), and has demonstrated efficacy for both civilians (Foa et al., 2005) and veterans (Eftekhari et al., 2013). CPT and PE are currently the first-line treatments for PTSD in the U.S. Department of Veterans Affairs healthcare system and have been widely disseminated. There are also promising briefer exposure-based treatments for PTSD, such as Written Exposure Therapy (WET; Sloan, Marx, Bovin, Feinstein, & Gallagher, 2012) that have demonstrated efficacy for PTSD.

All these treatments have robust evidence for their effectiveness in the treatment of PTSD, but they were not designed to target the full range of comorbid emotional disorders often seen in PTSD, and there is less evidence regarding the efficacy of these treatments for comorbid conditions. There is also some evidence that comorbid conditions may moderate the efficacy of treatments for combat-related PTSD. Specifically, there is some evidence that anxiety and anger may both predict PTSD symptom trajectories during treatment, but that the direction and magnitude of these moderating effects may vary as a function of the type of treatment delivered (Lloyd et al., 2014). The most promising evidence for these treatments regarding comorbidity is for the treatment of comorbid depression, with both CPT and PE being shown to also have an impact on symptoms of depression (e.g., Resick et al., 2002). Depression is just one of the many comorbid conditions commonly seen with PTSD. Therefore, there is a need to examine alternative treatment approaches for PTSD that may be more effective for comorbidity, which has been acknowledged in the National Research Action Plan (2013) developed by the U.S. Department of Defense and the Department of Veterans Affairs, which highlighted the need to study new treatments for PTSD.

The Unified Protocol for PTSD

The Unified Protocol for Transdiagnostic Treatment of Emotional Disorders (UP), therefore, holds great promise as a potential alternative treatment for PTSD, given that it explicitly targets transdiagnostic factors (e.g., neuroticism) that underlie all emotional disorders (Barlow, Sauer-Zavala, Carl, Bullis, & Ellard, 2014). As outlined in Chapter 1 of this volume, the UP is a modular treatment that can be flexibly delivered in 12 to 18 sessions, depending on the presenting problems of individuals. The modules are framed within the three-component model of emotions and incorporate many techniques that are common in existing CBT protocols. The sessions follow a consistent structure, in which the therapist and patient first review symptom monitoring and homework from the previous session, a new concept or skill is introduced and demonstrated, and homework activities are then collaboratively identified to help the patient learn to flexibly use more adaptive emotion regulation strategies. The details of modules are more thoroughly covered elsewhere in this book and in Barlow et al. (in press) so they will only be briefly outlined here.

After a thorough diagnostic and functional assessment, UP treatment begins in Module 1 with a focus on cultivating motivation, identifying clear treatment goals, and promoting self-efficacy regarding change. Module 2 focuses on psychoeducation, helping patients to understand the adaptive nature of emotions, recognize the three components of an emotional experience, and learn how to monitor the antecedents, components, and consequences (both short- and long-term) of their emotional experiences. Module 3 focuses on helping patients to cultivate nonjudgmental, present-focused awareness of their emotional experiences using mindfulness exercises and other emotion induction strategies. Module 4 uses cognitive therapy techniques such as the downward arrow to help patients identify maladaptive thinking traps in the form of probability overestimation and catastrophizing, and then use cognitive reappraisal skills to develop greater cognitive flexibility. Module 5 helps patients to recognize the variety of emotional avoidance strategies that they are using, to understand how avoidance and suppression can be ineffective and counterproductive in the long term, and to identify how engaging in alternative actions can break the cycle of disordered emotions. Module 6 uses interoceptive symptom induction exercises to help patients cultivate improved awareness and tolerance of physical sensations that often accompany PTSD and other emotional disorders. Module 7 is where patients practice all of the new emotion regulation skills they have learned while experiencing strong emotions and confronting feared stimuli through a combination of situational, imaginal, and interoceptive emotional exposure exercises.

The focus in these exercises is on new contextual learning and using coping skills to develop an increased tolerance of emotions more than habituation of the emotional response. Treatment concludes with a module focusing on recognizing accomplishments and looking to the future, in which progress and the skills covered in treatment are reviewed and patients are encouraged to begin functioning as their own therapist using the skills learned in treatment.

The UP has multiple potential advantages compared to current, gold-standard, PTSD-specific CBT protocols. In contrast to traditional CBT protocols, which primarily emphasize disorder-specific symptoms, the UP focuses on transdiagnostic dimensions of vulnerability (e.g., neuroticism) and dysfunctional emotion regulation strategies (e.g., experiential avoidance) that contribute to the development and maintenance of many emotional disorders. The UP, therefore, places greater emphasis on psychiatric comorbidity than existing PTSD treatment approaches and emphasizes the development of more adaptive emotion regulation strategies that are relevant across the full "neurotic spectrum" (Brown & Barlow, 2009).

The focus on these underlying mechanisms of vulnerability and maintenance may result in more robust long-term treatment effects, even in the absence of comorbid conditions. The UP may also have an advantage in terms of retention, which is a significant challenge in traditional CBT protocols for PTSD (Gutner, Gallagher, Baker, Sloan, & Resick, 2016), due to the UP starting treatment with a module that focuses on cultivating motivation and treatment engagement. Patients may also perceive the UP as more tolerable, given the focus on cultivating more adaptive emotion regulation skills prior to initiating exposure exercises in Module 7. Although there is promising evidence supporting the UP as a treatment for mood and anxiety disorders (e.g., Farchione et al., 2012; Barlow et al., under review), the UP has not been empirically studied as a treatment for PTSD.

Transdiagnostic Conceptualization of PTSD

Prior to discussing the results of the case series, it is worth briefly discussing how PTSD can be conceptualized as a disorder of emotion regulation in a manner that is consistent with current theories of emotion regulation (Gross, 2014) and how cases are conceptualized in the UP (Boettcher, Chapter 2 in this volume; Campbell-Sills, Ellard, & Barlow, 2014). PTSD, as currently defined in DSM-5, consists of five main criteria: the experience of a traumatic event; persistent reexperiencing symptoms; frequent efforts to avoid memories, thoughts, or feelings related to the trauma; negative alterations in cognitions and mood; and finally, symptoms of hyperarousal that can manifest in various forms.

From the perspective of the UP, it is understandable that individuals may experience intrusions, negative thoughts and feelings, and some elevated physiological arousal in the aftermath of a traumatic event. Efforts to avoid memories/reminders, suppress thoughts and feelings, and other problematic emotion regulation strategies contribute (among other risk factors) to the development of PTSD rather than the more normative recovery response. The introduction of more adaptive emotion regulation skills through the UP can counter the avoidance and other emotion-driven behaviors (EDBs) that serve to reinforce and maintain the symptoms of PTSD and help to promote more adaptive recovery. The UP is consistent with existing treatments such as PE in targeting avoidance during treatment, but it diverges from existing treatments by first emphasizing the development of more adaptive emotion regulation skills that are relevant across diagnostic boundaries, and then helping clients use these skills during emotional exposure activities that may focus on traumatic experiences, depression, phobias, or whatever else may be causing distress or impairment for the client.

CASE SERIES OF THE UP FOR PTSD

This chapter presents the results of a clinical replication case series of the UP for three individuals with a principal diagnosis of PTSD. These three individuals each sought treatment at the Center for Anxiety and Related Disorders (CARD) at Boston University and were treated by the author. All three individuals consented to participate in this case series, and the procedures were reviewed by the Institutional Review Board of Boston University. The names and other identifying information for each individual have been changed to protect confidentiality.

Two of the patients completed a full course of the UP treatment, and the third dropped out of treatment after nine sessions for reasons that were reported to be unrelated to treatment. The Anxiety Disorders Interview Schedule (ADIS; Di Nardo, Brown, & Barlow, 1994) was used at baseline and posttreatment to determine diagnostic status and severity in the form of clinical severity ratings (CSRs). In addition, each patient completed the Overall Anxiety Severity and Impairment Scale (OASIS; Norman et al., 2006), the Overall Depression Severity and Impairment Scale (ODSIS; Bentley, Gallagher, Carl, & Barlow, 2014), and the PTSD Checklist for DSM-IV (PCL; Weathers Litz, Herman, Huska, & Keane, 1993) prior to each treatment session. Previous research has indicated that scores of 8 may be a useful cutoff for identifying diagnostic levels of anxiety and depression using the OASIS and ODSIS, respectively, and that a score of 44 may be a useful cutoff for identifying diagnostic levels of PTSD using the PCL. For each case, an overview of the patient's presentation at the intake assessment is provided first. Specific examples of progress made and obstacles encountered that may be common when treating PTSD with the UP are then presented. Finally, outcome data for each patient and aggregating across the three patients is presented.

Case 1: Danielle

The first patient in this case series is "Danielle," an 18-year-old Asian female who presented for treatment and initially reported that a primary concern that led her to seek treatment was her difficulty sleeping due to nightmares. Prior to initiating the UP, Danielle had been receiving supportive psychotherapy focusing on her symptoms of depression, but she decided to seek out a more structured treatment focusing on PTSD and anxiety. The results of Danielle's ADIS indicated that she met diagnostic criteria for PTSD (CSR = 6), social phobia (CSR = 5), and major depressive disorder (MDD; CSR = 5). She also reported significant symptoms of worry that would have been sufficient to meet diagnostic criteria for generalized anxiety disorder (GAD), but these symptoms were subsumed into the diagnosis of PTSD due to the time course of these symptoms.

Danielle reported that her symptoms of PTSD were due to physical abuse by her father that occurred approximately 10 years prior to her seeking treatment. Her father contacted her roughly a month before she sought treatment, which she indicated may have led to an uptick in her symptoms. Danielle reported significant distress and impairment related to her PTSD, social anxiety, and depression, but identified the symptoms of PTSD as most disruptive to daily functioning. Specifically, she reported reexperiencing symptoms in the form of daily nightmares, constant efforts to avoid thoughts or discussions of her child-hood trauma, feeling unable to enjoy activities or fully engage in relationships, and hypervigiliance that caused her to always be on guard and that led to her frequently feeling exhausted. Her self-reported symptoms of PTSD (PCL = 43), anxiety (OASIS = 6), and depression (ODSIS = 5) at the start of treatment were slightly below the commonly used cutoffs, but Danielle reported after first com-pleting these questionnaires that she sometimes minimizes her symptoms as a means of avoidance.

Danielle successfully completed a full course of the UP in 17 sessions. In the initial discussion of goals for treatment and the potential pros/cons of change during Module 1, she was easily able to identify the potential benefits of complet-ing treatment, including being able to develop more open and trusting relation-ships with family and friends, being more optimistic about the future and not assuming that additional trauma is inevitable, and being less exhausted on a daily basis if she could sleep more and experience less hypervigilance and physiologi-cal arousal.

Not surprisingly, one of Danielle's major concerns about the potential cons of completing treatment and trying to change is that she recognized that treatment would involve her having to talk about her traumatic experiences and confront other aspects of her life that she typically tried to suppress or avoid. Although avoidance is a major focus later in treatment during Module 5, having an hon-est discussion about how treatment will involve countering feared and currently avoided memories, thoughts, and situations is always important during the UP, but it may be particularly relevant when treating PTSD. During the second mod-ule, Danielle reported that she often struggles to understand the different aspects of her emotional experiences, and that the confusion about her emotions is one of the reasons that she typically tries to suppress or avoid those feelings. By dis-cussing the function and adaptive benefits of emotions, Danielle was quickly able to recognize the benefits of developing an improved understanding of the components of her emotional experiences and expressed a greater willingness to start tracking her emotional experiences using the emotion monitoring work-sheets in order to understand when, where, and how she experienced strong emo-tions. During Module 3, brief mindfulness exercises conducted in session helped Danielle to understand how cultivating mindfulness could help to improve her ongoing, nonjudgmental awareness of emotional experiences. She recognized that her intrusions about past trauma and anxiety/worry about future situations both conspired to make her more disconnected from the present moment because she assumed that focusing on the present or fully engaging with her emotions would be intolerable.

Danielle initially reported difficulty identifying common cognitive apprais-als and the underlying beliefs driving some of her common thoughts. Using the downward arrow and other exercises in Module 4 helped her identify core cog-nitive distortions, such as the belief that she is unlovable and can't trust others or ever be trusted in relationships. Danielle was able to identify how these cata-strophic thoughts might be linked to her traumatic experiences and how thinking more flexibly about herself, others, and the future could have a dramatic impact on how she approaches relationships.

When discussing avoidance and EDBs in Module 5, Danielle expressed that in addition to avoiding thoughts, reminders, or discussion of her past trauma, she more generally made efforts to avoid interpersonal closeness due to the complicated emotions she felt when trying to connect with and trust others. She also identified that when she experienced anxiety, sadness, or other strong emotions, she would engage in various EDBs to push other people away in an attempt to isolate herself. She indicated that the exception to this was in interactions with her younger sister, who reportedly experienced similar traumas with her father and whom she therefore felt she could confide in and trust.

By developing a better understanding of these avoidance and EDB processes, Danielle was able to articulate how her responses to and avoidance of emotions were interfering with her goals. By completing a series of interoceptive exercises during Module 6, we were able to determine that heart palpitations, sweating, and lightheadedness were the most prominent physical sensations that she experiences during and after strong emotions. In addition to completing a series of planned interoceptive exposure (IE) exercises, Danielle had an unexpected opportunity to practice having an increased awareness of and tolerance of physical sensations in the aftermath of a minor surgical procedure that she coincidentally had while completing this module.

When developing an emotional exposure hierarchy in Module 7, Danielle reported that she had already made more progress in confronting feared social situations and responding more adaptively to feeling of sadness, but that she still had more anticipatory distress related to approaching her past trauma. Her hierarchy, therefore, initially consisted of tasks such as volunteering to give a speech in one of her classes prior to engaging in more difficult emotion exposures, such as writing about or discussing her trauma with her mother.

Danielle successfully engaged in a variety of emotion exposures but initially struggled when attempting to write a detailed account of her traumatic experience. She stopped her first attempt to do so when she reached the point of describing when her father started to hit her. We discussed how discontinuing this exercise was an example of avoidance, discussed the emotions that were brought up by this activity, and discussed how cognitions related to this traumatic experience continue to influence her ability to trust others in relationships. Danielle was encouraged to apply the skills that she had learned in treatment while expanding upon her written trauma account.

She was subsequently successful in both fully writing her trauma account and then having a conversation with her mother about what she had written, which was something that at the start of treatment, she reported that she doubted she would ever be capable of doing. After the series of successful emotional exposure exercises, a review of the course of treatment and skills learned was presented in Module 8. Danielle reported satisfaction with the progress that she had made in treatment and confidence that she would be able to continue to apply the skills from the UP going forward, so she agreed to end treatment.

Danielle's symptoms of PTSD, anxiety, and depression declined significantly over the course of treatment, as measured by the weekly PCL/OASIS/ODSIS assessments. Her self-reported symptoms at the end of treatment (PCL = 17, OASIS = 2; ODSIS = 1) were all dramatically lower than her initial scores and close to or at the minimum score possible on these measures. Danielle no longer met diagnostic criteria for PTSD, social phobia, or depression at the end of treatment based on the ADIS, and reported that she was no longer experiencing any significant interference or distress related to the symptoms that motivated her to seek treatment. A plot of the module-to-module averages of her self-reported levels of PTSD, anxiety, and depression can be seen in Figures 7.1, 7.2, and 7.3, respectively.

Case 2—Jaime

The second patient in this case series is "Jaime," a 39-year-old Hispanic female who also sought treatment for symptoms of PTSD related to childhood physical abuse that was perpetrated by her father. The results of Jaime's ADIS indicated that she met diagnostic criteria for PTSD (CSR = 6), social phobia (CSR = 5), MDD (CSR = 5), and obsessive compulsive disorder (OCD; CSR = 4). Jaime also reported significant symptoms of worry that would have been sufficient to meet diagnostic criteria for GAD, but these symptoms were subsumed into the diagnosis of PTSD due to the time course of these symptoms.

Jaime reported that recent conflict with coworkers at her job that she perceived as bullying had been very distressing, as it triggered memories of her past traumatic

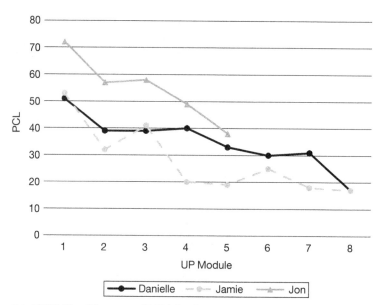

Figure 7.1 PTSD Checklist scores (PCL) for three cases across each module of the UP treatment.

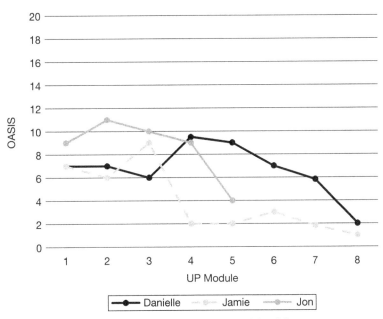

Figure 7.2 OASIS scores for three cases across each module of the UP treatment.

experiences. The increase in her symptoms of PTSD, anxiety, and depression in the aftermath of this conflict at work resulted in her being placed on short-term disability leave. Prior to initiating UP treatment, Jaime had been receiving supportive psychotherapy focusing on stress management skills as a component of her disability leave, but she reported that the increase in her symptoms had helped

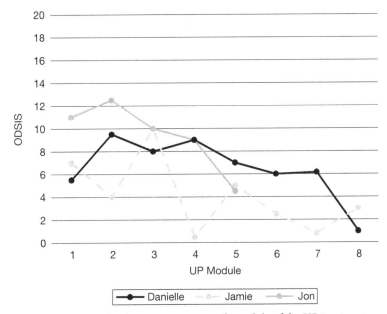

Figure 7.3 ODSIS scores for three cases across each module of the UP treatment.

her recognize that she may benefit from a treatment specifically targeting PTSD, anxiety, and depression. Her self-reported symptoms at the start of treatment (PCL = 53, OASIS = 14; ODSIS = 7) were consistent with clinically significant levels of PTSD, depression, and other anxiety disorders.

Jaime completed a full course of the UP in 17 sessions. During Module 1, she stated that major goals for treatment were to become more comfortable with her emotions in general, and specifically to develop skills to more adaptively cope with emotions that were triggered by stress at work, uncertainty in relationships, and by intrusions related to her past trauma. Jaime indicated that she had previously tried to engage in a regular practice of meditation to better understand her emotional experience, but that she found that to be difficult, as she didn't feel that she had the skills necessary to cope adequately with her emotions when she became aware of them. She was quickly able to understand the rationale for beginning treatment by focusing on improving understanding of emotions and had no difficulty articulating the pros of change and the cons of staying the same.

Jaime was very eager to begin tracking her emotions in Module 2 using the three-component ARC of emotional responses worksheet. She reported that the use of the three-component model worksheet provided clarity about the components involved in her emotional responses and also helped her to recognize how often she tries to suppress her emotions. Jaime had significant previous experience with meditation practice and was quickly able to understand the rationale behind cultivating mindfulness. We discussed how she could engage in additional exercises to develop a more mindful and nonjudgmental orientation to her emotional experiences. She reported good insight in response to the mood induction exercises in terms of recognizing the natural course of emotions when she mindfully attends to emotions rather than avoiding them and was able to complete and understand all the key components of Module 3 in just one session.

Prior to Module 4, Jaime had reported that she often felt that her thoughts while experiencing strong emotions were a jumbled mess. By discussing and monitoring her common automatic appraisals and identifying potential alternatives, she reported an increased flexibility in her thinking. Module 4 coincided with the date at which her short-term disability was set to expire and she was supposed to return to her job. Jaime reported that the cognitive skills learned in Module 4 gave her an improved understanding of the sources of her anxiety related to returning to work and increased her optimism about her capacity to successfully do so. She then had an unexpected opportunity to practice the cognitive reappraisal strategies in a very stressful situation, as she received unexpected news that she would be unable to return to work as planned. We discussed her reactions to this news and with the use of the downward arrow technique, she was able to identify a core cognition that drives much of her anxiety: "If I don't have complete control, then I can't protect myself and will ultimately suffer." Jaime was able to articulate how this belief may be linked to her past trauma and how it influenced her behavior at work, in relationships, and her identity more generally.

The stress and uncertainty regarding Jaime's return to work continued to provide valuable opportunities during Module 5 to practice the new approach to emotions. Jaime was successfully able to identify many of the avoidance strategies that she commonly uses, and we discussed the short- and long-term consequences of these avoidance strategies. She reported some initial success in identifying and implementing alternatives to avoidance, and we discussed how this allowed her to more effectively cope with the stress that she had recently experienced related to the process of returning to work. She stated that following discussions with human resources staff at her previous job, it was mutually agreed that she should accept a severance package rather than returning to her previous position. We discussed how she had applied the skills learned in treatment to date to manage this situation, and Jaime reported pride in her ability to effectively manage the stress related to this development while being nonjudgmentally aware of her emotions, not engaging in catastrophic thoughts about her future work prospects, and not engaging in the avoidance and EDBs that she previously used when experiencing significant stress.

For Module 6, we completed a series of exercises in order to determine which sensations were most similar to what she experiences while anxious, and Jaime reported that hyperventilation, shaking, and muscle tension in her jaw were most prominent. By conducting a series of IEs in which she used breathing and muscle tensing to induce these sensations, Jaime was able to quickly develop an improved awareness and tolerance of these physical sensations that she commonly experienced in the context of strong emotions.

At the beginning of Module 7, Jaime reported that she no longer feared many of the situations that she had struggled with when she started treatment. She said that despite multiple significant life stressors, she has been experiencing significantly less anxiety and depression in recent weeks and stated that she believed that she has experienced a "180 degree shift" in how she responds to her emotions. She ultimately was able to recognize that she still feared thoughts and feelings related to her previous traumatic experiences and had some ongoing anxiety related to finding a new job and social situations. Some of the initial emotional exposure exercises that she engaged in were attending and actively participating in networking situations and making efforts to rekindle relationships that she had avoided in recent years due to her fear of how others viewed her.

The final and most challenging emotion exposures exercises for Jaime focused on her past traumatic experiences and involved her repeatedly completing both verbal and written accounts of her trauma and engaging with activities and memories related to the trauma. These tasks allowed her to practice applying her new emotion regulation skills while experiencing all the intense thoughts, feelings, and reminders related to her past trauma. Jaime reported that her peak and post-exposure levels of distress were significantly less than her anticipatory distress, and we discussed what she could learn from these experiences. After four sessions focusing on emotional exposures, she reported that she was experiencing significantly less anxiety and distress when confronting all the situations initially identified on her emotional hierarchy and that she felt more capable of effectively regulating anxiety or depression regardless of the circumstances.

During Module 8, Jaime was able to clearly summarize the skills that she had learned in treatment, how they differed from the approach to emotions/coping that she previously used, and how she could continue to apply these skills in the future to better manage both her life stress and thoughts/feelings related to the physical abuse that she had experienced as a child. Jaime reported satisfaction with the progress that she had made in treatment and confidence that she was ready to terminate treatment. Her symptoms of PTSD, anxiety, and depression declined significantly over the course of treatment, as measured by the weekly PCL/OASIS/ODSIS assessments. Her self-reported symptoms at the end of treatment (PCL = 17, OASIS = 1; ODSIS = 3) were all dramatically lower than her initial scores and close to or at the minimum score possible on these measures.

Jaime no longer met diagnostic criteria for PTSD, social phobia, depression, or OCD at the end of treatment based on the ADIS, and she reported that she was no longer experiencing any significant interference or distress related to the symptoms that motivated her to seek treatment. A plot of the module-to-module averages of her self-reported levels of PTSD, anxiety, and depression can be seen in Figures 7.1, 7.2, and 7.3, respectively.

Case 3—Jon

The third and final patient in this case series was "Jon," a 24-year-old African American male who presented for treatment due to distress and impairment related to traumatic experiences that occurred while serving in the U.S. Marine Corps. His military occupational specialty was infantry, and he served two tours of duty in which he was deployed to Iraq and experienced a variety of traumatic experiences while deployed. He was honorably discharged from the Marines following his two tours and reported that he had struggled with the transition back to civilian life and had difficulty managing distress related to his traumatic military experiences, as well as other symptoms of anxiety and depression.

During his initial assessment, he reported that he often felt like he was stuck in "combat mode," where he believed that he needed to numb his emotions in order to get through each day. Jon reported that he often resorted to using substances (primarily cannabis and alcohol) and other forms of emotional avoidance due to his difficulty confronting his emotions, although he indicated that he had recently made some progress in decreasing his substance use prior to seeking treatment. The results of Jon's ADIS indicated that he met diagnostic criteria for PTSD (CSR = 6), MDD (CSR = 5), cannabis dependence with physiological dependence (CSR = 4), and alcohol dependence in partial remission (CSR = 4).

As with the two previous cases, Jon also reported significant symptoms of worry that would have been sufficient to meet diagnostic criteria for GAD, but these symptoms were subsumed into the diagnosis of PTSD due to the time course of these symptoms. Prior to initiating UP treatment, Jon reported that he had participated in some outpatient group treatments focusing on anxiety and anger at a

Veterans Administration (VA) hospital, but he was hesitant to initiate individual treatment at the VA for his symptoms of PTSD and anxiety. Jon's self-reported symptoms at the start of treatment (PCL = 72, OASIS = 9; ODSIS = 11) were consistent with clinically significant levels of PTSD, depression, and GAD.

Jon completed nine sessions of treatment and was in the middle of completing Module 5 when his participation in this case series was prematurely terminated so that he could receive more intensive care, for reasons explained subsequently. In Module 1, Jon indicated that his primary goals for treatment were figuring out how to reduce emotional numbing behaviors so that he could enjoy socializing with friends and generally be more engaged in relationships, could reduce reported "survivor's guilt" and related anhedonia and guilt associated with pleasurable activities, and learn how to better cope with physical pain and sensations associated with distress. Jon was also able to recognize the downsides of pursuing change, in that he had a strong preference for consistency that was further reinforced by his military service, so he was generally uncomfortable with change, and that even though he recognized numbing is detrimental over the long term, it can reduce short-term distress.

By discussing both his goals and the pros/cons of change, Jon was able to articulate how and why the approach to understanding, experiencing, and responding to emotions might differ from his current coping strategies that were carried over from his military service and how he may benefit from treatment. In Module 2, he quickly understood and recognized the benefits of tracking and viewing emotions as potentially adaptive. Although he struggled in some ways to fill out the emotion tracking forms accurately, he made a clear effort to practice this skill and reflected that his initial difficulties simply reflected how foreign it was for him to actively track his emotional experiences, as well as the antecedents and consequences of his emotions. After a week of practice, he reported that he was able to apply the concept of the ARC of emotional experience to better understand the major ongoing life stressors that he was experiencing related to academic stressors and conflict in his romantic relationships.

Jon indicated during Module 3 that he recognized why it may be helpful to have a present-focused, nonjudgmental awareness of his emotions, but he initially reported skepticism about his ability to develop this skill. During the first attempt to complete a mindfulness exercise in session, Jon reported that he quickly became overwhelmed by his emotions and appeared to have experienced a flashback or to have briefly dissociated. Grounding techniques were used to help Jon return to the present moment, and we discussed his reactions to the experience. This was done by asking Jon to focus on and describe tactile sensations (e.g., the feeling of rubbing his hands on his jeans) to help him reconnect and focus on the present moment. He reported that he was not able to identify exactly what thoughts/memories were triggered, but that he was trying extremely hard to suppress his feelings during the exercise. We discussed how Jon's experience fit within the model of emotional disorders that is presented in the UP and how he may be able to gradually shift how he engages with his emotions and memories of past experiences, which in turn may help lessen the resulting distress. Despite his initial skepticism, after additional exercises to cultivate mindfulness during and between sessions, Jon was subsequently able to develop an increased ability to maintain a present-focused and nonjudgmental awareness of his emotions, even while thinking about his past trauma.

During Module 4, Jon reported that he had started to develop a better awareness of some of his cognitions by using the emotion-tracking skills introduced in Module 2, but that he still sometimes struggled with identifying cognitions and that he rarely considered alternative thoughts when he did identify his thoughts. The use of the ambiguous picture exercise in session, which helped demonstrate how attending to different stimuli can influence appraisals, resonated with Jon, and he reported that he often assumes that there is only one possible way to think about things. After using the other exercises included in Module 4, including the downward arrow technique, Jon was ultimately able to identify an underlying belief that he doesn't believe that he deserves to be happy. He also was able to recognize how this leads to catastrophic thinking and probability overestimation in terms of how he approaches his undergraduate classes, his relationships, and his past trauma.

During Module 5, Jon reported that highlighting the short- versus long-term benefits of emotional avoidance was very helpful for him. He was able to articulate why some strategies for regulating emotions that were adaptive while on active duty and in combat situations were no longer as adaptive. The discussion of the importance of flexibility in approaching and responding to emotions in a manner similar to what was described in Module 4 also resonated with Jon and helped him to identify the importance of flexibly choosing behavioral responses to his emotions that were most adaptive and congruent with his goals.

The Boston Marathon bombings occurred on April 15, 2013, in the week between Jon's 9th and 10th sessions of treatment. The events and aftermath of the bombings were traumatic in many ways for individuals in the Boston area. Unfortunately, one such consequence was a significant increase in Jon's symptoms and a worsening of his functioning. Jon reported being overwhelmed in the days following the bombings, as the heavy military presence was very triggering for him and he was also very distressed because an acquaintance of his was injured and hospitalized as a result of the bombings. Jon reported a dramatic increase in dissociative symptoms, difficulty organizing his thoughts and behavior, and symptoms that were consistent with a manic episode.

In discussing the increase in and change in his symptoms following the bombings with both Jon and his healthcare providers in the Veterans Healthcare system, it was collaboratively decided that it was in Jon's best interest to receive a more intensive level of treatment, and Jon voluntarily hospitalized himself in order to help stabilize his mood. Jon's involvement in treatment as part of the formal case series therefore ended following his 9th session of the UP. The author continued to provide treatment for Jon after his hospitalization, and he confirmed his consent for his initial course of treatment to be included in this case series, even though he was unable to complete the full course of the UP. At the time of Jon's termination, he still met diagnostic criteria for both PTSD and MDD. A plot of the module-to-module averages of his self-reported levels of PTSD, anxiety, and depression can be seen in Figures 7.1, 7.2, and 7.3, respectively.

CONSISTENT THEMES IN TREATMENT

Some common themes were observed during treatment that would likely be commonly encountered when using the UP to treat PTSD. One of the first things that was noteworthy was that early in treatment, all three individuals expressed appreciation for the psychoeducation and conceptualization of PTSD as an emotional disorder that functioned in a manner similar to other symptoms that they were experiencing. They each indicated that they felt that this helped them to feel less defined by trauma and to have more personal agency regarding potential recovery.

Not surprisingly, minimizing avoidance was identified as a concerning disadvantage of pursuing treatment, but having a discussion about the pros/cons of change helped solidify the motivation to learn alternative strategies to avoidance. It only occurred in the case of Jon, but dissociative symptoms might be more likely to be encountered during the mindfulness exercises in Module 3 for individuals with PTSD than those with other emotional disorders. The incorporation of grounding exercises as an additional approach for promoting nonjudgmental awareness of and engagement with the present, therefore, might be helpful for individuals with the dissociative subtype of PTSD. The prominence of worry as a cognitive process was also consistent across all three participants.

None of the patients had a formal diagnosis of GAD due to the DSM decision rules regarding the overlap of PTSD and GAD symptoms, but the experience of worry was common for all three, so it is likely important to explore the frequency and function of worry in individuals with PTSD, even if there is no formal diagnosis of GAD. Physical symptoms were prominent in all three cases, and IEs appeared to be very helpful for the two cases that completed treatment. Despite the strong somatic component of many PTSD symptoms, IEs are typically not as widely used in existing CBT protocols for PTSD, but the anecdotal evidence from this case series is consistent with previous findings that the IEs used in Module 6 of the UP are relevant across the emotional disorders (Boswell et al., 2013).

Finally, when it came time to develop and execute a series of emotional exposure exercises, both patients who completed Module 7 reported that their self-efficacy and optimism for completing the emotional exposures related to PTSD, depression, and other forms of anxiety had increased dramatically as a result of the emotion regulation skills that they had developed in previous modules. The successful completion of a variety of emotional exposure exercises ultimately assisted patients in having the ability to clearly articulate the lessons learned in treatment during Module 8 and to have the perceived capacity to terminate treatment, as they felt confident that they understood not only how to apply the skills to the symptoms that initially led them to seek treatment, but also to apply the skills to future situations.

SUMMARY OF TREATMENT IMPACT

Although only two of the three participants in this case series completed a full course of treatment, all three displayed progress in terms of self-reported symptoms of PTSD (PCL pre-mean = 56; PCL post-mean = 23.3), anxiety (OASIS pre-mean = 9.7; OASIS post-mean = 1.7), and depression (ODSIS pre-mean = 7.7; ODSIS post-mean = 3). The two participants who completed a full course of treatment no longer met diagnostic criteria for any of the emotional disorders that they initially presented with and sought treatment for. Jon reported significant improvements in symptoms of PTSD, anxiety, and depression, but he was still experiencing clinically significant distress and impairment related to these symptoms when the decision was collaboratively made to end his participation in the case series so that more intensive clinical care could be provided in the aftermath of the Boston Marathon bombings. Jon reported that he had been optimistic that the UP treatment could have successfully addressed his symptoms if they hadn't escalated and changed following the Marathon bombings, but of course, there is no way to know the extent to which his symptoms may have changed had he received a full course of the UP.

CONCLUSIONS

The results of this case series provide promising preliminary evidence regarding the tolerability and efficacy of the UP as a treatment for PTSD and associated comorbid conditions. Although the effect sizes should be considered with caution, given that the results are from just three individuals, the pre- and post-effect sizes from this case series indicated robust effects for PTSD ($g = 1.53$), anxiety ($g = 1.57$), and depression ($g = 1.35$). Although one of the three individuals in this case series did not conclude treatment, all three reported high levels of satisfaction with the treatment protocol. They particularly expressed an appreciation for the more general focus of the treatment rather than exclusively focusing on trauma, and all three participants reported an improvement in their awareness of and ability to tolerate and effectively respond to different emotions.

The results, therefore, provide limited but promising evidence of potential extension of the UP as a treatment of PTSD. Future research is now needed to more rigorously test the efficacy of the UP for PTSD, to evaluate the relative efficacy of UP versus the current, gold-standard treatments for PTSD (i.e., CPT and PE), and to determine whether the UP does in fact effect change in symptoms of PTSD by targeting transdiagnostic mechanisms that underlie the emotional disorders.

8

The Unified Protocol for Comorbid Alcohol Use and Anxiety Disorders

TODD J. FARCHIONE, TRACIE M. GOODNESS,
AND KATELYN M. E. WILLIAMS ■

Alcohol use disorders (AUDs) are highly prevalent, with almost 18 million U.S. adults meeting diagnosis (Teesson, Hodder, & Buhrich, 2003; Teesson et al., 2010). Further, the past year's prevalence in the United States for moderate and severe AUD was estimated at 6.9% and 3.9%, respectively (Dawson, Goldstein, & Grant, 2013). Even after individuals diagnosed with AUD seek and complete treatment, relapse rates and treatment discontinuation are high (e.g., Bottlender & Soyka, 2005; Olfson et al., 2009).

ALCOHOL USE DISORDERS AND COMORBID ANXIETY DISORDERS

AUDs have a significant comorbidity rate with anxiety disorders (AXDs), with estimates of approximately 6 million U.S. adults having comorbid AUD/AXD (de Graaf, Bijl, ten Have, Beekman, & Vollebergh, 2004). Of those patients who seek treatment for AUD, over a third will be diagnosed with at least one concurrent AXD. Rates of AXD comorbidity in AUD-specific treatment settings exceed those numbers, with estimates of over 50% of patients suffering from comorbid AUD/ AXD (Kushner et al., 2005; Ross, Glaser, & Germanson, 1988).

Comorbid AUD/AXDs are associated with multiple negative outcomes (e.g., increased rates of disability, greater levels of drinking before and after treatment, interference in treatment engagement, higher rates of relapse, greater overall health care service utilization, and increased use severity) (Burns, Teesson, & O'Neil, 2005; Morley, Baillie, Sannibale, Teesson, & Haber, 2013; Kushner et al., 2005; Compton, Thomas, Stinson, & Grant, 2007; Magidson, Liu, Lejuez, &

Blanco, 2012; Buckner, Timpano, Zvolensky, Sachs-Ericsson, & Schmidt, 2008; Schneier et al., 2010; Gillihan, Farris, & Foa, 2011). Unique to either condition occurring in isolation, cooccurring AUD/AXD present a distinct set of difficulties for not only the individuals that are dealing with the disorders, but also for providers that seek to target both disorders in treatment. Given the large proportion of individuals who suffer from comorbid AUD/AXDs, as well as the severity of negative associations and outcomes, addressing the problem of how to best treat AUD/AXD could provide multiple positive outcomes for those meeting criteria for both diagnoses.

HYPOTHESIZED RATIONALE FOR COMORBIDITY

It is clear that AUD/AXD comorbidities exist at high rates. However, less clear is the underlying cause or causes that may account for this. There is a growing body of literature that suggests that the presence of one disorder may not necessarily put an individual at risk for developing the other; rather, the comorbidity may simply be different manifestations of similar underlying temperamental characteristics. Several constructs have been proposed to account for the high rates of comorbidity seen clinically, including (and most relevant to the current discussion) *neuroticism,* defined as the frequent experience of intense negative affect coupled with aversive reactivity to emotional experiences when they occur (Barlow, Ellard, Sauer-Zavala, Bullis, & Carl, 2014). These aversive reactions lead, in turn, to efforts to control or suppress emotional experiences, which has been shown to provoke rebound effects where emotions return with greater frequency and intensity (Rassin, Muris, Schmidt, & Merckelbach, 2000; Wegner, Schneider, Carter, & White, 1987), resulting in symptom maintenance.

Emotion regulation difficulties have been implicated in the development and maintenance of alcohol-related disorders (for reviews, see Kober, 2014; Sher & Grekin, 2007), and a growing body of evidence supports a relationship between emotion dysregulation and clinical alcoholism. For instance, emotion dysregulation is significantly elevated in alcohol-dependent subjects compared to social drinkers (Fox, Hong, & Sinha, 2008) and has been found to be related to the severity of alcohol dependence (Fairholme et al., 2013).

Patients with AUD also tend to score higher on self-report measures of neuroticism (Jackson & Sher, 2003; McCormick, Dowd, Quirk, & Zegarra, 1998; Prescott, Neale, Corey, & Kendler, 1997) and negative emotionality (Martin, Lynch, Pollock, & Clark, 2000; McGue, Slutske, & Iacono, 1999; Swendsen, Conway, Rounsaville, & Merikangas, 2002) than do nonalcoholic controls. Further, in a recent study by Petit and colleagues (2015), patients with alcohol dependence were shown to rely more on maladaptive emotion regulation strategies than did controls. Findings from this study also suggest that emotion dysregulation is associated with higher rates of craving and that abstinence is associated with a shift toward more adaptive emotion regulation patterns.

TRANSDIAGNOSTIC TREATMENTS
FOR COMORBID AUD/AXD

To date, effective psychological interventions for AUD/AXD comorbidity have remained elusive. Traditionally, single-diagnosis protocols or other approaches (e.g., twelve-step facilitation programs for AUDs) have been the predominant methodology of treatment for AUDs, AXDs, or both. In these treatments, individual disorders are treated either simultaneously or sequentially. However, findings regarding the efficacy of these approaches are quite mixed, with some indicating that parallel cognitive behavioral therapy (CBT) for anxiety and AUDs showed worse drinking outcomes relative to CBT for alcoholism only (Randall, Thomas, & Thevos, 2001), and other studies showing no differences in alcohol and anxiety outcomes (Bowen, D'Arcy, Keegan, & Senthilselvan, 2000). In a departure from this attempt to simply combine existing treatments, Kushner et al. (2006) developed a more integrated treatment approach, designated as *Hybrid-CBT,* that more explicitly examines the functional relationship between anxiety and AUD symptoms and focuses on weakening the links between the experience of anxiety and the motivation to drink. Using this integrated treatment protocol, Kushner and colleagues (2006, 2009) showed initial support for simultaneous treatment of AUD/AXD, including increased acceptability versus individual treatments, as well as significant clinical advantages (e.g., fewer total drinks, fewer heavy drinking episodes, and less severe relapse than the control group).

In the AXD area, there has been a similar movement toward the development of transdiagnostic treatments that can address comorbidity in a more comprehensive fashion. Recent meta-analyses found moderate to very large effects in pretreatment to posttreatment gains (Norton & Philipp, 2008) and large effects in comparative group differences between transdiagnostic treatments and controls (Newby, McKinnon, Kuyken, Gilbody, & Dalgleish, 2015).

Of the transdiagnostic treatments that exist for anxiety, depressive, and other "emotional" disorders, one of the most commonly utilized treatments is the Unified Protocol for Transdiagnostic Treatment of Emotional Disorders (UP; Barlow, Farchione, et al., in press). The UP is a cognitive behavioral intervention developed to address common underlying vulnerabilities across emotional disorders, particularly in those disorders where emotion dysregulation is central. It does this by targeting key aspects of temperamental characteristics, particularly those related to neuroticism (as defined previously). Initial findings suggest that the efficacy of transdiagnostic treatments, compared to the more traditional CBT models that focus on a single diagnosis, may be difficult to differentiate (Norton & Barrera, 2012; Farchione et al., 2012), but that transdiagnostic approaches afford several significant advantages to these existing treatments.

Further, the UP has some initial support in comorbid AUD/AXD (Ciraulo et al., 2013). In that study, investigators found that UP plus a placebo medication fared better in reducing days of heavy drinking in patients with AUD/AXD compared to several other groups: UP plus venlafaxine; a norepinephrine serotonin reuptake inhibitor with some support of effectiveness in AUDs; venalafaxine combined with progressive muscle relaxation; and placebo combined with progressive muscle relaxation.

CASE EXAMPLE

Tony was a 34-year-old, single, non-Hispanic Caucasian male who was self-referred to our center. His primary reason for seeking treatment was "anxiety and alcohol abuse." Tony completed a clinical assessment that included the Anxiety Disorders Interview Schedule for DSM-IV: Lifetime Version (Di Nardo, Brown, & Barlow, 1994), a semistructured clinical interview focusing on the diagnosis of AXDs and their accompanying mood states, and a set of standardized self-report inventories.

Tony reported a history of problems with alcohol use, starting in his mid- to late twenties. In the month prior to his assessment, he was drinking five days per week on average. On a typical drinking day, he would drink four to five servings of alcohol over about two to three hours, usually in the form of beer and some liquor. He reported drinking even more heavily at least once per week, often on the weekend. On those occasions, he would drink between four and six beers, as well as three shots of hard liquor, in less than four hours.

Tony reported that his drinking would "sometimes" affect his work performance, by making him feel "cloudy," and he was often late to work on days following a particularly heavy night of drinking. He stated that his current girlfriend of six months was unhappy with his alcohol use, and that it caused disagreements and conflict in their relationship. He reported that his use of alcohol also contributed to increased feelings of anxiety and depression. He experienced more anxiety in the early morning and then again in the early evening, often as he returned home from work.

He noted a clear relationship between his urge to drink and increased feelings of anxiety, stating, "They seem really connected. Sometimes I can't tell if I'm feeling anxious or just want a drink." Tony felt that he had built up a tolerance to the effects of alcohol in the six months prior to seeking treatment, drank larger amounts and/ or over longer periods of time than he intended to, and found it difficult to control his drinking on some occasions. His alcohol use also sometimes caused unpleasant withdrawal symptoms, including increased anxiety and sleep difficulties, which he would alleviate three to four times per month by taking 0.5 mg of Klonopin. While he did not believe that his alcohol use was greatly interfering with his life, he felt that it resulted in "moderate" interference in the prior year, as it caused him to engage in behaviors that he believed had a negative impact on his social reputation, and because it contributed to greater feelings of anxiety and depression.

In addition to these difficulties related to alcohol use, Tony reported a number of anxiety-related difficulties. In particular, he reported feeling moderately anxious in social situations, including giving presentations at work, participating in meetings, introducing himself to a group of people, attending parties, initiating and maintaining conversations, and asking others to change their behavior. He reported being afraid that he might "slip up" or that others might think badly of him. He stated, "I get concerned that other people might discover something bad about me . . . they won't like me."

Tony reported that in social situations, he often fears having intense physical symptoms of anxiety in these situations and that others might notice that he is feeling anxiety and think negatively about him as a result. He denied ever having a panic attack in social situations, though noted that he uses alcohol or Klonopin to help manage his anxiety. In addition to these difficulties in social situations, Tony reported occasionally having panic attacks when driving, some worries about his job (especially how well he's performing and the possibility of making mistakes), friendships, and, when he has a girlfriend, the quality of the romantic relationship. In addition, he reported occasionally experiencing low mood, but he did not meet criteria for a depressive disorder.

The results of baseline self-report questionnaires and additional clinician-administered measures are presented in Table 8.1. On the Depression Anxiety Stress Scales (DASS; Lovibond & Lovibond, 1995), a measure of general depressive, anxiety, and stress symptoms, his scores were 9, 19, and 24, respectively. These scores are indicative of "normal" levels of depression and "severe" levels of anxiety and stress. He obtained a score of 29 on the Anxiety Sensitivity Index (ASI; Reiss, Peterson, Gursky, & McNally, 1986), which reflects a "moderate" fear of the physical sensations of anxiety. On the clinician-administered Hamilton Anxiety and Depression Rating scales (HAM-A and HAM-D; Hamilton, 1959,

Table 8.1. BASELINE AND POSTTREATMENT
DESCRIPTIVE DATA

Assessment	Baseline	Post-Tx
ADS	21	–
ASI	29	17
DASS-A	19	8
DASS-D	9	3
DASS-S	26	15
HAM-A	18	10
HAM-D	11	6
Principal Dx CSR	7	4

NOTE: ADS, Alcohol Dependence Scale; ASI, Anxiety Sensitivity Index; DASS-A, Depression Anxiety Stress Scales–Anxiety subscale; DASS-D Depression Anxiety Stress Scales–Depression subscale. DASS-S, Depression Anxiety Stress Scales–Stress subscale. HAM-A, Hamilton Anxiety Rating Scale; HAM-D, Hamilton Depression Rating Scale (range 0–23). CSR, Clinical Severity Rating from the Anxiety Disorders Interview Schedule.

1967), two widely used severity measurements for assessing anxiety and depressive symptoms, his scores for anxiety and depression were in the "moderate" and "mild" ranges, respectively. The Alcohol Dependence Scale (ADS; Skinner & Horn, 1984) was used to assess severity of alcohol dependence within the last 12 months. His score of 21 on this measure fell within the upper level of the second quartile (just below the third quartile, which recommends intensive treatment) for alcohol dependence.

On the basis of the information obtained during the assessment, a principal diagnosis of alcohol dependence with physiological dependence [DSM-IV, 303.90; clinical severity rating (CSR) = 7 on a scale of 0 to 8, with 8 being most severe and interfering] was assigned. In addition, he was assigned a diagnosis of social anxiety disorder (nongeneralized; DSM-IV, 300.23; CSR = 4). As described previously, Tony reported additional anxiety symptoms, including panic attacks, particularly while driving, and worries about a number of areas in his life, and occasional low mood; however, he did not meet full criteria for any additional DSM-IV clinical diagnoses.

TRANSDIAGNOSTIC CONCEPTUALIZATION

Patients with AUD will often report using alcohol for coping motives and to reduce negative affect, which occurs frequently and intensely in response to situational triggers and cues. While these behaviors may reduce the patient's immediate emotional response in the short term, they fail in the long term and may contribute to maintenance of the patient's emotional difficulties, primarily through negative reinforcement. In our case example, for instance, Tony reported during the initial evaluation that he often used alcohol as "a means of escape" from difficult, anxiety-provoking situations. Later in treatment, he admitted that using alcohol in this way actually made him feel less able to cope and increased his perceived need for alcohol in social situations.

The primary focus of the UP is to help patients experience and respond to their emotions in more adaptive ways. Specifically with regard to alcohol use difficulties, as patients become better able to tolerate intense emotions and associated physical sensations, such as those accompanying withdrawal and cravings, it is expected that they will be in a better position to resist drinking urges and instead respond to their emotions in more goal-directed, adaptive ways. Over time, as emotional responses normalize, patients are also expected to see a reduction in presenting diagnostic symptoms.

Treatment

Module 1: Setting Goals and Maintaining Motivation

Following an introductory session reviewing the patient's presenting difficulties and providing an introduction to the UP, treatment begins with the application of strategies designed to increase both readiness for change in treatment and perceived self-efficacy to achieve change. The in-session exercises contained in this treatment module were derived from principles and techniques used in motivational interviewing (Miller & Rollnick, 2002) and have been found to enhance both client motivation to change and commitment to engage in therapy (Buckner & Schmidt, 2009; Korte & Schmidt, 2013; Marcus, Westra, Angus, & Kertes, 2011).

During this module, the therapist worked with Tony to identify problems associated with his drinking and frequent experience of anxiety, particularly in social situations. The "Decisional Balance" exercise from the workbook was used to help Tony explore and resolve ambivalence he might have with regard to changing his behavior and committing to therapy. Tony was easily able to identify the potential benefits of completing treatment, including fewer conflicts in his romantic relationship, better health, fewer difficulties at work and greater potential for career advancement, and increased time and money from a reduction in his alcohol use.

Through this exercise, it became apparent that while Tony recognized his drinking as being problematic, he was also concerned about what it might mean for him to stop drinking and whether this might exacerbate his anxiety symptoms. While identifying the "cons" of change, for instance, Tony stated, "If I stop drinking, I'm not sure I'll be able to go out with friends . . . I get too anxious." He followed this up by saying, "Honestly, I don't think I'm much fun when I'm sober." In exploring this further, he admitted that while he did not fully believe this statement to be true, it certainly contributed to his reluctance to reduce or stop his drinking. At this point in treatment, the therapist did not directly challenge this negative appraisal. Instead, identified reasons for not changing were discussed and simply juxtaposed against the potential "pros" of change. At a later point in treatment, during the cognitive flexibility module (Module 4), Tony's beliefs about himself were further evaluated in an effort to establish alternative appraisals.

Following the "Decisional Balance" exercise, the therapist and Tony then worked collaboratively to develop a treatment plan based upon a functional assessment of Tony's problem behaviors (based on information gathered during the introductory treatment session), his personal values, and his expressed goals for treatment. Because of his hesitation to give up drinking completely, a controlled-drinking model was used for treating Tony's alcohol dependency, which research has demonstrated to be at least as effective as alternative abstinence models in the treatment of alcohol addiction (Marlatt, Larimer, Baer, & Quigley, 1993; Sanchez-Craig, Annis, Bronet, & MacDonald, 1984). Consistent with the low-risk drinking guidelines established by the National Institute on Alcohol Abuse and Alcoholism (NIAAA), it was agreed that one of Tony's long-term goals for therapy would be to reduce his alcohol consumption to a weekly limit of 12 drinks, for which a daily limit of 3 drinks was set, and to reduce drinking to no more than four days a week. In addition to reducing his drinking, Tony further specified that he wanted to (a) reduce his anxiety in social situations, (b) learn how to manage anxiety without the use of alcohol or other avoidance behaviors, and (c) increase his sense of self-control with regard to drinking.

Module 2: Understanding Emotions

Module 2 of the UP provides an overview of the functional, adaptive nature of emotions and helps patients to identify and track their emotional experiences. During Module 2, acquisition of learned behaviors is discussed, including how they ultimately contribute to maintenance of nonadaptive patterns of behavior and emotional responding. Further, the therapist introduces the concept of emotional behaviors, which includes avoidance of emotion and what we've come to refer to as emotion-driven behaviors (EDBs), or the idea that emotions can lead to specific actions or behavioral tendencies that (in the case of psychological disorders) are maladaptive. This discussion sets the stage for identification of behavioral targets during subsequent modules.

Module 2 also introduces the three-component model of emotions (i.e., the way in which emotions are experienced not in isolation, but as an interrelationship among cognitions, physiological sensations, and behaviors), and explores the antecedents (or triggers) and consequences of emotional responses to help patients gain a better understanding of their emotions in context. In the following vignette, the therapist and Tony are discussing a three-component analysis of a situation that elicited a strong emotional response, which was later used to help him identify more adaptive ways of responding to similar situations in the future. In this situation, Tony had a "bad day" that culminated in an argument with his girlfriend later that night. He became so upset during the argument that he punched a hole in their bedroom door, causing her to leave for the evening, and that resulted in him drinking "whatever [he] could find in the house":

> TONY: *I just felt awful after she left. I was really angry but also ashamed that I'd lost control. She was really upset. I felt like a total jerk. Honestly, I didn't think she was coming back.*
>
> THERAPIST: *So the thoughts you identified were "I screwed things up," "What's wrong with me?" and "She's never coming back." I see you noted some feelings here, and also a strong urge to drink.*
>
> TONY: *At that point, all I wanted to do was drink.*
>
> THERAPIST: *What were you hoping for?*
>
> TONY: *I just wanted to feel better, and I did . . . at least for a while.*
>
> THERAPIST: *And then what happened?*
>
> TONY: *I guess I just kept drinking until I fell asleep. I woke up feeling like garbage the next day, and barely made it to work. That was a bad night.*
>
> THERAPIST: *Do you think you were drinking because of what happened with your girlfriend?*
>
> TONY: *Definitely.*
>
> THERAPIST: *No, what I mean is . . . what do you think were the emotions that actually led to the drinking behavior?*
>
> TONY: *Hmm. Yeah, I guess I was feeling ashamed. I felt bad about myself and what I had done. I wasn't really mad at her anymore. I just felt awful about losing control.*

THERAPIST: *I'm sorry you had such a tough night. I wonder if those feelings might have contributed, at least in part, to you drinking so heavily.*
TONY: *Yeah, that sounds about right.*

Upon further reflection, Tony noted that as the night went on and he continued to drink, he felt increasingly upset about what had happened and frustrated with himself for not being able to control his drinking. In turn, this led to increased anxiety and low mood (accompanied by feelings of shame), as well an even greater desire to drink. Initially, Tony was unable to identify how his thoughts, feelings, and behaviors in this situation were interrelated. However, discussing this example in session allowed Tony and his therapist to break down the seemingly overwhelming situation into individual components, which helped Tony to identify this "downward spiral" pattern. Ultimately, he was able to practice noticing his experiences over the next few weeks in other emotionally provoking situations.

For homework, Tony was asked to track his emotional responses in accordance with the three-component model. In addition, given his presenting alcohol use difficulties and his identified goals for treatment, he tracked the severity and frequency of his urges to drink and alcohol usage (i.e., number of drinks). In the following two vignettes, the therapist works with Tony to more explicitly examine the short- and long-term consequences of emotion avoidance, while identifying the primary components of his emotional responses. Tony recorded these situations, which occurred prior to beginning Module 3, on tracking forms from the treatment workbook:

TONY: *I was supposed to meet up with a friend of mine from work. We were planning to have dinner, but before I got to the restaurant, I started feeling really anxious. I ended up almost having a panic attack, so I just went home. I texted him and everything, but I still felt really bad about it.*
THERAPIST: *I'm sorry you weren't able to meet up with your friend. What happened after you left?*
TONY: *Just like that* (snaps his fingers), *I started feeling better. I actually thought about going back, but I was too embarrassed.*
THERAPIST: *And what did you identify as the long-term consequences of that behavior?*
TONY: *I definitely had a harder time with that part. I know I was feeling pretty down on myself. I mean, I should've been able to go for a few minutes at least. Also, I noticed that when I met up with my friend later in the week, I didn't want to go to the same place. So I made up an excuse.*
THERAPIST: *Any reason why?*
TONY: *I don't know. I just felt like I was going to feel anxious again. Plus* (slightly laughing) *they didn't serve alcohol at the first restaurant. I know that sounds ridiculous, but it makes me feel better to know it's an option.*

Similarly, in the following clinical example, taken from the same homework assignment, Tony explored the short- and long-term consequences of using alcohol to help manage his anxiety. In this example, Tony drank heavily during a work-related "mixer":

> TONY: *I just can't stand those types of things . . . all the small talk. I only went because my supervisor had mentioned it earlier in the day and asked if I was going. I don't do well in those situations. I was really worked up so I started drinking right away.*
>
> THERAPIST: *Did the drinking help alleviate some of your anxiety?*
>
> TONY: *Yeah, but then things got a little out of hand. I ended up having too many.*
>
> THERAPIST: *What happened?*
>
> TONY: *I mean, nothing terrible . . . but one of my friends told me I started acting a little too social. I didn't completely embarrass myself or anything, but I guess I got a little loud and had to take a cab home instead of driving.*
>
> THERAPIST: *Sounds like your drinking got away from you a bit.*
>
> TONY: *Yeah. No big deal, but I wish I had been [in] more control.*
>
> THERAPIST: *Maybe a middle ground?*
>
> TONY: *Yeah. I felt pretty embarrassed the next day. My boss sort of joked about it, but it's not a good way for me to be. I don't want people to think I'm an alcoholic or anything like that.*
>
> THERAPIST: *So from what you've told me, it sounds like the alcohol helped you feel less anxious in the situation initially, but then caused some problems for you in the end.*

In both of these examples, Tony's avoidant behaviors served to initially provide him with short-term relief from his anxiety, but they caused other long-term problems that likely maintained his emotional difficulties. In the first example, avoiding going into the restaurant resulted in an almost immediate reduction of his anxiety and panic; however, it ultimately reinforced the idea that he couldn't handle the situation in any other way and that he needed to leave in order to feel better. Tony's use of alcohol in the second example served a very similar function as leaving the restaurant did in the first, in that it allowed him to relieve (or escape from) the anxiety that he was experiencing in response to the feared social situation. In both cases, the behaviors resulted in negative long-term consequences, which Tony identified.

Initially, Tony found it difficult to connect with his emotions as they occurred; instead, he would often complete the tracking sheet following an emotionally provoking situation or at the end of the day. Over time, however, and with the extended awareness training provided in Module 3, he was able to gain greater awareness of his emotional responses as they developed. For Tony, Module 2 was also especially helpful in bringing greater awareness to the relationship between his emotions and desire to drink. Further, he reported that by gaining a greater understanding of why the drinking behavior was occurring, he felt more in control and in a better position to make a change.

Module 3: Mindful Emotion Awareness

Module 3 of the UP (the first core module of the protocol) is designed to help patients develop a more objective, nonjudgmental, and present-focused awareness of their emotional experiences, so as to (a) increase their tolerance and acceptance of intense emotions, (b) reduce the frequency at which they experience emotions about their own emotions, and (c) increase their ability to implement skills introduced later in therapy by bringing greater present-focused awareness to their emotional responses.

We have found that individuals with AUD/AXD have a tendency to ascribe negative attributions to emotions associated with uncomfortable experiences such as affective arousal, distress, and (specifically with regard to AUD) cravings. In the following vignette, Tony and his therapist discuss how his negative and judgmental thoughts about his emotional response to a perceived failure at work (in which he had to present in a staff meeting) served to exacerbate his emotional distress in the moment and (though not discussed here) his urge to drink:

> THERAPIST: *Last session, you mentioned feeling like a total failure because of what happened at work. Could you tell me more about that?*
>
> TONY: *I just feel like I can't do the most basic things sometimes without breaking down and panicking. Anxiety keeps me from being a normal person.*
>
> THERAPIST: *A normal person?*
>
> TONY: *Well I can't do normal, everyday things without being scared. I'd say that's not very normal.*
>
> THERAPIST: *I know it might feel that way, but as we discussed earlier, anxiety is a normal, adaptive emotion that everyone experiences. So one might argue that the fact you experience anxiety actually means you're a normal person, just like everyone else.*
>
> TONY: *I get that, but why do I get so anxious about stupid things?*
>
> THERAPIST: *We could talk more about how your fears got established, but for right now, let's focus a bit more on what may be maintaining them. A big part of it is how you think about your anxiety and other emotions. It's really hard to accept intense emotions, particularly when they're happening. But judging your feelings as abnormal, unwanted, or bad contributes to the problem. Let's take a presentation as an example. During presentations at work, do you notice yourself getting anxious?*
>
> TONY: *Definitely. I feel my heart beating, and I can't remember what I want to say. I just try to get through it as quickly as possible.*
>
> THERAPIST: *And how do you feel about the anxiety you're experiencing?*
>
> TONY: *I just want it to go away. I feel like everyone can see that I'm anxious. It's awful.*
>
> THERAPIST: *Are you able to focus on the presentation at all?*
>
> TONY: *Not really. Somehow I get through it. I don't know how.*
>
> THERAPIST: *Do you think being upset about your anxiety makes it worse?*

TONY: *Probably.*

THERAPIST: *How do you think?*

TONY: *I don't know, but I can't imagine it makes things any better.*

THERAPIST: *I would agree. You're trying to get rid of your anxiety by being anxious about it. It's like trying to put out a fire with gasoline, which doesn't work so well. I wonder what would happen if you tried to experience your anxiety differently in that situation, to not be so upset about it. I know it might hard to imagine, but how do you think things might have been different if you weren't as concerned about your anxiety . . . if it didn't bother you as much?*

TONY: *That's a good question. I guess I wouldn't be so focused on it. I'm not exactly sure, but it sounds like you think that's a better way to go.*

In this example, Tony's negative judgments about his emotions (that his anxiety is "abnormal," there's something wrong with him for feeling anxious, etc.) is conceptualized as contributing to a hyperfocus on how he feels during a presentation. This contributes to a shift in his attention away from his intended goal-directed behavior and toward his internal state, which unfortunately served to intensify his anxiety. Tony described feeling like a failure because, according to him, he allowed his anxiety to interfere with the presentation. In turn, he experienced frustration and shame that was associated with an increased desire to drink later that evening. After drinking heavily that night, he felt even more disappointed with himself and frustrated with his inability to control his drinking.

To provide Tony with a more adaptive way to cope with these thoughts and shift his attention to focusing more on the "big picture," an in-session mindfulness "body scan" exercise was used to demonstrate the skill of nonjudgmental awareness. Further, he was asked to engage in an in-session emotion induction exercise that entailed having Tony practice nonjudgmental, present-focused awareness while listening to a series of emotionally provoking songs. Tony did well with both of these exercises.

To strengthen his emotion awareness skills outside of therapy, Tony was asked to practice anchoring the present using the Mindful Emotion Awareness form from the workbook. In the following exchange between Tony and his therapist, which occurred prior to beginning Module 4, he describes an experience while completing this exercise that helped him to better appreciate the relationship between his negative emotions and his urge to drink:

TONY: *I decided to practice the awareness exercise while driving home from work. I had a really hard day, so it was actually pretty tough for me to stop thinking about it. Also, you know how much I love driving.*

THERAPIST: *Okay, let's take a look at your tracking sheet.*

TONY: *One thing I noticed is that my urge to drink was really high almost the entire drive home. Also, it got worse as I got closer to home.*

THERAPIST: *Did you notice any physical sensations associated with your desire to drink?*

TONY: *I did, but it was hard to notice exactly what I was feeling. I just know that I had a strong urge to drink. I think it may have had to more with what I was thinking as opposed to feeling. At one point, I noticed the thought "I can't wait to get home and drink."*

THERAPIST: *So what happened?*

TONY: *Well, it was actually kind of cool because I felt like I could sort of see the urge and just let it pass. It came in waves.*

THERAPIST: *And what happened after you got home? Did the urge continue?*

TONY: *Yeah, it was pretty bad, and eventually I had a couple drinks. But I actually felt good about being able to notice the urge. I've never experienced it like that before.*

Upon further discussion, Tony also noted feeling that he was becoming better able to experience his emotions nonjudgmentally. Further, when he did have a strong urge to drink, he was feeling more accepting of the urge and importantly, less compelled to drink. In later sessions, Tony engaged in mindful awareness exercises centered around his urges to drink. Consistent with the "urge surfing" exercises described by Marlatt (1994), these practices were designed to enhance his acceptance of uncomfortable experiences of cravings by increasing his awareness of their transient nature. As a result of practicing this exercise over subsequent weeks, Tony reported becoming better able to resist his urges to use alcohol.

Module 4: Cognitive Flexibility

The fourth module of the UP (the second core module) is designed to help patients develop more flexible ways of thinking by teaching them how to identify, interrupt, and reappraise anxious and negative cognitions and core automatic appraisals that contribute to the maintenance of their emotional difficulties. Through the integrated use of Socratic questioning and the downward arrow technique, the therapist helped Tony to identify automatic appraisals (and cognitive biases) associated with his anxiety in social situations. Further, Tony identified a number of positive drinking expectancies (i.e., expectations that drinking alcohol would result in desirable outcomes) and negative thoughts regarding himself because of his difficulty controlling his drinking.

In the UP, two primary cognitive distortions (or "thinking traps") are identified as generally capturing the cognitive-affective tendencies of clients with emotional disorders—*jumping to conclusions* (e.g., the tendency to overestimate the likelihood that something bad will happen) and *thinking the worst* (e.g., the tendency to automatically assume the worst-case scenario and underestimate one's ability to cope). We have found that patients with AUD (such as Tony) may perceive their drinking as a short-term strategy for reducing negative emotional states, including anxiety and low mood. Alternatively, patients might report that drinking can serve to enhance experiences or is associated with an increased positive mood or other pleasurable emotional state.

For instance, in this case, Tony once described drinking as a "social lubricant," noting that it made it easier for him to talk to people he didn't know at parties and to spend time with friends at the bar. He also felt that drinking made him feel better about himself (at least in the short term) and that it gave him greater confidence in social situations. These types of expectancies can be thought of as "probability overestimation" thinking errors, directly in line with the one of the thinking traps that patients work to identify in the UP, though labeling them as such is less important than helping patients examine these thoughts and consider alternatives.

In the following vignette, the therapist and Tony discuss specific thoughts regarding the perceived anxiolytic properties of his alcohol use. Notice that Tony also begins to identify some negative thoughts about his emotional reactions that appear to reflect a more general intolerance of negative affect:

> TONY: *I did a little pregaming before the party.*
> THERAPIST: *Pregaming?*
> TONY: *You know . . . my friends and I had a few drinks before going out.*
> THERAPIST: *I'm not sure I understand why you would do that.*
> TONY: *I guess it's just fun, and it definitely helps me feel less anxious.*
> THERAPIST: *And that was important to you . . . to feel less anxious before going out?*
> TONY: *[nods his head in agreement] Yeah, definitely. I hate feeling that way.*
> THERAPIST: *Maybe you could tell me a little more about that. What do you hate most about the anxiety?*
> TONY: *I don't know . . . I just hate it. I mean, no one likes feeling that way. I was trying to go out and have a good time with my friends. It sucks.*
> THERAPIST: *It can certainly be hard to feel like that . . . especially when it seems like no else is feeling the same way. Is there anything else that bothers you about it?*
> TONY: *I guess it just makes me feel weak, like I'm a wimp. No one else seems to struggle the way I do. I'm too old to be scared and anxious . . . there's no reason for it.*

In this example, the therapist was able to help Tony identify a number of cognitions regarding his emotions (in this case, anxiety) that became an important focus of cognitive restructuring throughout the remainder of treatment. Tony identified several core beliefs about himself in relation to his anxiety, including being different than others, feeling "weak" and being a "wimp." At other points in treatment, he noted feeling like a "failure" because of his anxiety and expressed concern that no one would want to be around him if they knew how "messed up" he really was.

After helping Tony identify maladaptive appraisals related to anxiety-provoking situations, his alcohol use, and (most important) his own emotions, the therapist worked with Tony to develop cognitive skills designed to increase flexibility in thinking (i.e., to consider alternative possibilities and look at situations from different perspectives). Self-monitoring homework was used to facilitate practicing these skills throughout the remainder of treatment. Initially, Tony would complete tracking sheets before going into difficult situations, such as giving presentations at work, when entering social situations where his friends might be drinking heavily, or after experiencing intense emotions. However, as treatment progressed, Tony reported that he was engaging in cognitive flexibility more "in the moment" and found that he was able to practice this before his emotions "got away from [him]."

Module 5: Countering Emotional Behaviors

The overall aim of Module 5 of the UP (the third core module) is to help patients identify and change maladaptive patterns of emotional responding, including avoidance of emotion and EDBs, which in the UP are broadly categorized as emotional behaviors. A large part of the module, then, is dedicated to helping patients understand how (primarily through the process of negative reinforcement) these behaviors ultimately serve to perpetuate and strengthen experiences of disordered emotion, despite their ability to provide momentary relief in the face of intense or uncomfortable emotional experiences.

In applying the UP to patients with AUD/AXD comorbidity more specifically, the therapist helps patients conceptualize their alcohol use as a maladaptive reaction to or attempt to avoid their emotions. Instead of using alcohol, the patient can "actively do nothing," practicing greater acceptance and tolerance of their emotional response (consistent with the skills developed in Module 3), utilize cognitive skills to adaptively alter the perceived threat associated with the situation (consistent with Module 4), or adopt an incompatible alternative action, often until the urge to use alcohol has passed.

In the current case example, the therapist discussed these concepts with Tony and demonstrated the paradoxical effect of emotion suppression using an in-session exercise from the workbook. The therapist then helped him identify typical patterns of emotion avoidance and EDBs that may be contributing to his emotional distress, problematic drinking, or both. This process is illustrated in the following example, in which the therapist helps Tony to identify potential EDBs while discussing an anxiety-provoking situation that had occurred in the prior week:

> THERAPIST: *In reviewing your self-monitoring record from last Friday, I noticed that your anxiety ratings were particularly high that day, and that your alcohol consumption was three drinks over the maximum limit that you had set for your daily drinking goal.*
> TONY: *Yeah, on Friday I went to a party with my friend and was really anxious. I didn't know anyone there except him.*

THERAPIST: *That's tough. How did it go?*

TONY: *Not as well as I would've liked. As soon as I got there, I had a drink to try to settle down. Other people weren't even there yet.*

THERAPIST: *And did your anxiety subside by the time everyone arrived?*

TONY: *No, not really. Not until I had a couple more drinks.*

THERAPIST: *So, by that time, you were maybe about three drinks in. Did you finally feel more comfortable?*

TONY: *I was definitely starting to feel more at ease, and eventually I started talking to other people.*

THERAPIST: *Were you able to stop drinking at that point?*

TONY: *I slowed down a little, but I noticed that even after that, I just felt better having a drink in my hand. That happens a lot.*

THERAPIST: *Any sense of why that was the case?*

TONY: *Well, I guess for a few reasons. Holding something stops me from fidgeting. It also helps me feel less anxious, maybe because I know that I have alcohol in case I start feeling anxious.* (Laughing) *It sounds weird, but it's sort of like a security blanket.*

THERAPIST: *Having the alcohol nearby helps you feel less anxious.*

TONY: *Yeah, I think so. Also, it gives me a good excuse if I want to get out of a conversation. I can always just finish my drink and leave to get another one.*

THERAPIST: *So it also gives you a means of escape.*

In this example, Tony clearly identifies drinking as an a response to feeling anxious in an attempt to "settle down". This is a common behavioral response for patients presenting with AUD/AXD comorbidity and fits well within the theoretical framework of the treatment model. It is also worth noting that Tony describes using alcohol as what is referred to in the UP workbook as a "safety signal," in the sense that simply having alcohol available to him made him feel more comfortable in an otherwise anxiety-provoking situation.

After helping Tony identify typical avoidance patterns and EDBs, the therapist worked with him to identify and implement more adaptive, approach-centered behaviors. Generally, these behaviors were incompatible with his more typical, maladaptive pattern of responding. For Tony, this included talking to unfamiliar people at parties instead of just hanging out with his friends, keeping his hands unoccupied during conversations, and coming out from behind the podium when engaged in formal presentations at work.

Module 6: Understanding and Confronting Physical Sensations

The primary aim of Module 6 (the fourth core module) is to increase both the patient's awareness and tolerance of physical sensations through the use of interoceptive exposure (IE) exercises. For patients with AUD, sensitivity to physical sensations may be especially important for understanding maladaptive reactions to physiological cues, such as those accompanying cravings. Typically, this module is completed over the course of one session, during which the therapist elaborates on the role of physical sensations as a core component of emotional experiences and the rationale for provoking these sensations repeatedly through "symptom induction exercises" designed to elicit physiological sensations that are distressing to the patient, most consistent with what they experience with intense negative emotions, or both.

Tony was especially sensitive to IE exercises designed to elicit feelings of disorientation, dizziness, and feelings of unreality, such as spinning and hyperventilation. During one of the hyperventilation exercises, Tony reported that when he experienced these feelings while driving, he sometimes got scared about possibly crashing the car. Also, the physiological sensations would often be interpreted as a sign that he was "out of control" and that the symptoms, therefore, were likely to increase in intensity and duration unless he did something to stop them, such as taking Klonopin or escaping from the situation.

Exposure to bodily sensations has been shown to increase alcohol-dependent individuals' tolerance of the uncomfortable physiological and emotional sensations associated with experiences of withdrawal and craving (Otto, O'Cleirigh, & Pollack, 2007). Consistent with this finding, Tony reported a greater ability to respond adaptively to cravings and to be less distressed by feelings of anxiety that he experienced the morning after a particularly heavy night of drinking following this module. Interestingly, however, this effect seemed more pronounced in situations where the cravings accompanied more negative (as opposed to positive) affect and distress. So, for instance, he continued to have difficulty resisting an urge to drink when approaching social situations at the end of treatment, but was better able to resist cravings that occurred outside of that context, such as after a hard day at work.

For homework, Tony was assigned a list of relevant IE exercises to complete throughout the week. This included sensations that he identified as being associated with cravings for alcohol and uncomfortable sensations associated with a state of withdrawal. Tony's list included a set of hyperventilation, spinning in place (to produce feelings of disorientation), breathing through a thin straw, and running exercises.

Module 7: Emotion Exposures

In Module 7 (the fifth and final core module), patients gradually engage in exposure exercises designed to (a) further increase awareness and tolerance of intense, uncomfortable emotions and (b) facilitate application of newly acquired, more adaptive emotion-regulation strategies. Procedurally, this module is typically carried out over the course of four to six sessions, during which the patient repeatedly confronts a range of avoided situations (and physical sensations) in a graded, bottom-up manner on the basis of an *emotion exposure hierarchy* designed collaboratively by the patient and therapist. After discussing the rationale of engaging in emotion exposures, the therapist typically guides the patient through a series of in-session exposure exercises corresponding to situations listed on the patient's hierarchy, with similar exposure tasks being assigned for homework each week.

For Tony, emotion exposures were explicitly designed to target intense emotional responses triggered by both internal and external cues; this included exposure to alcohol-related cues, social situations, panic-related sensations, and driving. In-session exposures allowed Tony to practice applying the skills that he had gained in treatment and gave him the opportunity to develop a plan for managing experiences of anxiety and cravings that might occur while completing exposure exercises in subsequent weeks.

Tony and his therapist conducted a number of in-session exposures designed to help him feel more comfortable in social situations and with being assertive. These included having a debate with a confederate, attending a mock party, and introducing himself to strangers. These situations were designed to closely resemble real-life situations that Tony encountered on a regular basis to encourage generalizability of treatment gains. In addition, imaginal and IE exercises were used to elicit intense emotions and physical sensations. For instance, Tony conducted an in-session exposure in which he imagined a recent past situation involving a verbal argument with his girlfriend about his alcohol use. Imagining this situation evoked feelings of embarrassment and guilt. During the exercise, Tony stated, "I hate feeling this way!" The cognitive flexibility skill (from Module 4) was used to help him think differently about the situation (including thoughts about his emotions) while conducting the exercise.

One exposure assignment near the top of Tony's hierarchy was to attend a poker night with friends while abstaining from alcohol. He felt that this situation would be especially difficult for him because it targeted several of his fears at once; specifically, he planned to (a) drive his car to the poker game and then back home, (b) abstain from alcohol (and practice assertiveness in refusing a drink from his friends) in the presence of alcohol-related cues, and (c) socialize with a number of people whom he did not know very well. In the following vignette, Tony describes how he did with this exposure. Notice that given the nature of the situation, the therapist was unable to create a similar in-session exercise. However, several in-session exposures were conducted to help prepare him more indirectly for this particular situation. Here, we see a "real-life" application of the skills learned in treatment:

THERAPIST: *Before we begin with the exposure exercises planned for today's session, I'd like to start by discussing the exposure task you completed for last week's homework. The first part of your assignment was to drive to your friend's poker game. How did it go?*
TONY: *Well, I had some panic symptoms, like racing heart and shortness of breath, about five minutes into the drive. But I kept going and tried to*

just let it wash over me. It didn't go away entirely, but I kept going, and eventually it subsided after I got to my friend's house.

THERAPIST: *That's great! How did things go at your friend's house?*

TONY: *For the first hour, it was pretty rough. Before we started playing, everyone was spread out across the kitchen and living room socializing, and because I only knew one person there, I felt really out of place. I was nervous that I looked awkward. It also didn't help seeing everyone else drinking. Standing around with nothing in my hand made me feel even more awkward.*

THERAPIST: *How did you go about managing the anxiety and cravings you were experiencing at that point, especially without alcohol?*

TONY: *It was tough. At one point, I even went to the bathroom for a little while to collect myself.*

THERAPIST: *And then what happened?*

TONY: *Well, I worked really hard to ride things out by just being mindful of the experience. I also practiced some of the cognitive skills, which helped bring my anxiety down a bit.*

THERAPIST: *That's great! What was the focus of the cognitive work?*

TONY: *I just kept reminding myself that the urges would pass after a little while, and I tried to remind myself of the reasons why I had set my goals in the first place. Also, I started thinking about how I had a really good friend there, and I'd met some of the people there at least a few times over the years. They weren't total strangers.*

THERAPIST: *Excellent, Tony! How did the rest of the night go?*

TONY: *It was pretty good. At one point, my friend asked if I wanted a drink. I told him no, which was fine. But after I refused, I started to really feel self-conscious and thought that the other guys around me might judge me for not drinking; but then, this other guy next to me said he wasn't drinking either because he was training for a triathlon. That helped me a lot.*

THERAPIST: *Wow, that's great! I'm happy you were able to hear that.*

TONY: *It definitely helped. I mean, I didn't have the same excuse, but I started thinking about how people might not really care about whether I drank or not. I thought to myself, "These guys don't even notice." Then once we started playing, I felt more comfortable. It gave me something else to focus on. Sitting between my good friend and someone I met at the last poker night also helped.*

THERAPIST: *How did you do socially?*

TONY: *Well, I actually ended up talking a lot with the guy who was training for the triathlon. And by talking to both him and my friend, I got into some conversations with people sitting next to them too.*

THERAPIST: *What did you take away from this experience?*

TONY: *I think it helped me challenge some of my beliefs about drinking. I was able to get along with people without drinking, which was good for me to see. Plus, I ended up winning a hundred bucks, which was awesome.*

THERAPIST: *That's great! Did you experience any anxiety during your drive home?*

TONY: *Actually, my drive home ended up turning into a social exposure as well. One of the guys from the game was too drunk to drive, so I volunteered to give him a ride. Normally, I wouldn't do that.*

THERAPIST: *That's great. It sounds like the exposure went really well. You did a nice job pushing yourself and stuck to your plan even though you felt some pretty strong emotions. You really did a great job!*

As illustrated here, Tony demonstrated greater awareness of his emotional experience. He was able to identify the physical sensations associated with his anxiety while driving, as well as in the social situation. Overall, he appeared to have a more open, nonjudgmental attitude toward his emotions. He also successfully reduced his engagement in emotional behaviors and continued with the task despite feeling anxious, whereas in the past, he might have escaped from the situation and returned home or used alcohol or Klonopin to help "take the edge off" and make him feel more comfortable.

Module 8: Recognizing Accomplishments and Looking to the Future

Treatment with the UP concludes with a final psychoeducation module focused on identifying and preventing high-risk situations for relapse, during which the therapist reviews the treatment principles and strategies that patients learned during treatment, acknowledges the treatment progress, and provides patients with recommendations for areas that could use further improvement. In order to maintain treatment gains, the therapist and patients additionally work together to develop a timeline, as well as exposures to help them successfully meet their long-term goals after treatment. Patients are also reminded that periodic experiences of intense emotion are inevitable and are not necessarily an indication of relapse.

In the current case example, the therapist reviewed Tony's progress by having him rerate the perceived difficulty of each situation listed on his exposure hierarchy, all of which were significantly lower relative to his initial ratings of these situations, particularly for previously avoided and feared situations involving driving. The therapist also worked with Tony to identify high-risk drinking and social situations, as well as weaknesses in his skill set for managing these situations. Although Tony had made great progress throughout treatment, he still struggled with significant cravings for alcohol during social interactions with individuals who he felt were "superior" to him in some way (e.g., acquaintances who were better at poker than he was or supervisors with whom he had to interact outside of work). To address these issues, part of Tony's long-term goal plan was to continue engaging in social exposure exercises involving low-drinking risks (e.g., asking a poker "buddy" to attend an event that was a shared interest), so as to further develop the skills that he had been taught during treatment.

For individuals with social anxiety disorder and AUD, lack of social support has consistently been found to be one of the strongest predictors of relapse after treatment (Beattie & Longabaugh, 1999; Dobkin, Civita, Paraherakis, & Gill, 2002; Kushner et al., 2005). Because many of the interests, social interactions, and activities of these individuals prior to treatment typically involved drinking, two other long-term goals established for Tony included (a) enlisting a group of family members and close friends to support and encourage him with maintaining his treatment gains, and (b) enrolling in a boxing class, which was an activity that was both incompatible with drinking and would allow him to socialize with new people.

In addition to these strategies planned and implemented around Tony's symptoms of craving alcohol in social situations, he noted that generally, he would like to continue to practice the skills that he learned throughout treatment in order to further reduce his drinking, both in frequency and in quantity. Tony noted wanting to be able to drink on a more controlled, regular schedule instead of in response to anxiety. The modules were reviewed with Tony, and plans for a general continued decrease were implemented (e.g., over the next month, cut drinking down by one day per week).

CLINICAL OUTCOMES

Tony responded well to treatment, experiencing marked decreases in diagnostic severity across all disorders, as well as improved psychosocial functioning. These improvements were reflected in his scores on both self-report and clinician-administered measures (see Table 8.1). Tony evidenced significant improvements on the DASS and both the clinician-administered HAM-A (Hamilton, 1959) and HAM-D (Hamilton, 1967) rating scales, which reduced to normal levels at posttreatment.

Similarly, scores on the ASI declined over the course of treatment and ultimately fell into the mild range. Using a controlled-drinking model, Tony's self-reported alcohol use also decreased over the course of treatment. Initially, Tony's level of drinking qualified as "heavy drinking" as defined by the Substance Abuse and Mental Health Services Administration (SAMHSA)—that is, five drinks in one drinking period for 5 or more days in the past 30 days) routinely; Tony met that criterion during the week and exceeded it in his heavier drinking episodes. In the two weeks prior to the posttreatment assessment, Tony evidenced a reduction in the amount that he drank and frequency of days drinking, drinking an average of 3 to 4 days a week, an average of two to three drinks per drinking occasion, and a maximum of four drinks on one occasion (decreasing the percentage of heavy drinking days from 80% pretreatment to 0% posttreatment). Further, he reported no heavy drinking episodes during that period, exceeding his original treatment goals. Despite significant improvements throughout the course of treatment, however, Tony still met levels for moderate drinking, which are often associated with some of the same negative outcomes associated with heavy drinking.

During the ADIS assessment, Tony reported experiencing fewer drinking-related consequences and less interference in social and occupational areas of his life. He also started exercising more often and reported feeling better about himself given his ability to better control his drinking. While he made large reductions in quantity and frequency of drinking and identified other positive outcomes, he also stated that he wanted to reduce his drinking further on his own using the skills from the UP. Overall, these changes dropped his CSR for his principal diagnosis of an AUD from a clinical level of 7 to a moderate level of 4.

Functionally, Tony was able to meet a number of his long-term treatment goals, which included reducing his alcohol consumption to an average of nine drinks per week (based on the two weeks prior to the posttreatment assessment), and increasing his perceived self-efficacy in his ability to manage experiences of anxiety without the use of alcohol or other avoidance behaviors.

By the end of treatment, Tony's engagement in social interactions had significantly increased, his girlfriend had noted more engagement by him in their relationship, and he had reported feeling "like a much more confident person," which was noticeably evident in both his demeanor and presentation at the time of termination. There was a slightly larger change in his comorbid diagnosis, and he no longer met diagnostic criteria for social anxiety disorder.

SUMMARY AND CONCLUSIONS

In this chapter, we presented a case study illustrating the application of the UP with a patient presenting with comorbid alcohol use and AXDs. The focus of the UP on addressing underlying temperamental factors and shared psychopathological processes reflecting aversive reactivity to intense negative affect is a clear departure from existing single-diagnosis protocols or other approaches to treatment that simply combine existing CBT elements or entire treatment protocols, either sequentially or simultaneously, without directly (and intentionally) targeting core underlying factors that may be shared by the various disorders.

Transdiagnostic (and other integrated) approaches to treatment for AUD/AXD comorbidity afford several advantages over existing psychological treatments for these disorders. First, by addressing comorbidity in a more comprehensive fashion, these treatments are more cost-effective and efficient for both patients and clinicians, and they arguably may lead to better treatment outcomes. Second, by providing a treatment that more adequately maps onto real-world patient presentations, transdiagnostic treatments may be more acceptable to clinicians in community settings, where treatments for comorbid AUD/AXD are sorely needed. Third, these treatments provide clinicians with the necessary skills to treat a broad range of problems with a single protocol, thereby greatly reducing the burden of training.

There has been some initial support for the efficacy of the UP to facilitate abstinence from alcohol consumption in individuals with comorbid AUD/AXD, as compared to that of a combined treatment with placebo (PLC) and progressive muscle relaxation (PMR) therapy, the control treatment condition (Ciraulo et al., 2013). Further evidence supporting the efficacy of this protocol is needed, however, particularly in real-world settings where implementation of the protocol may be more difficult. If found to be effective, the impact on AUD treatment would be substantial.

9

The Unified Protocol
for Eating Disorders

CHRISTINA L. BOISSEAU AND JAMES F. BOSWELL ■

INTRODUCTION

Disturbance in the experience of emotions is common with eating disorders. Specifically, individuals with these disorders demonstrate a biological and psychological predisposition toward experiencing negative affect more frequently and intensely than healthy controls (Brockmeyer et al., 2014; Harrison, Sullivan, Tchanturia, & Treasure, 2009; Svaldi, Griepenstroh, Tuschen-Caffier, & Ehring, 2012) and exhibit a tendency to view affective experiences as aversive, unpredictable, and uncontrollable (Brockmeyer et al., 2014; Svaldi, Griepenstroh, Tuschen-Caffier, & Ehring, 2012). This is coupled with maladaptive attempts to regulate and control emotional experiences and a tendency to underutilize adaptive emotion regulation skills (Danner, Sternheim, & Evers, 2014; Svaldi et al., 2012). Indeed, ecological momentary assessment research strongly implicates intense affective states (and an inability to cope with them effectively) as common antecedents to eating disorder behaviors (Berg et al., 2013; Engel et al., 2013; Kraus, Lindenberg, Kosfelder, & Vocks, 2015).

There is convincing evidence that the onset and maintenance of eating disorder pathology shares many of the same core features of common emotional disorders, such as anxiety and depressive disorders. Consistent with this, the lifetime comorbidity rates for various eating disorders and any anxiety disorder range between 48% (anorexia nervosa; AN) and 80% (bulimia nervosa; BN) (Hudson, Hiripi, Pope, & Kessler, 2007).

In terms of case formulation, diverse eating disorder behaviors (e.g., restriction, binge eating, and purging) serve a similar function of regulating and/or dampening distressing affect, which is thought to be driven by a vulnerability characterized by heightened negative affectivity and reactivity (Sauer-Zavala et al., 2012). In addition to accumulating empirical support in the area of eating disorders (e.g.,

Steinglass et al., 2011; Zucker et al., 2013), this formulation offers a theoretically and clinically useful functional model that can be cohesively integrated into a transdiagnostic treatment for diverse eating problems and commonly occurring comorbid conditions.

Using clinical case examples from both outpatient and residential treatment settings, we illustrate how the core principles of the Unified Protocol for Transdiagnostic Treatment of Emotional Disorders (UP; Barlow, Farchione et al., 2018) can be applied to eating disorders. We focus on the five core treatment modules: (a) increasing mindful emotion awareness, (b) promoting cognitive flexibility, (c) countering emotional behaviors, (d) understanding and confronting physical sensations, and (e) emotion exposures. We also outline the research supporting their utilization in eating disorders. Finally, we provide recommendations for future applications of the UP for eating disorders.

INCREASING MINDFUL EMOTION AWARENESS

Individuals with eating disorders evidence deficits in emotion and related interoceptive awareness (Brown, Smith, & Craighead, 2010). It is easy to underestimate the role of basic psychoeducation and objective monitoring (e.g., labeling and distinguishing) in developing a capacity for more adaptive emotion regulation. It may be difficult for many eating disorder patients to take full advantage of more complex skills (e.g., reappraisal and engaging in alternative action tendencies) in the absence of basic emotion awareness skills. Therefore, the first core module of the UP includes strategies to promote objective emotion awareness skills, including three-component monitoring that breaks a particular emotional response into its constituent elements: cognitions, physical sensations/feelings, and behaviors. This includes a functional analysis of emotions and behaviors, or the identification of antecedent and reinforcing factors that influence the occurrence of specific thoughts, feelings, and behaviors.

For example, individuals who suffer from BN are taught how to identify the antecedents (e.g., proximal and distal triggers), emotional responses (e.g., anxiety), and consequences of a binge eating/purging episode (arousal and tension reduction). In such cases, the short-term reduction in negative arousal is often followed by an increase in specific emotions such as shame or disgust, which is itself analyzed in a similar fashion. In the following vignette, the therapist works with a patient in a group setting to identify the three core components of emotional experience:

> THERAPIST: *Let's spend some time going over some examples from yesterday. Does anyone want to share an experience when they practiced the three-component monitoring?*
> PATIENT: *I had a really hard time yesterday.*
> THERAPIST: *Do you mind telling us about it?*

PATIENT: *I looked at my body in the mirror. I just wanted to crawl out of my skin . . .*

THERAPIST: *What else did you notice?*

PATIENT: *Sinking feeling in my chest.*

THERAPIST: *Any feelings?*

PATIENT: *I was angry . . . disgusted . . . disappointed . . . maybe shame . . .*

THERAPIST: *Thoughts?*

PATIENT: *I hate my body. I'm ugly.*

THERAPIST: *Behaviors?*

PATIENT: *I'm not sure I did anything with it. I stopped looking. I wanted to isolate . . . withdraw . . . disappear . . . If I had been at home, I would have binged and purged, or cut. I guess I felt like cutting.*

THERAPIST: *You are raising an important point. When we talk about behaviors in the context of strong emotions, it's not just the things you do, but can also be the things you have an urge to do that are important . . . like binging or purging.*

PATIENT: *Right.*

THERAPIST: *You said disappear?* [patient responds affirmatively] *That is powerful language. Do you think that might be related to the feeling of shame that you mentioned?* [patient responds affirmatively] *. . . The other really important thing about your experience is that it shows how we can have more than one emotion, and then emotions about emotions. So there are layers . . . If you think back, do you recall the sequence? You started with anger in your description . . .*

PATIENT: *I think that might have been what I noticed first. The disgust and shame came immediately after . . . I was kind of stuck in that place.*

THERAPIST: *Given your behavioral urges, does the disgust, or maybe even the shame, seem more core to you?*

PATIENT: *I agree. That captures it better . . .*

Individuals with eating disorders have elevated levels of alexithymia, or notable impairment in the ability to label and describe their own emotional experiences accurately (Bydlowski et al., 2005; Davies, Schmidt, Stahl, & Tchanturia, 2011; Harrison, Sullivan, Tchanturia, & Treasure, 2009; Nowakowski, McFarlane, & Cassin, 2013). Thus, the UP's focus on teaching patients to recognize and label their emotional experiences *as they unfold* is particularly relevant. Intrinsic to this approach is maintaining a present-focus, accepting emotions even when they are uncomfortable, and cultivating a nonjudgmental stance toward whatever emotions are experienced. It is not the emotional experience per se that is problematic, but the response to that experience. Here, the therapist uses an in-session emotion induction to help a patient practice mindful emotion awareness:

THERAPIST: *Now I am going to ask you to play one of the songs you brought to session. And really, the only goal is to notice how you are feeling—your emotions, but also any physical feelings.*

PATIENT: [plays part of the song]

THERAPIST: [after noticing patient looking around the room and playing with her jewelry] *Let's pause for a moment. Tell me a little about what's going on for you right now.*

PATIENT: *I don't know.*

THERAPIST: *Well, let's take a step back. Sometimes it helps to focus on what we are doing . . . on our behavior. What are you doing?*

PATIENT: *I'm playing with my bracelet . . . I guess it makes me feel better.*

THERAPIST: *Feel better? How so?*

PATIENT: *More calm. More in control.*

THERAPIST: *Were you feeling out of control?*

PATIENT: *I was feeling sad and anxious, I think . . . the refrain in the song where it's like "if it doesn't stop I'll go insane" is . . .* [trails off] *My heart starts pounding, I think about how fat I am and how that'll never go away, I feel so helpless . . . sad. I can't handle this. I don't want to feel this way.*

THERAPIST: *I can understand that you don't want to feel sad or helpless. So when you were listening to the song, you started to feel sad and anxious, you noticed your heart start racing, and you thought "I'm fat" . . .*

PATIENT: *And I guess my anxiety will never get better. Everything in my life is a mess. My job sucks. Normal people don't feel this way . . . it's stupid that I get this upset over things.*

THERAPIST: *So you had all these thoughts, these feelings, and started playing with your bracelet.*

PATIENT: *I see where you are going. I guess I did it to distract myself.*

THERAPIST: *What do you think would have happened if you had stayed with the emotion?*

PATIENT: *I don't know. Something bad.*

THERAPIST: *It seems like one of the things you do when you feel like you can't handle your emotions is to try to get rid of them in some way. In this case, you tried to distract yourself, because you are afraid that if you didn't, something bad would happen. We've also talked about binging and purging as a way to get rid of emotions, or to try to feel a different way.* [patient nods affirmatively]

THERAPIST: *One of the things that we will work on is trying to get you to fully experience those emotions without running away from them. And, also work on not judging your experience—so the "I'm stupid for feeling this way," the "I can't handle this," or the secondary reactions to your emotions. Really how you feel about having emotions. I'm going to propose that it's not actually the emotion that is problematic, but really it's how you react to your emotions. One of my goals is to teach you that you can have emotions, that it's okay to have them and fully experience them, and that if you sit through them, without avoiding them, then they will eventually subside.*

PATIENT: *I'm not sure I believe you.*

THERAPIST: *Is it something you'd be willing to test out?*

PATIENT: *I guess . . .*

THERAPIST: *Then let's play the song again, and this time, if you find yourself trying to distract yourself, try to bring your attention back to whatever you are feeling.*

Although initially reluctant to reengage in the emotion induction, with encouragement from the therapist, the patient continued to practice observing her emotional experiences. Over the course of several sessions, and with repeated practice, the patient was eventually able to listen to the song as well as other pieces of music, without avoidance, and observe all parts of her emotional experience. While music was a particularly effective emotion induction tool for this patient, other stimuli such as video clips and pictures can be used to help patients practice nonjudgmental, present-focused awareness.

PROMOTING COGNITIVE FLEXIBILITY

The second core module of the UP integrates cognitive interventions that are commonly included in CBT protocols for eating disorders and show specific benefits to address shape and weight concerns (Hilbert & Tuschen-Caffier, 2004), as well as anxiety and depression (McNally, 2001). Difficulties with cognitive flexibility are a hallmark of eating disorders (Roberts, Tchanturia, & Treasure, 2010; Tchanturia et al., 2004, 2012), including obsessive-compulsive traits thought to influence maintenance, symptomatic expression, and treatment outcomes (Anderluh, Tchanturia, Rabe-Hesketh, & Treasure, 2003; Halmi et al., 2005; Serpell, Livingstone, Neiderman, & Lask, 2002). Problematic cognitions characteristic of eating disorders concern symptom domains (e.g., body checking, thin-ideal internalization; Mountford, Haase, & Waller, 2006; Stice et al., 2001), personality characteristics (e.g., perfectionism, self-schemas; Mizes et al., 2000; Waller, Ohanian, Meyer, & Osman, 2000), and beliefs about emotions (e.g., the need to avoid; Wildes, Ringham, & Marcus, 2010).

In the UP, the antecedent-based strategy of cognitive reappraisal targets two core cognitive themes: (a) overestimating the probability of negative events happening, and (b) overestimating the consequences of that negative event if it did happen. Here, the therapist challenges the likelihood of a residential treatment patient's belief by introducing possible alternative appraisals:

PATIENT: *I know I'm going to make myself throw up tonight after dinner* [appears upset] . . .

THERAPIST: *You think you will make yourself vomit tonight? What makes you say that?*

PATIENT: *I just know it is going to happen. I'm really overwhelmed, and I don't think I can stop myself from doing it.*

THERAPIST: *Can you be 100% certain?*

PATIENT: *I guess not, but it feels certain.*

THERAPIST: *What is the feeling?*

PATIENT: *I'm feeling panicky . . . tense . . . I'm having an urge I need to act on . . .*

THERAPIST: *It sounds like these feelings, or your emotional experience, is strong enough to convince you that this is inevitable or out of your control . . . Is it possible that these feelings will subside by tonight?*

PATIENT: *I guess it's possible.*

THERAPIST: *Is there anything that you can do instead of purging if it remains or returns?*

PATIENT: *I can talk to staff . . . try to do an ARC [practice worksheet] . . .*

THERAPIST: *Those are great alternatives . . . It also seems likely that telling yourself that throwing up is inevitable increases the intensity of the feeling that it needs to happen . . . you can see the reciprocal piece of this.*

Importantly, strategies aim to promote cognitive flexibility, regardless of the content of the thoughts. Thus, therapists not only target eating disorder–related cognitions (e.g., "I'll gain a large amount of weight if I eat a meal prepared by someone else"), but also focus on more general identification and understanding of how patients' appraisals influence patterns of emotional responding:

PATIENT: *I found yesterday's group really depressing. Examining my thoughts more deeply just leads to catastrophizing . . . I don't get it . . . it seems to make things worse . . .*

THERAPIST: *Examining one's thoughts just leads to catastrophizing? Do you mind sharing an example?*

PATIENT: *Well, I found out that my insurance company is no longer going to cover a medication I need, and it is like the only medication that is helpful to me. My downward arrow was "This is unfair. I won't be able to get better. If I don't get better, then I won't be able to leave. If I can't leave, then I won't be able to go back to school. If I don't go back to school, then I won't be able to get a job. If I don't get a job, I won't be able to pay rent or bills. If I can't afford to live, then I will be broke on the streets." If it wasn't for this homework, I would never have been aware of those thoughts. This made me catastrophize, and so it was just depressing . . . I felt way worse . . . the homework made me have bad thoughts . . .*

THERAPIST: *You were feeling pretty bad . . . Has this chain of thoughts happened before? Do you think this is common for you?*

PATIENT: *Probably, but this forced me to think about that stuff . . . they would not have been there without the exercise, and it just made me feel depressed . . .*

THERAPIST: *Try to remember what we said about appraisals . . . our interpretation of events and experiences impacts our overall emotional response and the components of emotions that we have been practicing identifying . . . When you think about not getting your medication right now, what do you notice?*

PATIENT: *That it's unfair. I feel sad, maybe angry. Hopeless . . . but I think that has a lot to do with this downward arrow exercise . . .*

THERAPIST: *Let's try to step away from the exercise for a moment . . . Taking away this medication has left you feeling sad and hopeless. Something important was taken away from you in a way that was out of your control, and now you picture a future that is rather dark. Is that accurate?*

PATIENT: *Yes.*

THERAPIST: *I can understand why that would be depressing, but I'm not sure the exercise is the most relevant issue. You noted that this spiral of thoughts is pretty typical, right? What that might tell us is that whether or not you are aware of it, this is how your mind works. It seems like the implication is that you are better off being unaware. . .*

PATIENT: *Probably . . . it didn't feel good . . .*

THERAPIST: *I hear that. But I don't believe that a lack of awareness is a fail-safe solution for avoiding painful experience. It doesn't change the fact that this happened, and it has an impact on you . . . I would argue that lack of awareness through the same old avoidance strategies does not serve you in the long run . . . I expect that it leads to hopelessness that leads to more distress and less adaptive responses because it becomes entirely disconnected from the relevant issue . . .*

PATIENT: *I don't know . . .* [very quietly]

THERAPIST: *I know this is a lot. I am asking that you try to stay more open to be curious about how your mind works. These thoughts and feelings are there and have an impact regardless of your awareness . . . you have to trust that things will feel less out of control if you pay attention and learn from your experience . . .*

Based on these comments, the therapist devoted significant time in the remainder of the group session to practicing identifying emotion-incongruent alternative outcomes. Group members assisted one another in generating alternative outcomes related homework examples, and then in evaluating the probability of these outcomes. The patient in the example given here continued to struggle with these reappraisal strategies when she applied them to her own emotional responses, yet she demonstrated a capacity to generate alternatives and assess probabilities with regard to her fellow group members' examples. In an attempt to empathize with this patient, the therapist stated, "It can be easier to apply this flexibility to others than it is to apply it to ourselves . . . we kind of get stuck in our own experience in a different way."

This example demonstrates that for many patients, developing a willingness to connect with their thoughts and associated emotions is a crucial step toward learning more adaptive appraisal and reappraisal skills. In addition, it underscores how a "negative" homework experience can be grist for the therapy mill.

COUNTERING EMOTIONAL BEHAVIORS

The third core module addresses patterns of emotion avoidance and maladaptive emotion-driven behaviors (EDBs) that, from a UP perspective, result in the short-term reduction of intense emotion, but also contribute to the maintenance of the very emotions that the patient is seeking to change. Avoidance of situations that produce intense emotions, both positive (e.g., excitement, enjoyment) and negative (e.g., sadness, anger, anxiety) is common across the eating disorders (Corstorphine, Mountford, Tomlinson, Waller, & Meyer, 2007; also see Lavender et al., 2015 for review).

Emotion avoidance in eating disorders may be overt (e.g., refusing an invitation to go out to eat with friends, not eating "bad" foods) subtle (e.g., reading a menu ahead of time to plan what to order, wearing loose clothes), or cognitive (e.g., distraction). Safety signals (e.g., carrying chewing gum or water to consume if tempted by food) are also employed to keep emotions from becoming overwhelming. In the following vignette, the therapist helps the patient to see that she is engaging in emotion avoidance when she only wears baggy clothes:

> PATIENT: *My mom really wanted to take me shopping for new clothes, but I told her I didn't want to.*
> THERAPIST: *Why didn't you want to go?*
> PATIENT: *I don't need any new clothes. The ones I have are fine, but my mom was upset I didn't want to go. She kept talking about how she'd like to get me some summer clothes. I think she is just tired of me wearing sweats.*
> THERAPIST: *It does seem like sweatpants would be hot in the summer . . .*
> PATIENT: *Yeah, but I prefer comfy clothes.*
> THERAPIST: *What makes those clothes comfortable?*
> PATIENT: *They have a drawstring so I know they'll always fit. It's what I like.*
> THERAPIST: *Certainly, we all have personal preferences, but I'm wondering if there might be some emotional avoidance in there. Before the [eating disorder], did you wear different clothing?*
> PATIENT: *Well, I guess. When I was younger, I wasn't really concerned with how I looked. Now, no matter how much weight I lose, I feel like a blob. The whole dressing room thing causes me too much stress. What if I something doesn't fit? And then I have to deal with the mirrors and all the other people looking at me . . . so I guess, I'm avoiding it because I don't want to think about my body.*

In addition to binging, purging, and restriction, individuals with eating disorders often engage in ritualistic behaviors motivated by anxiety and perceived catastrophic outcomes should such behaviors not be completed (Johnson, Connors, & Tobin, 1987; Lawson, Waller, & Lockwood, 2007). These maladaptive EDBs often include body checking (e.g., using clothing fit or jewelry to evaluate shape

Table 9.1. EDBs Commonly Associated with Eating Disorders

EDB(s)	Incompatible Behaviors
Compensatory behavior (e.g., purging, compulsive exercise)	Alternative meaningful activity (e.g., journaling) or seeking out support
Eating at a regimented or slow pace	Engage in mindful eating without counting or timekeeping
Blotting food with a napkin	Holding food with both hands
Fidgeting	Hands on lap and feet on floor
Eating foods in a particular order	Eating food out of order
Body/mirror checking	Practice observing body in nonjudgmental terms
Perfectionistic behavior at work or home	Leaving things untidy or unfinished
Social withdrawal	Behavioral activation
Leaving (escaping from) a food/body image–related situation	Move to the center of the crowd; smile or put on nonfearful facial expressions

and weight, examining specific body parts, frequent weighing, and mirror utilization) to prevent or lessen distress arising from a preoccupation with body weight and shape (Mountford, Haase, & Waller, 2006; Reas, Whisenhunt, Netemeyer, & Williamson, 2002; Shafran, Fairburn, Robinson, & Lask, 2004); rituals around eating (e.g., eating food in a specific order, chewing a specific amount of times); purging (e.g., in a specific way, place, or until seeing a particular food); and weighing (e.g., repeatedly, at a specific time of day, after defecating) (Sunday, Halmi, & Einhorn, 1995).

Though these EDBs help eating disorder patients attenuate their emotional experience to some degree, in the long term, they serve to maintain disordered emotional experiences. Thus, facilitating incompatible action tendencies (e.g., sitting with emotions instead of purging) is a critical step in promoting emotional health. Table 9.1 lists EDBs that are commonly associated with eating disorders and incompatible responses.

In the following vignette, the therapist reviews a patient's EDB homework:

PATIENT: *I am not sure I can do this. Not avoid my emotions. And I am not sure it's helpful to write any of this stuff down. It just makes me feel bad about myself. I almost gave up midweek.*

THERAPIST: *I hear that. It's hard to think of doing something different. And I'm asking you to focus on and be aware of your feelings instead of automatically trying to get rid of them. It's something very different than you're used to.*

THERAPIST: [reviewing patient's homework] *Tell me a bit more about the first situation you wrote down—the fight with your boyfriend.*

PATIENT: *He was upset that I wouldn't go out to dinner with him and his coworkers. I felt guilty, so after he left, I drove to the supermarket and bought ice cream and some cookies. I didn't even wait until I got* home . . . I ate it all in my car. I guess that's both emotional avoidance and an EDB. I didn't go to dinner because I was scared I'd be anxious and wouldn't know what to order. And then I felt bad that I didn't go, and lonely, so I binged.

THERAPIST: Yes, it is both. You skipped dinner to avoid feelings of anxiety—that was emotion avoidance—and then you engaged in an EDB when you binged in response to feeling lonely.

PATIENT: Yeah, but I don't think I'm ever going to be able to do something different. How am I supposed to not avoid my emotions when it's what I always do?

THERAPIST: It's definitely a process. But the good news is that while you've learned to avoid your emotions, it's something that you can work to unlearn. Plus, you have already shown times when you did things despite feeling bad. Like you said you wanted to stop the homework midweek, but in front of me, I have a worksheet that's completely filled out. So we have a good example of when you wanted to avoid but acted opposite to your EDB.

PATIENT: [nods tentatively]

UNDERSTANDING AND CONFRONTING PHYSICAL SENSATIONS

The concept of *interoceptive sensitivity* has broadened beyond fear and anxiety (labeled *anxiety sensitivity* in such cases) to denote sensitivity to physical sensations associated with varied emotional responses (e.g., sadness, anger, or joy) and psychophysiological processes (e.g., appetite, hunger, satiety, or pain; Herbert, Muth, Pollatos, & Herbert, 2012; Matsumoto et al., 2006; Merwin, Zucker, Lacy, & Elliott, 2010; Zucker et al., 2013). Furthermore, all emotions have constituent somatic features (Barlow, 2002; Ekman & Davidson, 1994); as such, physiological arousal is relevant to any disorder with a core emotional component.

Eating- and digestion-specific physiological cues, such as hunger, satiety, nausea, fullness, and mechanoreception (e.g., pressure from clothing, stretching of skin) are gaining more attention and may represent a new frontier in exposure therapy for eating disorders (Zucker et al., 2013). Each of these eating-specific and emotion-based interoceptive cues is potentially relevant to the treatment of eating disorders. This, in conjunction with successful recent attempts to generalize interoceptive exposure (IE) strategies, supports IE as a transdiagnostically relevant intervention strategy that can be cohesively and effectively integrated into cognitive behavior therapy (CBT)–oriented treatments for eating disorders (Boswell, Anderson, & Anderson, 2015).

Research findings highlight the role of a general interoceptive sensitivity factor that encompasses both eating- and digestion-specific (e.g., gastric functions) and general autonomic (e.g., cardiac) physiological cues (Herbert, Herbert et al., 2012). This general interoceptive sensitivity factor is closely aligned with the construct of affect intolerance. For example, an individual who possesses an interoceptive sensitivity vulnerability may go on to develop AN if she or he learns maladaptive interpretations of weight gain, and physical cues related to digestion (e.g., fullness) are experienced acutely as strong signals that have become associated with weight gain.

Through interoceptive conditioning, the sensation of fullness serves as a cue for anxiety or fear (or negative affect, broadly). The intensity of the emotional experience itself will likely lead to maladaptive avoidance and EDBs (e.g., restricting, overexercising), yet both the sensation of fullness (which may be inaccurate due to hypersensitivity) and anxious arousal would, separately or in combination, trigger maladaptive behavioral responses, which are then negatively reinforced. Therefore, both eating/digestion-specific and emotion-based somatic cues represent viable targets for eating disorder treatment. Interoceptive cues related to anxious or fearful arousal, sadness, shame, hunger, satiety, scents, tastes, and mechanoreception that have become associated with weight gain or body image can all be coupled with and/or trigger amplified anxiety (Vocks et al., 2011). Sensitivity to these cues (including conditioned anxiety) and their negative meaning will be associated with maladaptive emotion regulation strategies that serve to control and suppress negative arousal. A variety of eating behaviors, from restriction to binging and purging, may serve this function.

Our experience suggests that the in-session symptom induction exercises contained in the patient workbook, like breathing through a thin straw (to elicit sensations of breathlessness, lightheadedness, or hyperventilation), hyperventilation (to induce feelings of dizziness and unreality), spinning in a chair (to produce lightheadedness, disorientation, and nausea), and running in place (to elicit rapid heart rate, shortness of breath, and feeling flushed or hot), are helpful in decreasing interoceptive sensitivity in patients with eating disorders, which may generalize across eating-specific and emotion-based cues. Next, the therapist introduces the concept of interoceptive awareness with an in-session symptom induction exercise:

THERAPIST: *I'm going to ask you to breathe through the straw for one minute. Notice any urges to stop or distract yourself. Try to stay with it as best you can. Keep going until I say "stop." OK, begin.*

[Patient stops several times, and each time, the therapist prompts her to "stay with it."]

PATIENT: [after one minute] *Oh my God, I am so panicky!*

THERAPIST: *What are some of the symptoms you are noticing or did notice?*

PATIENT: *I'm really anxious! . . . lightheaded, dizzy . . . frustrated because it felt like my body tried to get me to quit . . . like I did not have a choice.*

THERAPIST: *So the sensations were really intense?*

PATIENT: *Definitely! But at the same time, I noticed a lot of cognitive avoidance. I tried to distract myself even though I know I wasn't supposed to . . . again, it felt like my body and mind were tricking me or something.*

THERAPIST: *The urge to stop and the distress felt overwhelming?*

PATIENT: *Very distressing . . . but I kept trying to go back to it. That was good, I think . . .*

THERAPIST: *Yes, you stuck with it! What do you make of that?*

PATIENT: *I wanted to make it the minute . . . obviously, I was actually able to keep trying . . . I am still feeling tense and a little lightheaded, but I survived. I think that's a pretty good first try . . .*

Accumulating basic psychopathology research indicates that novel IE techniques designed to target eating and digestion-related physiology might prove to be effective supplements to traditional IE exercises (Boswell et al., 2015). In reality, some existing exposure strategies for eating disorders already evoke relevant physiological cues (e.g., exposure to binge foods); however, interoceptive awareness and tolerance are arguably indirect targets. Consequently, integrating an increased focus on interoception may enhance existing strategies, and new induction strategies can be tested and potentially utilized as stand-alone interventions. For example, we are currently piloting the following exercises: gulping water (fullness, bloating, gastric functions); wearing tight clothing (constriction, general tactile discomfort); and smelling salient foods (hunger, salivation, disgust, gastric functions).

EMOTION EXPOSURES

Building on the skills taught in previous modules, the final core module utilizes interoceptive and situational exposures to increase emotion tolerance, allow the adoption of adaptive emotion regulation strategies, and introduce new contextual experiences. The use of exposure hierarchies for feared foods and in-session meal exposures, in particular, are well-established components of CBT-based eating disorder protocols (Fairburn, 2008). Indeed, exposure-based treatments encouraging patients to eat feared foods while preventing maladaptive avoidance and EDBs have recently shown some promise for both AN (Steinglass et al., 2011, 2014) and BN (Martinez-Mallen et al., 2007; McIntosh, Carter, Bulik, Frampton, & Joyce, 2011). Guided mirror exposure, in which individuals are asked to observe and describe their bodies in nonjudgmental terms, also has gained empirical support (Delinsky & Wilson, 2006; Hilbert, Tuschen-Caffier, & Vogele, 2002; Hildebrandt, Loeb, Troupe, & Delinsky, 2012).

However, here, it is important to consider the variations that may occur within eating disorder patients. While some patients may engage in excessive mirror checking to monitor their body image, others may avoid their reflection. Although clinicians using the UP with eating disorder patients often incorporate feared foods and mirror exposures into treatment, it is important to note that the primary focus of the exposure is to the emotion itself, not on a specific situation. Thus, the therapist helps the patient create a hierarchy containing situations that trigger uncomfortable emotions, both positive and negative, and works with the patient to systematically confront those situations through in-session, imaginal, and in vivo exposure. Figure 9.1 shows an example of an emotion expo-sure hierarchy.

Dovetailing with the previous interoceptive awareness module, therapists also assign exposures to target physiological feelings that an eating disorder patient might associate with negative emotion, including eating/digestion-specific sensa-tions. Here, the therapist reviews IE homework with a group of residential patients:

> THERAPIST: *You've been working on the interoceptive exercises. Would anyone else like to share something from their hierarchy?*
> PATIENT: *I made the choice not to wear sweatpants everyday.*
> THERAPIST: *Is that something that you came up with [individual therapist]?*
> PATIENT: *Yes . . . Instead of wearing sweatpants every day . . . like to this group . . . because they are more comfortable and don't remind me of my weight because they are like so baggy . . . I chose to wear jeans instead, which are slightly uncomfortable . . . actually they fit correctly, but they are more snug against my legs . . . it reminds me that I have gained weight here.*
> THERAPIST: *That is a really clever idea. Remember, we talked a little bit about wearing belts to do something similar?*
> PATIENT: *Yes. I am exposing myself to this tighter sensation. Tight is OK . . . my pants don't need to be loose . . . I can learn to be comfortable wearing regular clothes at this weight.*

CONCLUSION AND FUTURE DIRECTIONS

Although preliminary data support the utility and efficacy of the UP with het-erogeneous emotional disorders (Farchione et al., 2012), efficacy and effective-ness evaluations in eating disorders are only beginning (Thompson-Brenner & Ice, 2014). Nevertheless, as illustrated by the clinical cases presented in this chap-ter, early indications suggest that the UP may provide an effective approach for addressing common underlying processes that cut across emotional disorders, simultaneously addressing multiple disorders and, thereby, providing a more par-simonious option for the treatment of a range of cooccurring diagnoses.

In addition to demonstrating effectiveness, we offer several recommenda-tions for future work involving the UP for eating disorders. The standard treat-ment approach for eating disorders is multimodal, particularly in residential and intensive outpatient settings. Patients receive individual and group psychotherapy, nutrition monitoring and counseling, pharmacotherapy, and complementary com-ponents such as creative-expressive arts. Future research should examine the feasi-bility, process, and outcomes of fully integrating the UP principles in multimodal treatment contexts. In addition, the implementation of eating/digestion-specific IE interventions should be examined through both basic and applied research.

Finally, additional research is needed to identify and directly test target mecha-nisms of eating disorder UP outcomes. Theoretically, these mechanisms would

Do Not Avoid	Hesitate To Enter But Rarely Avoid	Sometimes Avoid	Usually Avoid	Always Avoid
0		**5**		**10**
No Distress	Slight Distress	Definite Distress	Strong Distress	Extreme Distress

	Description	Avoid	Distress
1 **WORST**	Eating food at a sporting event and keeping it down	9	10
2	Wearing a bathing suit in public	9	9
3	Eating at a restaurant or another public place	7	8
4	Eating what significant other cooks without knowing the ingredients	6	8
5	Going clothing shopping	5	5
6	Telling other people when I'm upset (not faking happiness)	5	5
7	Going grocery shopping	4	5
8	Watching a sad movie	3	4

Figure 9.1 Example of an emotion exposure hierarchy for a patient with bulimia nervosa.

be consistent with other emotional disorders, but this remains to be tested. Given recent promising work in the area of exposure therapy for AN (Steinglass et al., 2012, 2014), isolating emotion-focused exposure mechanisms in the UP for eating disorders (as well as other disorders) may lead to more effective interventions in a problem area that historically has been extremely difficult to treat.

10

The Unified Protocol
for Insomnia Disorder

JACQUELINE R. BULLIS AND SHANNON SAUER-ZAVALA ■

INTRODUCTION

Insomnia is one of the most common complaints among adults in primary care settings (Morin & Benca, 2012). Individuals with chronic insomnia report impaired health-related quality of life that is comparable to people with clinical depression or congestive heart failure (Katz & McHorney, 2002). Chronic insomnia is also associated with impaired mood, perceived deficits in functioning, and elevated rates of absenteeism in the workplace, as well as increased healthcare utilization (Walsh, 2004). In a recent study of a large cohort of adults that were followed for 20 years, individuals who experienced persistent insomnia for at least 6 years were 58% more likely to die than their peers without insomnia (Parthasarathy et al., 2015).

Insomnia disorder is characterized by dissatisfaction with sleep quality or quantity, including at least one of the following symptoms: difficulty falling asleep at the beginning of the night, difficulty staying asleep throughout the night, or waking in the morning earlier than intended (American Psychiatric Association, 2013). In addition, the sleep difficulty must be associated with significant distress or interference in important areas of functioning (e.g., social, educational, occupational, and behavioral). The problem must occur at least three nights a week, for a minimum of three months, and within the context of sufficient opportunity for sleep (i.e., dissatisfaction with sleep quantity that is not due to sleep deprivation).

Prior to the introduction of DSM-5, insomnia was characterized as either a primary or secondary condition; an individual whose chief complaint was sleep disturbance, in the absence of any other psychological or medical conditions, was diagnosed with primary insomnia, whereas an individual who was experiencing sleep disturbance associated with another condition or viewed as a symptom of another disorder (e.g., depression, stress, chronic pain, side effect of a medication) was assigned a diagnosis of secondary insomnia. In DSM-5, primary insomnia was renamed as *insomnia disorder*, reflecting a decision to no longer distinguish between primary and secondary insomnia within this classification system. Experts in sleep medicine hope that this change will both encourage mental health and medical clinicians to recognize sleep disturbance as an important treatment target and improve treatment approaches for it when it is comorbid with another condition (Reynolds, Redline, and the DSM-V Sleep-Wake Disorders Workgroup and Advisors, 2010).

Sleep disturbance is highly comorbid across many psychiatric disorders and is consistently recognized as a core symptom across anxiety and depressive disorders (National Institutes of Health, 2005). On average, individuals reporting to health facilities and community samples report rates of comorbidity between insomnia and psychiatric disorders of 53% and 41.7%, respectively (Harvey, 2001). Perhaps due to its ubiquitous nature, insomnia is frequently conceptualized as a symptom of other disorders, particularly when it presents with anxiety or depression (Harvey, 2001). It is often assumed that diagnosis and treatment of the primary diagnosis or underlying psychological disorder will result in the remission of sleep difficulties as well. However, studies show that even among disorders where sleep disturbance is a diagnostic criterion, such as posttraumatic stress disorder (PTSD), depression, and generalized anxiety disorder (GAD), effective treatment of the anxiety or depressive disorder does not result in full remission of insomnia symptoms (Belanger, Morin, Langlois, & Ladouceur, 2004; Harvey, 2001; Stepanski & Rybarczyk, 2006; Zayfert & DeViva, 2004). In addition, insomnia is a well-established predictor for depression (Baglioni et al., 2011) and is associated with increased suicidal ideation and suicide attempts, independent of depressive severity (Peterson & Benca, 2006). These studies suggest that it is insufficient to simply treat the anxiety or depressive disorder when insomnia is present as well, but also that individuals who continue to experience sleep difficulties following successful treatment of the comorbid condition may be more vulnerable to reoccurrence in the future.

This chapter will present a rationale for why the Unified Protocol for Transdiagnostic Treatment of Emotional Disorders (UP; Barlow et al., 2018) may be an effective treatment approach for addressing insomnia disorder, followed by a review of how traditional treatment targets for insomnia may be conceptualized from a transdiagnostic perspective. Then we will present a case example of an individual with insomnia who was treated with the UP.

INSOMNIA AS AN EMOTIONAL DISORDER

It is now well established that sleep disturbance is a transdiagnostic process that is highly comorbid with many psychiatric disorders (Dolsen, Asarnow, & Harvey, 2014; Harvey, Murray, Chandler, & Soehner, 2010). However, emerging research suggests that many of the mechanistic processes responsible for the development and maintenance of symptoms in emotional disorders are present in insomnia as well.

As discussed in greater detail in Chapter 1, individuals with emotional disorders tend to experience more negative affect, react negatively to their own emotional experiences, and subsequently engage in efforts to suppress or downregulate the emotional experience (i.e., avoidant coping). A number of studies have demonstrated that people with insomnia report more negative affect and higher levels of neuroticism than healthy individuals (Buysse et al., 2007; Duggan, Friedman, McDevitt, & Mednick, 2014; Gurtman, McNicol, & McGillivray, 2013; LeBlanc et al., 2007; Ramsawh, Ancoli-Israel, Sullivan, Hitchcock, & Stein, 2011; Vincent, Cox, & Clara, 2009; Williams & Moroz, 2009). People with insomnia also tend to exhibit more emotional reactivity to stress than good sleepers, which is observable even before the onset of insomnia symptoms (Fernandez-Mendoza et al., 2010).

Despite experiencing an equivalent number of stressful life events as good sleepers, individuals with insomnia rate the impact of these daily minor stressors higher, view their lives to be more stressful overall, and report low control over daily stressors. This reflects both a heightened negative emotionality and a perceived inability to cope in response to stress (Morin, Rodrigue, & Ivers, 2003). Indeed, heightened stress-reactivity and an avoidant coping style appear to be among the strongest predictors of insomnia (Harvey, Gehrman, & Espie, 2014), and recent research on environmental and genetic contributions suggests that the genetic vulnerability for insomnia appears to influence how the sleep system is affected by stress, rather than affecting the sleep system itself (Drake, Friedman, Wright, & Roth, 2011).

TRANSDIAGNOSTIC TREATMENT TARGETS IN INSOMNIA

Research on the causes of insomnia often focuses on predisposing, precipitating, and perpetuating factors (Morin & Benca, 2012). *Predisposing factors* are factors that may increase the likelihood of experiencing sleep difficulties, such as a family history of insomnia or an anxiety-prone personality. *Precipitating factors* are associated with the initial onset of symptoms and may include an increase in stress (e.g., illness, promotion at work) or a lifestyle changes (e.g., birth of a baby). Once the triggering event is resolved, insomnia symptoms typically remit. However, some individuals continue to experience sleep disturbance even after the initial stressor is gone, due to the presence of *perpetuating factors*, which consist of maladaptive coping strategies that actually exacerbate or maintain the sleep difficulties.

For the purposes of this chapter, we will be focusing on perpetuating factors, for two reasons. First, although predisposing and precipitating factors are highly relevant to acute insomnia, they become increasingly less so as an acute episode of insomnia transitions to a chronic condition over time. Second, perpetuating factors reflect the mechanisms responsible for chronic insomnia and therefore represent appropriate targets for intervention. We will now review the treatment targets commonly discussed in the context of cognitive behavioral therapy for insomnia (CBT-I) and discuss how these same targets can be conceptualized from a transdiagnostic perspective using the UP.

Dysfunctional Beliefs About Sleep

Individuals with insomnia reliably endorse more dysfunctional beliefs and excessive worry about sleep than good sleepers (Edinger et al., 2000; Espie, 2002; Morin, Vallieres, & Ivers, 2007). Dysfunctional beliefs often consist of unrealistic expectations about the quantity (e.g., "I need eight hours of sleep to feel good") or quality (e.g., "If I wake up in the middle of the night, I won't feel refreshed in the morning") of sleep required, which in turn drives worry about the effect of a poor night's sleep on individuals' functioning the next day (e.g., inability to perform at work, irritable mood).

As a result of these negative beliefs about sleep and associated consequences of insufficient sleep (e.g., "If I don't fall asleep soon, I'll be a complete mess at work tomorrow"), people with insomnia experience an increase in negatively toned cognitive activity while they are in bed and attempting to fall asleep that interferes with sleep onset (Wicklow & Espie, 2000). Studies have shown that changes in beliefs and attitudes about sleep are associated with improvement in insomnia symptoms, suggesting that dysfunctional beliefs about sleep are an important perpetuating factor to target in the treatment of insomnia (Edinger, Wohlgemuth, Radtke, Marsh, & Quillian, 2001; Morin, Blais, & Savard, 2002).

Dysfunctional beliefs about sleep reflect a lack of cognitive flexibility that prevents alternative, more objective interpretations of a situation. For example, someone with insomnia who feels anxious is likely to conclude that the anxiety is a direct result of not sleeping well the night before. However, there are many other possible interpretations of why he or she is feeling anxious (e.g., upcoming performance review, fight with friend that has not been resolved yet). Other dysfunctional beliefs about sleep, particularly those related to the consequences of not getting enough sleep, tend to reveal low self-efficacy and an inability to cope with negative consequences. Module 4 of the UP, which focuses on cognitive flexibility, is well suited to help patients identify their negative automatic thoughts about sleep and then adopt a more flexible approach to evaluating their thoughts. By countering probability overestimation and decatastrophizing in the context of thoughts related to sleep, patients learn to generate more objective predictions of how likely it is that a negative outcome will occur (e.g., "Even though I haven't fallen asleep yet, I will likely get at least a few hours of sleep before I need to get up for work"), as well as their ability to cope with a negative outcome (e.g., "If I don't get eight hours of sleep tonight, I can find ways to cope with my fatigue tomorrow").

Hyperarousal

Insomnia is also associated with a state of increased physiological arousal that is referred to as *hyperarousal.* Research has demonstrated that individuals with insomnia demonstrate increased secretion of cortisol (a stress hormone associated with numerous poor health outcomes), greater activation of brain areas associated with emotion, and elevated heart rate (Bonnet & Arand, 2010). It has been proposed that this autonomic arousal in individuals with insomnia is a direct result of the excessive worry and rumination that occur prior to sleep onset (Harvey, 2002a).

Due to their fear of sleep-related impairment, people with insomnia also tend to display hypervigilance for sleep-relevant cues. For example, they might monitor their bodies for signs that they are falling asleep (e.g., decrease in heart rate) or check for signs of poor sleep the next day (e.g., bodily sensations consistent with fatigue, concentration difficulties). Unfortunately, this hypervigilance has the undesirable effect of increasing autonomic arousal and intrusive thoughts about sleep (e.g., "I feel terrible today, so I need to make sure I get a good night's sleep tonight").

The hyperarousal described here is driven by negative reactions to emotional states or somatic symptoms that are incongruent with sleep. In other words, individuals with insomnia are judging their emotional experiences as "bad" or "unacceptable" and then worrying about what might happen in the future (e.g., "I'm going to blow my sales pitch tomorrow") or ruminating on what went wrong in the past (e.g., "Last time I had to give a sales pitch on only a few hours of sleep, I really blew it"). Module 3 of the UP introduces mindful emotion awareness skills, with the goal of helping patients develop skills to observe their emotional experiences in a nonjudgmental way while remaining in the present moment. By applying these skills to the hyperarousal that is typically experienced at bedtime, patients with insomnia can learn to acknowledge the symptoms of autonomic arousal (e.g., racing heart, muscle tension) without evaluating them as a threat to sleep or engaging in efforts to control or change them.

Research also has shown that anxiety sensitivity is associated with sleep difficulty and medication use among individuals with insomnia (Vincent & Walker, 2001), and there is some evidence suggesting that interventions targeting anxiety sensitivity can produce some reduction in insomnia symptoms (Short, Allan, Raines, & Schmidt, 2015). Accordingly, targeting emotional reactivity to symptoms of hyperarousal using interoceptive exposure (IE), as is done in Module 6 (Understanding and Confronting Physical Sensations) may help patients with insomnia gain a greater understanding of the role that these somatic symptoms play in triggering their emotional response, as well as increase their tolerance of the symptoms.

Safety Behaviors

In order to prevent feared outcomes associated with disruptive or nonrestorative sleep, individuals with insomnia develop a variety of coping strategies (Harvey, 2002b). These strategies, also referred to as *safety behaviors*, range from using a sleep medication or having a glass or two of wine before bed to napping during the day or canceling plans to provide plenty of time to relax and wind down before going to bed. Although people with insomnia view these strategies as helpful, they are often in fact counterproductive because they can interfere with sleep (e.g., alcohol consumption and napping both disrupt the normal sleep/wake cycle) and they prevent individuals from disconfirming their dysfunctional beliefs about sleep (e.g., if someone with insomnia cancels a meeting with her boss because she did not sleep well, she will not have an opportunity to learn that she is able to perform well even when fatigued).

Insomnia is also associated with greater use of avoidant cognitive coping strategies (e.g., thought suppression or distraction), and this relationship is particularly strong when insomnia is comorbid with an anxiety disorder (Belanger, Morin, Gendron, & Blais, 2005). Indeed, research has demonstrated that engaging in efforts to fall asleep (as opposed to allowing sleep to happen naturally) is associated with more severe symptoms of insomnia (Hertenstein et al., 2015).

These safety behaviors can function to either avoid the negative emotional experience entirely (e.g., taking a sedative or hypnotic medication before bedtime as a preventative measure) or to reduce the intensity of a distressing emotional experience (e.g., canceling social obligations when feeling fatigued). Modules 5 and 7, which focus on emotion avoidance and emotion exposures, respectively, are designed to reduce both forms of emotion avoidance. In Module 5, patients learn how their emotion-driven behaviors (EDBs) influence their emotional experiences and then begin to identify and counter maladaptive EDBs with alternative actions.

For patients with insomnia, safety behaviors can be conceptualized as EDBs that allow short-term reduction in anxiety, but over time, maintain symptoms of insomnia by reinforcing dysfunctional beliefs about sleep. For example, going to bed early may reduce a patient's anxiety about being able to fall asleep in time to get eight hours of sleep, but ultimately strengthens the patient's beliefs that the consequences of not getting eight hours of sleep would be catastrophic. Similarly, patients who nap to alleviate daytime fatigue or irritability may feel better for the rest of the day, but they are likely to experience increased difficulty falling asleep at night due to a decrease in sleep drive.

Module 7 provides patients with an opportunity to confront distressing emotions in a gradual manner without engaging in avoidance. Accordingly, many of the traditional components of CBT-I, such as maintaining a regular wake-up time, getting out of bed when unable to sleep, or reducing the total time spent in bed, can be introduced as emotion exposures with the UP. However, it is important to clarify the difference between the UP and CBT-I with regard to the rationale for engaging in these exercises. For example, in CBT-I, getting out of bed when unable to sleep is framed as behavioral intervention to regulate the sleep-wake cycle more effectively by reducing the association of the bed with emotion distress. In the UP, getting out of bed when unable to sleep is framed as an emotion exposure where the patient confronts the anxiety about getting out of bed, as many patients with insomnia are fearful that getting out of bed will result in greater arousal and reduce the likelihood of being able to fall asleep later.

The overall goal of emotion exposures for patients with insomnia is to facilitate the modification of previously held beliefs about sleep (e.g., catastrophic consequences of poor sleep) and to develop greater tolerance of distress through repeated practice confronting strong emotions. The expectation is that, over time, by reducing emotion avoidance and EDBs, patients will reduce sleep effort and, as a result, be able to fall asleep naturally.

CASE PRESENTATION

Introduction

Jonathan is a 38-year-old, married Caucasian male with two-year-old twin daughters. When he presented for treatment, he was employed full time in the banking industry. Jonathan indicated that he was seeking services to cope with anxiety and depression related to difficulty sleeping. He was referred to our Center by a nearby psychiatric hospital following a four-day inpatient stay that was precipitated by two weeks of very little sleep, during which he experienced marked feelings of depression and thoughts of suicide. These symptoms were alarming to Jonathan's wife, who urged him to seek immediate treatment at the hospital.

While at the hospital, he was prescribed Ativan (a benzodiazepine commonly prescribed for anxiety, depression, or insomnia) and Seroquel (an atypical antipsychotic that is also prescribed for depression) to be taken at bedtime to aid him in falling asleep. Upon calling to initiate services at our center, Jonathan stated that he continued to have difficulty falling asleep and was still bothered by worries about his sleep throughout the day following his discharge from the hospital.

Diagnostic Assessment

The Anxiety Disorders Interview Schedule for DSM-5 (ADIS-5; Brown & Barlow, 2014) was used to perform a semistructured diagnostic interview. Each diagnosis is then assigned a clinical severity rating (CSR) ranging from 0 (no symptoms) to 8 (extremely severe symptoms), where a CSR of at least 4 (definitely disturbing/disabling) represents the clinical threshold.

During the diagnostic assessment, Jonathan endorsed symptoms consistent with a diagnosis of insomnia disorder. He recalled that before the onset of the sleep difficulty, he had experienced two consecutive nights of almost no sleep due to repeated disturbances from the family cat; the cat's nocturnal activity may have been a precipitating factor. Jonathan reported that even after he began locking the cat in the basement at night, he continued to experience sleep difficulties due to anxious thoughts about whether he would be able to fall asleep and how it would affect his mood, work, and family life if he didn't get enough sleep. The insomnia continued for several weeks, during which he reported getting less than two hours of sleep most nights. Jonathan then began experiencing panic attacks at bedtime, triggered by lying in bed awake.

He also stated that he experienced a depressed mood and, most notably, passive thoughts of suicide (e.g., "I can't take this anymore, I'll probably be dead in the next month"), which prompted his aforementioned hospitalization. He stated that he was able to sleep for the four days that he was hospitalized, but he experienced severe anxiety upon his discharge regarding his ability to sleep at home. Jonathan reported that this anxiety had lessened somewhat since returning home, but he noted that he was still experiencing intrusive worries throughout the day regarding his ability to sleep (e.g., "I'll have another bad night's sleep and I'll feel depressed, and then it will snowball out of control"). He indicated that he was currently sleeping about four hours per night, and that it took him around two hours to fall asleep.

Jonathan also continued to experience significant symptoms of depression and fatigue, particularly in the mornings. He reported that the depression was most severe during the initial onset of his insomnia; he cited depressed mood, lack of interest in usual activities, decreased appetite, difficulty sitting still, fatigue, and thoughts of suicide. Jonathan indicated that since the modest improvement in his sleep following his hospitalization, he wasn't experiencing these symptoms as frequently. However, he stated that the symptoms of depression still interfered with his ability to concentrate at work and reported that he was particularly distressed by his lack of interest in engaging with his daughters. Jonathan denied any previous depressive episodes.

Finally, Jonathan endorsed symptoms of social anxiety disorder. He indicated that he experiences anxiety while giving a presentation, introducing himself to others, prior to attending parties, talking to persons of perceived authority, and initiating and maintaining conversations. He stated that currently, he is most bothered by anticipatory anxiety prior to weekly meetings at work. He reported that he largely copes with his social anxiety by avoiding situations that trigger it (e.g., screening phone calls, refraining from participating in meetings, avoiding parties). Jonathan stated that his social anxiety did not cause him much distress, as he has felt it since he was in junior high school.

Diagnostic feedback was given following the assessment. Jonathan met criteria for insomnia disorder with nonsleep disorder mental comorbidity (CSR = 5). An episodic specifier was assigned to reflect that his insomnia symptoms were present for at least one month, but less than three months. He also met criteria for a major depressive disorder (MDD) with anxious distress in partial remission (CSR = 5). Finally, Jonathan met criteria for social anxiety disorder (CSR = 4), although he indicated that he was not interested in making social concerns a focus of treatment.

Treatment with the Unified Protocol

Jonathan's principal goal for treatment was to address his insomnia as quickly as possible due to concerns about the cost of treatment, so his therapist elected to utilize a cognitive-behavioral protocol, *Overcoming Insomnia*, from Oxford's "Treatments That Work" series (Edinger & Carney, 2008). However, during the first treatment session, it became apparent that Jonathan was not willing to engage in insomnia-specific treatment components due to his anxiety about getting "enough" sleep each night. For example, he expressed an unwillingness to keep a sleep log or to avoid excessive time in bed. He stated that keeping a sleep log could lead him to feel even more distress if he realized that he was in fact sleeping less than he thought, and that this distress would then further interfere with his ability to sleep.

In addition, although Jonathan appeared to understand the rationale for stimulus discrimination (a behavioral strategy for reducing the association between being in bed and emotional distress, as well as enhancing the association between the bed and sleep), he was not willing to wait until he felt sleepy to go to bed or to get out of bed if 20 minutes elapsed and he hadn't fallen asleep yet; he maintained that limiting time spent in bed would interfere with the opportunity to get as much sleep as possible.

Since Jonathan was not ready to engage with the *Overcoming Insomnia* strategies, his therapist made a decision to utilize the UP, with the hope that developing a better understanding of the functional relationships between his negative reactions to emotional experiences and subsequent attempts to downregulate the experience would result in greater treatment engagement. Therapists may also consider using the UP instead of a disorder-specific insomnia protocol when a patient is presenting with more than one diagnosis or when they feel comfortable with the UP and would prefer not to learn a new protocol.

UNDERSTANDING EMOTIONS

The second half of the first session was spent helping Jonathan develop a greater awareness of his own emotional experiences. The therapist asked Jonathan to describe his experience the previous night when he had been lying in bed trying to fall asleep, and then utilized a three-component model to illustrate how to break an emotional experience into cognitions, somatic sensations, and behaviors (Figure 10.1). Applying the three-component model to the anxiety that he experiences at bedtime helped Jonathan to begin viewing his emotional experiences, which felt overwhelming and uncontrollable, from a more objective perspective.

Next, the therapist discussed the interaction of Jonathan's thoughts, physical sensations, and behaviors in order to demonstrate how one component of the emotional experience can amplify another. For example, Jonathan reported that when he was lying in bed, his thoughts typically centered on how he would sleep that night and the implications of not being well rested the next day. As time passed and he remained in bed worrying, he would also begin experiencing physical symptoms of anxiety and hyperarousal. Jonathan then interpreted those physical symptoms as a sign that he would not be able to fall asleep, which then led to greater anxiety about how much sleep he would get and the associated consequences, as well as more autonomic arousal.

Since he viewed the consequences of not getting enough sleep to be disastrous, Jonathan engaged in a series of emotion-driven behaviors (EBDs), such as lying down hours before his typical bedtime, to prevent his insomnia. When the therapist inquired whether these behaviors were effective, Jonathan responded

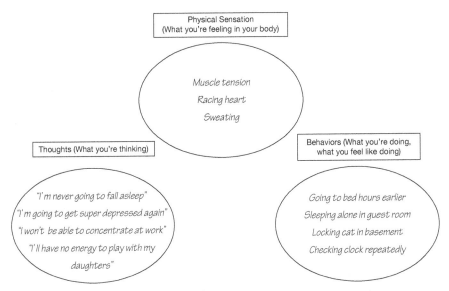

Figure 10.1 Three-component model of emotions.

affirmatively (e.g., "The only reason I'm getting any sleep at all these days is because I'm going to bed much earlier!"). The therapist then asked Jonathan to elaborate on how going to bed hours before he expected to feel sleepy was helpful, and Jonathan explained that when he went to bed earlier, he felt more in control of the situation, which in turn reduced some of his anxiety in the moment.

Through the use of Socratic questioning, Jonathan eventually agreed that although these EDBs helped him manage his anxiety in the short term, the long-term effect was that he was reinforcing his negative beliefs about sleep—specifically, that sleep was extremely elusive and that he would be unable to function at work or at home if he did not get enough sleep the previous night. The therapist then discussed how Jonathan's refusal to monitor his sleep or to restrict his time spent in bed were EDBs that helped him cope with some of the acute anxiety associated with his insomnia, but they also prevented him from learning that his anxiety would diminish on its own with time, as well as accumulating sufficient sleep drive. Although he remained unwilling to make any changes to his sleep routine, Jonathan did agree to complete a three-component model of emotions worksheet each evening for homework.

MINDFUL EMOTION AWARENESS

The next two sessions were spent introducing and then practicing an objective, present-focused, nonjudgmental awareness of Jonathan's emotional experiences, particularly his anxiety about whether he would be able to fall asleep each night, how much sleep he would get, and the associated impairment the following day. The racing thoughts that Jonathan experienced at bedtime, which drove his anxiety, were often related to past experiences (e.g., ruminating about his hospitalization) or concerns about the future (e.g., worry over his ability to perform at work the next day), so it was particularly important for him to learn how to anchor himself in the present.

During the in-session practice, Jonathan was instructed to allow himself to fully experience his emotions as they happened, remain present, and to notice the thoughts, feelings, and behaviors as they occurred. The therapist also advised him to let his emotions come and go, without judging them as good or bad or trying to push them away. It was emphasized that practicing mindful emotion awareness is not meant to be a relaxation exercise and that it may initially produce distress, particularly during the experience of negative emotions, but over time and with practice, it will allow the emotion to pass more quickly. Jonathan agreed to practice the exercise on his own twice a day, with one practice occurring prior to bedtime, and to record his experience using the "Mindful Emotion Awareness" worksheet.

When Jonathan returned to session the following week, he reported that he found the emotional awareness practice to be quite uncomfortable, stating that it was hard to observe his thoughts and physical sensations at bedtime without immediately feeling stressed and anxious, and then interpreting those negative emotions as a sign he would not be able to fall asleep, which triggered further worry about how he would be able to get through the day tomorrow. Jonathan was encouraged to adopt a more objective view of his anxiety (e.g., "It makes sense that I feel anxious about getting enough sleep because it's helpful to be well rested when I have to give a presentation at work") instead of allowing the anxiety to trigger future-oriented worry (e.g., "My depression will get worse and I'll end up back in the hospital"). He also worked on grounding his anxiety in the context of the present moment (e.g., "I am worrying about giving a presentation at work tomorrow on no sleep, but right now I am lying in bed"). For Jonathan, when he noticed that his thoughts were being pulled away from the present moment, it was helpful for him to label these thoughts as either "past" or "present" and to direct his focus on his breathing to ground himself.

The therapist also used the ARC of emotions to review with Jonathan how his reluctance to wait until he felt sleepy to go to bed, or to get out of bed if he was unable to fall asleep within 20 to 30 minutes, resulted in him spending a great deal of time lying in bed awake. Over time, doing this weakens the bed as a cue for sleep and strengthens the association between the bed and emotional distress. A consequence of this association is that the bed itself becomes an antecedent or automatic trigger for anxious thoughts about sleep, which then results in the somatic sensations of hyperarousal and leads to attempts to control the anxiety, which unfortunately only exacerbates the insomnia.

Cognitive Flexibility

The fourth and fifth sessions were spent on developing greater cognitive flexibility. The therapist introduced the reciprocal relationship between negative automatic thoughts and emotions, discussing how Jonathan's interpretations of a situation influenced his emotional reaction (and vice versa). For example, Jonathan was prone to interpret any somatic sensations that he experienced while lying in bed as a threat to sleep, which then resulted in worry and anxious distress. On nights when he lay in bed tossing and turning until early morning, his automatic thoughts focused on how impaired he would be the next day and the cost of not performing well (e.g., being laid off from work, his wife leaving him). With the help of the therapist, Jonathan learned to become more aware of his negative automatic thoughts and replace them with more objective alternatives. For example, the automatic thought "I won't be able to fall asleep tonight" was countered with "I am awake now, but I don't know for certain whether I'll stay awake all night."

As discussed earlier, dysfunctional beliefs about sleep (e.g., "After a poor night's sleep, I know it will interfere with my daily activities the next day," "I am concerned that chronic insomnia may have serious consequences on my physical health") are an important treatment target for patients with insomnia. Accordingly, the therapist explored a number of Jonathan's specific beliefs related to sleep:

> THERAPIST: *It sounds like you view your ability to perform at work as directly dependent on how well you slept the night before.*
>
> JONATHAN: *Yes, but that's because it is—on nights that I only get a few hours of sleep, I can't concentrate at work the next day. I spend most of the day just staring at my computer screen. I'm a total mess.*
>
> THERAPIST: *And has your boss talked to you about it?*
>
> JONATHAN: *What do you mean?*
>
> THERAPIST: *Has your boss spoken to you about missing deadlines or your lack of productivity?*
>
> JONATHAN: *Well, I haven't actually missed any deadlines. I guess I am still getting things done.* [pause] *Okay, so maybe I was blowing things out of proportion a bit there, but I know that the insomnia is 100% what caused this depression. So even if I am doing okay at work, I am still scared that I'll get depressed again if I'm can't sleep.*
>
> THERAPIST: *What about when the twins were born? How much sleep were you getting then?*
>
> JONATHAN: [laughs] *Not enough! My wife and I felt like we were sleepwalking for those first few months.*
>
> THERAPIST: *And what was your mood like during those months?*
>
> JONATHAN: *I was so happy. I had always wanted to be a dad.*
>
> THERAPIST: *So it sounds like even though you were only getting a few hours of sleep each night, you weren't depressed. In fact, you were really happy.*
>
> JONATHAN: *I guess you're right—I never thought about that before.*

Jonathan found it particularly helpful to remind himself of the times when he didn't perform well at work or felt down when he had slept well the night before, which allowed him to be more flexible in his predictions related to sleep. At this point in treatment, Jonathan had developed greater awareness of his emotional experiences and was able to use anchoring in the present and cognitive flexibility skills to manage the anxiety surrounding bedtime more effectively. However, it was still taking him up to an hour to fall asleep, and he reported that he was getting around five hours of sleep a night.

COUNTERING EMOTIONAL BEHAVIORS AND EMOTION EXPOSURES

Sessions six and seven focused on identifying emotion avoidance strategies and replacing those strategies with alternative actions. Some of Jonathan's EDBs included looking up articles on the long-term effects of insomnia, taking a sleeping pill every night, rescheduling meetings at work when he hadn't slept well the previous night, driving to work instead of riding his bike to conserve energy, and worrying about the consequences of poor sleep while he was in bed. Jonathan was also sleeping separately from his wife, locking the cat in the basement at night, and going to bed early to give himself plenty of time to fall asleep.

By this point in treatment, Jonathan recognized that these behaviors were all forms of avoidance, and although he reported that these behaviors tended to provide short-term relief from his anxiety, he agreed that they were likely maintaining his symptoms over the long term. However, he remained very anxious about making any behavioral changes to his sleep routine due to a fear that he would revert to the severe insomnia that preceded his hospitalization.

The therapist helped Jonathan generate an emotional and situational avoidance hierarchy (Figure 10.2) that would provide opportunities for him to experience his emotions fully without engaging in his patterns of avoidance. While some items on his hierarchy involved reducing his avoidance behaviors, others involved the use of physical exercises to help him develop a new set of nonfearful associations between physical symptoms of anxiety and his predicted outcome (i.e., insomnia). Jonathan and the therapist discussed how he would implement the skills he had learned thus far in treatment during exposures (e.g., cognitive flexibility and mindful emotion awareness). For example, when he became highly anxious about implementing a behavioral change to his sleep routine, he practiced anchoring himself in the present moment and being more flexible in his prediction of the possible outcomes.

For his first exposure, Jonathan agreed to return to bed with his wife, rather than sleep in the guest room. He also agreed to keep a sleep log to determine the total amount of time that he should spend in bed. At this point, Jonathan understood that the rationale for completing these exposures and the success that he had experienced with the other UP treatment components helped to increase his buy-in for exposures as a critical mechanism of treatment. Even though he was highly apprehensive about confronting these previously avoided situations, he was able to see how doing so fit into the larger treatment model of the UP.

When he returned to clinic the following week, he found that he was sleeping, on average, six-and-a-half hours each night. To determine the amount of time that he should spend in bed, 30 minutes were added to his average sleep time. In

Do Not Avoid	Hesitate To Enter But Rarely Avoid	Sometimes Avoid	Usually Avoid	Always Avoid
0		**5**		**10**
No Distress	Slight Distress	Definite Distress	Strong Distress	Extreme Distress

	Description	Avoid	Distress
1 **WORST**	Not taking sleep medicine	8	9
2	Letting cat roam around the house at night	8	7
3	Going to bed at 1am	7	7
4	Doing jumping jacks 30 minutes before bed	6	7
5	Getting out of bed if unable to fall asleep within 30 minutes	6	6
6	Using a sleep diary to monitor sleep	5	4
7	Getting up at by 8am on the weekends	5	4
8	Sleeping in bedroom with wife	4	3

Figure 10.2 Emotion exposure hierarchy.

other words, by limiting his time in bed to seven hours, Jonathan would be giving himself sufficient time to fall asleep and then achieve approximately six-and-a-half hours of sleep. Previously, Jonathan was getting into bed around 11 PM when he needed to be up at 8 AM the following morning for work. After calculating the total time that he should be spending in bed, Jonathan agreed to go bed at 1 AM as an emotion exposure.

From a CBT-I perspective, this exercise is a behavioral strategy for decreasing the amount of time spent lying in bed awake, which in turn reduces the strength of the bed as a cue for sleep. Within a UP framework, the goal of this exercise was for Jonathan to expose himself to the emotion triggered by facing an anxiety-provoking situation without engaging in any EDBs. By limiting the total time spent in bed, Jonathan was able to learn that his anxiety will diminish on its own, without his trying to get rid of it. He also was able to test whether his feared consequence (i.e., he won't be able to fall asleep if he doesn't give himself "enough time") was accurate.

RELAPSE PREVENTION

Due to financial concerns, Jonathan indicated that he would like to terminate treatment after eight sessions. During the final session, the therapist discussed the progress that he had made in treatment to date, including becoming more aware of his emotional experiences and how the way he responded to his emotions influenced the intensity of the experience. With regard to long-term goals, Jonathan indicated that he would like to go back to "normal" and "not think about sleep so much." The therapist emphasized the importance of continuing to address items on his hierarchy (e.g., getting out of bed if he was unable to fall asleep within 30 minutes and decreasing his reliance on sleep medication). Although Jonathan felt confident that he would be able to continue making progress on his own, his therapist informed him that he could schedule booster sessions if he experienced difficulty completing his hierarchy independently.

CONCLUSION

Whether it presents in isolation or along with another condition, insomnia is associated with numerous poor health outcomes, and as such, represents an important target for treatment. Unfortunately, sleep difficulty is often neglected as an explicit treatment target when it is comorbid with anxiety or depression, due to the commonly held belief that it is a symptom that will remit once the other presenting condition is successfully treated. However, as discussed earlier, research has demonstrated that sleep difficulties frequently persist following remission of depression and anxiety.

One reason for the persistence of sleep symptoms following CBT for other disorders is that the skill of cognitive reappraisal does not appear to generalize to dysfunctional beliefs about sleep. For example, Carney, Harris, Friedman, and Segal (2011) found that patients who received CBT for depression evidenced a significant decrease in general negative beliefs but no change in maladaptive beliefs about sleep.

Although more systematic evaluation of the UP for the treatment of sleep disturbance is necessary, existing empirical evidence of the shared mechanistic processes between insomnia and other emotional disorders provides a strong basis of theoretical support for the clinical utility of a transdiagnostic treatment approach. A benefit of the UP is that sleep-related negative automatic thoughts and EDBs can be seamlessly woven into the course of treatment for an individual presenting with a comorbid emotional disorder. Alternatively, the UP can be used to address insomnia when it is the patient's primary concern, as was illustrated by Jonathan's case.

11

The Unified Protocol for Nonsuicidal and Suicidal Self-Injurious Thoughts and Behaviors

KATE H. BENTLEY, SHANNON SAUER-ZAVALA,
CLAIR CASSIELLO-ROBBINS, AND STEPHANIE VENTO ∎

DEFINITIONS AND PREVALENCE OF NONSUICIDAL AND SUICIDAL SELF-INJURIOUS THOUGHTS AND BEHAVIORS

Self-injury can be defined as any behavior that is directly and deliberately harmful to the self (Nock, 2010). Under the umbrella of self-injury, there is an important distinction made between nonsuicidal and suicidal behavior. *Nonsuicidal self-injury (NSSI)* refers to self-injurious behavior in which there is no intent to die, and it includes both thoughts of engaging in NSSI and actual NSSI episodes (Nock, Cha, & Dour, 2011; Nock & Favazza, 2009). *Suicidal self-injury* assumes that there is at least some intent to die, and the term also can refer to a broad range of thoughts and acts (e.g., suicide ideation, suicide plans, suicide attempts, complete suicides; Nock, 2010).

Nonsuicidal and suicidal self-injurious thoughts and behaviors are common. For example, a recent meta-analysis of NSSI prevalence showed lifetime rates of 17.2% in adolescents, 13.4% in young adults, and 5.5% in adult populations (Swannell, Martin, Page, Hasking, & St. John, 2014). In terms of suicidal self-injury, 40,000 individuals take their own lives in the United States each year, and over 1 million die by suicide worldwide [Centers for Disease Control and Prevention (CDC), 2011; World Health Organization (WHO), 2012]. In addition to completed suicides, 3% of individuals engage in nonfatal suicidal behaviors, and 9% experience serious thoughts of suicide during their lives (Borges et al., 2010; Nock et al., 2008). Taken together, both NSSI and suicidal self-injury are significant, prevalent public health problems warranting our immediate attention.

A number of psychological treatments for self-injurious thoughts and behaviors have been developed and tested to date. Dialectical behavior therapy (DBT; Linehan, 1993) is a multifaceted, cognitive behavioral therapy (CBT) treatment designed to address both nonsuicidal and suicidal self-injurious behaviors. Overall, substantial evidence indicates that DBT effectively reduces suicidal behavior among patients with borderline personality disorder (BPD); however, the effects on NSSI specifically have been more mixed (Lynch, Trost, Salsman, & Linehan, 2007; Turner, Austin & Chapman, 2014).

In terms of treatments specifically targeting NSSI, emotion regulation group therapy (Gratz & Gunderson, 2006), which is administered as an adjunct to treatment as usual (TAU), and manual-assisted cognitive therapy (MACT; Evans et al., 1999) have both been shown to effectively reduce NSSI in comparison to control conditions (usually TAU alone) in female subjects with BPD (Turner et al., 2014). Regarding treatments specific to suicidal thoughts and behaviors, recent studies testing time-limited CBT interventions have produced promising results (e.g., Brown et al., 2005; Rudd et al., 2015), whereas problem-solving interventions have resulted in more inconsistent findings (Ward-Ciesielski & Linehan, 2014). Although recent years have witnessed exciting new developments in treatment research for nonsuicidal and suicidal forms of self-injury, the rates of these behaviors have unfortunately not yet reduced. Thus, a need remains to identify not only the most effective but also the most efficient and disseminable approaches for addressing these problems across the full range of self-injuring patients.

NONSUICIDAL AND SUICIDAL SELF-INJURIOUS THOUGHTS AND BEHAVIORS WITHIN THE EMOTIONAL DISORDERS FRAMEWORK

There is literature suggesting that nonsuicidal and suicidal self-injurious thoughts and behaviors are functionally similar to core processes defining one particular category of psychopathology—emotional disorders. As described throughout this text, Sauer-Zavala and Barlow (2014) define *emotional disorders* as psychopathology characterized by the frequent experience of intense negative emotions (e.g., fear, anxiety, sadness), coupled with strong aversive reactions and efforts to escape these emotional experiences. *Neuroticism,* or the traitlike tendency to experience intense negative emotions accompanied by a sense of uncontrollability of such emotional experiences, is thought to underlie the development and course of these disorders (Barlow, Sauer-Zavala, Carl, Bullis, & Ellard, 2014).

First, there is a large body of evidence supporting the functional overlap between NSSI and the avoidant coping strategies used to manage negative emotional experiences characterizing emotional disorders. Although a number of theories have been proposed to explain why NSSI occurs, there is a consensus that these behaviors most often serve to reduce or escape aversive affective or cognitive states (Chapman, Gratz, & Brown, 2006; Klonsky, 2007; Nock & Prinstein, 2004; Selby, Anestis, & Joiner, 2008). This escape-based function of NSSI is similar to the avoidant strategies used by individuals with other emotional disorders to manage their emotions (e.g., avoidance, suppression, rumination). For instance, an individual with social anxiety disorder may experience heightened anxiety at a party and choose to leave early to relieve this aversive emotional state. Another individual may cut his or her skin in order to regulate acute distress about an upcoming "high-stakes" event (e.g., an important work- or school-related task or interpersonal interaction). In these examples, both leaving early and cutting serve as forms of maladaptive, avoidant coping with emotional distress, in that although these strategies may reduce negative affect in the short term, they are likely to increase and maintain such emotions over time (e.g., Crowell, Derbridge, & Beauchaine, 2013; Sauer-Zavala, Bentley, & Wilner, 2015; Weiss, Sullivan, & Tull, 2015).

A number of theories have been proposed to understand suicidal self-injury, including the interpersonal-psychological theory of suicide (Joiner, 2005), the hopelessness theory (Beck, 1986; Abramson et al., 2000), the escape theory (Baumeister, 1990), the psychache theory (Shneidman, 1993), and the emotion dysregulation model (Linehan, 1993). Although distinct, these theories share one overarching commonality—the role of *emotional pain* in contributing to suicidal self-injury (Selby, Joiner, & Ribeiro, 2014; Ribeiro, Bodell, Hames, Hagan, & Joiner, 2013).

Emotional pain also plays a central role in emotional disorders, as these individuals' symptoms are generally maintained by the use of avoidant coping strategies to reduce or suppress intense, unwanted feelings. In the emotional disorders framework, suicidal thoughts and behaviors can be conceptualized as extreme forms of emotion avoidance, associated with similar short- and long-term consequences. Whereas completed suicide may be the ultimate escape from emotional distress, fantasizing about suicide, developing a suicide plan, or engaging in nonfatal suicidal behavior may serve to temporarily distract from or reduce a negative emotional state but is unlikely to provide sustained relief, and may even worsen negative affect, in the long term.

Given these functional similarities, it is no surprise that accumulating research supports a relationship between neuroticism and both nonsuicidal and suicidal forms of self-injury. First, cross-sectional findings indicate that neuroticism distinguishes individuals who engage in NSSI from those who do not across a range of clinical (e.g., outpatient, inpatient; Claes, Vandereycken, & Vertommen, 2004; Claes et al., 2010) and nonclinical (e.g., undergraduate, medical student; Allroggen et al., 2014; Brown, 2009; MacLaren & Best, 2010; Mullins-Sweatt, Lengel, & Grant, 2013) populations.

Neuroticism also has been shown to prospectively predict suicide ideation (e.g., Handley et al., 2012), attempts (e.g., Holma et al., 2014; Wedig et al., 2012), and deaths (e.g., Fang, Heisel, Duberstein, & Zhang, 2012; Tanji et al., 2014). In sum, there is empirical support for the role of strong, negative emotions in nonsuicidal and suicidal self-injury. Further, self-injurious thoughts and behaviors can function as maladaptive responses to negative affect—whether acute, temporary negative arousal for NSSI, or pervasive, stable negative emotions for suicidal thoughts and behaviors. Next, we explore the clinical implications of conceptualizing suicidal and nonsuicidal self-injury as avoidant strategies for coping with strong emotions in the context of a transdiagnostic treatment for emotional disorders.

Application of Unified Protocol Skills to Nonsuicidal and Suicidal Self-Injurious Thoughts and Behaviors

The Unified Protocol for Transdiagnostic Treatment of Emotional Disorders (UP; Barlow et al., 2018) is an emotion-focused, CBT intervention designed to address the range of emotional disorders—conditions that frequently cooccur with NSSI and suicidality (e.g., Bentley, Cassiello-Robbins, Vittorio, Sauer-Zavala, & Barlow, 2014; Borges et al., 2010; Kanwar et al., 2013; Selby et al., 2012). Given the functional similarities between core emotional disorder processes and self-injury, it stands to reason that the UP also may be applicable for self-injuring individuals, and moreover offers a flexible framework from which clinicians can target self-injurious thoughts and behaviors directly while simultaneously addressing coexisting emotional disorder symptoms.

The UP aims to help individuals adopt a more accepting attitude toward uncomfortable emotions while identifying and altering maladaptive reactions to the experience of strong emotions—thereby breaking the cycle of maladaptive emotional responding. For individuals who use self-injury to relieve or escape unwanted emotions, UP strategies that facilitate more effective management of negative emotions may not only reduce reliance on self-injury, but also address core factors underlying continued engagement in self-injury and related symptoms (e.g., frequent/acute negative emotions, perception of intense affect as intolerable).

Of note, though there is an important distinction between nonsuicidal and suicidal self-injury (Nock, 2010), both are targeted similarly within the UP. This represents another potential advantage of using the UP to treat self-injurious thoughts and behaviors, as individuals who engage in NSSI are also prone to suicidal thoughts and behaviors (and vice versa; e.g., Muehlenkamp, 2014). Accordingly, in the discussion to follow, we use the umbrella term *self-injury* to refer to the application of UP modules to both types of self-injurious thoughts and behaviors. When the distinction between NSSI and suicidal self-injury is critical to delivering a particular concept, however, that is explicitly noted.

Over the following paragraphs, we highlight specific aspects of UP modules that are particularly applicable to self-injury. First, in Module 1, patients' motivation for behavior change and belief in their ability to enact change successfully are targeted. For self-injuring patients, during the "Decisional Balance" exercise, it can be validating to acknowledge the reinforcing nature of self-injury, in that it is often quite effective in providing immediate relief from distress. Changing, which will involve *resisting* self-injurious behaviors, is likely to present significant challenges (i.e., potential cons). Along these lines, identifying the pros and cons of changing provides an opportunity to discuss any ambivalence about treatment focused on reducing self-injury. For suicidal individuals specifically, the decisional balance may be extended to explicitly address the pros and cons of living versus ending one's life (e.g., reasons for living).

Module 2 consists of psychoeducation on the functional nature of emotions, and patients learn to break down their emotional experiences into thoughts, physical sensations, and behaviors. This module provides the opportunity to discuss antecedent and reinforcing factors maintaining self-injury (e.g., both proximal and distal triggers, short-term relief from unwanted feelings) that may be contributing to not only continued engagement in these behaviors, but also sustained negative emotion. Patients also begin to explore how emotions that contribute to self-injury may be communicating important information to them. For example, when working with suicidal individuals, thoughts of ending one's life can be framed as one response to overwhelming feelings of loneliness, which could be indicating the need to seek out more positive relationships. The aim of this discussion is for patients to begin to view their emotions as adaptive or functional, albeit painful, and thus not necessarily warranting maladaptive efforts to avoid or escape them.

Next, Module 3 (the first core UP module) aims to help individuals adopt a more mindful (i.e., nonjudgmental and present-focused) awareness of their emotions through a combination of brief emotion awareness and mood induction exercises. For self-injuring patients, learning to shift attention to their emotional experiences as they unfold in the present (rather than ruminating about past events or worrying about future consequences) can prove extremely beneficial. Specifically, with increased mindful awareness, it is expected that these individuals become better able to accept and engage more productively with their ongoing emotional experiences instead of getting carried away by or reacting negatively to them, thereby reducing the need to use self-injurious thoughts and behaviors as strategies to relieve distressing emotions.

Module 4 focuses on cognitive flexibility during and about emotion-provoking situations (and emotions themselves). For self-injuring individuals, maladaptive thoughts can have a strong influence on emotional responding (namely, engagement in NSSI, suicidal behaviors, or both). For example, for an individual who draws catastrophic interpretations about conflicts (e.g., "They don't love me anymore"), these cognitions may set in motion or exacerbate cycles of increased negative emotion that culminate in urges to self-injure. Patients are encouraged to consider other more flexible, realistic interpretations of emotion-laden situations—not replacing their negative automatic thoughts, but allowing such alternative interpretations to coexist (e.g., "One fight doesn't mean that they are going to leave me"). Cognitions with content specific to self-injury also may be directly addressed; for example, patients may be asked to reevaluate thoughts such as "Cutting is the only thing that makes me feel better" or "People would be better off without me."

During Module 5, the focus is on identifying and changing two types of problematic, emotional behaviors—emotion avoidance and emotion-driven behaviors (EDBs). This module is highly relevant to self-injuring individuals, as NSSI and suicidal self-injury are explicitly framed as behavioral responses that may provide short-term relief, but over time, paradoxically increase the frequency and intensity of the emotions that the individual is trying to escape or reduce in the first place. After generating personally relevant alternative actions (e.g., calling a loved one, vigorous exercise, self-soothing activities), patients are asked to begin implementing more adaptive responses. It can be very challenging, of course, for individuals who have come to rely on self-injury to change patterns of emotional responding; thus, the therapist and patient must work collaboratively to establish small, realistic steps toward new responses.

Modules 6 and 7 offer the opportunity to practice applying previously learned UP skills in the context of experiencing strong emotions during a combination of interoceptive, situational, and imaginal exposures. By beginning with lower-intensity, more manageable exercises in controlled settings and with the therapist, patients learn that they can apply helpful strategies (e.g., anchoring in the present, cognitive flexibility) when faced with strong emotions without using self-injury or another maladaptive form of avoidance to escape or otherwise control their experiences. As exposure tasks gradually become more challenging and less controlled, this new learning translates into patients' real-world emotional experiences. For example, an individual with a history of suicidal behavior may begin with an in-session exposure in which he or she vividly imagines thoughts, feelings, and behaviors during a suicidal episode. The patient may then imagine implementing alternative, adaptive responses (e.g., noticing a suicidal thought in a nonjudgmental way or engaging in an alternative action, such as consulting a safety plan). Another individual may first engage in a role-play with his or her therapist of a previous emotionally laden interaction with a loved one that resulted in an NSSI episode; this exercise may serve as a stepping stone to an in vivo conversation with the same person, applying more helpful responses. Through graduated emotion exposure, in which adaptive skills for coping with strong emotions are practiced, it is expected that the degree to which these individuals can tolerate negative emotions without resorting to self-injurious thoughts or behaviors increases.

Factors to Consider When Using the UP to Treat Self-Injury

It is important to acknowledge that the UP—at least in the way that it is traditionally delivered—may not be an appropriate stand-alone intervention for all self-injuring individuals. First and foremost, the UP was originally developed as a time-limited, outpatient treatment delivered in weekly 50- to 60-minute sessions. This level of care is not recommended for patients presenting with medically severe NSSI, resulting in major injuries, or who are determined to be at high risk for imminent suicidal behavior, as these individuals are likely to require more intensive treatment to ensure safety (e.g., inpatient, partial hospitalization and more frequent sessions or monitoring). For outpatients with less acute self-injury (e.g., superficial NSSI or passive or active suicide ideation without a very recent attempt) or otherwise deemed low to moderate risk for immediate suicidal behavior, however, the UP may be more appropriate as a stand-alone treatment. The UP or its elements also may function well as an adjunctive intervention (in an individual or group-based format; see Chapter 15 of this book) to the usual care provided by clinicians in the community or acute inpatient settings, as we discuss in the second case presentation in this chapter.

In addition, the UP is unlikely to be an appropriate treatment approach for patients with self-injury performed stereotypically and at high frequencies in the context of developmental disabilities (e.g., head banging in autism). Finally, when NSSI is enacted for functions other than affect regulation (e.g., social reinforcement; Nock & Prinstein, 2004), other strategies (e.g., interpersonal skills building) may be warranted.

CASE PRESENTATION 1: NSSI

A recent study examined the effects of Modules 3 (mindful emotion awareness training) and 4 (cognitive flexibility) on NSSI (Bentley, Nock, Sauer-Zavala, Gorman, & Barlow, in press). Although all core UP modules focus on adaptive, nonavoidant strategies for responding to intense emotion, these two modules were selected because of the notable deficits in mindful emotion awareness and cognitive flexibility among self-injuring populations documented in the literature (e.g., Heath, Carsley, De Riggi, Mills, & Mettler, 2016; Voon, Hasking, & Martin, 2014). In addition, mindfulness and cognitive restructuring procedures are included in existing, multicomponent NSSI treatments (e.g., DBT, MACT), but there is little understanding of the unique effects of each therapeutic strategy when delivered in isolation.

After a baseline phase, patients were randomly assigned to four weekly, individual outpatient treatment sessions of either module; based on the degree of improvement in NSSI during these four sessions, they then either immediately entered a four-week follow-up period or received four sessions of the alternative module before a follow-up. At the intake, self-injury was assessed using the clinician-rated Self-Injurious Thoughts and Behaviors Interview (SITBI; Nock, Holmberg, Photos, & Michel, 2007). Psychiatric diagnoses were assessed using the Adult Anxiety Disorders Interview Schedule for DSM-5 (ADIS-5; Brown & Barlow, 2014) and the Structured Clinical Interview for DSM-IV Axis II Disorders (SCID-II; First, Gibbon, Spitzer, Williams, & Benjamin, 1997). Throughout the study, nonsuicidal self-injurious thoughts and behaviors were monitored daily on a smartphone using ecological momentary assessment (EMA) methods. The Southampton Mindfulness Scale (SMQ; Chadwick et al., 2008) and the Emotion Regulation Questionnaire—Reappraisal subscale (ERQ-R; Gross & John, 2003) were also used to capture levels of treatment skills each week. A case presentation of one patient who was randomized to initially receive Module 3 follows. Potentially identifying details have been altered to protect confidentiality.

E. K. is a 22-year-old, single, Asian female enrolled as a full-time college student (in her senior year). She is captain of her school's track team and hopes to attend a masters program in cognitive science after graduation. During the intake, she reported first engaging in NSSI when she was 16, and the last time was three weeks before the interview. E. K. described experiencing urges to engage in NSSI about once per week and engaging in NSSI about six times in the past year. She reported always cutting or scraping her inner thighs or forearms with a razor blade. With regard to functions, she reported most often engaging in NSSI to "escape negative feelings" (e.g., acute anxiety, intense sadness) or "wanting to be in control over [her] feelings" when overwhelmed. She also described occasionally engaging in NSSI in order to "feel something" when emotionally numb or empty. E. K. reported significant distress associated with NSSI, including intense guilt and shame about her engagement in this behavior. Based on information obtained during the intake, E. K. also met DSM-5 criteria for persistent depressive disorder, generalized anxiety disorder (GAD), and social anxiety disorder. She denied suicidal ideation or intent. Of note, E. K. did not meet criteria for a BPD diagnosis, as she endorsed only two symptoms of BPD at a clinical level: frantic efforts to avoid abandonment and NSSI behavior.

During the study's four-week baseline phase, E. K reported experiencing between one and four urges to engage in NSSI each week, and one cutting episode (Figure 11.1). In the intervention phases, the beginning of each individual treatment session was spent reviewing any NSSI thoughts and behaviors that had occurred since the previous meeting in graph format. In addition to discussing triggers during this review, we were able to address the short- and long-term consequences of her NSSI. For example, when reviewing her first cutting episode at the initial session, E. K. described experiencing momentary relief from her negative emotions, but the next day feeling "so silly and weak for doing that." She also readily noticed her pattern of experiencing urges to engage in NSSI more frequently than actual behaviors.

Over further discussion, E. K. speculated that thoughts of engaging in NSSI often arise in situations when she faces anxiety-producing tasks perceived as "more important" than her own needs (e.g., finishing a time-sensitive assignment for school). By focusing her attention on the task at hand, however, she began to notice that her urges often passed.

These observations gleaned from reviewing her urges and acts of NSSI transitioned smoothly into an introduction to mindful emotion awareness (Module 3), the first UP skill presented. During the first two sessions and corresponding between-session homework, E. K. initially struggled to remain nonjudgmental of her experiences (e.g., "I was feeling anxious about my anxiety"), especially when already feeling a strong negative emotion before attempting a present-focused emotion awareness exercise. With continued practice, however, E. K. described becoming better able to take an objective stance toward her thoughts, feelings, and behaviors, particularly in terms of noting judgmental thoughts and comparisons to other people.

During the second session, E. K. considered applying this skill to situations that elicit urges to engage in NSSI; she speculated that it may be helpful to try to "step

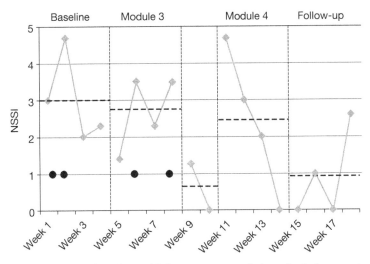

Figure 11.1 E. K.'s NSSI thoughts and behaviors measured via ecological momentary assessment.

Shaded circles reflect NSSI episodes. Shaded diamonds (and connecting solid lines) reflect the number of NSSI thoughts each week. The dashed horizontal lines reflect the average number of NSSI thoughts per week as a function of phase. Module 3 = mindful emotion awareness. Module 4 = cognitive flexibility. Of note, no treatment sessions occurred during weeks 9 and 10, as E. K. was at home for a school vacation.

SOURCE: Bentley, K. H., Nock, M. K., Sauer-Zavala, S., Gorman, B. S., & Barlow, D. H. (in press). A functional analysis of two transdiagnostic, emotion-focused interventions on nonsuicidal self-injury. *Journal of Consulting and Clinical Psychology*.

back" and objectively observe her emotions (including how, in particular, worrying about graduate school applications heightens anxiety or ruminating about past interpersonal conflicts increases low mood) when faced with external and internal triggers for NSSI.

Along these lines, the third and fourth sessions were dedicated to translating more formal mindful emotion awareness practice into anchoring in the present during emotional situations that naturally occur. E. K. reported that this skill was generally helpful in noticing when she was caught up in the past or future, being judgmental, or both, including in many emotion-provoking situations (e.g., before a race and in social situations). She noted that anchoring allowed her to "let [her] emotions pass" and respond more adaptively in these more common situations. However, she found this skill to be less helpful during the more rare, acute negative emotional states that elicit strong urges to engage in NSSI. This observation is shown in the following vignette:

E. K.: [After describing a conflict with her roommate] *I was just starting feeling really frustrated because I felt like there was no way to make it go away.*

THERAPIST: *Make what go away?*

E. K.: [Pause] *Well, I guess, thinking about how I can't do anything right. And how I felt—I was so sad and just, like, hopeless. Totally hopeless.*

THERAPIST: *Okay. Are those thoughts and feelings what led to you wanting to cut?*

E. K.: *Yeah, completely. I just couldn't handle feeling that way anymore . . . and I tried, you know, to anchor in the present. Like we've been working on. But it felt, like, way too hard.*

THERAPIST: *Can you tell me more about what felt too hard about it?*

E. K.: *Well, it was almost like, I felt so bad in that moment, I just focused on how bad everything was . . . like focusing on my thoughts, feelings, and behaviors almost made everything feel more intense.*

THERAPIST: *I think I understand. It sounds like by this point, your emotions had built up to a really high level. That same level we've talked about, when it feels like you can't tolerate your feelings, and self-harming is the only thing that you feel like will make it better.*

E. K.: *Exactly.*

THERAPIST: *That makes sense. Once you've gotten to that "breaking point," anchoring in the present may not seem to really* work *(and here, even made your emotions feel even* more *intense). Thinking about the whole night, though, are there times when it might have been more helpful?*

E. K.: [Pause] *I guess, like, earlier on. When everything was actually happening with my roommate, I could've probably tried to focus on what I was feeling and what was going on in front of me . . . instead of, like, trying to pretend I was okay but really being so upset.* [Therapist nods] *And also, probably in the couple hours after we talked. I mean, I didn't cut right when she left. I got really worked up after she left, crying and alone, you know, back in my room.*

THERAPIST: *Okay, got it. So maybe, in future situations, trying to practice mindful awareness of your emotions earlier on, like when you first start to feel more emotional and your feelings aren't super intense yet, is when it's going to be most helpful [and] important for you.*

E. K.: [Nods] *Yeah. As, like, more of a way to keep me from getting to that breaking point.*

Consistent with this discussion, E. K. found that observing and accepting her emotions as they occur on an ongoing basis, instead of suppressing negative thoughts and feelings (especially in social settings), helped to prevent negative affect from escalating to a point where self-injurious urges arise. For example, during the last session of Module 3, she noted: "General emotion awareness really helps me because, it's like, you know what, I'm sad today. Whatever comes my way, I've already accepted that that's today and it'll get better." In addition to applying this skill to negative emotions, E. K. noticed that mindful emotion awareness helped her purposefully tune into positive emotions resulting from experiences such as praise from a professor.

Based on E. K. experiencing no significant changes in frequency of NSSI urges and acts during Module 3 (Figure 11.1), we proceeded with Module 4 (cognitive flexibility) when she returned from a two-week vacation. E. K. immediately evidenced a strong understanding of the reciprocal nature of automatic thoughts and emotions, perhaps due to her heightened emotional awareness after four weeks of mindful emotion awareness training. Through downward arrow exercises, E. K. identified her core beliefs of "I'm a failure" and "I'm worthless," and was quickly able to recognize how these underlying thoughts drive negative, automatic surface-level thoughts (e.g., "Everyone in the lab treats me badly," "My friends don't want me around") in more ambiguous or trivial interpersonal situations. She also noted how this thinking process leads to maladaptive responses (e.g., excessive irritability, completing her work carelessly, withdrawing). In addition, E. K. readily grasped the concept of thinking traps and the utility of noticing when she is jumping to conclusions (e.g., "He doesn't respect my science") or catastrophizing (e.g., "I don't matter"), especially when faced with triggers, like feeling slighted by a friend, that often elicit urges to cut.

During our seventh and eighth sessions, we focused on reevaluating E. K.'s negative automatic thoughts with the aim of generating more flexible, alternative interpretations of situations that can lead to NSSI. For example, regarding her automatic thought of "I'm a terrible person" after she forgot to bring coffee to a friend, E. K. used challenging questions to generate alternative thoughts, such as "Everyone is forgetful sometimes." We also began promoting greater cognitive flexibility with negative cognitions tied to NSSI specifically; for example, in one homework assignment, E. K. recorded the automatic thought of "Cutting is the only way I can make myself feel better" that contributed to a strong urge to cut. Here, the therapist works with E. K. to question this particular thought, and thus facilitate more adaptive behavioral responses in future situations that trigger urges to engage in NSSI:

THERAPIST: *What was going on that led to you wanting to cut that night?*

E. K.: *Well, I had to finish a report, and was in the library till midnight . . . it was awful. I was already really depressed, which was making it really hard to focus, but I had to get it done.*

THERAPIST: *It sounds like this was a stressful night.*

E. K.: *Yeah.* [pause] *It was really nice though because one of my friends stayed. She was going to go home, but then was like, "I'm going to stay with you for a while." She could tell that something wasn't right. But I was thinking, "Well, I sort of wish you would just go away, because it would be so much easier to just cut, and then not feel sad."*

THERAPIST: *Right.*

E. K.: *But I knew that was unreasonable, so I said she could stay. Then, there was one point when someone texted me about the team noticing I was late to practice . . . I just lost it. I started bawling.*

THERAPIST: *Then what happened?*

E. K.: *Well, she just looked at me and asked, "Are you OK?" and I was immediately like, "I'll be fine!" but I didn't think I would [be fine]. Then, a few minutes later, I actually was okay. I felt better. I think that was like, a different kind of release . . . [trails off]*

THERAPIST: *Crying was a different kind of release than cutting?*

E. K.: *Yeah, exactly. When I cry, especially in front of other people, I feel so vulnerable. With my friend, I was surprised at how okay I was with it. [pause] I think that was good to learn—that I'm okay with crying and being vulnerable around her.*

THERAPIST: *Right. It's so interesting that you said that crying was a different kind of release—letting your emotions out in front of him. It sounds like before she ended up staying, and you were thinking about cutting, you noticed the automatic thought, "It would be so much easier if she left, and I could just cut, and feel less sad."*

E. K.: *Yeah—that was when I was like, "cutting is the only good way to cope right now."*

THERAPIST: *But then, she stayed . . .*

E. K.: *She stayed, and I felt so much better afterwards. I still felt sad, really tired, and frustrated that I had stuff to finish, but better . . . I feel like I don't appreciate the little interactions, like this one, that I have with my really close friends. That was really powerful.*

THERAPIST: *Very powerful. [pause] How could you use that powerful experience to help you think more flexibly during other times when you feel like cutting is the only good option to feel better?*

E. K.: *Well, I think part of it with cutting is that I have to be in the right place, physically—so usually at home, by myself. In the same way, to be vulnerable like I was then, I have to physically be in the same place with someone I trust. [pause] I think that as purposefully as I would seek out a place to cut, I need to seek out a place to just cry or do something else.*

THERAPIST: *And it sounds like this time, you got a good, helpful release from that. So, would you say that there are other ways to get that same release, even if they take purposeful action?*

E. K.: *Completely. Even in those moments, to ask myself, "Really? Is cutting the only thing that will help me?" I know the answer is no.*

Consistent with this exchange, over the last two sessions, E. K. reported confidence in her ability to generate more flexible, balanced thoughts to help her respond more adaptively (e.g., expressing emotion or reaching out to a close friend) when urges to cut arise in the future. Interestingly, E. K. also found the mindful approach that she developed toward her emotions during the first four sessions to facilitate her subsequent experiences with cognitive flexibility.

Toward the end of treatment, E. K. described no longer "being afraid of [her] depression," as she was better able to notice and accept thoughts like "I feel depressed right now" or "I may be sad tomorrow" without the secondary, judgmental reactions that previously contributed to thoughts and feelings of hopelessness, as well as urges to engage in NSSI to control her emotions. At our final session, E. K. observed: "It's easier when I see being depressed or anxious as something that's going to pass . . . that *in itself* is an alternative thought, instead of, 'Oh my gosh, it's going to last forever.'" She also framed nonjudgmental, present-focused emotion awareness and cognitive flexibility as a two-part process of "taking the first step of noticing 'I'm feeling depressed today,' and then being on the look-out for thinking traps and using [cognitive flexibility]." In sum, E. K. appeared to benefit from mindful emotion awareness training before the cognitive flexibility module, consistent with the full UP treatment format.

Overall, E. K.'s data were generally consistent with her verbal assessment of progress. In terms of self-injury, she did not engage in NSSI during the final 10 weeks of the study (Figure 11.1). Further, when we contacted her about four months after study monitoring ended, she denied any acts of NSSI following treatment termination. Despite a notable decline in thoughts of NSSI (and also, per her report, the intensity of urges) during the cognitive flexibility phase, E. K. experienced an increase in urges during the last two weeks of follow-up, which she attributed to several specific stressors, including a big conflict with her longtime roommate.

Although these situations led to "the strongest urge to hurt [herself] in a while," it is noteworthy that she did not act on this urge. E. K.'s ability to take a nonjudgmental, present-focused approach to distressing emotions, as measured weekly by the SMQ, also increased steadily throughout treatment, reaching the highest level during the cognitive flexibility phase. This suggests that in addition to mindful emotion awareness enhancing her subsequent experiences with cognitive flexibility (as E. K. described in session), cognitive flexibility may have improved her ability to adopt a more mindful approach to her emotions. Her flexibility levels as measured weekly with the ERQ-R, however, remained relatively unchanged during treatment. Given her consistently positive feedback regarding this skill in session, it is possible that this particular measure did not capture how she used cognitive flexibility in her daily life.

CASE PRESENTATION 2: SUICIDAL THOUGHTS AND BEHAVIORS

The UP was recently modified for delivery in an inpatient setting (specifically, a crisis stabilization unit) to individuals who had recently experienced intense suicidal ideation or made a suicide attempt as part of an initial feasibility and acceptability trial (N = 10) comparing the modified UP (in addition to all usual services at the unit) to treatment as usual. Patients were excluded from this study if they were currently experiencing severe symptoms of mania or psychosis, or if they were detoxing from a substance.

The original protocol was condensed into five one-hour individual treatment sessions and delivered over a four-day period. Session 1 included an introduction to treatment, discussion of the functional nature of emotions, and motivation enhancement (namely, the decisional balance), per Modules 1 and 2. Session 2 covered selected content from Modules 2 and 3: breaking down an emotion into its three components, as well as antecedents and consequences, and anchoring in the present. Session 3 focused on cognitive flexibility (Module 4), and Session 4 introduced emotional behaviors (Module 5). Session 5 (and, in some cases, part of Session 4) included emotion exposure (Module 7), providing the opportunity for skills rehearsal and consolidation in the context of a strong emotion, and plans for future practice (Module 8, relapse prevention). Patients were also provided with a modified UP workbook. In light of evidence that suicide prevention programs must explicitly target suicidality to be effective (e.g., Tarrier, Taylor, & Gooding, 2008), each skill was applied directly to suicidal thoughts and behaviors, in addition to related emotional experiences contributing to suicidal episodes (e.g., depression, anxiety, and anger).

In the study, patients were assessed at pretreatment, posttreatment, and one month and six months after discharge. A modified version of the SITBI (Nock et al., 2007) was used to capture the occurrence of suicidal thoughts and behaviors at pretreatment, one-month, and six-month follow-up assessments. The following self-report measures were also administered at each time point: Beck Scale for Suicide Ideation (BSI; Beck & Steer, 1991), Beck Hopelessness Scale (BHS; Beck & Steer, 1988), Beck Depression Inventory (BDI; Beck, Steer, & Brown, 1996), Beck Anxiety Inventory (BAI; Beck & Steer, 1993). The self-report Work and Social Adjustment Scale (WSAS; Marks, Connolly, & Hallam, 1973), an indicator of functional impairment, was administered at all time points except posttreatment. Patients who received the UP completed two additional questionnaires that assessed skill comprehension and satisfaction at posttreatment.

A case example illustrating the application of the modified UP to one patient with longstanding suicidal thoughts and behaviors follows. Potentially identifying details have been altered to protect confidentiality.

H. T. is a 49-year-old, single, African American male. He is currently unemployed with two children and lives at his uncle's apartment. H. T. reported a long history of substance use (alcohol, cocaine, opiates) and depression and has been incarcerated multiple times. He originally presented at the emergency department stating that he had been experiencing intense suicidal ideation and "hearing voices" while intoxicated, after recently relapsing.[1]

As he was determined not to be at imminent risk, H. T. was admitted to the unlocked acute crisis unit in order to stabilize and reinitiate medications. During the pretreatment interview, he described past and current suicidal ideation (including in the prior week, when he thought about jumping in front of a train or off a bridge); developing a suicide plan on about 15 days in his life; and four prior attempts, in which he intentionally overdosed on drugs with some hope of

---

1. Drug-induced hallucinations were neither reflected in this patient's diagnoses nor addressed during UP treatment delivery for this patient because this symptom occurred rarely and was not particularly distressing to him.

Table 11.1. H. T.'s TREATMENT OUTCOME SCORES

	Pretreatment	Posttreatment	One-Month Follow-up
BSI	21	5	7
BHS	7	5	2
BDI	39	11	23
BAI	40	15	30
WSAS	18	–	14

NOTES: BSI = Beck Scale for Suicidal Ideation; BHS = Beck Hopelessness Scale; BDI = Beck Depression Inventory; BAI = Beck Anxiety Inventory; WSAS = Work and Social Adjustment Scale. Responses to the first 19 items of the BSI were summed to yield a total score, which could range from 0 to 38. The WSAS (an indicator of functional impairment) was not administered at posttreatment because the entire UP intervention was administered during H. T.'s stay at the crisis unit. For all measures, higher scores are reflective of higher severity or impairment.

dying—the most recent being about one week before his admission. Although a formal diagnostic assessment was not conducted as part of the study, clinicians at the unit diagnosed H. T. with a substance use disorder and depression. His self-report questionnaire data are presented in Table 11.1; at pretreatment, H. T. reported prominent suicidal ideation, mild hopelessness, severe depressive and anxiety symptoms, and moderate levels of impairment across a variety of life domains.

During the initial session, we provided the UP treatment rationale. H. T. was readily able to identify the utility of each emotion (fear, anger, sadness, etc.), which he summarized by saying "Emotions are like blinkers on your car," providing important information to guide us through life. Next, when discussing the potential functionality of his suicidal ideation, H. T. suggested that suicidal thoughts might alert him to the fact that changes need to be made in his life. In the following vignette, the therapist and H. T. considered how suicidal thoughts and behaviors may be one way to deal with life's difficulties, especially guilt about his substance use; however, the UP treatment focuses on new, more helpful ways to cope:

THERAPIST: *What do thoughts of suicide do for you? What purpose might they serve?*

H. T.: *Thoughts of suicide* [pause] *let you know that you have some bottled-up feelings that you need to vent.*

THERAPIST: *Tell me more about that.*

H. T.: *I feel like every emotion that you go thorough (depression, feeling suicidal, whatever) is like trash in your house—once it gets filled, you have to take it out. If you don't take it out on trash day, it's going to sit around, have an odor, and make trouble around the neighborhood. That's the way life and emotions are—you have to vent, channel thoughts, talk about it, and get it off your mind.*

THERAPIST: *That's a great example of how to think about emotions.*

H. T.: *You know, it's crazy you just asked me about this. I was sitting here thinking that I wanted to kill myself. That's crazy . . . wanting to take your own life. That's sad. Now that I'm venting, it seems so crazy, but when you get caught up in your emotions, all types of things seem overwhelming that you can't help [thinking about suicide].*

THERAPIST: *That's a good point. When you're experiencing lots of emotions and you've got a lot of problems, and you don't deal with them and it piles up like [a] big trash can, thoughts of suicide come up as a last resort. You think, "I can't even look at that pile of trash, so what's one thing I can do? I can kill myself."*

H. T.: *Right—suicide means I ain't gonna have that worry no more.*

THERAPIST: *It's like your brain is giving you a way of solving this problem. During this treatment, we're going be talking about other, more healthy ways to respond to strong emotions so they don't pile up like this.*

This discussion transitioned into enhancing motivation for treatment by H. T. considering the pros and cons of ending his life/not seeking treatment versus staying alive/learning new coping strategies in treatment. We conducted the "Decisional Balance" exercise by first generating pros of staying alive/treatment, which for H. T. generated "more time with my kids" and "not using [substances] to deal with emotions." In terms of cons of staying alive/treatment, we discussed how choosing to live and learn new skills (instead of, for example, using substances or attempting suicide) may involve feeling more uncomfortable emotions in the short term. H. T. expressed surprise when asked to weigh these pros and cons: "I can't believe I'd give up all that good because I sometimes feel pain."

During the second session, H. T. quickly grasped relationships between thoughts, physical sensations, and behaviors through examination of a recent emotion-evoking situation. Specifically, he discussed the emotional response following a reminder of his time spent in jail, a commonly occurring trigger for him. H. T. described thoughts of time lost while incarcerated (e.g., "I really missed out"), leading to feelings of loneliness, urges to go back to his old neighborhood, and, eventually, using substances. We also explicitly addressed the consequences of his behavioral responses to these feelings of sadness and loneliness. H. T. stated that going "down to the corner and using" alleviates his negative mood immediately (which is why he keeps doing it—i.e., maintained by negative reinforcement) but leads to his feeling even worse over time.

We extended this discussion to consider the short- and long-term consequences of suicide, and H. T. was able to identify a similar pattern of immediate relief from temporary emotions, followed by a long-term cost of losing everything that he identified as benefits for staying alive. During the second part of this session dedicated to present-focused emotion awareness, we discussed how emotional experiences can be influenced and augmented by thoughts about the past or worries about the future. H. T. learned concrete steps for bringing his attention to the present, including (a) taking an anchoring breath, (b) tuning in to what is happening in front of him, and (c) reminding himself that the past is over, tomorrow is a new day, and the future hasn't happened yet. This skill was applied to the triggering situation examined during the three-component model, and H. T. was encouraged to anchor in the present when he finds himself reminiscing about what he missed out on in the past.

The third treatment session introduced automatic thoughts, emphasizing the interactive relationship between one's thoughts and emotions. H. T. evidenced a strong understanding of these concepts; for instance, he explained, "when you feel like shit, you paint a negative picture." Here, the therapist works with H. T. to generate an example of a recent time when he experienced automatic negative thoughts that contributed to intense suicidal ideation and behavior:

THERAPIST: *People who are vulnerable to experiencing strong emotions like depression or anxiety, or thinking about ending their lives, tend to fall into patterns of negative thinking—latch on to negative ways of interpreting situations. You and I are going to walk through a skill to come up with more flexible thoughts that aren't just negative, so other ways to think about situations. To start, I'd like you to think of a time, recently, when you felt a strong emotion—particularly sad or anxious?*

H. T.: *The day before I came here.*

THERAPIST: *Okay. What was going on? What was the situation?*

H. T.: *I was living aimlessly. I wasn't doing what I know I should be doing . . . beating myself up.*

THERAPIST: *So the situation was a few days before you came to the hospital. Do you remember where you were? Let's try to get down some more details.*

H. T.: *I was walking around the city, crying and sh**. Just depressed. Like, thinking about walking in front of the bus. Jumping on the train tracks. It's so sad because somebody always says something to me to try to cheer me up . . . I'm sitting here, beat down emotionally. I want to pick up the phone to call somebody, but who do I call? . . . I have a lot of sh** that's on my mind. Honestly, I've never spoke to anyone about it . . . It's really tough.*

THERAPIST: *That is really tough. So, you've said that a few days before coming to the hospital, you were walking around the city, feeling extremely depressed. What were some of the negative thoughts that were going through your mind?*

H. T.: *I just wanted to end my life.*

THERAPIST: *Why?*

H. T.: *Just because, it's like my computer is out of order. It's like I've been hacked. I can't tune myself out.*

THERAPIST: *You were thinking, "I just want to end my life because . . ."?*

H. T.: *"Because I can't focus or tune back in . . . I just can't." [pause] It's hard— I feel like haven't put myself in the right situations or with the right people. I haven't gotten the help that I really need.*

THERAPIST: *So, "I just want to end my life because I can't focus or tune back in" and "I haven't put myself in good situations"?*

H. T.: *Exactly. I haven't put myself in the best of situations—I keep putting myself in harmful situations.*

THERAPIST: [writes thoughts on worksheet] *And when you were thinking "I haven't put myself in good situations," were you also thinking anything else?*

H. T.: *Yeah . . . I think I've told you, my biggest fear is ending up in the street homeless. It's just so lonely.*

THERAPIST: *Is that something you were afraid was going to happen last week?*

H. T.: *Yeah.*

THERAPIST: *So was another thought "I'm going to end up homeless"?*

H. T.: *Yeah—I feel like I am.*

THERAPIST: *Good* [writes thought on worksheet]*—these are all perfect examples of automatic thoughts for us to talk about some more.*

After this exchange, we proceeded to highlight the role that these automatic negative thoughts played in contributing to suicidal urges and behavior (in this scenario, making a plan to walk in front of a train) and discuss the importance of challenging patterns of "thinking negative and beating [himself] up." We then practiced using relevant questions to generate more balanced, flexible interpretations. For example, in response to discussing whether he could cope if he did end up homeless for a period of time, H. T. began to identify specific steps that he could take to improve his situation, such as going to a church or a housing shelter. In turn, he was able to generate the alternative possibilities about his ability to cope in future situations that in the past had elicited thoughts and feelings of hopelessness and/or suicide.

In the fourth session, we focused on H. T.'s emotional behaviors, with an emphasis on the behavioral responses that have served to avoid or escape his painful emotions during past suicidal episodes. First, he identified using substances, withdrawing from others, "bottling [his] emotions up," and lashing out as relevant emotional behaviors. From a UP perspective, we explicitly framed developing a plan to end his life as an emotion-driven response that may provide some temporary relief from his emotional pain, but not an effective long-term solution for managing strong emotions. H. T. readily acknowledged the short- and long-term consequences of these responses; for example, although acting on his suicidal urges would "end all emotions" and offer relief in the moment, he explained that it would be "harmful . . . and cause so many problems," including missing out on time with this children in the long term.

Next, we discussed the role of alternative actions to break the cycle of negative emotion and suicidal thoughts and behaviors, and then generated specific actions to counter his emotional behaviors. During this exercise, H. T. identified calling someone who doesn't use (e.g., a friend, sister, sponsor), playing basketball, watching television, being present with his breath, and caring for a pet as alternative actions when he feels suicidal. He also noted the potential helpfulness of consulting this list if and when he experiences suicidal thoughts in the future, and added "looking back at [his] notes" as another alternative action.

After discussing the importance of "learning by doing" by practicing his skills learned thus far while experiencing strong emotions, we conducted two in-session emotion exposures, one during each of the last two sessions. The first consisted of viewing images online to trigger urges to use substances (e.g., pictures of cocaine, street corners), given that H. T. consistently reported that drug use often leads to or exacerbates his suicidal thoughts. During this exercise, he was asked to imagine implementing helpful alternative actions (e.g., calling his sponsor), as well as practice challenging automatic thoughts as they arise ("I always end up falling on my face") and stay anchored in the present, rather than focusing on his past failures.

The second in-session exposure consisted of an imaginal exercise, in which H. T. was asked to play out his core fear of becoming homeless, which, if it occurred, he expected that it would lead him to want to kill himself. The aim of this particular task was for H. T. to experience intense negative emotion without distracting himself or pushing his uncomfortable feelings away, and while experiencing this high level of emotion, practice applying his new, more adaptive skills for responding to strong emotions; in turn, it was expected that this exposure would facilitate adoption of effective emotion regulation strategies and bolster his ability to tolerate negative affect.

Once H. T. was vividly imagining what his life be like if he were homeless (including specific thoughts, feelings, and behavioral urges), he proceeded to imagine engaging in relevant alternative actions to using drugs and taking steps toward ending his life (e.g., talking to a priest, going to the hospital, and calling his daughter), and generate more flexible alternative thoughts about this seemingly hopeless situation. He also practiced using his breath to stay anchored in the present instead of "worrying about tomorrow" during this exercise. After the exposure, when asked what he learned, H. T. reported, "I'm a lot stronger than I thought" and elaborated: "I was able to defer from [substances] too, because I was really just focused on me and my homeless situation . . . it could be something good that comes out of all this—it makes me stronger."

Overall, this exercise appeared to improve H. T.'s confidence in his ability to apply treatment skills and cope if his feared outcome occurred. Given that this task was completed during the fifth (final) session of the adapted protocol, it is unknown whether he continued to practice this imaginal emotion exposure on his own for homework (as recommended by his therapist).

The second half of the last session included developing a plan for future skills practice, in which following through with outpatient providers was framed as an alternative action to H. T.'s previous patterns. Of note, he was consistently non-compliant with between-session assignments, which he attributed to not sleeping well and distractions at the unit. Despite this, he evidenced a relatively strong understanding of UP concepts, scoring 80% on the measure of skill acquisition. H. T. also rated the treatment as "very acceptable" and reported being "very satisfied." When asked to indicate the most helpful thing he learned, he wrote, "Life is all about dealing with your emotions"—a statement in line with the overall UP framework. Overall, these data indicate that, for H. T., the modified UP was a feasible and acceptable adjunctive treatment approach.

H. T. showed clinically significant reductions in suicidal ideation, depression, and anxiety at posttreatment, falling in the minimal or mild ranges on each of these measures (Table 11.1). He also demonstrated a small reduction in hopelessness, which started in the mild range at pretreatment. Of note, his response to the specific BHS item assessing reasons for living/dying changed from "My reasons for dying outweigh my reasons for living" at pretreatment to "My reasons for living outweigh my reasons for dying" at posttreatment—consistent with his in-session reaction to the "Decisional Balance" exercise.

Of note, given that in this study, the modified UP was delivered over the course of four days while patients stayed at the crisis unit, functional improvement was not assessed at the final treatment session. In terms of follow-up data, despite multiple attempts to contact at both time points, H. T. never completed a clinician-rated interview after being discharged from the unit. Accordingly, it is unknown whether he made a suicide attempt or was readmitted to the hospital after treatment. However, H. T. did return self-report questionnaires via mail at the one-month follow-up (Table 11.1).

These data indicate that he had largely maintained his treatment gains in terms of suicidal ideation and hopelessness. Although he reported moderately severe depressive symptoms and severe anxiety symptoms at this time point, his scores were not back at pretreatment levels. H. T. also reported less overall functional impairment; however, because he never completed a clinician interview, knowledge of specific potential examples of functional improvement (e.g., maintained sobriety, employment, better relationships) is lacking. Unfortunately, we did not receive self-report data from H. T. at the six-month follow-up; thus, it is unknown whether he continued to benefit from the UP treatment.

CONCLUSION

The aim of this chapter was to illustrate applications of the UP to self-injuring individuals. It was theorized that the UP (or its elements) may be a promising approach for addressing NSSI and suicidal self-injury due to the functional overlap between self-injurious thoughts and behaviors and the avoidant, maladaptive processes characterizing the emotional disorders. Specifically, individuals often engage in nonsuicidal and suicidal self-injurious thoughts and behaviors to relieve or escape unwanted, intense emotional experiences. Although in the short term, these responses may temporarily relieve negative emotion, in the long term, NSSI and/or suicidal self-injury are likely to maintain or even worsen negative affect. Because nonsuicidal and suicidal self-injury often cooccur with one or more emotional disorders, the UP may represent an efficacious and efficient framework for treating these maladaptive thoughts and behaviors, while simultaneously addressing comorbid emotional disorder symptomatology.

In the two clinical case presentations presented here, the UP was well received (e.g., acceptable, feasible) and produced clinically meaningful reductions in self-injurious thoughts and behaviors. However, research on the efficacy of the UP in treating self-injury is in its infancy, and as such, continued work in this area remains a priority.

Specifically, future research is needed to determine which self-injuring individuals are most likely to benefit from treatment with the UP. As previously noted, the relatively brief UP, at least how it is traditionally delivered (16–20 weekly outpatient sessions), is not a suitable stand-alone treatment for patients at immediate, high risk for lethal or medically serious self-injurious behavior, who are likely to require more intensive care to ensure their safety (e.g., hospitalization, residential treatment). However, adapting the traditional UP for use in inpatient settings that typically provide a combination of individual psychotherapy, skills groups, and medication management warrants further empirical attention.

The UP also may function well as an adjunctive, individual or group-based intervention to the usual care (e.g., supportive therapy, medications) provided to self-injuring individuals in the community. Moreover, individuals presenting with less acute self-injurious thoughts, behaviors, or both in outpatient settings may be appropriate candidates for the UP as a stand-alone treatment. In conclusion, it is our hope that this chapter encourages clinicians who work with self-injuring individuals (or who may see these urges or behaviors emerge during the course of treatment focused on other symptoms or diagnoses) to consider ways in which the UP principles may be used to address self-injury.

12

The Unified Protocol for Borderline Personality Disorder

SHANNON SAUER-ZAVALA, KATE H. BENTLEY,
AND JULIANNE G. WILNER ■

BORDERLINE PERSONALITY DISORDER IS AN EMOTIONAL DISORDER

Borderline personality disorder (BPD) is a severe psychiatric condition characterized by impairment across several areas of psychosocial functioning (American Psychiatric Association, 2013); these include emotional difficulties (mood lability, intense anger), interpersonal problems (efforts to avoid abandonment, unstable relationships), behavioral dysregulation [chronic suicidality, nonsuicidal self-injury (NSSI)], other impulsive actions), identity disturbance (unstable sense of self, chronic emptiness), and cognitive abnormalities (transient dissociation or paranoia). BPD is quite common, with recent studies indicating that the prevalence of this disorder in the United States may range from 0.5% to 5.9% (Crawford et al., 2005; Grant et al., 2008; Lenzenweger & Pastore, 2007; Samuels et al., 2002; Swartz, Blazer, George, & Winfield, 1990). This population also makes up a large proportion of individuals seeking treatment, comprising at least 10% of outpatient and 20% of inpatient treatment samples (APA, 2013). However, despite being highly treatment-seeking, patients with BPD are often described as difficult to work with, evidence high dropout, and are often treatment-resistant (Cambanis, 2012).

Evidence suggests that the treatment resistance seen in BPD may be the result of complex comorbidities that are common in this disorder. BPD is characterized by extremely high rates of comorbidity with other mental disorders (Zanarini et al., 1998; Zimmerman & Mattia, 1999); for example, Grant and colleagues (2008) found that 75% of individuals with a lifetime BPD diagnosis will meet criteria for a lifetime mood disorder, and 74.2% of individuals with a lifetime BPD diagnosis will meet criteria for a lifetime anxiety disorder.

Comorbid BPD has been determined to exacerbate the severity of, and the treatment response for, other disorders (e.g., mood, anxiety; Sadock & Sadock, 2000). Specifically, cooccurring BPD has been shown to increase the severity of panic disorder (Weiler et al., 1988; Ozkan & Altindag, 2005), posttraumatic stress disorder (PTSD; van Dijke et al., 2012; Vignarajah & Links, 2009) obsessive-compulsive disorder (OCD; McKay, Kulchycky, & Danyko, 2000) and depressive disorders (Joyce et al., 2003), which appears to lead to decreased treatment effectiveness (Ozkan & Altindag, 2005).

A recently articulated explanation for the high rates of comorbidity among BPD, anxiety, and mood disorders (Brown & Barlow, 2009; Sauer-Zavala & Barlow, 2014) may inform the development of efficient interventions geared toward addressing BPD and comorbid conditions simultaneously. Several authors have suggested that the pattern of comorbidity described here may be best accounted for by a general neurotic syndrome (Andrews, 1990, 1996; Tryer, 1989), and that symptom heterogeneity among these disorders (e.g., individual differences in the prominence of interpersonal conflicts, panic attacks, and anhedonia) can be viewed as trivial variations in the manifestation of this broader syndrome (Barlow, Sauer-Zavala, Carl, Bullis, & Ellard, 2014).

At first glance, the symptoms of BPD may not appear to resemble those of anxiety and mood disorders; however, a large body of literature (for a review, see Sauer-Zavala & Barlow, 2014) supports the notion that these symptoms arise from similar underlying vulnerabilities and fulfill similar functions. Specifically, individuals with BPD, like individuals with anxiety or depressive disorders, endorse high levels of neuroticism (the frequent experience of negative emotions) and tend to evaluate their emotional experiences negatively. Due to these negative reactions to their emotions, they are more likely to engage in avoidant coping strategies to manage emotional experiences, and these strategies, in turn, paradoxically increase the frequency and intensity of negative emotions.

In fact, much of the clinical presentation of BPD can be accounted for by these emotional factors (Linehan, 1993). For example, the impulsive behaviors that characterize BPD, such as self-harm, substance abuse, and binge eating, are often understood as maladaptive attempts to escape from intense negative affect (Chapman, Gratz, & Brown, 2006). Albeit more severe, these BPD characteristic behaviors function similarly to leaving a social situation or taking a benzodiazepine among individuals with anxiety disorders. Finally, there is emerging evidence to suggest that BPD appears to share a substantial, genetically mediated underlying variance with anxiety and mood disorders (Eaton et al., 2011; James & Taylor, 2008) that is represented by an underlying neuroticism factor. The term *emotional disorder* has been used to classify the types of psychopathology that exhibit these functional and genetic similarities (Barlow, 1991; Barlow et al., 2011, Brown & Barlow, 2009).

EXTANT TREATMENTS FOR BPD

Over the past 20 years, a variety of treatment protocols addressing the severe, life-threatening dysregulation characterizing BPD have emerged. Dialectical behavior therapy (DBT; Linehan, 1993) has accumulated considerable empirical support, and treatments such as transference-focused therapy (TFT; Clarkin et al., 2001), mentalization-based treatment (MBT; Bateman & Fonagy, 2004), schema-focused therapy (SFT; Young, Klosko, & Weishaar, 2003), and general psychiatric management (GPM; McMain et al., 2009) also appear promising (for a review, see Neacsiu & Linehan, 2014). The aforementioned approaches are all intensive, long-term (usually at least 1 year in duration), and focused on targeting the life-threatening and therapy-interrupting behaviors that often characterize this complex disorder.

BPD, however, is a heterogeneous disorder with diagnostic criteria that can be combined to create over 300 unique symptom presentations (Ellis, Abroms, & Abroms, 2009); further, most individuals with this disorder never attempt suicide or need hospitalization (Zanarini, Frankenberg, Hennen, & Silk, 2004). To date, no treatments have been explicitly designed to target more stable presentations of BPD—that is, those patients who are not at acute risk for suicide. Patients presenting with less severe symptoms of BPD may represent a unique opportunity to explore core, mechanistic deficits underlying this diagnosis, as they are less likely to display life-threatening behavior that may shift the focus of treatment to safety.

In addition, time-limited, once-weekly outpatient intervention, like the standard format of the UP, may be sufficient for this population. Of course, it is important to note that conceptually, the mechanisms addressed by the UP are also relevant for suicidal thoughts and behaviors (see Chapter 11); the UP has been adapted for use in inpatient settings where patient safety is ensured or could be considered as an adjunctive, mechanism-focused intervention to more intensive outpatient care.

Application of Unified Protocol Skills to BPD-Related Problems

Advances in intervention development have suggested that a transdiagnostic approach to treatment, targeting common processes across disorders (as described previously), may offer an efficacious and efficient solution for the treatment of both principal and cooccurring disorders. The Unified Protocol for Transdiagnostic Treatment of Emotional Disorders (UP; Barlow, Sauer-Zavala et al., in press) is a cognitive-behavioral intervention recently developed to address underlying vulnerabilities across the emotional disorders. There are strong data to support using this approach across the spectrum of anxiety and unipolar mood disorders (Barlow et al., in press; Ellard, Fairholme, Boisseau, Farchione, & Barlow, 2010; Farchione et al., 2012). Given that these same commonalities appear to be present in BPD, it stands to reason that the UP, an emotion-focused treatment for neuroticism, would address the symptom-level features of BPD that may result from the same underlying vulnerability.

As previously described, emotional disorders appear to arise from strong emotions coupled with negative reactions to these experiences, leading to maladaptive avoidant coping that paradoxically exacerbates symptoms. As such, the central goal of the UP is the cultivation of a more accepting attitude toward emotional experiences by providing patients with skills to manage and regulate them effectively as they occur. The UP's treatment goal is consistent with Linehan's major treatment target in Stage 2 DBT, when patients are no longer engaging in self-injurious and other risky behaviors. This overlap lends support to the notion that the UP may be a reasonable treatment for more stable presentations of BPD and may be a more efficient way to address core, maintaining mechanisms in a BPD population.

The UP consists of eight treatment modules delivered across weekly sessions designed to target maladaptive negative responses to emotions and subsequent avoidant coping. A detailed account of each module has been described elsewhere (Allen, McHugh, & Barlow, 2008; Payne, Ellard, Farchione, Fairholme, & Barlow, 2014); however, aspects of each module that are particularly relevant to BPD symptoms are highlighted in the following sections. Treatment begins with an introductory module (Module 1) that emphasizes the importance of enhancing motivation to ensure engagement in treatment (Miller & Rollnick, 2012). This is accomplished through two guided exercises, in which patients weigh the pros and cons of changing versus staying the same and articulate concrete treatment goals.

Module 2 provides a greater understanding of the functional, adaptive nature of a range of emotions (anger, anxiety, sadness, joy), and these experiences are broken down into three components—physical sensations, cognitions, and behaviors—that serve to make the experience more manageable and provide points of intervention. The interaction between these three components is discussed in session, particularly how negative reinforcement due to decreased emotional arousal occurs following behavioral efforts at avoidance. This module may be particularly useful for patients with BPD, as these individuals are likely to view their emotions as problematic, criticism-eliciting events rather than normal, adaptive experiences. As astutely observed by Linehan (1993), individuals with BPD are accustomed to having others minimize, trivialize, and criticize their emotional expressions, which has been shown to result in heightened anxiety focused on emotions (Sauer & Baer, 2009). Further, individuals with BPD engage in avoidance-motivated behaviors and can benefit from understanding that such activities are short-term solutions that are likely to lead to increased discomfort in emotional situations in the future.

Module 3 introduces the concept of mindful emotion awareness, and patients are told that the goal is to engage in present moment–based, nonjudgmental attention. Given that individuals with BPD are particularly prone to deficits in mindfulness, which have been shown to account for important variance in BPD symptoms (Wupperman, Neumann, & Axelrod, 2008; Wupperman, Neumann, Whitman, & Axelrod, 2009), mindfulness training may represent a useful tool for addressing such deficits. Module 4 provides skills for directly coping with thoughts that arise as part of an emotional experience. Although this module involves skills for identifying thinking errors and engaging in cognitive restructuring, the emphasis is primarily on developing cognitive flexibility; accordingly, patients are instructed to move past initial, automatic appraisals by generating other possible interpretations of the situation.

This approach to cognitive therapy is particularly well suited to patients with BPD, who may have frequently been accused of distorting or misperceiving situations by significant others and may respond poorly to a therapist pointing out "irrational" thoughts (Linehan, 1993). Despite the reluctance to address them with traditional cognitive therapy, distorted cognitions are common in BPD, particularly core beliefs regarding the self as vulnerable, bad, or unlovable (Beck & Freeman, 1990; Klosko & Young, 2004). The UP also includes efforts to address core beliefs by assisting patients in identifying self-relevant misappraisals and uncovering how they can trigger emotional reactions in certain situations.

Next, Module 5 provides skills for countering emotional behaviors—that is, avoidance and escape behaviors that may maintain or exacerbate emotional disorder symptoms. This module involves the identification and prevention of any behaviors that function to reduce or downregulate emotional experiences. Behavioral avoidance is common in BPD; literature suggests that the *Diagnostic and Statistical Manual of Mental Disorders,* fifth edition (DSM-5; American Psychiatric Association, 2013), lists diagnostic criteria for BPD including recurrent suicidal behavior/self-injury and self-damaging impulsivity that function to reduce negative emotions (Bentley, Nock, & Barlow, 2014). Further, the interpersonal criteria of BPD (frantic attempts to avoid abandonment and alternating between extremes of idealization and devaluation) also may function in this manner. As such, the UP, as a treatment for emotional disorders, may provide a useful framework for addressing these behavioral manifestations of BPD.

Finally, Modules 6 and 7 encourage patients to engage in emotion exposure exercises, providing an opportunity for them to develop new associations with the experience of strong emotions through extinction learning. First, in Module 6, interoceptive sensitivity is targeted by asking patients to engage in exercises that create physical symptoms of anxiety; for example, patients might breathe through a thin straw to experience symptoms of shortness of breath or spin in a chair to cultivate dizziness. Module 7 involves entering into situations or engaging in activities that elicit strong emotions. Previously learned UP skills (i.e., generating alternative appraisals about a situation before entering, tolerating physical sensations, thoughts, and behavioral urges that may arise over the course of the exposure, or acting counter to urges to avoid) provide a framework that facilitates new learning about emotions during the exposure exercise.

The UP approaches exposure in a graduated fashion, starting by creating manageable, controlled situations in collaborating with a therapist in which to practice. This may be particularly useful for patients with BPD, who may have a hard time finding a suitable, low-level situation for practice in their often chaotic lives. For example, a therapist might encourage a patient to engage in an exposure in which she tolerates being alone in the office for five minutes. Finally, Module 8, consistent with most CBT protocols, allows patient and therapist to review progress made during treatment and discuss ways to prevent relapse.

CASE PRESENTATION

Our research group has applied the UP clinically to five cases of BPD and comorbid anxiety and mood disorders. Patients received 16–20 weekly sessions of treatment with the UP. Initial diagnoses were confirmed using the BPD module from the Diagnostic Interview for Personality Disorders—4th Edition (DIPD-IV; Zanarini et al., 1987) and the Adult Anxiety Disorders Interview Schedule for DSM-IV (ADIS-IV; Di Nardo, Brown, & Barlow, 1994), two clinician-rated measures of psychopathology. Severity of BPD, anxiety, and depressive symptomatology was assessed at pretreatment and posttreatment via well-validated and widely administered self-report measures: The Zanarini Rating Scale for Borderline Personality Disorder (ZAN-BPD; Zanarini, 2003) and the Depression Anxiety Stress Scales (DASS; Lovibond & Lovibond, 1995). In addition, the Difficulties in Emotion Regulation Scale (Gratz & Roemer, 2004) was used to assess pretreatment and posttreatment acquisition of emotion regulation skills. For a detailed account of this study, see Sauer-Zavala, Bentley, and Wilner (2015). Given the heterogeneity of BPD presentations, two cases were selected to highlight the ways in which UP skills may be applied to individuals with this diagnosis; cases are described in detail next. Specific, potentially identifying details in each case have been altered to protect patient confidentiality.

Case 1: I. R.

I. R. is a 35-year-old, married, Caucasian female who presented to the Center for Anxiety and Related Disorders for psychological treatment for the first time. She is self-employed, and over the course of treatment, she was reportedly building up her business after a recent move to the Boston area. I. R. indicated that she sought treatment at the request of her husband, who believed that her mood swings were interfering with their marriage, and found our center by consulting her primary care doctor. In our initial phone consultation, I. R. described her emotions as escalating from "0 to 10, with nothing in between." She stated that her strong emotions have affected her relationship with her husband, other family members, and business clients, and that she copes by withdrawing (e.g., sleeping) to avoid conflicts. I. R. indicated that her overarching goal for treatment was to develop better strategies to modulate her emotional experiences in order to relate better to the people in her life.

The results of the initial diagnostic assessment revealed that I. R. met criteria for BPD and social anxiety disorder. She endorsed clinical levels of the emotional difficulties that characterize BPD, including inappropriate intense anger and affective instability. She described herself as quick to experience anger, particularly in response to relatively minor interpersonal situations (e.g., friends arriving late to plans or not returning her calls right away, client complaints, her mother calling too frequently), and explained that she copes with this by venting to her husband. I. R. indicated that another source of anger is when her husband expresses frustration with her venting, which leads her to yell at him and occasionally throw objects such as her phone.

She reported that her mood shifts several times a day, and that her mother and husband have often described her as moody. I. R. also endorsed BPD interpersonal difficulties at a clinical level (e.g., frantic attempts to avoid abandonment and relationship instability) and reported a pattern of unstable, intense relationships within the context of previous friend groups, with her mother, and, as described earlier, with her husband. Of note, she described intense close relationships with several members of a club to which she belonged, which all ended after a falling out and physical fight with another woman.

I. R. indicated that she currently has a small group of friends with whom she texts, and that she begins to worry about the status of the relationship if she doesn't hear back in a timely manner, leading to more frequent texting. She also noted that when her husband expresses disappointment in her behavior, she begs him not to leave her. With regard to her BPD identify disturbance, I. R. endorsed clinically significant levels of chronic emptiness and an unstable sense of self. In addition, she noted that others have commented that she looks sad, but she has difficulty identifying her "blank" feelings. I. R. further reported that, beyond her profession, she doesn't know who she truly is, and that she believes other people in her life also see her only as her job title.

Finally, I. R. endorsed chronic, frequent thoughts of suicide, particularly with regard to easing the burden on close friends and family; however, she denied having a history of suicidal behavior or engaging in NSSI or impulsive behavior in other domains. She also reported subthreshold symptoms of cognitive difficulties— namely, transient dissociation in response to stress. For example, I. R. stated that after experiencing strong emotions, she feels "numb and spaced out."

In terms of her social anxiety disorder diagnosis, I. R. endorsed significant anxiety attending parties, speaking with unfamiliar people, eating in public, being assertive, and initiating and maintaining conversations. She stated that this has caused problems in building her business, as it is difficult for her to attend networking events. In addition, I. R. described her husband as very social, and she stated that she has difficulty accompanying him to dinners and other events with his friends. Finally, in our interview, I. R. also endorsed depressive symptoms at a subclinical level. She stated that she had experienced depressed mood and lack of interest in her usual activities for most of the day in the two weeks prior to our assessment; however, she denied the associated symptoms required to meet criteria for a DSM-IV depressive disorder. I. R.'s initial self-report assessment scores indicated high levels of BPD and depressive symptoms, moderate levels of anxiety, and a high degree of emotion regulation deficits (see Table 12.1).

Table 12.1. PRETREATMENT AND POSTTREATMENT OUTCOME SCORES

Comorbid Diagnoses	Case 1 (I.R) GAD		Case 2 (R.B) MDD		Case 3 SOC		Case 4 SOC		Case 5 SOC	
	Pre	Post	Pre	Post	Pre	Post	Pre	Post	Pre	Post
ZAN-BPD	22	16	16	8	18	2	7	3	17	17
DASS-D	23	3*	32	21	22	0	9	8	19	22
DASS-A	13	3*	21	17	12	4	5	1	15	20
DERS	136	116	98	92	106	54	121	65	99	95

NOTES: GAD = generalized anxiety disorder; MDD = najor depressive disorder; SOC = social anxiety disorder; ZAN-BPD = Zanarini Rating Scale for Borderline Personality Disorder (self-report version); DASS-D = Depression Anxiety Stress Scales–Depression subscale: DASS-A = Depression Anxiety Stress Scale–Anxiety subscale; DERS = Difficulties in Emotion Regulation Scale (higher scores reflect greater difficulty).

* Patient failed to complete back side of questionnaire, so data for week 12 have been substituted.

After I. R.'s level of motivation to change was assessed using the "Decisional Balance" exercise (identifying pros and cons of changing), she struggled with setting concrete goals, citing that she didn't know how to translate her motivation into action (Module 1). To assist her, the first three treatment sessions were spent in efforts to better define her difficulties, followed by the development of goals to address them. For instance, we reviewed I. R.'s relationship with her husband, as conflict in this area had prompted her to seek treatment. We delineated a pattern in which I. R. would experience conflict with clients and her mother and, instead of handling it directly, would vent to her husband. This, in turn, would lead to conflict with her husband that was described as much more distressing than the original conflict. Clearly defining problematic patterns for I. R. helped direct the focus of goal setting, and she indicated that she would like to develop skills for disengaging from work stress when enjoying time with her husband in order to minimize fighting.

Following completion of homework geared toward identifying steps to accomplish her goal of being able to disengage from situations causing strong emotions (e.g., work, her mother), I. R. expressed concern that these efforts would lead to getting rid of negative emotions altogether, preventing her from expressing herself and honoring her feelings. This allowed us to transition into our next treatment topic, the function and nature of emotions (Module 2, for two sessions).

While dissecting a recent emotional experience into its component parts (thoughts, feelings, and behaviors), I. R. noticed her tendency to evaluate her friend's behaviors as personal slights (thoughts) but refrain from expressing her displeasure with the situation (behavior). For example, when a friend was 20 minutes late meeting her for lunch, I. R. did not describe this as an inconvenience and ask her friend to change her behavior. In the short term, refraining from expressing her emotions may avoid arguments with friends, but in the long term, it appears to lead to feelings of helplessness, subsequent venting to her husband, and repeated lateness from friends.

Through this discussion, it became clear to I. R. that expressing her emotions (and therefore validating them) in the moment, and to the offending individual, may actually help her in the service of her goal to disengaging from stressors when she is with her husband. This realization is illustrated in the following vignette:

I. R.: *I know that it is leading to conflict with my husband and I need to stop, but I feel like I'll just be stuffing my feelings if I don't vent.*

THERAPIST: *So, it sounds like your emotions are telling you something important—that your friend wasn't valuing your time—and that it would be really hard not to do something about it.*

I. R.: *Yeah, I feel like if I didn't vent, it would be like telling myself that I shouldn't be upset.*

THERAPIST: *I wonder if there is another way you could respond that would still feel like you're taking your emotion seriously.*

I. R.: *[Pause] I guess I could have talked to [my friend] directly.*

THERAPIST: *What would that have been like for you?*

I. R.: Really hard—I'd be afraid of upsetting her.

THERAPIST: *So in the short term, confronting your friend about her lateness might be anxiety provoking. Are there any benefits in the long term?*

I. R.: Maybe she wouldn't be late next time. And I might not feel the need to complain to my husband after the fact.

In addition, I. R. found that the mindful emotion awareness skill of anchoring in the present (Module 3, for two sessions) was useful for putting aside work concerns, particularly future worries about clients leaving bad reviews online, in order to engage productively with her husband. She also reportedly enjoyed the formal meditation practice, describing it as a "safe place" to sit with her emotions.

Midway through treatment, I. R. reported that she had become pregnant, but she was unsure of whether to keep the baby; this topic became a major focus of treatment on which subsequent UP skills were applied. I. R. endorsed a great deal of distress regarding the uncertainty of this decision. We returned to the "Decisional Balance" exercise (Module 2) to examine the pros and cons for both keeping and terminating the pregnancy. Although the most favorable decision remained unclear, this exercise allowed I. R. to identify her worst-case scenarios for either decision (e.g., my husband will leave me after the baby is born, but I'll become depressed if I have an abortion) and use her cognitive flexibility skills (Module 4) to address worries around these scenarios. This strategy increased her confidence in her ability to handle these unlikely outcomes, reducing her anxiety.

I. R. eventually decided to terminate her pregnancy, and during a subsequent session, she reported feeling intense sadness associated with the loss. We returned to a discussion of the functional nature of this emotions (Module 2) and clarified the difference between taking time to process her feelings as opposed to engaging in behaviors that might cause long-term problems. Consequently, I. R. was encouraged to act inconsistently with her emotion-driven behaviors (EDBs) to withdraw from work and to sleep (Module 5). She completed homework to counter EDBs by engaging in self-care (showering, eating), regular exercise, completing procrastinated work, and refraining from napping, and she reported that her feelings of unrelenting sadness had abated by our next session. Although we conducted the interoceptive symptom induction test (Module 6), I. R. denied distress associated with the sensations generated; in fact, she described the exercises as "fun." This is consistent with her previous self-report that physical sensations are not a particularly salient component of her emotional experience.

The final phase of treatment was focused on utilizing the skills that I. R. had learned thus far through emotion exposure tasks (Module 7). Specifically for I. R., exposures were designed to elicit anxiety around social situations (attending networking events and parties with her husband) and losing both personal and work relationships (setting limits with clients, her mother, and her husband). She displayed the greatest ease completing exposures related to work situations and demonstrated an improved capacity to tolerate uncertainty with clients and provide negative feedback. She also demonstrated similar assertiveness with her husband and by standing up to him in an appropriate manner, she was able to see that expressing her opinions does not always lead to a fight and in fact, can improve their relationship in the long term. She also attended several professional networking events and was surprised by her ability to engage in small talk during these events.

At the time of treatment termination, I. R. reported significant improvement in her ability to challenge the validity of her negative thoughts and to act inconsistently with maladaptive behavioral urges driven by emotional experiences. She stated that, consistent with her treatment goal, her relationship with her husband had improved; however, I. R.'s husband was reportedly apprehensive about the termination of her treatment, and she discussed her intention to pursue additional treatment. I. R.'s self-report data were consistent with her verbal assessment of treatment gains. She evidenced reductions in symptoms and increases in her ability to regulate her emotions (see Table 12.1).

Case 2: R. B.

R. B. is a 26-year-old, married, Caucasian female who was referred for cognitive-behavioral therapy (CBT) by her supportive counselor. She is currently employed part time as a customer service representative and is pursuing her associate's degree in health care administration. R. B. reported that she sought treatment to cope with jealousy that arises when she and her husband are around other women, despite there being no history of infidelity; she further indicated that, in such situations, she begins to feel insecure in their relationship, and that this can lead to panic attacks. R. B. stated that anxiety with regard to fidelity has caused tension in her marriage, as well as in previous romantic relationships. In addition, she has distanced herself from her family for fear that her husband might be attracted to her sister, sister-in-law, and mother.

At the start of treatment, a thorough diagnostic interview was conducted. Based on the assessment, R. B. met criteria for BPD and major depressive disorder (MDD). In terms of her BPD diagnosis, R. B. endorsed clinical levels of BPD emotional symptoms: inappropriate intense anger and affective instability. She reported easily triggered anger that occurred most frequently when her husband is looking at or talking to other women, and that she becomes unable to refrain from pointing out his problematic behavior and forces them to leave the situation immediately. In addition, she reported that her mood shifts several times a day from neutral to panicky in response to small triggers, including issues with her husband, magazines that reportedly diminish her self-worth, and work and school stress.

R. B. also endorsed BPD interpersonal difficulties at a clinical level. As noted previously, she reported that "all [her husband] has to do is see another woman and [she] feels like he will be unfaithful and leave [her]." She stated that they generally avoid going out in public together in order to minimize contact with other women. R. B. also reported a pattern of unstable, intense relationships within the context of previous romantic relationships. She stated that, in her current relationship with her husband, they fight frequently, and she often threatens to end the marriage. R. B. also endorsed clinically significant levels of chronic emptiness, particularly with regard to her firm belief that she will never find love.

Finally, R. B. reported clinically significant evidence of suicidal thoughts and gestures, describing both thoughts of suicide (e.g., it would be easier on both me and my husband if I were gone) and frequent threats made to her husband in the context of their fights (when she had no intent to engage in suicidal behavior). However, she denied suicide attempts or a history of engaging in NSSI or impulsive behaviors in other domains. In addition, she denied symptoms of cognitive difficulties, such as dissociation or transient paranoia in response to stress.

In terms of her diagnosis of MDD, R. B. stated that she had experienced depressed mood and lack of interest in her usual activities for most of the day in the two weeks prior to our assessment. She also endorsed associated symptoms of weight loss, difficulty sleeping, feelings of worthlessness, difficulty concentrating, and, as noted earlier, thoughts of suicide. R. B.'s initial self-report assessment scores indicated high levels of BPD, depressive, and anxiety symptoms and a high degree of emotion regulation deficits (see Table 12.1).

In our first treatment session, R. B. indicated that her goals for treatment were to be less insecure and jealous in her marriage. She was encouraged to define her goals in terms of concrete observable behaviors (e.g., going out in public with her husband and engaging in fewer instances of reassurance seeking) and to brainstorm smaller intermediate steps toward these goals (Module 1). Also, following a discussion of the pros and cons of changing through treatment, R. B. indicated that developing a more trusting relationship with her husband outweighs the small protection that vigilance against infidelity might provide.

R. B. arrived at our second treatment session reporting a high level of distress. She indicated that her mother, with whom R. B. and her husband are currently living, had just hired a new female babysitter for her little sister earlier in the day. Prior to our session, R. B. had reportedly texted her husband repeatedly ("Don't interact with her") and had begun looking for apartments in order to move out. Her distress in this situation provided a useful opportunity to explore the three components of her emotional response and how they contributed to the intensity of her experience (Module 2). In particular, this exercise highlighted for R. B. the relationship between behaving as if her husband will be unfaithful (e.g., monitoring his behavior via text message and preventing him from interacting with women) and the conviction with which she holds negative thoughts (e.g., "My husband will disrespect me by flirting with other girls").

R. B. also noted that physical sensations associated with anger and anxiety, such as shaky hands and rapid heart rate, also increase the believability of her negative thoughts and the urgency to perform anxious behaviors. These discoveries became the focus as we sought to increase her ability to mindfully observe emotion-related stimuli (Module 3). R. B. was particularly encouraged to notice catastrophic predictions about her husband's fidelity, label them as thoughts, and allow them to be there without responding to them as if they were true. We also discussed the nature of thoughts and how it made sense that she would have such thoughts, given her father's history of infidelity, allowing R. B. to be less judgmental about her anxiety. In addition, she reportedly found anchoring in the present to be a useful strategy for combating negative predictions about schoolwork (e.g., "I'm going to fail") and work (e.g., "I'm never going to be able to finish all this work") by noting that these feared outcomes had not yet occurred.

R. B. was able to quickly integrate the use of cognitive flexibility (Module 4) in response to worry thoughts about school or work, but she exhibited greater difficulty challenging predictions about her husband's fidelity. Several sessions were spent discussing R. B.'s core beliefs around the importance of her vigilance against infidelity. She indicated her worry that her husband will have impure thoughts (e.g., considering another woman attractive) and her subsequent monitoring of his behavior reflect a greater fear that she will be "played for a fool"—or worse, that she is a fool. Also, she reported believing that if her husband did cheat on her, she would be unable to ever trust anyone again and therefore be unable to have a romantic relationship, again prompting her intense reactions to seemingly minor offenses (e.g., her husband being in the same store as other women).

In a related effort, we conducted a behavioral experiment in which R. B. was asked to objectively evaluate the attractiveness of men that she encountered between sessions in order to determine whether this behavior led to sexual thoughts or cheating. We further explored the behavioral contributions to R. B.'s emotional experiences by asking her to act inconsistent with her behavioral urges. For example, instead of monitoring her husband's behavior in stores, R. B. challenged herself to complete her errands. Finally, interoceptive exposures (IEs; e.g., hyperventilation, straw breathing, and muscle tensing) were used to increase R. B.'s comfort level with the physiological component of her strong emotions and to increase her ability to objectively observe her tendency to rate her automatic thoughts as more believable in the presence of physiological cues.

Unfortunately, following session 12, R. B. and her husband moved farther away, and she was unable to make the commute to finish our final four sessions. As such, despite being able to complete an emotion exposure hierarchy (which included running errands with her husband, looking at women's magazines in the presence of her husband, going to the beach with her husband, and being assertive about her schedule at work), we did not complete any exposures together in session (Module 7).

At the time of treatment termination, R. B. reported some improvement in her ability to tolerate and respond to strong emotions, leading to fewer fights with her husband and less anxiety regarding school and work success. In addition, R. B. and her husband had been going out together on the weekends more frequently, and she was able to complete errands without being overly focused on his behavior, though this was reportedly still anxiety provoking. R. B.'s self-report data was consistent with her verbal assessment of treatment gains. She evidenced reductions in symptoms and increases in her ability to regulate her emotions (see Table 12.1). Finally, R. B. expressed a desire to complete exposures on her own to continue to become more comfortable on outings with her husband.

EMPIRICAL SUPPORT

As noted, our team has treated five individuals with BPD to date. Outcome data are presented in Table 12.1. Overall, treatment with the UP was well received. Four of the five cases treated, including the two cases described in this chapter, evidenced reductions in BPD, depressive, and anxiety symptoms (see Table 12.1). Large effect sizes (standardized mean gain, ES_{sg}) were found for change in BPD symptoms and emotion-regulatory capacity from pretreatment to posttreatment ($ES_{sg} = 1.06$, 95% CI .01: 2.11 and $ES_{sg} = 1.29$, 95% CI .01: 2.59, respectively), whereas changes in anxiety and depressive symptoms represented medium effects ($ES_{sg} = .51$, 95% CI −.18: 1.19 and $ES_{sg} = .70$, 95% CI −.69: 2.08, respectively).

Confidence intervals of the effect sizes for change in anxiety and depressive symptoms included zero, indicating that this may not be a reliable effect. This is likely due to the small sample size, suggesting that future studies with larger, controlled samples are necessary. In sum, results from this preliminary investigation suggest that increasing BPD patients' capacity to observe their emotions without avoidant responding (facilitated through mindfulness training and cognitive restructuring) allows them to move toward the goals established early in treatment (e.g., better relationship with significant others, moving toward education and social goals).

CONCLUSION

The purpose of this chapter was to present clinical case examples illustrating the application of the UP, a transdiagnostic treatment for emotional disorders, with patients with BPD and comorbid depressive and anxiety disorders. Both BPD and other emotional disorders are characterized by the tendency to experience strong emotions, coupled with finding these emotional experiences aversive. As such, individuals with emotional disorders (BPD included) engage in strategies, often maladaptive, designed to escape or avoid strong emotions.

The UP was developed specifically to target these negative reactions to emotions that can lead to paradoxical increases in symptoms. Patients are encouraged to tolerate emotions rather than push them away, and they are given skills (e.g., mindfulness training, cognitive restructuring, acting inconsistent with emotion-driven urges) to facilitate adaptive responses. Because of the functional similarities among BPD and other emotional disorders, it was theorized that the UP may be an appropriate treatment to address BPD symptoms in a relatively stable population, as well as simultaneously addressing coexisting emotional disorders (e.g., depressive and anxiety disorders). In general, patients treated with the UP saw meaningful reductions in their BPD symptoms, as well as their symptoms of depression and anxiety (Sauer-Zavala, Bentley, & Wilner, 2016).

It is notable that, in most of these cases (including the two described in detail here), unanticipated significant life stressors (e.g., an unexpected move, an unplanned pregnancy and subsequent abortion, job loss) occurred during the course of treatment with the UP. These types of stressors are consistent with the life chaos described by Linehan (1993) that is often experienced by individuals with BPD. Although these stressors were largely addressed within the context of the UP skills, their presence may have shifted the patients' focus from skill acquisition to crisis management. It is possible that this may have limited the gains made, particularly in the present research trial, in which all modules were covered within an arbitrary limit of 16 to 20 sessions.

In addition, it is important to note that one patient in this study (not described here) did not improve. Although this individual appeared somewhat less engaged in treatment activities than the other four patients, the specific reasons for this lack of improvement remain unclear. One possibility is that he was not intrinsically motivated to complete treatment, as he was mandated by his university to be in therapy. Another potential explanation is that he was qualitatively more severe than the other patients, given his history of and current engagement in NSSI, and that once weekly, outpatient treatment may not have been the appropriate level of care for this individual. Future research is needed to clarify what patients with BPD are likely to benefit from treatment with the UP. As previously noted, our expectation is that patients with less severe and risky presentations of BPD may be ideal candidates for this relatively brief, CBT approach.

In summary, treatment with the UP, a transdiagnostic, emotion-focused CBT treatment, appears to be a promising approach to the treatment of BPD. The outcomes of the cases presented here suggest that the UP is both a feasible and acceptable approach in this population. However, future, controlled studies will be needed to formally assess both the short- and long-term efficacy of the UP in managing BPD symptoms, as well as to evaluate specific moderators and mediators of treatment (e.g., severity) in this difficult-to-treat population. If the UP proves efficacious, this may offer a parsimonious, cost-effective approach for individuals presenting with less severe (e.g., less life-interfering) BPD symptoms.

13

The Unified Protocol
for Chronic Pain

LAURA A. PAYNE ∎

CHRONIC PAIN

Chronic pain, typically defined as pain lasting three months or longer without identified tissue damage (International Association for the Study of Pain, 2012), is a significant and costly public health problem, affecting an estimated 100 million American adults and resulting in costs of up to $635 billion annually in medical expenses and lost productivity [Institute of Medicine (US) Committee on Advancing Pain Research, 2011]. Short-term effects of chronic pain include missed work, withdrawal from social and physical activities, and family stress and tension. However, long-term effects of chronic pain may be even more deleterious, leaving many individuals suffering with inadequate treatment, ongoing functional impairment, and disability.

The biopsychosocial model of pain purports that chronic pain represents a complex interaction of biological, psychological, and social factors (Gatchel, Peng, Peters, Fuchs, & Turk, 2007). Pain itself is a multidimensional construct incorporating both sensory (e.g., intensity, duration) and affective (emotional) aspects. Recognition of the affective dimension of pain has focused attention on the ways in which mood states influence the pain experience, and research over the past several decades has begun to provide support for the concept of shared mechanisms underlying both pain and emotions (Asmundson & Katz, 2009; Ribeiro, Kennedy, Smith, Stohler, & Zubieta, 2005). In brief, evidence supporting the relationship of pain and emotional dysfunction is found in the high rate of psychological comorbidity in chronic pain populations (Riegel et al., 2014; Tegethoff, Belardi, Stalujanis, & Meinlschmidt, 2015; van Hecke, Torrance, & Smith, 2013); common neurobiological underpinnings and genetic polymorphisms underlying pain and anxiety/depression (Narasimhan & Campbell, 2010; Ribeiro et al., 2005; Strigo, Simmons, Matthews, Craig, & Paulus, 2008); evidence of emotion dysregulation associated with chronic pain (Cioffi & Holloway, 1993; Lumley, Beyer, & Radcliffe, 2008; Mattila et al., 2008; Sullivan, Rouse, Bishop, & Johnston, 1997; Tuzer et al., 2010; van Middendorp et al., 2008); and the efficacy of cognitive behavior therapy (CBT) strategies for managing chronic pain (e.g., Williams, Eccleston, & Morley, 2012).

Neuroticism and Pain

Neuroticism, or "negative affect," a higher-order personality trait, may be one of the shared vulnerabilities that contributes to the development and progression of mental and physical disorders. *Neuroticism* is typically defined as a personality trait with symptoms of negative or unstable emotionality, including anxiety, depression, irritability, and hostility (Costa & McCrae, 1992; John & Gross, 2004). Decades of research have linked neuroticism to an increased risk for and greater comorbidity with mental disorders (Lahey, 2009). However, neuroticism is also associated with physical outcomes. Higher levels of neuroticism predict the likelihood of having a physical impairment (including pain) 25 years later (Charles, Gatz, Kato, & Pedersen, 2008). Neuroticism has been associated with foot and ankle pain (Shivarathre, Howard, Krishna, Cowan, & Platt, 2014), labor pain (Yadollahi et al., 2014), recall of variability in pain unpleasantness in people with persistent low back pain (Lefebvre & Keefe, 2013), and brain activity during visceral pain (Coen et al., 2011). Levels of neuroticism uniquely predict pain in adolescents (Wilner, Vranceanu, & Blashill, 2014). In addition, high levels of neuroticism are associated with poorer treatment outcomes in individuals with chronic prostatitis/chronic pelvic pain syndrome (Koh et al., 2014). Neuroticism is independently predictive of both pain catastrophizing and pain anxiety (two cognitive-affective constructs that are implicated in the development of chronic pain conditions), above and beyond the effects of depression and self-reported pain severity (Kadimpati, Zale, Hooten, Ditre, & Warner, 2015). Taken together, these data highlight the potential critical role that neuroticism plays in the development of both psychological and pain conditions.

Given these findings, a psychological treatment that directly targets neuroticism/negative affect may be a more comprehensive and affective method of addressing physical pain and associated emotional symptoms. The Unified Protocol for Transdiagnostic Treatment of Emotional Disorders (UP; Barlow et al., in press) specifically focuses on negative automatic thoughts, eliminating emotional avoidance strategies, and correcting emotional behaviors—techniques that are applicable to both emotional and physical disorders. This chapter presents the case of "Lisa" and describes how the UP was applied to her particular presenting concerns.

CASE PRESENTATION

"Lisa" was a 25-year-old, single, Caucasian woman who presented for treatment for pain "all over" her body at a local integrative and multidisciplinary pain treatment center. She described experiencing constant whole body pain with accompanying fatigue, although she noted that the pain was often worse in her neck, back, and shoulders following even mildly strenuous activities (i.e., brisk walking and standing for longer than 5–10 minutes). Lisa described the constant pain as dull and "achy," with occasional sharp, piercing, or burning sensations. She reported that the pain began several years earlier, when she was completing her senior year in college. After a long weekend of studying, she reportedly felt very fatigued and "achy" and had trouble getting out of bed the following Monday morning. The pain had been present since.

Despite repeated visits to primary care physicians, neurologists, and orthopedists and a multitude of clinical examinations and tests, there were no abnormal findings. Lisa was unable to finish her classes due to significant impairment in her ability to move, walk, and sit for long periods of time. She ultimately withdrew from school prior to completing graduation requirements. Over the past several years, she had become even more impaired and was avoiding most physical activities due to pain and fatigue. She also stated that her social life had diminished since she often cancelled plans, either due to pain or because of her fear that pain would become "intolerable" and she would not be able to return home easily. As a result, Lisa spent little time with friends and spent most of her time at home with her parents and younger sister.

Lisa also described a history of anxiety, with onset during childhood. She reported often worrying about her performance in school, the health of her family members (particularly her parents), and her relationships with friends. Lisa always performed well in school, noting that she was a "straight A student" throughout high school and college. However, she often would stay up quite late to finish assignments and prepare for exams. She described her worry and anxiety as "uncontrollable" and reported accompanying physical symptoms of fatigue, restlessness, irritability, muscle tension, and difficulty sleeping. Lisa was a self-described "perfectionist" and noted that she typically pushed herself very hard to meet the expectations that she set for herself.

Integrative Evaluation

Lisa's medical history and all her past related laboratory and radiographic studies were reviewed by a pain physician. Based on these records, as well as a physical assessing multiple widespread muscle tender points, Lisa was diagnosed with fibromyalgia. She was also given a diagnosis of generalized anxiety disorder (GAD) to categorize her ongoing, uncontrollable worry and anxiety. Lisa was referred for psychological treatment to help her manage pain and anxiety symptoms and to improve her overall level of functioning.

Assessment

As part of her assessment, Lisa completed a number of self-report measures designed to assess various aspects of her functioning, including overall pain levels, anxiety, depression, positive and negative affect, and pain anxiety. Measures were administered immediately prior to treatment and immediately following treatment completion. Each measure is detailed next.

Numeric Rating Scale (NRS). Lisa was asked to rate her overall pain in the last week using a 0 (none) to 100 (worst or most possible) NRS. This scale captured her overall level of pain, regardless of location on the body. The NRS has been shown to be a reliable and valid method of assessing pain levels in adults (Bijur, Latimer, & Gallagher, 2003; Hollen et al., 2005; Jensen, Karoly, & Braver, 1986; Williamson & Hoggart, 2005).

Brief Symptom Inventory—18-Item Version (BSI-18) (Derogatis, 2001). The BSI-18 measures distress about various symptoms over the past week. Two subscales of the BSI-18, the anxiety and depression subscales, were used to evaluate Lisa's levels of anxiety and depression.

Positive and Negative Affect Scale (PANAS) (Crawford & Henry, 2004; Watson, Clark, & Tellegen, 1988). The PANAS is a 20-item measure that assesses dimensions of positive affect (e.g., interested, enthusiastic, inspired, etc.) and negative affect (i.e., upset, guilty, afraid, etc.). Each emotion is rated on a five-point scale indicating the extent that the participant has experienced that feeling over the past week.

Pain Anxiety Symptom Scale—20-Item Version (PASS-20) (McCracken & Dhingra, 2002). The PASS-20 was used to assess Lisa's fear of pain and pain-related anxiety symptoms. It consists of a total score, as well as four five-item subscales (cognitive, escape/avoidance, fear, and physiological anxiety).

Treatment Approach

Given Lisa's chronic physical pain, as well as her comorbid anxiety symptoms, it was determined that she would benefit most from the transdiagnostic approach of the UP, which could address both pain-related and emotional dysfunction. A transdiagnostic approach may represent a more efficient, and possibly more efficacious, way to ameliorate overlapping emotional disorder symptomatology (comorbidity) (McManus, Shafran, & Cooper, 2010; Wilamowska et al., 2010). Chronic pain disorders naturally fit within this transdiagnostic paradigm, given that many patients present with multiple chronic pain complaints (Johannes, Le, Zhou, Johnston, & Dworkin, 2010; Yunus, 2012), as well as significant symptoms of anxiety and depression (Asmundson & Katz, 2009; Riegel et al., 2014; Tegethoff et al., 2015; van Hecke et al., 2013).

The treatment presented here describes how the UP can be applied to physical pain by emphasizing emotional reactions to emotional *and* physical discomfort—an area that is typically addressed in the UP in the context of interoceptive exposure (IE) and panic attacks. Given that pain is a very complex phenomenon involving various emotional, neurobiological, and sensory pathways, an additional psychoeducation component focusing specifically on pain was included to help conceptualize pain in a way that makes it amenable to a transdiagnostic approach.

MODULE 1: SETTING GOALS AND MAINTAINING MOTIVATION

Following her medical and psychological assessment, Lisa met with the therapist for a first treatment session. In this session, the nature of the treatment and the importance of homework completion were reviewed. Lisa expressed concern about the effectiveness of the therapy for reducing her pain and associated distress and noted that it had been challenging to follow through with other prescribed therapies (i.e., physical therapy and acupuncture) when she did not see an immediate benefit. Therefore, the first module focusing on connecting Lisa with her most significant symptoms and then identifying treatment goals (as well as potential obstacles to treatment) was particularly relevant. Rather than attempting to "convince" Lisa that the therapy would be helpful, the therapist encouraged Lisa to consider each new skill as one potential step toward improving functioning. Her concerns were acknowledged as valid, and the therapist also spent time exploring some of Lisa's fears that she would not improve. In addition to building motivation by "rolling with resistance," the relationship between Lisa and the therapist was strengthened by encouraging her to discuss her concerns openly.

The Treatment Goals Form was assigned for homework, and Lisa returned the following week with a single goal completed of "becoming pain-free." In session, Lisa and her therapist worked together to make the goal more concrete by focusing on identifying specific activities that made the goal more concrete, such as walking her dog, engaging in an exercise regimen, and taking a class at a local art school. They then identified a series of steps that Lisa could take to help achieve her goals, including attending therapy sessions (a step that she had already taken), looking at class availability at the art school, getting out of the house at least once per week, walking around the block twice per week, and, finally, walking her dog daily. Lisa and her therapist also discussed the actual likelihood of achieving the goal of becoming completely pain free, given that pain is (a) necessary for adaptive functioning and (b) an experience that everyone has at various times. Lisa was able to consider this and adjust her goal to having her pain become more manageable.

For additional goals, Lisa's therapist inquired whether she also wanted to work on reducing symptoms of anxiety. Lisa agreed that she did want to feel less anxious, although she saw the anxiety as a function of her body pain. When asked how to make this goal of being less anxious more concrete, Lisa struggled to consider what concrete behaviors would change if she felt less anxious. Her therapist asked whether anxiety was an obstacle to completing her college degree or spending time with friends. Lisa hesitantly agreed that it was, although she still focused on pain and anxiety about developing pain symptoms as the primary obstacles to engaging in those activities. However, Lisa and her therapist were able to identify other steps that she would need to take to address anxiety, including practicing awareness of anxiety, changing perfectionistic behaviors (including repeatedly checking assignments), and not avoiding social situations due to anxiety and worry.

Subsequently, Lisa and her therapist completed the Decisional Balance Worksheet, focusing specifically on the pros of staying the same and the cons of changing, since these would likely identify the biggest obstacles to treatment. Lisa was initially confused by the concept that there may be obstacles to treatment, but after some reflection, she acknowledged that the idea of going back to school and finishing her degree caused significant anxiety. She also stated that it was very easy for her to live with her parents, as her mother prepared most of her meals and she did not have to concern herself with financial issues (e.g., paying bills, creating a budget, etc.). Moving out of her parents' home would require her to take on a great deal more responsibility, which also caused anxiety. These obstacles, as well as the pros of changing and cons of staying the same, were all documented on the worksheet.

MODULE 2: UNDERSTANDING EMOTIONS

This psychoeducation module was particularly relevant for Lisa, as she had trouble recognizing her emotions, including lower levels of stress and anxiety that could be contributing to pain. This module began with an introduction to the nature and function of emotions, as well as a description of how pain fits into this conceptualization. Specifically, pain was described as a signal that indicates the potential for or the occurrence of tissue damage from a harmful stimulus. Nerves send information about the stimulus to the brain, where that information is processed and evaluated in combination with many other factors, including expectations about pain, mood and anxiety, previous experiences with pain, and neurobiological sensitivity to pain. The output of this processing is the response to pain—whether it is to move quickly away from the stimulus, yell, cry, or ignore it. However, when pain becomes *chronic* (i.e., lasting three months or longer) and dysfunctional, the brain may still be signaling that there is pain, even though there is no harmful stimulus or ongoing tissue damage. This is why localized interventions (such as surgery) may not be helpful for chronic pain, while treatments such as psychotherapy can help the brain "turn off" the pain-signaling system. As with anxiety, fear, sadness, or anger, the goal of treatment is to bring the pain-signaling system back to a functional level, not eliminate it entirely.

Lisa found this information helpful but still expressed a concern that her pain was arising from a physiological injury. In line with motivational enhancement strategies, her therapist used the technique of "rolling with resistance" and did not challenge Lisa on this belief. Instead, Lisa was asked only to consider that other factors may be contributing to her pain experience and that there may be value in addressing those other factors to help reduce pain.

Next, the three-component model of emotions/pain was described by reviewing thoughts, physical sensations, and behaviors associated with emotions and pain responses. The cycle of pain was then discussed in relation to the concept of negative reinforcement. For Lisa, the relationship between physical sensations (body pain), thoughts (e.g., "If I go out with my friends, my pain will get worse and it will become unmanageable"), and emotional behaviors (i.e., staying home) were explicitly identified, with an emphasis on how this cycle contributes to more frequent and intense levels of body pain. In addition, her *emotional* response to body pain (i.e., anxiety) was discussed as an additional factor that contributes to the cycle of pain.

These concepts were extended to include the antecedents, responses, and consequences of emotions and pain. However, Lisa struggled to identify clear antecedents or "triggers" for her body pain. Occasionally, she acknowledged that she may have had more stress on days when she had pain flare-ups, but this was not a consistent phenomenon. Again, her therapist did not get "stuck" on this particular issue and asked Lisa to continue to monitor her experience as best she could, even if she could not identify a specific trigger for pain.

Similarly, Lisa had trouble identifying triggers for anxiety and worry, although a similar approach was used to have her monitor these experiences, regardless of whether she could identify a trigger. However, Lisa's therapist did encourage her to consider additional factors that may be related to her pain, including fluctuations in her hormonal levels over the course of her menstrual cycle, changes over the course of a day, or differences with regard to her sleep patterns. To the extent that a trigger for pain and/or anxiety could be identified, it may be useful information for Lisa to know so that her symptoms could have some level of predictability.

Through completion of the Following Your ARC form, it became clear that Lisa typically withdrew from activities or social interactions in response to both pain and anxiety. She noted that she would engage in distracting activities (watching television, sleeping) or avoid leaving her house when she felt either pain *or* anxiety. These responses were identified as "learned," and this was the first time that Lisa appreciated how her habit of reacting to discomfort (whether physical or emotional) was contributing to her overall functioning. She found this concept of learned responses particularly useful for more clearly evaluating the patterns of avoidance and subsequent impairment in her life.

Module 3: Mindful Emotion Awareness

Given her difficulty identifying more subtle cues that she was feeling anxious, developing skills of emotional awareness seemed to be particularly relevant to Lisa's presenting problems. In this module, she was provided with psychoeducation about primary emotions and secondary reactions and how these related to both pain and anxiety. When applied to body pain, Lisa's therapist changed the term *primary emotion* to *primary experience* to capture the initial sensations that triggered the cascade of pain and anxiety. For Lisa, she was able to identify that she could experience a sharp, stinging pain in her neck (primary experience), which then almost immediately triggered anxiety and a sense of hopelessness (secondary reaction). Lisa was encouraged to observe that her judgments about pain were creating a cycle of increasing attention to her body and physical functioning that led to heightened anxiety.

The first exercise in this module skill involved a Mindful Emotion Awareness Meditation, focusing on her breath as an opportunity to become more aware of what she was feeling, both physically and emotionally. Consistent with an emotional acceptance–based approach, and in contrast to other methods, the UP does not emphasize breathing as a way to relax, as this may have the unintended effect of creating increased levels of anxiety/stress because of the implied goal of suppressing any "nonrelaxing" experiences. In this sense, breathing is used only as a tool to increase awareness. Lisa was instructed in the use of other mindfulness exercises to help bring her attention and awareness to the present moment instead of getting caught up in judgments about her experience.

Lisa also was asked to engage in some mood and pain induction exercises, with the goal of practicing being aware of *emotional* responses to the pain. She practiced slowly stretching her limbs until she began to feel the sensation of pain in her body, noticing those sensations and her emotional reactions for a few moments, and then returning her body to a resting state. As she continued to practice this exercise, she became more aware that even subtle sensations in her body triggered anxiety, and thus she was better able to understand the connection between her physical sensations of pain and anxiety. Lisa also brought in a recording of a popular song from when she attended college. She identified that the song itself triggered feelings of joy and happiness (primary experience), although the memories connected to this song quickly led to feelings of sadness and regret (secondary reaction). So Lisa's primary experience (in this case an emotion) was happiness because she recalled such experiences in her own life. Her secondary reaction, however, was sadness as she then quickly reflected on her current experience, which highlighted missing aspects of her life. In her *evaluation* of the primary experience, she elicited the secondary reaction of sadness.

MODULE 4: COGNITIVE FLEXIBILITY

Module 4 addressed the cognitive component of Lisa's pain and emotional experiences. First, Lisa's thoughts were described as "negative automatic thoughts," and she was asked to consider how her thoughts were subject to personal experience and emotional reactions. This notion was illustrated through the presentation of an ambiguous picture, where Lisa was asked to identify her negative automatic thought about what was happening in the picture, as well as several alternative interpretations. Lisa was given the picture from the UP Client Workbook of a person lying in a bed while others stood outside the door. She immediately became tearful and reported that her negative automatic thought was that the person was a young man near death, lying in a hospital bed. She identified that she first focused on the shape of the bed and mattress as a clue that it was a hospital bed, and the blank expression and closed eyes on the person's face indicated to her that he was dying or very sick. Her therapist then asked her for additional possible interpretations (even if she didn't necessarily believe these new interpretations). Lisa considered that the person could be lying in bed resting or taking a nap; she also suggested that the person may have fallen down on the bed. She and her therapist then discussed each interpretation as a function of what information she focused on to generate that appraisal.

Lisa's therapist also noted that Lisa had mentioned that she was feeling particularly sad and hopeless during this session, which may have had an influence on her appraisals. The idea of emotional experiences affecting subsequent appraisals was a very profound concept for her. She was able to connect her emotions of sadness, anxiety, and frustration to how she viewed daily experiences, which led to a continuous cycle of hopelessness. For the first time, Lisa was able to consider that her thoughts were just one of many ways of looking at a situation, and this realization engaged her in the treatment process in a new way.

At the next session, Lisa's therapist reviewed specific skills for responding to negative automatic thoughts, including identification of "thinking traps" (i.e., negative or unhelpful ways of thinking that are easy to get stuck in, such as "jumping to conclusions" or "thinking the worst") and cognitive reappraisal strategies (i.e., using evidence from past experience to consider whether automatic appraisals are likely or accurate, or whether she could cope with negative outcomes). Since the previous session, Lisa had seen how her thoughts were skewed and often led to behaviors of social withdrawal and isolation. Her therapist helped her begin to challenge these negative automatic thoughts in her daily life by gathering evidence based on Lisa's specific experience (i.e., how, even though she still had ongoing pain, her pain never remained at its highest level following a pain flare-up) *and* helped her to consider her ability to cope with the negative consequences or impact of pain (i.e., encouraging Lisa to consider how she would develop a meaningful life if she did become bedridden).

MODULE 5: COUNTERING EMOTIONAL BEHAVIORS
The concept of emotional behaviors proved difficult for Lisa to grasp initially. Her therapist first described various emotional avoidance strategies that may be contributing to Lisa's pain and anxiety, although Lisa was unable to clearly identify with any of these strategies aside from worry and rumination. However, when her therapist probed further, she discovered that she had a range of subtle behavioral avoidance strategies, including procrastination on tasks until she was in less pain, avoiding any physiological arousal (such as drinking caffeine or walking up several flights of stairs without stopping), and avoiding a television show that was about a group of students attending college. Lisa, however, was adamant that these strategies were useful and helpful in managing her emotions, and therefore were not avoidance.

Again, following the motivational enhancement strategy of rolling with resistance, Lisa's therapist encouraged her to notice how often she engaged in these and other strategies to manage her emotions and to simply note her reaction (without challenging Lisa on whether they were avoidance strategies). At the following session, Lisa noted that she was aware of her reactions and still believed that procrastination was ultimately not problematic for her and that she didn't mind avoiding physiological arousal or the one television show. Given Lisa's firm opinions about these behaviors, Lisa's therapist decided to move on to the next part of the module.

However, Lisa immediately connected with the examples of perfectionistic behavior (particularly when she was in school) and social withdrawal as examples of emotional behaviors related to anxiety. Even though withdrawal is often associated with depression, Lisa felt that this emotional behavior was a result of feeling "overwhelmed" and anxious. She also identified with hypervigilance, noting that she felt she was often "on guard" for something bad that might happen (physically or otherwise). Lisa and her therapist discussed how these emotional behaviors, despite providing momentary relief or a sense of preparedness or control, ultimately perpetuated the cycle of pain and anxiety by (a) preventing her from learning that she can tolerate physical sensations, anxiety, or both, and they will eventually diminish on their own; and (b) behaviorally reinforcing anxiety- or pain-related appraisals (e.g., "If I experience too much pain, I won't be able to tolerate it").

During the session, Lisa gave a recent example of having been invited to an outing with people from her high school, whom she had not seen since she graduated. She immediately felt anxious about experiencing pain and not being able to leave the situation easily, so she declined the invitation and stayed in bed at home. Engaging in the emotional behavior of withdrawing from the situation supported and strengthened her maladaptive evaluation of her pain and anxiety. She prevented herself from having the opportunity to tolerate the physical symptoms and seeing that she may be able to tolerate more than she first assumed. Lisa and her therapist discussed how these emotional behaviors had kept Lisa stuck by consistently reinforcing maladaptive appraisals of the impact of pain and anxiety.

When discussing countering emotional behaviors, Lisa became tearful and communicated that she was feeling very anxious about the prospect of being "forced" to go out when she was in pain. Her therapist reminded her that she would never be forced to do anything that she did not agree with, and also that the purpose of the upcoming sessions would be to challenge her. Lisa expressed being very worried that she would have to sign up for an art class or a college class before she was ready, which would lead to another severe "breakdown." Lisa's therapist used this as an opportunity to practice cognitive flexibility; acknowledging that Lisa's interpretation is a possibility, although not a likely outcome, and that it is based at least partly on how she was feeling at the present moment (anxious), and there may be other more likely and less catastrophic outcomes.

Next, Lisa's therapist returned to her Treatment Goals Form and Decisional Balance Worksheet for review. Lisa saw that she had listed the challenge of taking a class as a con of changing. Lisa's therapist reminded her that this was a predictable obstacle that was a natural part of the change process. She agreed to continue to move forward with the sessions and was informed that the following session would involve repeated, controlled exposure to uncomfortable physical sensations.

MODULE 6: UNDERSTANDING AND CONFRONTING PHYSICAL SENSATIONS

The first session of Module 6 was aimed to provoke strong physical and emotional responses. Lisa had previously expressed significant reservations about this session, and she ultimately cancelled it the day before. Lisa's therapist spoke to her on the phone extensively using the motivational enhancement strategies outlined in Module 1. She validated Lisa's fear and anxiety and encouraged her to come to session as soon as possible, even if she was not able to complete the scheduled exposures. Lisa agreed, and the missed session was rescheduled for the following day.

Lisa arrived to session appearing tearful and anxious. She reported she had not slept well, was experiencing more body pain, and was concerned that the exercises may make her "overreact" to the physical sensations. Lisa's therapist agreed that her reactions may be different from day to day, but it was still important to continue with the treatment as planned. Lisa hesitantly agreed to try the first exercise on the Physical Exercise Test Form, which involved hyperventilation. After her therapist demonstrated how to engage in hyperventilation, Lisa engaged in the exercise for 15 seconds before stopping. She rated her anxiety about the physical sensations at an 8 on a 0 (none) to 8 (severe) scale, noting she felt dizzy and lightheaded and was experiencing pain in her arms. She was encouraged to observe these sensations as she rested quietly for the next few moments. Her therapist also noted that she engaged in some avoidance by not breathing in and out very deeply during the exercise. Lisa agreed but stated that she was too fearful to fully bring on the sensations as directed.

The next exercise involved straw breathing, which Lisa was able to successfully complete for two minutes. She reported minimal anxiety (rated at a 2) and no physical sensations. Finally, Lisa was asked to run in place, which she agreed to do despite feeling significantly anxious about the exercise. She ran in place for 60 seconds and noted that she felt quite anxious about the pain that she was feeling in her legs and arms. However, she also felt very proud of herself, as she had not attempted running at all since she developed body pain. Lisa was amazed she was able to do the exercise for a full minute. Although she was reluctant, Lisa agreed to practice the hyperventilation exercise and running in place over the next week using the Physical Exercise Practice Form.

MODULE 7: EMOTION EXPOSURES

When Lisa returned to session to begin Module 7, she had not completed the physical exercises assigned from the previous module. Lisa and her therapist discussed the obstacles to completing these tasks, which were both external (i.e., lack of time on one particular day) and internal (i.e., anxiety about experiencing pain and general physical discomfort). Lisa's therapist encouraged her to conduct a mindful emotion awareness meditation and recall the feeling of anxiety, as well as pride and satisfaction she had felt during the last session, when she was able to run in place. Lisa's therapist guided her through the process of recalling running in place and asked her to notice her thoughts, feelings, and behaviors in the moment.

Following the exercise, Lisa acknowledged that she was able to connect with her previous emotions about running in place, although she was still experiencing many negative appraisals of what would happen as a result of completing the exercises. However, Lisa used cognitive flexibility skills without prompting and entertained the possibility that she could have another positive experience. Lisa and her therapist agreed that it would be useful to practice the same physical exercises again right away. This proved very beneficial for Lisa overall and was a significant turning point in her willingness to engage in the process of behavior change.

She ran in place for another full minute without stopping, and rated her anxiety about her painful sensations at a 4. Lisa was also willing to try hyperventilating again. This time, she was able to hyperventilate for 45 seconds and rated her anxiety about the sensations at a 6. Following this practice, she felt much more confident and agreed to try both exercises again for homework.

Lisa returned the following week having completed all the physical exercise practices. She stated that she was able to elicit strong sensations in her body but did not feel very anxious about them because they quickly went away. This gave her a greater sense of control over her body and, as a result, she was able to push herself to intensify the sensations. Lisa felt confident and "strong," and she was ready to experiment with additional exercises and situational exposures.

As described in the UP, the seventh module of the UP involves specifically designing and executing situational exposures that trigger uncomfortable emotions so behaviors that occur during the experience of emotion or pain (i.e., emotional behaviors such as escaping during the experience of fear or discomfort) can be modified, and emotional avoidance and safety behaviors are reduced or eliminated. In this module, triggers can vary from interoceptive (e.g., pain) to situational (e.g., in vivo), so that the therapist has flexibility to design effective emotion exposures.

Lisa and her therapist agreed to first focus on tasks and activities that Lisa was avoiding due to fear of pain. The session was spent exploring various physical activities and social activities that she potentially could engage in. She had recently been in touch with an old friend through Facebook, and Lisa agreed that a first emotion exposure practice would be to make plans to meet the friend for coffee. She felt that this would be manageable since it would be for a limited time and close to her home.

Over the next several sessions, Lisa engaged in a number of pain and emotion exposures that directly addressed her avoidance and emotional behaviors. For in-session exposures, Lisa watched an episode of the television show that she had avoided, she conducted an imaginal exposure to the memory of the morning that she woke up feeling pain all over her body (which she subsequently paired with hyperventilation exercises), and she sent out several text messages to friends whom she had been avoiding. For out-of-session practice, Lisa began walking around her block and eventually joined a yoga class, she scheduled several activities with close friends (including attending a party), and she contacted her college to determine what requirements she would need to fulfill to get her degree. She signed up for a local art class that met once per week.

Prior to the final session, Lisa actually registered for an online class that would complete one of her remaining degree requirements. Lisa had avoided this task for years, and she noted that she felt like a "weight had been lifted" when she ultimately completed it.

MODULE 8: RECOGNIZING ACCOMPLISHMENTS AND LOOKING TO THE FUTURE

The final module was Lisa's final treatment session and focused on reviewing her progress and anticipating future difficulties. At this session, Lisa's therapist highlighted Lisa's progress over the course of treatment. Although Lisa was still experiencing body pain, her overall functioning had improved and her pain anxiety and general anxiety and worry had decreased. Lisa and her therapist reviewed the most important skills learned, particularly the relevance and power of emotion awareness practice for focusing on how she felt when she did not avoid anxiety-provoking tasks. Lisa and her therapist discussed future obstacles (e.g., perfectionism) as she planned to continue taking classes to complete her degree. She connected this tendency to want things to be perfect with feeling "overwhelmed" and anxious, which typically led her to withdrawing from activities. Lisa and her therapist identified several warning signs that this pattern could be happening and the skills that Lisa could use to counteract the cycle. Overall, Lisa expressed a great satisfaction with her treatment outcome and the benefits that she had received with regard to pain, functioning, and anxiety.

Treatment Outcome

Lisa's pretreatment and posttreatment outcome measures are represented in Figure 13.1. At the beginning of treatment, Lisa's self-report measures demonstrated a significant degree of pain, anxiety, negative affect, and pain-specific anxiety. She reported her pain level at an 85 out of 100 on the NRS. On the BSI-18, she obtained a raw score of 13 on the Anxiety subscale (T score = 67, female oncology norms) and a raw score of 9 on the Depression subscale (T score = 65, female oncology norms) (Derogatis, 2001). Lisa's Anxiety subscale was consistent with her self-reported significant anxiety and worry, although her Depression subscale was higher than expected, given that she did not endorse clinical symptoms of depression. On the PANAS, Lisa scored 18 on the Positive Affect subscale and 28 on the Negative Affect subscale, suggesting minimal positive affect and significant levels of negative affect. She also scored 83 out of a possible 100 points on the PASS-20, indicating severe anxiety about the experience and implications of pain.

At posttreatment, Lisa made significant improvement on a number of the measures. Interestingly, she rated her average pain as 60 on the NRS, suggesting

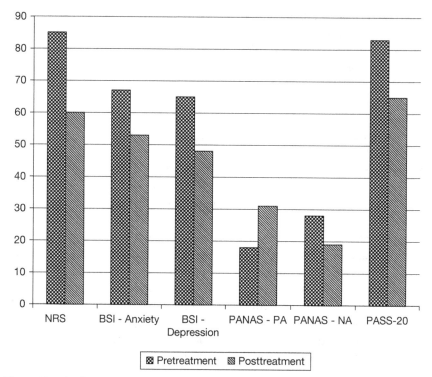

Figure 13.1 Lisa's pretreatment and posttreatment scores on relevant self-report measures.
NOTES: NRS = Numeric Rating Scale; BSI = Brief Symptom Inventory; PANAS = Positive and Negative Affect Scale; PA = positive affect; NA = negative affect; PASS-20 = Pain Anxiety Symptom Scale—20-Item Version

that she was still experiencing more than moderate pain, despite improvement compared to her pretreatment level. The Anxiety and Depression subscale scores of the BSI-18 improved dramatically (Anxiety subscale raw score = 4, T score = 53; Depression subscale raw score = 2, T score = 48). She also scored 31 on the Positive Affect subscale and 19 on the Negative Affect subscale of the PANAS, which approximate community norms for women (Crawford & Henry, 2004). Lisa still evidenced notable pain anxiety, with a posttreatment score of 65 on the PASS-20, although this measure also showed some improvement from pretreatment.

CONCLUSIONS

Overall, Lisa demonstrated an excellent response to treatment. At the first treatment session, she indicated high levels of impairment in social, occupational, and personal functioning as a result of pain and anxiety. She initially struggled to connect to the treatment principles, although the motivational enhancement skills of rolling with resistance (i.e., not challenging Lisa directly about her reluctance), developing discrepancy (i.e., by identifying and clarifying her goals for treatment, as well as potential obstacles), and supporting self-efficacy (i.e., allowing her to make clear choices about which steps she wanted to take in treatment) were very beneficial in allowing her to engage with the various interventions.

Mindful emotion awareness meditations proved useful during the initial process of designing and executing exposures, as Lisa was able to disengage from worry enough to experience positive emotions as a result of her work. Although she initially did not find cognitive flexibility strategies helpful, she was able to use them to motivate her to engage in exposures. The physical exercise tests and practices resulted in substantial changes in her approach to the therapy, as they allowed her to develop some confidence and momentum in the treatment.

She still struggled with occasional avoidance and notable levels of pain; however, she was able to recognize these patterns much more clearly and quickly, which allowed her to utilize some of her new skills. Although she maintained perfectionistic behaviors, she also (a) became aware that these responses were developed as a way of avoiding anxiety and (b) understood that they made it easier for her to fall back into old patterns of avoidance. At the conclusion of treatment, Lisa reported significantly less functional impairment, anxiety, and pain-related anxiety, although she still noted relatively significant levels of pain in her body.

An emotion regulation–based treatment approach targeting neuroticism/negative affect represents a new and potentially more comprehensive treatment approach to improving pain, disability, and emotional disorders in adults with chronic pain. The treatment described here incorporated specific emotion regulation skills that aimed to reduce the *affective* component of pain in Lisa, as well as cooccurring anxiety symptoms through psychoeducation, emotional awareness, cognitive flexibility, countering emotional behaviors, and engaging in pain-related and emotional situations to practice her newly learned skills.

Although the UP has not yet been tested in a larger sample of adult chronic pain patients, data from a pilot study (Allen, Tsao, & Zeltzer, 2009) and case examples (Allen, Tsao, Seidman, Ehrenreich-May, & Zeltzer, 2012; Payne, Tsao, & Zeltzer, 2014) suggest that the UP treatment approach may jointly target pain and anxiety/depression in adolescents with chronic pain conditions. This, along with the case presentation of Lisa, certainly suggests that a transdiagnostic treatment formulation and approach may work well for the population of individuals struggling with chronic pain and related conditions.

There may be several potential mechanisms by which the UP is able to address a broad range of emotional and physical symptoms. It is possible that the strategies used target common, underlying processes contributing to both pain and emotional dysfunction. Another possibility is that teaching a core set of skills allows a client to apply those skills to each disorder individually. However, regardless of the mechanism, the evidence to date suggests that broadening the scope of applicability of emotion regulation skills and CBT strategies may be both feasible and helpful for individuals with complex medical and psychological conditions. Future research should further explore the utility of transdiagnostic approaches to various pain conditions, as well as the applicability of the UP to adults with diverse pain, emotional disorders, and other chronic health conditions.

14

The Unified Protocol for Complex, Highly Comorbid Cases

HEATHER MURRAY LATIN AND CLAIR CASSIELLO-ROBBINS ∎

INTRODUCTION

The presence of extensive comorbidity among emotional disorders (i.e., mood, anxiety, posttraumatic, and obsessive-compulsive disorders) is well established (e.g., Kessler, Chiu, Demler, & Wlater, 2005). In one study, 57% of patients who met criteria for an anxiety or mood disorder met criteria for at least one additional mood or anxiety disorder (Brown, Campbell, Lehman, Grisham, & Mancill, 2001). In another study, over 90% of patients with posttraumatic stress disorder (PTSD) met criteria for an additional diagnosis (Gallagher & Brown, 2015). Further, there is also a high degree of comorbidity between emotional disorders and nonemotional disorders. For example, in a study of older adults with attention deficit hyperactivity disorder (ADHD), about 50% of the subjects also had a comorbid anxiety, a depressive disorder, or both (Michielsen et al., 2013).

Comorbidities often present challenges in clinical work. The presence of comorbid diagnoses is associated with greater symptom severity (Allen et al., 2010). Although comorbid diagnoses experienced in patients receiving cognitive-behavioral therapy (CBT) for panic disorder did not have detrimental effects on outcomes of panic disorder at 6-month follow-up assessment (Tsao, Mystkowski, Zucker, & Craske, 2002), this trend may not persist in the long term. In one study of CBT for panic disorder, patients with comorbid diagnoses experienced a decline in comorbidity at posttreatment but experienced an increase in comorbidity at 24-month follow-up, suggesting that treatment did not reduce their comorbidity in the long term. Patients with comorbid diagnoses were also more likely to seek additional treatment over the follow-up period than those without. Taken together, these results suggest that the treatment focused solely on one disorder (in this case, panic disorder) might not sustainably reduce interference caused by other disorders (Brown, Antony, & Barlow, 1995). An evidence-based protocol equipped to treat comorbidity may parsimoniously address these conflicting findings by providing an efficient method for treating multiple diagnoses, should they be adversely affecting an individual's treatment.

Efforts to disseminate evidence-based psychological treatments are often met with resistance, and one of the most common challenges to these dissemination efforts is the pervasive idea that these protocols are not equipped to handle this aforementioned comorbidity. A common criticism is that samples included in treatment studies tend to be highly selective; these studies often exclude patients with extensive comorbidity, particularly comorbid psychotic disorders or suicidality (Gunter & Whittal, 2010).

The Unified Protocol for Transdiagnostic Treatment of Emotional Disorders (UP; Barlow et al., 2018) is uniquely suited to target this barrier because it was specifically designed to address the comorbidity often seen in community settings. As discussed in Chapter 1, the UP was designed to address common mechanisms that underlie emotional disorders (i.e., strong experience of negative emotions, aversive reaction to the experience of negative emotion, and efforts to suppress or avoid negative emotions), instead of focusing on surface-level differences between diagnoses (Barlow, Bullis, Comer, & Ametaj, 2013). Thus, the UP may be the ideal protocol to treat patients who present with multiple comorbid diagnoses.

Further, targeting comorbidities simultaneously in this manner may result in more efficient treatment. In an effort to battle the perception that evidence-based protocols are useful for only a select group of patients, our research efforts have sought to include patients with a variety of comorbidities in order to fully examine the efficacy of this mechanism-based protocol (Barlow et al., in press); Ellard, Fairholme, Boisseau, Farchione, & Barlow, 2010; Farchione et al., 2012). One such case is described in this chapter.

CASE PRESENTATION

Joe, a 22-year-old, single, non-Hispanic Caucasian male, was referred to our center by his psychiatrist. He completed a diagnostic evaluation at the Center for Anxiety and Related Disorders (CARD), which entailed the administration of the Anxiety Disorders Interview Schedule for DSM-5 (ADIS-5; Brown & Barlow, 2014), a semistructured clinical interview that focuses on the diagnosis of anxiety disorders and their accompanying mood states. On the basis of the information obtained during the assessment, a principal diagnosis of panic disorder (DSM-5, 300.01) was assigned. Additional diagnoses of agoraphobia (DSM-5, 300.22), generalized anxiety disorder (GAD; DSM-5, 300.02), obsessive-compulsive disorder (OCD; DSM-5, 300.3), major depressive disorder (MDD), and single-episode, mild (DSM-5, 296.21), and other specified ADHDs (DSM-5, 314.01) were also assigned. At the time of the evaluation, Joe was taking a therapeutic dose of a stimulant for his ADHD symptoms and a selective serotonin reuptake inhibitor (SSRI) for his anxiety and mood symptoms.

Conceptualization of Joe's Case

As discussed in Chapters 1 and 2, the diagnostic evaluation provides useful categorical information. The diagnostic labels efficiently communicate Joe's experiences with anxiety and depression. When conceptualizing symptoms of emotional disorders using a transdiagnostic approach, focusing on the similarities of experiencing intense emotions and identifying maladaptive reactions and efforts to control emotions provide a framework to better understand the development and maintenance of a range of cooccurring mental health disorders. As outlined in the Case Conceptualization Chapter, emotional disorders stem from an aversive reaction and effort to change or control negative emotions. See Figure 14.1 for the Functional Model of Emotional Disorders as it applies to Joe.

When conceptualizing Joe's case using this model, one sees that Joe clearly experiences frequent and intense negative emotions and responds to his negative emotional experiences by attempting to change or control them because he perceives them as intolerable or unacceptable. While these attempts may have resulted in short-term relief, they also maintained his symptoms in the long term. Moreover, Joe's judgment of his emotions and inability to control his negative emotional experiences in turn increase the intensity and frequency of these experiences.

Joe demonstrated many strengths. He was very intelligent and intellectually curious, highly motivated to change and willing to try treatment recommendations, and was surrounded by a good support system comprised of family, friends, and other providers. A few barriers arose during the course of treatment, however. First, the severity of Joe's symptoms and his degree of avoidance interfered with session attendance. At the beginning of the treatment, Joe would often cancel at the last minute due to heightened anxiety about driving in to the center. In addition, his need to "feel right" before leaving his house often resulted in him arriving to session 20–30 minutes late. Joe also exhibited difficulties with organization and planning, likely due to his ADHD and significant sleep deprivation. These symptoms interfered with his treatment, as he would forget about scheduled appointments, attend appointments at a time other than the scheduled time, and forget to complete homework assignments or to bring the homework assignments to session.

The presence of ADHD symptoms represented a unique challenge in this case, as ADHD is not traditionally considered an emotional disorder. However, the ADHD symptoms interacted with Joe's emotional disorder symptoms, and parts of his ADHD presentation were consistent with the aforementioned model of emotional disorders. For example, if Joe was experiencing symptoms of ADHD, he would often become frustrated (negative affect) and experience this emotion as intolerable, leading to him avoiding his schoolwork if he wasn't "in the

Avoidance	Subtle Behavioral Avoidance	Cognitive Avoidance	Safety Signals	Emotion-Driven Behaviors
Crowded places	Sitting near exits	Planning exit strategy (from party)	Going places with sister	Leave a situation early
Driving	Cleaning room	Asking for details of event or plan	Carrying medication	Berate self
Barbers	Playing with puppy	Using cell phone for distraction	Carrying hand sanitizer	Washing hands
Not touching "contaminated" things	Opening door with elbow	Excessive worry		
Declining invitations for plans with friends	Backing up files multiple times	Not committing to plans in advance		
	Participating in low-key activities with friends	Ruminating on experiences that haven't gone well		

Figure 14.1 Functional model of emotional disorders applied to Joe's case.

correct mindset" (efforts to suppress or avoid), but then he would feel guilty for not completing his work (efforts to suppress fail). So while Joe could have benefited from traditional treatments for ADHD (such as task prioritization, problem-solving skills, medication compliance, and time-management skills) his emotional response to his symptoms of ADHD fit into the model of emotional disorders and served as appropriate treatment targets within this transdiagnostic framework.

Transdiagnostic Treatment as Applied to Joe

Joe underwent 12 sessions of the UP as part of a large treatment study, and the following section describes the application of the UP treatment strategies to his case. To illustrate the delivery of concepts included in the UP treatment program, patient worksheets, therapist-patient dialogue, and exercises completed have been included.

The first session with Joe focused on gaining a better understanding of his experiences with specific symptoms and how these symptoms affected his life. In addition, an overview of the core treatment skills and the application of these skills to Joe's specific emotional experiences were discussed. Joe understood the treatment components and rationale for the components, including the exposure modules. He also understood that the goal of the treatment was not to eliminate unpleasant emotions, but rather to better understand his emotional experiences and learn to respond to the emotions in a functional and adaptive way. The importance of intersession practice, to reinforce the learning that has occurred within the session, was emphasized. Joe agreed that applying the skills to his "real" life would increase the benefits of treatment.

MODULE 1: SETTING GOALS AND MAINTAINING MOTIVATION

In the next session, as with every session hereafter, Joe completed the Overall Depression Severity and Interference Scale (ODSIS) and Overall Anxiety Symptoms and Interference Scale (OASIS) at the outset. Joe's scores on the ODSIS and OASIS across the treatment program can be seen in Figure 14.2. This next session covered content from Module 1, which includes an explicit discussion of the pros and cons of changing and staying the same, as well as the development of specific treatment goals to target a patient's belief in his own ability to change. Joe was able to identify external factors that affected his motivation. He noted that his motivation significantly declines (which led to procrastination or avoidance) when he feels tired, has difficulty concentrating, notices increased anxiety, and when "things aren't right" or he doesn't feel fully prepared. We agreed that keeping track of these identified factors and the potential impact on motivation for treatment would be a good idea.

Next, Joe explored the cost and benefits of changing and staying the same by completing the Decisional Balance Worksheet. The benefits of changing were related to changing his response to emotional experiences associated with the symptoms

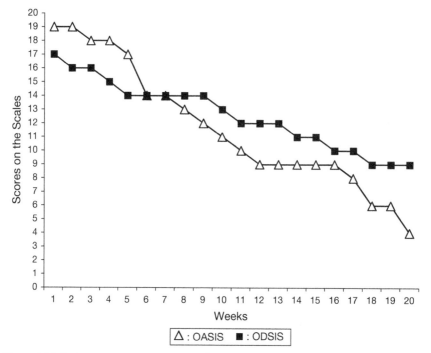

Figure 14.2 Joe's treatment progress record.

of his psychological disorders. More specifically, these benefits included being able to attend class, submitting assignments, socializing with friends regardless of the context, going to crowded places, increasing his efficiency (i.e., by decreasing his checking behaviors and procrastination), and becoming more independent.

Joe had difficulty identifying costs related to changing, as he had primarily considered only the benefits of the treatment program prior to the session. With assistance, he was able to recognize that time requirements related to attending sessions and completing homework assignments was a cost of this type of treatment. Joe also acknowledged that this type of treatment required feeling distress, in the service of learning how to better cope with that distress, although Joe was insistent that he was willing and motivated to do this. At the end of the exercise, Joe was clearly motivated for the treatment program, as his benefits of change outweighed the costs.

Next, the rationale for setting realistic treatment goals, with specific steps to reach each goal, was reviewed. During session, Joe generated several treatment goals, including:

- Not to let fear of a panic attack prevent me from participating in the things I want to do (i.e., getting a haircut, going to the dentist, baseball game, family functions, class, etc.)
- To complete a class
- Learn to let go of worrying about the minutia and not let the worry interfere with my productivity.

Module 2: Understanding Emotions

Module 2 consisted of one session, which focused on psychoeducation and tracking emotional experiences. Joe was 15 minutes late for this session. Given Joe's absence the previous session and tardiness for this session, some time in session was devoted to discussing the importance of attendance and identifying barriers to attending sessions on time. Joe was able to recognize that difficulty with time management and worry about having a panic attack while driving contributed to his absence and tardiness. He agreed to recruit a family member to drive him to the center for his appointments. The between-session assignments were reviewed. Joe completed the reading assignments and clearly grasped the concepts discussed.

The majority of the module focused on discussing the functional nature of emotional experiences and learning to monitor emotional experiences. In discussing the adaptive function of emotions, Joe was able to recognize that the range of emotional experiences served to alert him to important internal and external events or situations. These emotions motivated him to respond; the concept of emotion-driven behaviors (EDBs) was reviewed.

The ARC of emotional experiences was then introduced, highlighting that emotions are not coming out of the blue, albeit it sometimes feels like it; rather, emotions are triggered by events, situations, or sensations referred to as *antecedents*. Next, the response to the trigger was discussed and broken into the three-component model: thoughts, feelings, and behaviors. Finally, the short- and long-term consequences of typical responses were reviewed, highlighting that most often, our responses result in a positive short-term consequence (i.e., relief), though paradoxically they also contribute to negative long-term consequences (i.e., maintaining fear). Joe was able to apply the ARC worksheet to a recent emotional experience, as illustrated in the following conversation between the therapist and Joe.

Joe identified the antecedent as attending an upcoming Red Sox game, for which his dad had bought tickets for him and his family. He noted that he was not able to attend a previous game for which he had tickets because of significant anticipatory anxiety about having a panic attack at the ballpark:

> THERAPIST: *Now that you've identified the antecedent, let's think about your emotional response using the ARC. What are some thoughts that you are having about going to the game?*
>
> JOE: *Well, I'm worried that the same thing will happen this time; that I won't be able to go to the game. I really feel like I should be able to go, though if I can't control myself, I won't be able to go and it's Father's day.*
>
> THERAPIST: *OK, good. It seems like you are having a lot of thoughts in the form of predictions about what is going to happen on game day. And what would happen if your predictions were to come true?*
>
> JOE: *I'll disappoint my dad and my whole family.*
>
> THERAPIST: *It sounds like you are having some thoughts that if you are feeling too anxious and I can't go, you'll be a disappointment to your family*

JOE: *Not only that, but not being able to go will mean that there is something really wrong with me, and they will feel guilty.*

THERAPIST: *Just to clarify, your prediction is that you won't be able to go to the game and your family will feel guilty.*

JOE: *Yah.*

THERAPIST: *When you have this prediction, what physical sensations do you notice right now?*

JOE: *I'm feeling anxious, guilty, also frustrated.*

THERAPIST: *OK, and when you notice these emotions, what sensations do you feel?*

JOE: *I don't know . . . I guess I feel tense, kind of revved up.*

THERAPIST: *When you notice these thoughts and feelings, what type of things are you doing to feel better?*

JOE: *Generally speaking, I try not to think about it . . .*

THERAPIST: *Ah—sounds like distraction.*

JOE: *Yah, though thinking about things now makes me feel a little bit better.*

THERAPIST: *Now that you've been able to identify your response to this trigger, does it make sense that you are feeling these emotions, given your negative predictions?*

JOE: *Yes.*

THERAPIST: *Even though it makes sense that you may have this response, given your previous experiences going to a Red Sox game, let's thinking about the short- and long-term consequences of your response to this trigger.*

JOE: *OK.*

THERAPIST: *What is the short-term consequence of your predictions, physical sensations, and behaviors? Particularly, the thoughts that "I'll disappoint my family" or "There is something wrong with me" and the physical sensations of tension and your attempts to distract yourself to feel better?*

JOE: *I'm not sure?*

THERAPIST: *Let's think about your behavioral response. Why do you think that you want to distract yourself?*

JOE: *I think that I'll get a break from the anxiety, though it doesn't actually work that way.*

THERAPIST: *Right, so in the short term, you are responding this way to try to find some relief, though this strategy doesn't work that well for you. What about the long-term consequences of this response?*

JOE: *Typically, I just feel worse.*

Applying the ARC of emotions to experiences of anxiety is an ideal opportunity to distinguish the differences between thoughts, physical sensations, and behaviors in effort to make emotional experiences less overwhelming. As illustrated in this conversation, Joe was interchanging emotional feelings with physical feelings. The ARC is also a great tool to provide clarification of the role that thoughts, physical sensations, and behaviors play in the overall emotional experience, as well as the bidirectional relationship between these three components.

If time had permitted, a discussion of the short- and long-term consequences of Joe's predictions would have been useful to illustrate reasons why these thoughts are reinforced. Before ending the session, a discussion regarding the lasting impact of learned experiences ensued in order to illustrate how various behaviors are maintained over time, even though they produce substantial interference and distress (e.g., compulsions).

MODULE 3: MINDFUL EMOTION AWARENESS

At this session, Joe reported a slight reduction in his anxiety symptoms and a slight increase in his mood symptoms. The session started with reviewing his experience completing his between-session monitoring. As Joe described his difficulties starting the homework assignment, it became clear that his distress related to "needing things to feel just right" before being able to start a project was keeping him from completing the assignments. Joe eventually was able to apply the three-component model to this emotional experience. He was able to identify thoughts that included, "I don't feel ready to complete the assignment," "I need to find the right place for things before I can start working on this," "I can't do anything until things are in place," and "I can't start until my working space is right." Joe also noted physical feelings of a headache and shortness of breath.

Joe's behaviors included spending time cleaning and organizing his workspace (including resaving documents on his computer) and making lists of things that he had to do before starting the monitoring assignment. He was able to recognize that the compulsive behavior to organize his working space before starting the task only led to increased distress and more work for himself. He was also able to recognize that being easily distracted from his task of cleaning his workspace resulted in organizing taking up quite a bit of time. With some distance from the experience, Joe noted that he was "making prework for [himself] before [he] could begin working on the task." He also noted that taking his ADHD medication helped with his ability to stay on task. Joe was encouraged to continue to monitor his emotional experiences to better understand his triggers and responses.

When asked how the Red Sox game went, Joe nonchalantly reported that it "went well." He noted mild anticipatory anxiety the day of the game, though he said that once his dad informed him of the detailed plan of getting to the game, he felt relieved, saying, "If I don't know the details, I won't know how to get out of the situation." The baseball game had a rain delay, and Joe attributed his ability to get through the day partly to the delayed start. Joe's attribution provided an opportunity to discuss locus of control and, in particular, how misattributing success to external circumstances (i.e., luck, other people, medication) maintains anxiety instead of providing corrective feedback that he was able to handle the situation because of his internal ability to cope.

The remaining time of the session was dedicated to introducing and practicing mindful emotion awareness. Joe recognized that his judgment of his primary emotional experiences led to more complex secondary emotional experiences. He discussed the example of completing his homework assignment and stated that when noticing that he was distracted, he judged himself for not being able to stay focused. This judgment led to frustration, and he took the experience as confirmation that there was something wrong with him. He noted that in general, he interprets and judges his intense emotional experiences—whether they be panic, worry, disgust, or shame—to mean that there is something "wrong" with him.

An in-session emotional awareness exercise was conducted. Joe was encouraged to bring curiosity to, and reserve judgment of, his experiences as they occurred during the exercise. Joe was also instructed to practice taking note of when his mind wandered, and to deliberately bring his attention back to his experiences in the present moment. After the emotional awareness exercise was completed, the experience was debriefed.

MODULE 4: COGNITIVE FLEXIBILITY

Joe arrived to his next session late and was clearly anxious about his tardiness, apologizing profusely. He reported elevated symptoms of both anxiety and depression on the OASIS and OADIS. He discussed recent experiences that contributed to his elevated symptoms, including avoiding a friend's large Fourth of July party and avoiding a last-minute party hosted by a good friend with professional athletes in the area.

In talking about these experiences, Joe was able to recognize the relationship between attempting to avoid his emotional distress (by not attending the parties) and his hopes of feeling better, though ultimately he felt worse about himself. He stated, "I felt a sense of responsibility to attend my friend's party, and since I didn't go, I know that I let my friend down." In addition to feeling bad about not attending the parties, Joe noted that since then, his "background anxiety was raised a little bit and that [he] was having a hard time rebounding from these kinds of things," resulting in additional avoidance—namely, missing the first few classes of summer term.

Joe also expressed hesitation to use strategies from previous modules (particularly the ARC) to these situations because "I didn't want to think about it and make myself feel worse." A discussion of the short- and long-term consequences of Joe's attempts to avoid feeling anxious and depressed led to increased willingness to approach his distress in the moment by agreeing to complete the ARC for one of the experiences together in session. After completing the ARC, Joe reported feeling better and agreed to record and dismantle upcoming emotional experiences using it.

The remaining time of the session was devoted to content included in Module 4. "Cognitive Appraisal Exercise #1: Making Meaning" was completed in session to illustrate the tendency to rely on initial interpretations or appraisals of situations, though with increased cognitive flexibility, a number of different interpretations of the same situation are possible. When asked for his snapshot interpretation of an ambiguous picture of a person lying in bed in a hospital room (Figure 8.1 in the workbook), Joe responded, "Someone is receiving some medical care and these people are comforting each other." He identified several factors that led to this initial negative automatic thought, including his sister's obsession with watching the TV show *Grey's Anatomy* "priming me to think that there is a medical story with a tragedy." Joe also reported that his own experiences in hospitals visiting sick people contributed to this automatic appraisal.

Then Joe was asked to generate alternative interpretations about what the picture might mean. He came up with several, including "The person in the hospital bed has died, and the two people walking down the hallway embracing each other don't know the person in the hospital room," "One of the people in the hallway started to fall and was caught by the other person in the hallway," and "The people in the hallway are whispering to each other about the person in bed—how lazy she is." It was noted that all these interpretations were negative; Joe was encouraged to consider some positive alternative interpretations. Joe recognized that it was possible that the woman in the hospital room could have just had a baby, and her husband and mother were hugging. He was able to appreciate how these different appraisals led to very different emotional experiences.

A discussion of common thinking traps and questions to ask to counter those traps ensued. Applying the cognitive reappraisal skills to Joe's recent experience avoiding the Fourth of July party with his friends was completed in session. Joe's homework, completing the Identifying and Evaluating Automatic Appraisals worksheet was reviewed in session as well. Figure 14.3 illustrates his initial attempts to complete the worksheet and also indicates corrective feedback (italicized) provided during the session. In subsequent sessions, content from Module 4 was reviewed and practiced.

Module 5: Countering Emotional Behaviors

Joe's OASIS and ODSIS scores continued to be elevated. In addition, he reported difficulty sleeping, increased procrastination about sending emails to professors and the dean, difficulty recording and completing between-session assignments, and difficulty with medication compliance.

Given previous discussions highlighting the long-term consequences of avoidance strategies, Joe clearly understood the paradoxical effects of emotion avoidance. For him, his avoidance strategies often made him feel worse about himself, including increased guilt, frustration, and sadness, and they also maintained his anxiety and beliefs that he couldn't handle his triggers and difficult situations.

The different types of emotion avoidance were discussed, and Joe was able to identify several of the avoidance strategies that he used for a variety of emotional experiences. See Table 14.1 for examples of Joe's subtle behavioral avoidance, cognitive avoidance strategies, and use of safety signals. He was also insightful when identifying his maladaptive EDBs. Together, alternative action tendencies were identified for a variety of his common EDBs. For homework, Joe was encouraged to practice engaging in behaviors that were counter to his typical EDBs.

Module 6: Understanding and Confronting Physical Sensations

The next session focused on understanding physical sensations and the role of physical sensations in emotional experiences. Joe's OASIS score continued to be

SITUATION / TRIGGER	AUTOMATIC APPRAISAL(s)	IS THIS A THINKING TRAP?	ALTERNATIVE APPRAISAL(s)
Anxiety about going to dinner with friends	If this treatment doesn't work, I'll be stuck in a state of paralysis indefinitely	Yes	This treatment will probably work This treatment has already helped and if I keep doing what I do, it will continue to help
Anxiety about going to dinner	What if I panic at the restaurant with my friends? **If I go to the restaurant with my friends, I'll panic**	Yes	I've been able to handle panic attacks in the past, I can handle them at a restaurant with friends
Responding to emails	Since I haven't responded to my professors, I can't move forward with my other emails	Yes	It's okay if I respond emails but of order
Taking medication	If I eat now to take my medication, I won't be able to eat lunch with my friends	Yes	It's okay if I don't eat with gusto!
Responding to emails	When people are nice + understanding of m anxiety, it makes it worse if I can't email them **Because people are nice and understanding of my anxiety they deserve more from me**	Yes	People that are understanding recognize that these are challenging for me. I'll try my best regardless

Figure 14.3 Joe's initial attempts to complete the worksheet are written in regular type, and corrective feedback from the therapist is written in bold.

Table 14.1. JOE'S IDENTIFYING AND CHANGING EDBs WORKSHEET

Overt Avoidance	Subtle Behavioral Avoidance	Cognitive Avoidance	Safety Signals
Crowded places	Sitting near exits	Planning exit strategy (from party)	Going places with sister
Driving	Cleaning room	Asking for details of event or plan	Carrying medication
Barbers	Playing with puppy	Using cell phone for distraction	Carrying hand sanitizer
Not touching "contaminated" things	Opening door with elbow	Excessive worry	
Declining invitations for plans with friends	Backing up files multiple times	Not committing to plans in advance	
	Participating in low-key activities with friends	Ruminating on experiences that haven't gone well	

elevated, though his ODSIS score dropped significantly. The majority of the session focused on a discussion of the role of internal sensations in emotional experiences and completing symptom induction tests to identify exercises that elicited sensations most similar to sensations experienced during intense emotional responses.

Given Joe's experience with panic attacks, he demonstrated an acute awareness of his internal sensations when experiencing the emotions of anxiety and fear. Also, given previous conversations about the three-component model, Joe was familiar with how his hypervigilance about physical sensations and misinterpretations of his physical sensations (i.e., "I'm going to pass out") contributed to the emotional experience of anxiety and panic. To regulate his physical sensations, he developed a variety of avoidance behaviors and EDBs, including avoiding situations, lying down, and sitting near the exit in class.

With regard to other emotional experiences that Joe encountered frequently, it was more challenging to identify the physical sensations associated with the emotion, as well as his interpretation or behavioral response. By reviewing the three-component model, the role of the physical sensation in the emotional experience became clearer. For example, with regard to Joe's ADHD symptoms, he noticed the emotion of frustration when he had difficulty concentrating, which was associated with physical feelings such as forehead tension and jitteriness. His interpretation of the sensations was something along the lines of "I won't be able to get anything done in this state of mind," leading to procrastination of the task or disengaging from it altogether. With regard to depression, Joe noted often feeling tired and weighed down, which decreased his motivation to complete necessary tasks.

Joe clearly understood how his attempts to avoid or alter his physical sensations backfired, actually intensifying his emotional experiences, and therefore he grasped the concept of increasing his tolerance to the physical sensations that he associated with intense emotional experiences. Joe was instructed to approach and allow himself to fully feel his physical sensations during the exercises and note any attempts to control or decrease physical sensations. He denied having any medical conditions that may interfere with the completion of the symptom induction tests.

Joe had reported feeling palpitations, sweating, trembling, shortness of breath, chest discomfort, stomach distress, depersonalization, and fear of going crazy or dying during a panic episode. The initial symptom induction tests targeted these sensations. Surprisingly, Joe reported low levels of intensity, distress, and similarity to his naturally occurring symptoms when completing the hyperventilating exercise and the straw breathing exercise. When talking through his symptoms, Joe reported that the smothering sensations were most distressing during a panic episode.

Next, he tried an exercise to induce these sensations. Lying on the floor of the office, he placed a few textbooks on his chest. He reported feeling the following sensations: pressure on his chest, difficulty breathing, increased heart rate, and pronounced rapid breathing. He rated the intensity of the sensations to be a 6 (out of 8), the level of distress caused by the sensations to be an 8, as well as the degree of similarity of these sensation to his naturally occurring symptoms. To elicit the depersonalization sensations, Joe stared at this hand (placed a few inches from his head) for about two minutes. He rated the sensation of feeling detached from himself as somewhat intense, distressing, and similar to his emotion of panic.

For homework, Joe was instructed to continue to complete symptom induction exercises to identify sensations that were similar to sensations noticed during a variety of emotional experiences. Joe agreed to try drinking larger quantities of caffeine to induce sensations associated with his ADHD and related emotional experiences. He also agreed to wear wrist weights to induce physical sensations associated with feeling depressed (i.e., heaviness). In addition to completing a variety of symptom induction tests, Joe agreed to repeatedly engage in the physical sensation exercises that elicited sensations similar to his panic (i.e., putting textbooks on his chest, hand staring) and record his experiences using the Symptom Induction Practice form.

Upon reviewing his practice tolerating the physical sensation, Joe noted that his tolerance to these sensations translated into feeling more comfortable in situations when there sensations came up organically. Joe discussed attending a friend's birthday party at a crowded bar. Joe reported that he noticed the sensations associated with anticipatory anxiety before heading to the party, though he was able to tolerate them in a different sort of way than before. He went to the party and reported having a good time. He noted that he learned several things during this experience:

- He could tolerate the sensations of anxiety.
- The sensations of anticipatory anxiety did not predict his future emotional experience (i.e., he didn't have a panic attack at the party).
- He could experience a range of emotions, including feeling anxious and enjoyment, at the same time.

MODULE 7: EMOTION EXPOSURES

The next several sessions focused on reviewing the application of strategies and completing emotional exposures. During this time, Joe reported the greatest reduction in anxiety and mood symptoms, as indicated on the OASIS and ODSIS. This improvement was likely due to learning how to flexibly apply the strategies of mindfulness and cognitive reappraisal when encountering intense emotional experiences related to his panic disorder, agoraphobia, OCD, GAD, MDD, and ADHD.

Joe demonstrated an understanding of the rationale for confronting specific situations, images, activities, and sensations that produced strong emotional reactions. Prior to starting this section of treatment, Joe had been systematically approaching difficult situations (i.e., attending class, social activities, etc.) and reported successfully tolerating the intense emotional experience, often learning that the perceived consequence did not come true.

In session, Joe developed an emotional and situational avoidance hierarchy. As can be seen in Figure 14.4, the emotional experiences included on this hierarchy reflect distress as it related to Joe's panic disorder, agoraphobia, OCD, GAD, MDD, and ADHD, with some exposures representing distress associated with more than one disorder. When reviewing his hierarchy, the role of neuroticism across the emotional and situational experiences was profound.

Based on Joe's emotional and situational avoidance hierarchy, several exposures were chosen to complete in session. The following dialogue between the patient and therapist is derived from a session identifying and completing an emotion exposure:

THERAPIST: *Today, we are going to spend time completing an exposure task. We've discussed potential exposures targeting your anxiety about feeling contaminated. What do you think would be a good exposure to focus on today?*

JOE: *I'm OK if my hands get oily when working on my bike, though if my hands are oily, I can't touch anything else. For example, I can't touch my phone until several hand washes after working on my bike.*

THERAPIST: *OK, how about practicing touching [an] oily substance and sitting with the emotional discomfort?*

JOE: *OK.*

Do Not Avoid	Hesitate To Enter But Rarely Avoid	Sometimes Avoid	Usually Avoid	Always Avoid
0		**5**		**10**
No Distress	Slight Distress	Definite Distress	Strong Distress	Extreme Distress

	Description	Avoid	Distress
1 **WORST**	Submitting homework assignment on time regardless of quality of work (i.e meeting perfectionist standards)	7	9
2	Attending events with crowds	7	7
3	Responding to emails within 24hrs (without rewriting or double checking)	6	6
4	Writing assignments in one document (without backing up files)	6	6
5	Approaching tasks regardless of ability to concentrate	6	6
6	Touching "contaminated" surfaces without washing hands	5	6
7	Making plans in advance with friends	4	4
8			

Figure 14.4 Joe's Emotion Exposure Hierarchy.

THERAPIST: *Great. I happened to have Indian food for lunch. How about touching the chicken tikka masala sauce and practicing responding differently to the sensations and emotions, without engaging in the washing?*

JOE: *I guess I'd be willing to give it a try.*

THERAPIST: *Is there a particular area on your body that would be challenging to touch the chicken tikka masala sauce?*

JOE: *My face and neck.*

THERAPIST: *How long do you want to practice approaching the emotions in this exposure?*

JOE: *10 minutes?*

THERAPIST: *Great, we've identified the task. How high is your anticipatory distress right now?*

JOE: *5, I have some backup pencils that are made of plastic that are less porous.*

THERAPIST: *Oh, you are already engaging in safety behaviors . . . let's think about what you are thinking, feeling, and behavior right now.*

JOE: *My breathing is no longer a background function. I'm feeling tension in [my] chest.*

THERAPIST: *What thoughts are you having?*

JOE: *I'm thinking about what I can and won't touch.*

THERAPIST: *Okay, what are the actual thoughts?*

JOE: *I'll touch porous materials and they will be contaminated or stained.*

THERAPIST: *Ruined?*

JOE: *No, not ruined. Just difficult to clean . . . particularly insidious materials. And later on, when I would touch it again, the oil would transfer back to my hands.*

THERAPIST: *So, not only does the oil bother you now, but will forever?*

JOE: *I would feel it nearly forever.*

THERAPIST: *Just to clarify, the thought is that the oil will spread and porous materials will be contaminated forever, [leading] to being continuously grossed out and bothered.*

JOE: *That sounds about right.*

THERAPIST: *Okay, what about behaviors? Are you noticing any behaviors right now?*

JOE: *I'm avoiding aspects of the exposure. I've noticed that I'm writing down things over and over.* (Joe was taking notes about the exposure on the Record of Emotion Exposure Practice Form)

Further discussion led to reevaluating Joe's automatic thoughts. He eventually was able to identify a more helpful and evidence-based thought that he could remind himself of during the exposure. The reappraisal was "Even if something is marred, it isn't the end of the world." Before starting the exposure, Joe was reminded to anchor himself in the present moment. He was also encouraged to approach his emotional distress without trying to change or control it. He rated his anticipatory distress at a 7 before starting the exposure. For the exposure, Joe smears the Indian food on his face and neck and reports that his distress reaches an 8. Joe is encouraged to practice applying his coping strategies:

JOE: *This feels so wrong!*

THERAPIST: *I bet—this is a new and different experience for you. How can you apply your coping strategies?*

JOE: *Well, I'm noticing that I have to blow my nose soon and will have to touch my nose with my hands.*

THERAPIST: *Sounds like you are already preparing for the future. Practice bringing yourself back into the present moment. Thank your mind for trying to prepare you for the future.*

Joe practices applying mindfulness and sitting with the emotional distress for a few minutes.

THERAPIST: *How high is your distress right now?*

JOE: *I'm starting to acclimate. It's about a 6.*

Joe is encouraged to continue to approach his emotional experience without trying to control or alter it. After 10 minutes pass, Joe wipes off the residue of the Indian food with tissues (though not water or soap). The therapist and Joe agree that he can wash with water and soap after the session is over. Together, the emotional exposure is debriefed.

THERAPIST: *What did you take away from this exposure task?*

JOE: *I was able to resist the urge to wash my hands. I learned to draw myself into discomfort, almost embrace the feelings of distress. And I was able to acclimate to the distress.*

THERAPIST: *Did anything bad happen during the exposure?*

JOE: *Not really—just grossed out.*

After debriefing the emotion exposure, Joe identified a goal of increasing the amount of time feeling contaminated and gross. For homework, he agreed to practice washing with just water when feeling oil on his hands, continuing to touch gross things in a systematic way, and to complete the Record of Emotion Exposure Practice form when completing the exposures.

During the remaining sessions, Joe's practice completing exposures was reviewed. Additional emotional exposures were completed in session, targeting a range of emotional experiences. See Figure 14.5 for an additional exposure completed in session.

MODULE 8: RECOGNIZING ACCOMPLISHMENTS AND LOOKING TO THE FUTURE

As previously mentioned, since Joe was a participant in a large treatment outcome study, regular diagnostic assessments were completed. At his posttreatment assessment, Joe's symptoms of panic, agoraphobia, GAD, and MDD had significantly decreased. Joe no longer reported any symptoms of depression. He continued to report symptoms of panic and worry at a clinical level, although the symptoms were less intense and interfering than during his baseline evaluation. His symptoms of OCD and ADHD continued to persist at the same clinical level as reported at his baseline assessment. The clinical severity ratings obtained during the ADIS were consistent with Joe's self-reported symptoms of anxiety and depression on the OASIS and ODSIS at the 12th session. Joe's OASIS score was a

10, indicating occasional anxiety, moderate intensity, occasional avoidance, and mild interference. He reported a score of 0 on the ODSIS, indicating that he did not experience any depressive symptoms in the past week.

During the last session, Joe's progress was reviewed. He was pleased with the treatment gains made in the 12 sessions, particularly with regard to his panic and depression symptoms. His confidence in "handling" the panic had changed remarkably. A review of the skills for coping with emotions learned in the treatment program ensued.

Since Joe continued to exhibit symptoms of panic disorder, GAD, OCD, and ADHD at a clinical severity, the majority of the termination session focused on how to continue to apply strategies to these symptoms with a focus on ways to realistically and practically incorporate the strategies into his lifestyle. For example, to increase the likelihood that Joe would practice present-focused emotional awareness, he committed to practicing mindfulness strategies during tasks that he was already engaging in daily (i.e., playing with his dogs, showering, or eating). He believed that this systematic daily practice would facilitate mindfulness practice when he was experiencing more intense emotions. Similarly, Joe committed to practicing using cognitive flexibility for one emotional experience per day.

Throughout treatment, Joe increased his awareness of his tendencies to avoid emotional experiences and his EDBs. Once he was able to become aware of these behavioral tendencies, he identified a goal of responding differently by approaching the feared experience or engaging in an opposite action. Joe noted that in the past, he would create justifications for avoiding, and that moving forward, he would practice approaching situations even in less than ideal circumstances. Finally, he agreed that completing regular and systematic emotional exposures would be necessary for maintaining his treatment goals. He identified a range of emotional exposures, targeting anxiety, panic, frustration, guilt, shame, and loneliness.

Joe was encouraged to think of himself as his own therapist and to continue to challenge himself, particularly in situations that he wanted to avoid due to intense emotional experiences. He was able to identify long-term goals and steps that he could take on his own to achieve his goals.

Finally, termination issues were discussed. Joe disclosed apprehension about ending treatment due to his continued symptoms. Even though he was aware that he would receive only 12 sessions through the research study, he noted that the time had gone by very quickly, and he felt less than 100% prepared to continue to work on applying the strategies on his own. This experience was normalized. Joe was able to recognize that he understood the concepts included in the treatment, and he had demonstrated multiple times that he knew how to apply the strategies during intense emotional experiences. Joe was reminded and encouraged to stay in contact, particularly if he noticed an increase in his symptoms.

Exposure Tasks: _Spending 5 minutes to draft a response to an email_

from my professor and send even if it is not perfectly worded or contains errors

Prior to the task:

Anticipatory Distress (0–8): _6_

Thoughts, Feelings, and Behaviors you noticed before the task:

"My email won't makes sense"

"My professor will think I'm incompetent"

anxiety, behaviors include urge to draft email in separate document.

Reevaluate your automatic appraisals about the task:

Responding to the email, even if it isn't perfect, is better

than not responding at all.

After completing the task:

Thoughts, Feelings, and Behaviors you noticed during the task:

"this isn't good enough"

reassurance seeking "what do you think"?

Number of minutes you did the task: _5_

Maximum distress during the task (0–8): _7_   Distress at the end of the task (0–8): _4_

Any attempts to avoid your emotions (distraction, safety signals, etc.)?

Reassurance seeking with therapist

What did you take away from this exposure task? Did you feared outcome occur? If so, how were you able to cope with them?

I can send an email even when I feel anxious.

I can send an email even when it's not "perfect"

I actually feel better having sent the email

Sending emails doesn't have to take so much time!

Figure 14.5 Record of Emotion Exposure Practice.

CONCLUSION

The presence of comorbidity among emotional disorders is well established, necessitating a treatment approach that can address comorbid disorders in an integrated fashion to increase the efficiency and efficacy of treatment. This chapter provided an illustration of the application of the UP to a complex case in which several comorbidities were present. In this case, the UP provided an efficient treatment approach by targeting similar symptoms associated with a range of intense emotional experiences, maladaptive reactions, and attempts to control or suppress these emotional experiences. Joe's ability to anchor himself in the present moment and bring compassion to his emotional experiences not only brought clarity to the experiences, but also allowed him the opportunity to choose how to best respond to an emotional experience.

For example, Joe's recognition of the role that pervasive negative automatic appraisals played in generating and maintaining his emotional distress in the present moment allowed him to reappraise his cognitions, thus facilitating his willingness to approach physical and situational exposures that he would have avoided previously. With repeated, systematic exposure to a range of emotional experiences, Joe learned that he could tolerate the emotional experiences and, further, that the perceived consequences did not come to pass. This new learning increased his willingness and confidence to approach more challenging emotional exposures.

In Joe's case, the UP produced clinically meaningful reductions in symptoms of GAD, MDD, panic, and agoraphobia in 12 individual sessions. Importantly, while he did not experience reductions in the symptoms of OCD and ADHD, nor did his GAD and panic reach subclinical levels, he was able to understand how the skills that he learned in treatment might be applied to these symptoms, and then develop a plan to continue practicing these skills in the hope of continuing to see improvement.

15

Group Treatment Applications of the Unified Protocol

JACQUELINE R. BULLIS, KATE H. BENTLEY, AND KATHERINE A. KENNEDY ∎

INTRODUCTION

Despite the development of many evidence-based psychological treatments, less than 40% of individuals suffering from a mental illness receive treatment in a given year (Wang, Lane, et al., 2005). Even with those who do receive treatment, the time from the onset of the disorder to the initiation of treatment ranges from 5 to 9 years for substance use disorders, 6 to 8 years for mood disorders, and 9 to 23 years for anxiety disorders (Wang, Berglund, et al., 2005). There is both a scarcity of therapists and an inequitable distribution of practitioners who are trained to administer evidence-based treatments, which greatly limits the public health impact of these protocols (McHugh & Barlow, 2010; Shapiro, Cavanagh, & Lomas, 2003).

Transdiagnostic treatments like the Unified Protocol for Transdiagnostic Treatment of Emotional Disorders (UP) represent a more efficient and cost-effective way to increase the availability of therapists trained in evidence-based care, as proficiency in only one protocol would allow a practitioner to apply one evidence-based treatment to a variety of clinical presentations. Another approach to increasing the availability of resources is delivering empirically supported treatments in a group format, since one practitioner can deliver a treatment to group of individuals at the same time. However, many treatment clinics do not have a sufficient patient flow to consistently run a therapy group for multiple diagnoses (e.g., one group for social anxiety, another group for panic disorder). At our own Center, which is located in a metropolitan area, it can take months to accumulate enough patients with a specific anxiety disorder to begin a treatment group. However, a transdiagnostic treatment approach more easily allows the development of a group that can accept patients with a range of anxiety or depressive disorders, therefore significantly decreasing the wait time for treatment.

There are other advantages to delivering treatment in a group format as well (Whitfield, 2010). Group therapy facilitates normalization of experiences from listening to others with similar problems, which serves to reduce the stigma associated with treatment. During exposures that require an audience, such as public speaking, the other group members provide a natural audience and can provide feedback that is often viewed as more impartial or objective than feedback from the therapist. The group dynamic can also promote engagement; a patient who is initially reluctant to complete an exposure can be motivated by the support of the group or by watching another group member complete a challenging exposure. For some individuals, it also may be easier to apply treatment concepts or skills to another group member's situation. In other words, patients can practice becoming their own therapist by approaching other group members' problems from the perspective of a therapist.

Although the UP was developed with the intention that it could be delivered in both individual and group formats, the research conducted to date has focused almost exclusively on delivery in an individual format. Recently, our research team conducted a pilot test of the effectiveness of the UP when delivered in a group format (for a detailed account of this study, see Bullis et al., 2015). This chapter will present clinical case summaries for a group of patients who recently received group treatment with the UP, discuss challenges encountered during group-based delivery of the UP, and provide recommendations for future implementation in a group format.

CASE PRESENTATION

We will present case summaries for six diagnostically heterogeneous patients who were treated using a group format of the UP over the course of 12 two-hour sessions. Due to our Center's status as a specialty clinic for anxiety and related disorders, most patients who present for treatment are struggling with anxiety and depressive disorders. As a result, we were not able to include patients with other emotional disorders, such as borderline personality disorder (BPD) or posttraumatic stress disorder (PTSD), who likely would have benefited from the UP. All patients were recruited from our Center's treatment waitlist and were offered either transdiagnostic group treatment (immediately) or individual therapy (in approximately two to three months).

Patients provided their written consent for questionnaire data and case information to be used for the purposes of clinical research and publication; they received no compensation for sharing their information and were charged for treatment per usual Center practices.

ASSESSMENT

As discussed in Chapter 2, assessment is a critical component of case formulation, treatment planning, and evaluation of treatment response. All patients who present to our Center seeking treatment receive a thorough diagnostic evaluation using the Anxiety Disorders Interview Schedule for Diagnostic and Statistical Manual of Mental Disorders (DSM-IV; American Psychiatric Association, 1994): Lifetime Version (ADIS-IV-L; Di Nardo, Brown, & Barlow, 1994). (Although the latest edition of the ADIS is based on DSM-5 criteria, patients in this case presentation were evaluated prior to its release and therefore were assessed with ADIS-IV.) Each diagnosis is assigned a clinical severity rating (CSR) ranging from 0 (no symptoms) to 8 (extremely severe symptoms), where a CSR of at least 4 (definitely disturbing/disabling) is used to indicate the clinical threshold.

Patients who elected for immediate treatment with the UP were also administered several self-report questionnaires to assess treatment response; these questionnaires were completed at pretreatment (Session 1), midtreatment (Session 6), and posttreatment (Session 12). This questionnaire battery included the Depression Anxiety Stress Scale-21 (DASS-21; Lovibond & Lovibond, 1995), which assessed symptoms of depression, anxiety, and stress; and the Positive and Negative Affect Schedule (PANAS; Watson, Clark, & Tellegen, 1988), which was used to capture positive and negative affect. The Multidimensional Experiential Avoidance Questionnaire (MEAQ; Gamez, Chmielewski, Kotov, Ruggero, & Watson, 2011) measured the tendency to avoid negative emotional experiences (e.g., behavioral avoidance, distress aversion, procrastination, distraction/suppression, repression/denial), and the Anxiety Sensitivity Index (ASI; Peterson & Reiss, 1993; Reiss, Peterson, Gursky, & McNally, 1986) assessed fear and perceived dangerousness of anxiety-related physical sensations.

The Work and Social Adjustment Scale (WSAS; Marks, Connolly, & Hallam, 1973; Mundt, Marks, Shear, & Greist, 2002) measured functional impairment due to symptoms across a range of life domains. The Overall Anxiety Severity and Impairment Scale (OASIS; Norman, Cissell, Means-Christensen, & Stein, 2006) and the Overall Depression Severity and Impairment Scale (ODSIS; Bentley, Gallagher, Carl, & Barlow, 2014) were administered weekly to capture symptoms of anxiety and depression, respectively.

Finally, patients completed a survey at the last session that solicited their feedback on the treatment, as well as overall acceptability of and satisfaction with the UP group.

INTRODUCTION TO THE GROUP

Tom

Tom was a 22-year-old, single, Caucasian male who was applying to graduate programs in business and presented seeking treatment for social anxiety. He reported that his social anxiety led him to avoid networking and dating situations. Tom also endorsed several symptoms of alcohol abuse, including difficulties controlling his drinking and occasionally driving while under the influence of alcohol. Based on these symptoms, he was assigned a principal diagnosis of social anxiety disorder, generalized type (CSR = 5) and an additional diagnosis of alcohol abuse (CSR = 4). At the onset of treatment, Tom identified his primary goal for treatment as "eliminating [his] social anxiety and negative thoughts."

Karen

Karen was a 27-year-old, single, Caucasian female working full time at a marketing company. At the intake, Karen reported frequent, highly distressing panic attacks and agoraphobic avoidance of fear-inducing situations. She described excessive, uncontrollable worry about a number of domains and significant fear and avoidance of a variety of social situations. Karen also endorsed significant symptoms of depression, which make her feel "worthless and lost" on a daily basis. Based on these symptoms, she was assigned a principal diagnosis of panic disorder with agoraphobia (PDA; CSR = 5) and additional diagnoses of generalized anxiety disorder (GAD; CSR = 4), social anxiety disorder, generalized type (SOC; CSR = 4), and depressive disorder not otherwise specified (DD-NOS; CSR = 4). Her goals for treatment included feeling confident in group situations, no longer "feeling like a burden" to others, and reducing "negative talk."

Ginnifer

Ginnifer was a 57-year-old, single, Caucasian female working full time at a pharmaceutical company. During her initial interview, she reported notable anxiety before entering and in situations where it would be difficult to escape should she need to use the bathroom. Ginnifer denied avoidance of these situations but described limiting her liquid/food intake and using the bathroom up to six times before entering these meetings, as well as beginning to worry and experience stomach distress up to one week before meetings. Accordingly, Ginnifer was assigned a principal diagnosis of agoraphobia without a history of panic disorder (CSR = 5). Her primary goal for treatment was to "reduce or eliminate anxiety in meetings."

Ed

Ed was a 63-year-old, single, Caucasian male working in a leadership position at a local museum who presented at our Center seeking treatment for "anxiety attacks." He reported experiencing uncued panic attacks on a regular basis, as well as symptoms of social anxiety that negatively affected his job performance. In addition, Ed described significant symptoms of depression that interfered with his overall quality of life and a moderately distressing fear of heights. Based on these symptoms, he was assigned a principal diagnosis of PDA (CSR = 6), as well as additional diagnoses of social anxiety disorder, generalized type (SOC;

CSR = 5), major depressive disorder (MDD; CSR = 4), and specific phobia, heights (CSR = 4). Ed's primary goal for treatment was to develop new friendships and sources of social support.

Alexa

Alexa was a 33-year-old, single, Caucasian female working in hotel management. She presented to our Center seeking help for obsessive thoughts and compulsive behaviors that interfered with her efficiency at work, as well as her overall quality of life. In addition, she endorsed repetitive hair-pulling behaviors that she found moderately bothersome. Based on these symptoms, Alexa was assigned a principal diagnosis of obsessive-compulsive disorder (OCD; CSR = 5) and an additional diagnosis of trichotillomania (CSR = 4). Her primary goal for treatment was to reduce the OCD behaviors that were holding her back from achieving her "full life potential," which would include a more vibrant social life, spending less time at work, and having more energy.

Peter

Peter was a 48-year-old, married, Caucasian male with two children who was recently unemployed at the time of the intake. He reported significant fear and occasional avoidance of having blood drawn, receiving injections, and invasive medical procedures. He described clinically significant symptoms of inattention and hyperactivity, as well as excessive and interfering worry about minor matters, work, and finances. Based on these symptoms, Peter was assigned a principal diagnosis of specific phobia, blood-injection-injury type (CSR = 5) and additional diagnoses of attention deficit hyperactivity disorder, combined type (ADHD; CSR = 5) and GAD (CSR = 4). His primary goal for treatment was to be able to undergo medical procedures, such as blood draws and colonoscopies.

TREATMENT DELIVERY

The length and number of treatment sessions utilized in previous UP studies (e.g., Ellard, Fairholme, Boisseau, Farchione, & Barlow, 2010; Farchione et al., 2012) were adapted for a group-based application. Specifically, instead of a maximum of 18 60-minute sessions, the eight UP modules were delivered over the course of 12 two-hour weekly sessions; the majority of the diagnosis-specific treatment groups that are run at our Center are 12 weeks long, with two-hour sessions, so we chose to use the same structure for the UP. All sessions were delivered by three advanced doctoral students who were trained in administration of the UP. All patients were provided with the UP Client Workbook (Barlow, Ellard, et al., 2011).

Table 15.1. Outline of UP Content Delivered by Session

Session	Content
1	Unified model of psychopathology; motivation enhancement strategies; treatment goal setting (Module 1)
2	Psychoeducation on adaptive function of emotions; three-component model of emotional experiences (Module 2)
3	Natural course of emotions and role of avoidance; present-focused, nonjudgmental emotion awareness (Module 3)
4	Cognitive appraisal; thinking traps and countering questions; downward arrow (Module 4)
5	Identification of emotional avoidance strategies; rationale for replacing EDBs with incompatible behaviors (Module 5)
6	Psychoeducation on interoceptive conditioning; symptom induction test; IE exercises (Module 6)
7–11	Exposure rationale; create and review individual hierarchies; situational, emotion-focused exposures (Module 7)
12	Skill review; emphasis on continued implementation of exposures; review of progress and future goals; relapse prevention strategies (Module 8)

Sessions were structured such that each one, with the exception of the first, began with a brief review of previous session material and a collaborative review of homework that targeted issues with homework completion as needed. Homework review was followed by introduction of new material and completion of any in-session exercises, and then sessions concluded with homework assignment.

An outline of specific topics addressed in the group each week is presented in Table 15.1. We did not modify the treatment content, learning objectives, or homework assignments from those presented in the UP Therapist Guide (Barlow, Farchione, et al., 2011), and in general, treatment proceeded in a manner that was consistent with an individual format. However, delivering the UP in a group format required modifications to how some of the content was delivered or homework was assigned. We will discuss those modifications next and propose additional options for improving the delivery of the UP in a group format.

Unified Model of Psychopathology

Research has demonstrated that patients' initial beliefs about how much they will benefit from a particular treatment (i.e., expectancy) and how much a particular treatment approach makes sense to them (i.e., credibility) are important predictors of treatment response for cognitive-behavior therapy (CBT; e.g., Greenberg, Constantino, & Bruce, 2006; Newman & Fisher, 2010). Studies also suggest that providing patients with a treatment rationale (i.e., an explanation of how the treatment results in symptom reduction) enhances patient credibility and expectancy (Ahmed & Westra, 2009; Arch, Twohig, Deacon, Landy, & Bluett, 2015). Most patients are familiar only with group treatments that focus on a particular diagnosis or set of symptoms, so it is important to spend sufficient time during the initial session presenting the rationale for a transdiagnostic treatment approach.

The UP is based on the notion that it is our *reactions* to emotions (as opposed to the emotions themselves) that influence the frequency and intensity of future emotions and emotion-driven behaviors (EDB). Consequently, the primary goal of the UP is to develop a greater willingness to experience emotions and respond to them in more adaptive ways. We explain that the goal of treatment is not to eliminate negative emotions, but rather to gain greater awareness of emotional experiences. By developing more emotion awareness, patients begin to understand how certain learned behaviors provide short-term relief from distress but ultimately contribute to the persistence of symptoms over the long term.

During Session 1, we highlighted that although the specific symptoms or feared situations differed from person to person, the processes that were responsible for maintaining those symptoms were the same. For example, although Tom and Ed differed greatly from one another—Tom was a young, recent college graduate whose social anxiety was holding him back from engaging with peers in professional and romantic settings, while Ed was approaching retirement, coping with the recent loss of his partner, and suffering from panic attacks—they both utilized alcohol to dampen their anxiety. Tom feared that others would judge him if he appeared anxious in a social situation, so he often drank on his own prior to meeting with friends. Ed was fearful of the anxiety itself, in that he was afraid that the physical symptoms associated with anxiety (e.g. increased heart rate, feeling flushed) would escalate to a full-blown panic attack. Consequently, he drank almost daily, beginning at lunchtime, to manage his anxiety symptoms.

The UP is an emotion-focused intervention, and as such, it is possible to apply the unified model to any situation in which someone experienced a strong emotion. This flexibility is not only useful for reinforcing the treatment rationale, but also for providing a framework for patients to discuss sources of stress or difficulty that were not directly related to psychopathology. For example, Peter was experiencing increasing levels of marital discord during treatment, and during homework review, he would frequently launch into a detailed description of a recent disagreement with his wife. During these disagreements, which often revolved around his wife's spending habits, Peter reported that he would become highly agitated and end up saying things that further fueled the contentious nature of their relationship. Although these conflicts were entirely unrelated to why he initially sought treatment, they were often at the forefront of his mind during group.

Normally, structured group therapy is unable to address these types of interpersonal stressors without deviating significantly from the treatment protocol and possibly alienating the other group members by spending too much time on one individual's problem. However, with the UP, we were able to use the ARC of emotions to facilitate skill acquisition. Peter had recently been laid off from his job as an accountant and was having a difficult time finding another one, which was an antecedent for these conflicts with his wife over finances—he was feeling more concerned about money than he did when he was gainfully employed.

We explored the short- and long-term consequences of his response; although chastising his wife made him feel less upset in the moment because it provided an illusion of control (i.e., that his angry criticism of her would deter her from unnecessary spending in the future), it ultimately resulted in further deterioration of communication between the two of them and exacerbated the marital discord. We then invited other group members to help Peter generate a list of incompatible behaviors he could utilize in place of his EDB of lashing out verbally, such as going for a walk around the block or waiting 24 hours before discussing the credit card bill with her.

One challenge that arose was that from the onset of treatment, Ginnifer was unwilling to discuss her presenting complaint in any level of specificity in the presence of other group members and instead referred to her symptoms vaguely as "anxiety" that arose in work meetings and while traveling. During Session 8, a group leader conducted an exposure with Ginnifer that involved her sitting in a closet that could not be opened from the inside; this was the first exposure that she had completed where the other group members were not nearby. In this one-on-one setting, the group leader probed explicitly about her stomach distress. The following is an example of how the group leader utilized the downward arrow exercise in an attempt to get Ginnifer to disclose her feared outcome:

THERAPIST: *So what is it that you are afraid of happening during these meeting?*

GINNIFER: *I don't know, that I will get an upset stomach.*

THERAPIST: *And what would be so bad about getting an upset stomach?*

GINNIFER: *I don't know, I just—I don't want to say it.*

THERAPIST: *Are you afraid of passing gas during the meeting?*

GINNIFER: [shakes head no]

THERAPIST: *Then what? What would be the worst-case scenario?*

GINNIFER: *I just—do I have to say it?*

THERAPIST: *In order for me to be helpful, I need to understand what it is that you [are] afraid will happen.*

GINNIFER: *Well, I wouldn't want people to see me leave the meeting.*

THERAPIST: *Why not?*

GINNIFER: *Because, you know, they would think—I can't say it. I don't want to say it.*

THERAPIST: *Why don't you want to say it?*

GINNIFER: *It's too embarrassing!*

THERAPIST: *That's OK. It's OK to feel embarrassed; it won't last forever. They would think what? That you were leaving the meeting to go to the bathroom?*

GINNIFER: *Yes, but not just that.*

THERAPIST: *What else?*

GINNIFER: *Can I just write it down? I don't want to say it.*

> THERAPIST: *You're afraid that people will think you're leaving because you're going to have diarrhea?*
>
> GINNIFER: [covers face with her hands and nods yes] *But you have to prom-ise not to tell anyone else in the group, and you can't ask me about it in front of them!*

Her discomfort discussing her symptoms with other group members was espe-cially unfortunate because she demonstrated considerable difficulty grasping core UP skills throughout the course of treatment, but the group members were una-ble to provide instruction on how to apply skills to her specific situation while in session.

Although the unified model of psychopathology can be flexibly applied across myriad symptom presentations, including nonclinical experiences (e.g., inter-personal stress), Ginnifer is an illustrative example that clinical judgment may be necessary to determine an individual's ability to engage in and benefit from a transdiagnostic treatment like the UP in a group format. If a therapist were using the UP with Ginnifer in an individual format, she likely would have ben-efited from multiple sessions focused on mindful emotion awareness (whereas the group format spent only one session on this skill).

Homework

For the first few sessions, the group leaders spent approximately 15 minutes col-laboratively reviewing homework and then reserved the bulk of the two-hour session for introducing new material. However, a copy was made each week of group members' homework for a more thorough review outside of session. While reviewing homework forms, it became apparent that although they reported a strong grasp of the material during session, some group members were not imple-menting the treatment skills appropriately. For example, Ginnifer completed an Identifying and Evaluating Automatic Appraisals worksheet where she described her response to receiving an email about an upcoming work meeting. She recorded her automatic appraisal as "crowded room, hot/stuffy," her emotion as "rush of adrenaline," the thinking trap as "not going to feel comfortable," and her alternative appraisal as "try not to think about it." Ginnifer failed to fully articulate her automatic appraisal (what would happen if the room was hot/stuffy and felt uncomfortable?), her emotion (fear? anxiety?), or whether she was jumping to conclusions or assuming the worst. The goal of this exercise is to increase cogni-tive flexibility by generating other possible explanations, but instead of generating an alternative prediction, Ginnifer wrote that she should try to avoid thinking about it, which could in fact be conceptualized as a maladaptive EDB.

In response to the observation during the first few weeks that some group mem-bers were consistently struggling with skill acquisition, as evidenced by review of homework assignments, we elected to shift the structure of the group so that the first hour of session was spent reviewing homework. Doing so provided the group leaders with more opportunities to gauge comprehension and to provide corrective feedback as necessary. This change in session structure left less time for the introduction of new material each week, but it allowed the group leaders to review homework in greater depth after group members had attempted the practice on their own for a week, which appeared to enhance concept and skill acquisition. It also changed the expectations for participation; instead of asking for a few group members to volunteer an example from their homework practice, we began going around in a circle so that each group member had an opportunity to review their homework in detail. Finally, although the rationale for a transdiagnostic treatment approach is discussed explicitly only during the first session, we strove to highlight the commonalities among group members' experiences each week, and extending homework review provided more opportunities to do so.

It is also recommended that group leaders hold brief (approximately 10–15 minutes), individual meetings before or after sessions with group members who evidence difficulties grasping treatment material, applying skills in their daily lives, and/or are hesitant to disclose personal information in front of other group members. Although individual meetings were held only when group members missed the previous session or requested to meet one on one with a leader during the study described in this chapter, utilizing such "check-ins" on a more frequent, as-needed basis may help with time management and maximizing treatment response.

Exposures

Module 6 of the UP targets anxiety sensitivity by helping patients gain a greater understanding of the role that internal physical sensations play in determining their emotional response. To accomplish this, patients complete symptom induction exercises (e.g., hyperventilating, spinning, breathing through a straw) to identify the physical sensations that are the most strongly associated with their emotions and then repeatedly engage in symptom induction exercises (also referred to as interoceptive exposure, or IE) to increase their tolerance.

For the group format, we began by having everyone (i.e., both group members and group leaders) breathe through a thin straw for 60 seconds while holding their nose closed. The group then discussed the symptoms that they experienced and rated the symptom intensity and level of distress that the symptoms produced. One of the group leaders then continued repetitions of straw breathing with the group members who found the exercise to be at least moderately distressing and similar to their naturally occurring symptoms, while the other two group leaders worked with the remaining group members to practice more idiosyncratic symptom induction exercises. By the end of session, each group member had identified an effective symptom induction exercise that they were instructed to practice daily, using repeated trials.

Emotion exposures were introduced the following week, in Session 7, and completed both in-session and during homework practice for the following four weeks. Unlike a diagnosis-specific group, where each patient might complete the same exposure in session (e.g., each patient gives a speech in front of the group one week and then approaches strangers to ask for directions the following week) and then complete more personalized exposures for homework, the goal was for each UP group member to complete a personally relevant exposure from his or her exposure hierarchy during session each week. For example, the following reflects the exposures that were completed for each group member during one session: (a) watching phlebotomy videos (Peter); (b) turning a toaster on and off without engaging in any checking behavior (Alexa); (c) hyperventilating while sitting inside a small filing closet that could not be opened from the inside (Karen); (d) approaching a group of strangers at a bar (Tom); (e) riding the underground train (Ed), and; (f) eating "unsafe" foods prior to speaking in front of a group (Ginnifer).

In order to accomplish so many different exposures during one session, we utilized a variety of strategies. First, the group leaders brainstormed some possible exposures for each group member to complete during the first emotion exposure session (Session 6) based on clinical information accumulated during each group member's initial diagnostic evaluation and from the group itself. We did this because the emotional and situational hierarchy is introduced for the first time during Session 6, and we wanted to make sure that we had suggestions available if the group members weren't able to generate any ideas on the spot.

Because it is important to construct and prepare for emotion exposures appropriately to maximize the opportunity for new learning to occur, we elected to go around in a circle and plan each exposure as a group during the first session of in vivo exposures. Once the exposures were planned, one group leader remained in the group room while the other two group leaders worked individually with group members to execute each exposure. However, doing so left little time to process the exposure afterward or discuss which exposures should be completed for homework, which was problematic.

In subsequent sessions, the group members were divided into three pairs of two, and one group leader assisted each of the pairs with the construction and execution of the exposure. After the exposures were completed, the group reconvened to debrief and assign homework. To maximize the efficiency of this process, we utilized photocopies of the group members' exposure hierarchies before each session to strategize how to best pair group members. Sometimes we paired group members based on the type of exposures being conducted, and other times we paired group members such that a group leader could accompany one group member who needed more guidance while the other group member who had demonstrated greater mastery of exposure exercises conducted his or her own exposure independently.

We also encouraged group members to help plan each other's exposures, which provided an opportunity for us to assess their acquisition of treatment concepts. In this scenario, the group leader assumed a more passive role and let the group members problem-solve on their own before providing feedback. This was especially helpful in determining whether a group member understood a treatment skill but was struggling to implement it in personally relevant situations, or whether further instruction in the skill itself was necessary. For example, Karen often struggled with generating alternative interpretations of events and remained stuck in her initial, negative automatic appraisal during homework review. However, when observed assisting another group member in reevaluating their automatic appraisals about an upcoming exposure, Karen was unable to generate a single challenging question to ask her partner. This observation provided valuable clinical information on how to conceptualize Karen's suboptimal response to treatment (discussed next) and helped to guide recommendations for additional treatment following completion of the group.

TREATMENT RESPONSE

Clinical Outcomes

Most group members appeared to benefit from 12 sessions of treatment, as evidenced by self-report measures of depression, positive and negative affect, and functional impairment; pretreatment and posttreatment scores are displayed in Table 15.2. Tom displayed the strongest response to treatment, with posttreatment scores falling within normal ranges across all measures. He displayed strong skill acquisition; for example, during an emotion exposure where his goal was to initiate a conversation with other customers at a bookstore, he decided independently that he would deliberately make an awkward comment in the middle of the conversation to assess the social consequences.

On his feedback form, he wrote that the most important thing he learned during treatment was that "it is OK to feel anxious," reflecting a true willingness to experience the full range of emotional experiences. He also reported that he looked forward to beginning business school next year and felt prepared to use the skills that he learned in treatment to manage his anxiety in new social environments.

Peter experienced meaningful reductions in his levels of depression, stress, negative affect, and experiential avoidance, all of which fell into the normal, nonclinical range at posttreatment. Although he reported more severe functional impairment and anxiety sensitivity, his scores on both measures still fell within the mild range. It is important to note that Peter initially sought treatment for interference related to ADHD, which was not addressed during treatment with the UP and likely continued to contribute to his interference. Following completion of the group, he was referred to another Center therapist for individual therapy to address his attention difficulties.

Ed also appeared to benefit from treatment, with particularly notable increases in his level of positive affect and decreases in functional impairment, anxiety sensitivity, and experiential avoidance. However, his posttreatment scores continued to reflect moderate symptomatology and associated interference, except for measures of anxiety sensitivity and experiential avoidance, which fell within normal ranges. It became apparent to group leaders that Ed had initially underreported

Table 15.2. PRETREATMENT AND POSTTREATMENT OUTCOME SCORES

	Tom		Karen		Ginnifer		Ed		Alexa		Peter	
	Pre	Post	Pre	Post	Pre	Post	Pre	Post	Pre	Post	Pre	Post
DASS-ANX	3	1	14	12	0	0	12	13	0	0	3	4
DASS-DEP	10	0	11	9	0	0	10	7	0	1	13	4
DASS-STR	6	0	23	20	1	1	18	16	1	1	20	8
PANAS-PA*	15	33	22	32	44	41	23	31	40	40	34	32
PANAS-NA	25	12	30	22	10	10	17	22	15	15	28	17
MEAQ	248	116	235	176	113	94	204	151	146	123	230	147
ASI	18	2	40	30	5	2	43	13	20	10	15	19
WSAS	14	2	28	21	3	0	21	11	12	8	4	9

NOTES: DASS-ANX = Depression Anxiety Stress Scales–Anxiety Scale; DASS-DEP = Depression Anxiety Stress Scales–Depression Scale; DASS-STR = Depression Anxiety Stress Scales–Stress Scale; PANAS-PA = Positive and Negative Affect Schedule–Positive Affectivity; PANAS-NA = Positive and Negative Affect Schedule–Negative Affectivity; MEAQ = Multidimensional Experiential Avoidance Questionnaire; ASI = Anxiety Sensitivity Index; WSAS = Work and Social Adjustment Scale

* For this measure, higher scores are reflective of less impairment.

his alcohol consumption during the diagnostic evaluation and was likely suffering from alcohol dependence (e.g., he would develop hand tremors and begin sweating during the second hour of group). He was unwilling to discuss his alcohol use as an EDB either during group or in private with group leaders, but he was provided with a referral for substance dependence at the conclusion of treatment.

Karen's questionnaire scores indicated some improvement from pretreatment to posttreatment, most notably an increase in positive affect and decrease in negative affect. Her level of experiential avoidance was comparable with community norms. Her report of anxiety and depressive symptoms largely remained in the moderate range, and her functional impairment score continued to indicate significant interference at posttreatment. Karen was alert and attentive during group, but she was also highly sensitive to how her behavior would be perceived by group members. For example, she refrained from speaking about her romantic relationship because she did not want to upset Ed, whose husband had committed suicide the past year. During homework review, she would wait until all other members had spoken or until directly called upon by a group leader to share her experiences. Although Karen was attentive during group and participated when prompted, it is likely that her discomfort with being the center of attention prevented her from fully engaging in the treatment. At the conclusion of the group, she requested additional treatment to work on her "self-worth issues" and core beliefs, and she was assigned to another Center clinician for individual therapy.

For Alexa, her level of functional impairment, which was the only measure at pretreatment that fell in the moderate range, did decrease to a mild level at posttreatment. However, because she reported essentially no symptomatology at pretreatment (with the exception of moderate functional impairment), it is difficult to ascertain from her questionnaire scores how much benefit she derived from participation in the group. Alexa was informed that she could contact our Center at any point in the future for additional treatment.

A review of Ginnifer's pretreatment to posttreatment scores reflected essentially no change. At pretreatment, Ginnifer reported scores that were at least one full standard deviation lower than average scores for healthy controls (i.e., their scores indicated that they were functioning significantly better at pretreatment than individuals without a psychiatric diagnosis). These scores starkly contrast with other indicators of her distress; for example, Ginnifer was clearly distressed enough by her symptoms to contact our Center, complete a lengthy diagnostic evaluation, pay for treatment, and commute over an hour in traffic each way to attend treatment. She was informed that she could contact our Center at any point to request additional treatment or referrals.

Both Ginnifer and Alexa appeared to significantly underreport their symptoms, as evidenced by scores reflecting optimal functioning on a number of self-report measures, which may represent a severe deficit in their ability or willingness to identify, experience, and express their emotions. Although the UP is well suited for individuals with high levels of emotional avoidance since emotion awareness training is introduced early in treatment to facilitate the subsequent application of other treatment skills, it is likely that Ginnifer and Alexa were so unwilling to engage with their emotional experiences that the single session focusing on emotion awareness was insufficient.

It is quite possible that in an individual setting, with flexibility to spend multiple weeks on one skill and to provide individual attention, Alexa and Ginnifer would have evidenced a more favorable response. Therefore, it may be helpful to discuss the expectations of fully participating in the group, including sharing specific information about symptoms, with potential patients before determining whether they are appropriate for the UP in group format.

Patient Feedback

At the end of treatment, the group members completed a feedback form assessing how acceptable the group was (i.e., how much did the treatment approach and activities make sense and feel reasonable) and their overall satisfaction with the group. Tom and Ed rated the group treatment as "extremely acceptable/satisfied" and Peter and Alexa rated it as "very acceptable/ satisfied." Karen found it "moderately acceptable/satisfied." Ginnifer stopped attending treatment after Session 9, when she was laid off from her job, and did not complete the feedback form.

Group members were also asked to report, in their own words, what they thought of the group overall, which elements were most helpful and which were less helpful, what were the most important things they learned during the group, and any recommendations for improving the group. The majority of group members expressed a positive reaction to the group's diagnostic heterogeneity, reporting that "it was very helpful to hear the experiences of others" and "it [was] nice to be able to have a variety and understand that issues always come to a common center." Tom felt differently, stating that "sometimes [he] had trouble relating to some of the problems the other patients in group dealt with" and that it was most helpful when he was able to receive instruction from the therapists that was more specific to his personal experiences. Karen, Peter, and Ed all suggested that additional sessions, particularly sessions focused on emotion exposures, would be helpful.

CONCLUSIONS

The aim of this chapter was to provide guidance on the implementation of the UP in a group format using illustrative examples from six patients with diverse anxiety and mood disorder diagnoses. Results from our preliminary open clinical trial demonstrated that the UP delivered in group format results in moderate to strong effects on anxiety and depressive symptoms, functional impairment, quality of life, and emotion regulation skills (Bullis et al., 2015).

It is important to consider these findings in the context that the patients who participated in this open clinical trial were clinically challenging for a number of reasons. All group members presented with more than one diagnosis, had previous experience with psychotherapy, and many patients had received CBT within the past five years. Patients with multiple diagnoses are often excluded from psychotherapy research, and it is common practice in psychotherapy research to exclude patients with prior CBT experience because they may be "treatment resistant" and therefore less likely to respond to any intervention. As a result, it is often argued that patients in clinical trials do not represent the typical patient seen in community settings (Goldstein-Piekarski, Williams, & Humphreys, 2016; Odlaug et al., 2014).

Therefore, the patients presented in this chapter are more representative of the typical treatment-seeking adult than the patients traditionally recruited for clinical trials. Group members also indicated that the UP group was acceptable and satisfactory—an important finding, given that most patients tend to prefer individual treatment (e.g., Semple, Dunwoody, Sullivan, & Kernohan, 2006; Sharp, Power, & Swanson, 2004).

As discussed earlier, the majority of individuals suffering from psychological disorders do not receive treatment. Two of the foremost initiatives to improve access to evidence-based psychological treatments include stepped care models, where a patient is first provided the most effective and least resource-intensive treatment, and then progress is monitored continuously throughout treatment for referral to higher-level care if necessary, and mental health care is integrated into primary care (Haaga, 2000; Kerner, Rimer, & Emmons, 2005). However, one barrier to integration efforts is that physicians must identify the psychopathology and make the appropriate referral under enormous time constraints (Thielke, Vannoy, & Unutzer, 2007). A transdiagnostic treatment like the UP is optimally suited for the implementation integration of these two initiatives; a simple screening measure could be used in primary care settings to identify and triage patients into a UP group treatment. Patients who need additional treatment after completion of the group can then be referred for individual therapy.

In summary, there is preliminary empirical support that delivering the UP within a group setting is an effective, feasible treatment approach for the range of emotional disorders. Given the promising implications of transdiagnostic, group-based treatment for training and dissemination, the UP group may represent a cost-effective, efficient intervention to target core mechanisms underlying the emotional disorders. Future research is needed to evaluate the effectiveness of UP group administration and identify further areas for refinement, as well as explore whether there are specific patient characteristics that predict the ability to engage in a group-based delivery of the UP.

16

Cross-Cultural Applications
of the Unified Protocol

Examples from Japan and Colombia

AMANTIA A. AMETAJ, NINA WONG SARVER,
OBIANUJUNWA ANAKWENZE, MASAYA ITO,
MICHEL RATTNER-CASTRO, AND SRIRAMYA POTLURI ■

WHY DO WE NEED CULTURAL ADAPTATIONS?

Clinical guidelines recommend an evidence-based practice (EBP) approach for clinicians administering psychological treatments. This approach emphasizes the integration of up-to-date research findings with patients' preferences and characteristics, including patients' culture (American Psychological Association, 2006). The centrality of culture in psychological interventions, however, is a disputed topic. On one end of the spectrum, the assumption is that evidence-based interventions (EBIs) are universal and can be successfully applied to any patient from any cultural background because these treatments are devoid of the influence of culture (Falicov, 2009). On the opposite end of the spectrum, the argument is that EBIs are not recommended for culturally diverse individuals.

Historically, EBIs have not been tested with culturally diverse or minority individuals (La Roche & Christopher, 2008); thus, the inference is that these interventions may not work for those who differ in their cultural identification from the typical research participant (Horrell, 2008). An integrated outlook recognizes that EBIs can be efficacious with culturally diverse individuals if adapted to the particular culture where they are being applied. The premise for cultural adaptations is that, inevitably, EBIs contain cultural assumptions that at times may be at odds with different cultural perspectives. Thus, cultural assumptions ought to be identified and conflicts between differing assumptions resolved (Miranda et al., 2005).

The cultural assumptions in cognitive-behavioral therapy (CBT), of which the Unified Protocol for the Transdiagnostic Treatment of Emotional Disorders (UP) is an example, tend to include a focus on individualism, independence, assertiveness, logic and rationality, and behavior change (Hays, 2009). Some cultures, however, emphasize the opposite: importance of context/environment, interdependence, agreeableness, fitting in as opposed to standing out, a spiritual worldview, and acceptance of status quo behavior (Hays, 2009; Jackson, Schmutzer, Wenzel, & Tyler, 2006). Research suggests that a mismatch between patients' cultural perspective and interventions, or at times the therapist's perspective, can lead to lower treatment engagement, attendance, and overall effectiveness of interventions (Castro, Barrera, & Martinez, 2004; Kaysen et al., 2013).

Research in this area is in its early stages, but several explanations have been put forth as to why a patient who experiences a mismatch with a treatment's or provider's cultural perspective may drop out or disengage from care. For example, without incorporating the patient's worldview into the intervention, the clinician may fail to obtain the patient's agreement about the source of her/his suffering and thus, cooperation about instituting the planned intervention elements (La Roche, 2013). Similarly, even with the patient's agreement, a failure to create a cultural case conceptualization may lead to the clinician providing treatment elements that could be seen as irrelevant, unhelpful, or even insensitive. Although the clinician runs the risk of encountering the above mentioned issues in any therapeutic relationship, this risk may be even greater for those patients that experience a mismatch between their cultural perspectives and those of the intervention or of the provider. Thus, a sensitive cultural case formulation that takes into account the patient's worldview may be imperative, in some cases, to the patient's success in engaging with the intervention (Sue, Gallardo, & Neville, 2013).

HOW DO WE UNDERSTAND CULTURE ANYWAY?

To begin to untangle who needs culturally adapted treatments, which EBIs need adaptation, and how much adaptation is needed, the complexities of culture first must be visited. Culture is made up of many dimensions (from the institutional to the individual). More specifically, *culture* has been defined as a system of beliefs, values, rules, and norms, as well as traditions and customs that often are passed from one generation to the next (Betancourt & Lopez, 1993). Each individual has several dimensions to his/her cultural identity (e.g., race, gender, sexual orientation, nationality, immigration status, etc.) (American Psychiatric Association, 2013). However, it is important to note that ethnicity, race, and nationality do not narrowly define one's culture, and these terms are not automatically equivalent to culture (Betancourt & Lopez, 1993; La Roche, 2013). In addition, cultural dimensions are constantly affecting and shaping one another. As a result, each individual has a unique identity that is based on different aspects of one or more cultures to which that individual is exposed (Sue et al., 2013).

Although there may be group-based characteristics that may stem from belonging to a cultural group (or subcultural group), there are also many individual or idiosyncratic characteristics that are unique to the client (Muñoz & Mendelson, 2005). Thus, culture is a dynamic process that is constantly changing, shaping and being shaped by individuals. All of this taken together speaks to the complexity of culture and warns against overgeneralizing and stereotyping culture. This also points to the importance of a cultural case formulation. It is not sufficient to know that a patient is from a different cultural background. It is important to understand each patient's perspective of their symptoms and other relevant cultural views.

RECOMMENDATIONS FOR THE PRACTICING CLINICIAN FOR CULTURAL CASE FORMULATION WITHIN THE FRAMEWORK OF THE UP

A cultural case formulation incorporates culture in the understanding of patients' challenges and strengths. Given the complexity of culture (as described previously), it is important to take into account patients' unique cultural makeup. Patients' understanding of their psychopathology also may be influenced by their cultural perspectives, and this information could be useful to incorporate into treatment planning. In the UP, this information gathering can be incorporated easily in the first session, when the therapist asks about patients' symptoms.

Outlined next are some general guidelines for developing a cultural case formulation and for assessment and treatment of culturally diverse individuals. An emphasis on a respectful stance is recommended during both assessment and psychological intervention for any patient, but especially for a patient from a different cultural background than that of the clinician. Research suggests that respect, even more than rapport, is important for the therapeutic relationship for several cultures, including Asian, Native American, African, African American, Latino, Southern European, and Middle Eastern cultures (Hays, 2009).

Assessment Recommendations

Culturally informed assessment is the first step to better understand individuals' cultural identification and how it may be shaping their understanding of mental illness and help-seeking behaviors (Chapman, DeLapp, & Williams, 2014; Asnaani & Hofmann, 2012). Included in the *Diagnostic and Statistical Manual— 5th Edition* (DSM-5; American Psychiatric Association, 2013) is an outline of a cultural formulation to aid clinicians in considering culture in their case formulation. To create a cultural case formulation, clinicians should gather information on the patients' own cultural identification, cultural conceptualization of their own distress, psychosocial stressors, and cultural features of vulnerabilities. A helpful tool to achieve this can be the Cultural Formulation Interview (CFI), included in

DSM-5, which is a semistructured interview made up of 16 questions to assess the impact of cultural factors on the individual. This interview is person-centered, in that it is focused on the views of individuals and the people in their social groups. The focus on patients' views is intended to avoid overgeneralizing and stereotyping and to call attention to how the patients' idiosyncratic cultural perspective affects their understanding of their symptoms and help-seeking behaviors.

There are four domains in the CFI, and they can be used individually or conjunctly. The first domain assesses a patient's cultural definition of the problem (e.g., how the patient would describe his/her problems to his/her family, friends, or others in the community). The second domain is cultural perceptions of the cause, context, and support for the psychological problem (e.g., the thoughts of other individuals in family/friends, or community circles about the psychological problem). The third domain is cultural factors affecting self-coping and past help-seeking behaviors (e.g., how the patient has tried to cope with the problem on his/her own). Finally, the fourth domain is made up of questions that assess current help-seeking behaviors (e.g., what the patient thinks may be helpful now). This assessment tool can help the practicing clinician shape a cultural case formulation and address culture within the therapeutic relationship.

This information gleaned from the CFI can be utilized to tailor the UP to individual patients by explaining the treatment content in a way that is relevant to them and their worldview. Other options for gathering similar or additional information for practicing clinicians who face strict time demands on their assessment process can include the use of self-report measures instead of (or in conjunction with) clinician-administered measures for the initial cultural case formulation. Self-report measures could be provided to all patients at intake to understand their identified culture and its importance in their view of their mental health problems and help-seeking behaviors. Based on the information gleaned from these self-report measures, clinicians then could probe further about individuals' culture and its influence on their perspective of mental health problems and treatment.

Recommended self-report measures include the Multigroup Ethnic Identity Measure (MEIM; Phinney, 1992), which was developed to assess "ethnic identity" across diverse samples and translates well to the current construct of cultural identity. In addition to an overall ethnic identity score, this measure assesses two subsets of identity: (a) belonging and high identity achievement—the extent that a person has a secure view of his/her own ethnic identity; and (b) behaviors or activities that the person engages in with his/her ethnic group (Roberts et al., 1999). If a patient scores high on the overall score of either subscale, the clinician could utilize this information to start a conversation about the importance of culture to the patient.

For patients who have immigrated to the United States or their children, an acculturation scale, such as the Stephenson Multigroup Acculturation Scale (SMAS; Stephenson, 2000), may help the therapist to gauge their acculturation. Patients fall on two separate cultural spectrums, the new host culture spectrum and the native culture spectrum (Oetting & Beauvais, 1991). For example, it is possible for one individual to highly identify with both cultures. Regardless of the profile, this information could be incorporated into the UP case formulation and addressed with patients.

Other important aspects of patients' cultural identities include gender identity, sexual orientation, religious affiliation, and socioeconomic status (for more information, see Sue et al., 2013). Just as with cultural identity and acculturation, identification with a particular group would not suffice to draw conclusions about an individual's identity but can serve to identify individuals who may benefit from tailoring of the UP (or any protocol). Self-report measures can be a helpful first step for factoring the degree of identification with these various aspects of identity. An open and respectful conversation with patients about their cultural views would likely be the most beneficial.

Treatment Recommendations

General treatment recommendations for cognitive-behavioral interventions include an emphasis on respect that is translated through collaboration rather than confrontation or irreverence, especially with attention being paid to client-therapist differences (Asnaani & Hofmann, 2012; Hays, 2009). This recommendation fits well within the UP, where clinicians help patients to develop their ability to assess if emotional responses fit the situation/context that is provoking these emotions. The emphasis of the UP on the adaptive nature of emotions and modification of responses to emotions to become more adaptive in the long term also encourages autonomy and fosters respect between patient and therapist. The focus is, thus, not on telling patients what they may be doing wrong. In the UP, even more than other CBT protocols, patients' autonomy and a collaborative therapeutic process is emphasized.

Other recommendations for culturally sensitive interventions include questioning how helpful the patient's thoughts are, as opposed to challenging how valid they are. The UP manual emphasizes this exact approach by highlighting cognitive flexibility instead of errors in thinking. If the patient and therapist do not share cultural assumptions, the therapist may appear to lack empathy or an understanding of the patient's worldview by challenging the validity of the patient's thoughts.

For example, if a patient is afraid that her son will be arrested for speeding, the therapist could focus on the helpfulness of the thoughts (e.g., "How helpful is it for you to repeat this thought to yourself many times daily?"). If the therapist jumps to questioning the validity of the thoughts without assessing the likelihood first, the therapist is relying on his/her own cultural assumptions about the likelihood of this event. By focusing on whether thoughts or behaviors are helpful, as opposed to whether they are valid, as is emphasized in the UP, the therapist upholds the client's autonomy to choose the best behaviors in the particular context (Wood & Mallinckrodt, 1990). Similarly, inadvertent challenging of core cultural beliefs by the therapist may not be well received by a patient. For patients whose cultures emphasize connectedness as opposed to independence, a therapist who encourages a patient to disconnect from the family by not talking to them anymore because of the family's problematic behavior runs the risk of alienating the patient. In the UP, the clinician empowers patients to make their own decisions about how adaptive their behaviors are and whether these behaviors fall in line with their goals. Therefore, in this case as well, the UP aligns with following culturally informed treatment adaptations.

Theoretical Models of Cultural Adaptations: How Much Adaptation Is Needed, What Needs Adapting, and for Whom?

Given the complexity of culture, answering the question of who needs culturally adapted treatments is not simple. Some research suggests that cultural adaptations may be helpful for those living in a new host culture (e.g., immigrants or children of immigrants) or for those who belong to a subcultural group within the dominant culture. In addition, cultural adaptations may be needed for those cultures that differ significantly from the culture where the EBI was originally developed (e.g., another country). Research that suggests that culturally adapted interventions are effective has found that patients who are low in acculturation in the new adopted culture (e.g., do not speak English) may receive the greatest advantage from cultural adaptations (Castro, Barrera, & Steiker, 2010).

Cultural adaptations have been categorized into one of two categories: surface structure adaptations or deep structure adaptations (Resnicow, Soler, Braithwait, Ahluwalia, & Butler, 2000). Surface structure adaptations typically include changes to EBIs that are more superficial in nature or relate to easily identifiable cultural aspects, such as language, clothing, food and the like. Adaptations to EBIs that include deep structure changes are focused on cultural meaning-making, as well as how social, historical, contextual, traditional, and similar factors affect individuals' worldviews and help-seeking behaviors (Castro et al., 2010; Resnicow et al., 2000).

In their review of cultural adaptations, Castro and colleagues (2010) point out that there are several frameworks with promising results for cultural adaptations. The frameworks vary on specific steps but share similar major elements. The cultural adaptations frameworks include a mix of qualitative and quantitative statistical methods of developing a successful adaptation. Each framework includes the target population for the adapted protocol in the adaptation process through focus groups and other "market" research methods. Maintaining the core elements and mechanisms of action for the EBI is also highlighted by several of the frameworks. Pilot testing is used to test preliminary revisions to an original EBI and assess if further changes should be made. The frameworks are intended to zero in on distinct risk factors and strengths of the culture. Most of the frameworks incorporate stakeholders from the culture to aid in the adaptation process.

How Should and Shouldn't the UP Be Adapted?

Identifying core elements of an EBI, such as the UP, can help to strike the right balance between integrity to the original treatment and adaptation to accommo-date cultural differences, otherwise known as *fidelity* and *flexibility* (Barrera & Castro, 2006). More research may be needed on striking the ideal balance, and yet there are hypothesized core elements of the UP that are integral to the treatment's success according to preliminary research on putative mechanisms of actions for this intervention. Nonjudgmental, present-focused awareness is one such mecha-nism of action that may facilitate improvements in symptoms, although a min-imum dose may be crucial to its efficacy (Boswell, Anderson, & Barlow, 2014; Brake et al., 2016). Other core mechanisms of the UP include the psychoeduca-tion module (Module 2), which provides information on the adaptiveness and monitoring of emotions (Boswell et al., 2014). The remaining core modules in the UP are empirically supported CBT elements, including cognitive restructuring, alternative actions, interoceptive exposures, and emotion exposures. Distilling the essence of each module to ensure some fidelity to the original treatment may be crucial to an adaptation's success.

Cultural Adaptations to the UP

The UP has undergone preliminary testing and cultural adaptations in Japan and Colombia with some collaboration from the UP research team at Boston University, where the treatment was originally developed. In Japan, the proto-col has undergone mostly surface-level adaptations that include translating the protocol into Japanese, as well as adding illustrations and changing the structure of the treatment goals by revisiting them more consistently throughout treat-ment in the UP Client Workbook. However, the Japanese researchers, headed by Dr. Masaya Ito, decided not to change many details of the protocol, including patient descriptions in the workbook and therapist guide, because they believed the protocol to be sufficiently transcultural. However, to enhance the understand-ing and motivation of Japanese patients, they added illustrations to the workbook. Illustrations in books tend to be more common in Japanese culture and are seen as an essential part of published works for the general public. For an example of one of these illustrations, see Figure 16.1, which depicts an analogy comparing strong emotions to being stuck in the middle of a bowl of gelatin and the work in treatment to observing the bowl from the outside. A pilot feasibility clinical trial of UP was started in Japan in 2012 with 17 participants, 15 of whom completed it. The overall results suggested good feasibility and acceptability, as well as pre-liminary effectiveness of the UP among Japanese patients (for further details, see Ito et al., 2016).

The Colombian adaptation was made more specifically for victims of the armed conflict in this country. These victims tend to be from rural areas of Colombia and typically have lower levels of education, and many of them have faced several traumas and forced displacement. The UP was adapted through the translation and inclusion of examples and vignettes that would be more relevant to victims (e.g., trauma, displacement). The protocol was also shortened to 12 sessions, given the difficulty of retaining the patient population in treatment for extended periods of time for a variety of reasons, including transportation difficulties and high mobility among this population. Also, another session (session 0) was added prior to the 12 sessions of protocol content to allow patients to discuss their history in depth and establish rapport.

Given that a majority of the patients in the trial have faced one or more traumas and thus may potentially be distrustful of others, session 0 was dedicated to establishing trust between the patient and the clinician. Overall, this adaptation too would fall under a surface-level adaptation. A pilot feasibility clinical trial of UP was started in Colombia in 2016, sponsored by the Colombian government. It is projected that in this study, 50 participants will receive the UP and another 50 a waitlist delayed treatment condition.

CASE PRESENTATIONS

It is important to note that both therapists from these case presentations belonged to the same broader cultural context as their patients, although differences likely existed at the intersection of cultural factors (e.g., gender, socioeconomic status, and the like).

A Japanese Case

H. S. is a 28-year-old, single, Japanese woman. She lives in Tokyo, near one of the city's ports, and is employed part time as an office clerk by her family's small seafood company. Although she had been prescribed psychiatric medications, such as selective serotonin reuptake inhibitor (SSRIs) and benzodiazepines, for five years from a psychiatric clinic, her anxiety and depressed mood had not improved. Therefore, she presented to the National Hospital in Tokyo seeking CBT as an alternative to the medications. Her chief complaints were anxiety in social situations, persistent irritability, and depressed mood. She also felt intense fear in situations in which she could not easily escape (e.g., crowded places, department stores) and reported binge-eating episodes and shame over her body shape and weight. She had difficulty forming close relationships with friends and reported feeling distant from her parents as well. She avoided most social situations due to almost constant distress in these situations. Overall, she did not engage in many activities and reported little enjoyment when she did.

H. S.'s social anxiety presentation was in accordance with a cultural concept of distress called *Taijin kyofusho*. This syndrome is characterized by anxiety and avoidance of interpersonal situations based on beliefs that one's appearance and actions are unfit or offensive to others. *Taijin kyofusho* is defined in a broader sense than social anxiety disorder because the patients' focus is often on how their characteristics (e.g., body odor) or behaviors (e.g., manners) are affecting other people (DSM-5). H. S. reported an extremely high standard for social behavior and appearance, including the clothes that she wore, the way she smiled at people, and how she spoke. She typically wore formal clothing when attending sessions at the hospital, and her behavior could be described as overly polite.

The symptoms of *Taijin kyofusho* first became prominent when H. S. experienced bullying in junior high school. Her classmates made fun of her for being overweight and commented on her appearance with harsh words, like "You are so ugly. Go away." She was deeply hurt by these events and as a result stopped attending school for a year. Additional contributing factors may have included the fact that her father and mother had been very strict and critical as she was growing up. She also described almost daily arguments that at times escalated into physical altercations between her two "stubborn" parents throughout most of her childhood.

In addition, her parents strongly influenced almost all her decisions. Although she had wanted to study literature at her university, her father had compelled her to enter the university's branch of business administration. Her only show of resistance toward her parents was entering a university that was far from her home. She reported that she enjoyed life at the university and did not experience interfering symptoms of anxiety and depression during the time she spent studying there. When she returned home after graduation, she found that her parents' relationship was not as contentious as it had been in her childhood. However, she began to feel stress when interacting with her parents because they were still critical and emotionally distant. Her symptoms of anxiety, irritability, and depression reportedly started five months after her return home following her graduation from college.

Her initial assessment at the National Hospital resulted in diagnoses of social anxiety disorder, agoraphobia without panic disorder, and major depressive disorder (MDD), according to criteria in the fourth edition of the *Diagnostic and Statistical Manual* (DSM-IV-TR; American Psychiatric Association, 2000). Pretreatment assessment showed a score of 28 on the Structured Interview Guide for the Hamilton Anxiety Scale (SIGH-A; Shear et al., 2001); 25 on the GRID-Hamilton Depression Scale (Williams et al., 2008); 90 on the Liebowitz Social Anxiety Scale (LSAS; Liebowitz, 1987); and 45 on the Beck Depression Inventory-II (BDI-II; Beck, Steer, & Brown, 1996). H. S. was then referred to the National Center of Cognitive Behavior Therapy and Research within the National Hospital. The recommendation was that her medications remain the same following this initial assessment, but that she also receive CBT. At the National Center of Cognitive Behavior Therapy and Research, she was screened for eligibility for the UP clinical trial, and she initiated treatment soon after.

During the first session, the therapist explained emotional disorders (i.e., anxiety, mood, and related disorders), the treatment structure, and the importance of objective monitoring. H. S. identified with the label of emotional disorders, given that she had continually experienced negative emotions of various kinds, such as anxiety in social interactions, fear and anger toward her parents, and continuous sadness. By her report, these emotions dominated her as though they were a large dark cloud. It was a relief for her to know that treatment exists for such emotional difficulties. Simultaneously, she insisted that it was impossible to change her "mentally weak personality."

Here, the therapist incorporated this information into his case formulation of the patient; specifically, that she had negative and self-critical beliefs about her symptoms (i.e., how she explained her symptoms). The therapist emphasized that she need not change her personality, but she would likely benefit from learning new skills to understand and experience her emotions without feeling overwhelmed by them. In terms of objective monitoring, she liked the analogy of "standing outside the bowl of gelatin" described and visually depicted in the Japanese version of the UP Client Workbook (as shown in Figure 16.1 earlier in this chapter).

At session 2, H. S. discussed her motivation for treatment and completed the Decision Balance Worksheet on her own (Module 1). She found the exercise especially useful because it allowed her to consider the costs of continuing the same behavior in the same contexts. She wrote, "If I will stay the same, I will have no choice but to die. Experiencing tremendous loss of energy and feeling always tired. I have to continuously pretend to be nice but I am unable to do what I want to do. Above all, I always have to be fearful of what others think." Her treatment goals were centered around increasing social activities. For example, one of her goals was to "Get to know friends better," which she made more concrete by stating, "Go to a musical with a friend." With the therapist's assistance, she developed five steps to accomplish that goal and agreed to "obtain the information about the musical from one of her old friends" as the homework of the week.

Figure 16.1 Analogy of "being out of the bowl" in the Japanese version of the UP Client Workbook.
SOURCE: IOJIN Youko Komaki, Masaya Ito, and Masaru Horikoshi, (2012) Unified Protocol for Transdiagnostic Treatment of Emotional Disorders Workbook Japanese Ed. Tokyo: SHINDAN TO CHIRYO SHA. Reprinted with permission.

H. S. quickly grasped the rationale for the nature, function, and three-component model of emotions (Module 2). Understanding the function of emotions and how responses are learned over time was a very validating experience for her. She said to her therapist, "I have never thought that fear and anxiety are important. I'm relieved to know about emotion-driven behavior. Now I think my physical responses were reasonable because I had been in a really fearful situation in my childhood." In fact, her parents had fought almost daily during her childhood. She was increasingly sensitive to any sign of interpersonal conflict as a result. She also came to believe that she must be the cause of her parents' fighting and that she needed to behave perfectly to prevent it. In addition to hypersensitivity about her own behavior at home, she experienced bullying and exclusion from her classmates. These experiences had enhanced her cognition of *Taijin kyofusho* such as "I will bother someone in some way" and "I make other people feel bad."

Although H. S. could report on her emotional experience in retrospect (e.g., the three-component model of emotions), she reported difficulty in engaging in the in-session nonjudgmental emotion awareness exercise. The therapist aided her by shortening the exercise to a shorter, eight minute-version that H. S. recorded on her smartphone. This helped her to practice the exercise outside of session. Through daily practice, she slowly acquired increased emotional awareness. She realized that most of her anger was secondary to feelings of sadness when her parents said something invalidating to her.

The other exercise that helped H. S. cultivate a present-focused awareness was the mood induction exercise. Fortuitously, one of her hobbies was listening to songs from musicals. The first time she practiced the mood induction exercise in session, she experienced intense anxiety and shame because she was so concerned about the therapist observing her. However, she gradually became able to sense joy and pleasure in place of anxiety and shame as she refocused her attention and listened to her favorite song from the popular musical *Wicked*.

H. S. quickly identified automatic appraisals and tracked how often they arose (Module 4). She stated that she frequently thinks, "I make trouble for other people," "I appear a strange person to others," and "I have to be polite at all times." She experienced some difficulty with increasing cognitive flexibility. Although she was able to generate cognitive reappraisals, she reported, "This seems artificial to me and it feels disappointing. Maybe I was unable to reappraise well. I can develop alternative appraisals in my head, but it doesn't change my emotions."

The therapist asked her about the differences in emotions when she thinks "I must be polite all the time and everywhere," as opposed to "I must be polite when needed. However, I need not suppress my emotions all the time and everywhere." She acknowledged that the emotions differed, although slightly, based on her thoughts. Moreover, when she accessed her core negative automatic appraisal, "I will be alone forever," via the downward arrow technique, she was moved to tears and reported deep sadness and loneliness. The therapist asked her to stay with the sadness and loneliness nonjudgmentally. The following is a transcript of the conversation between the therapist and H. S. describing how this unfolded:

H. S.: *My thought is that other people see me as strange.*

THERAPIST: *OK, that is an automatic appraisal that came up for you during the week when facing social situations. I wonder if we could try the downward arrow technique since we both agree that such an appraisal comes up often in your daily life. We might be able to find an important core belief tied to it.*

H. S.: *I'm not sure if that will help, but I guess I should try it.*

THERAPIST: *OK, what will happen if your appraisal is true? Other people see you as strange.*

H. S.: [pause] *That's horrible. It's proof that I'm a strange person.*

THERAPIST: *OK, "I'm strange." Then, what will happen?*

H. S.: *I don't know . . .* [pause] *I just feel like I'm the worst. person* [H. S. starts crying]

THERAPIST: *So, what does this mean to you? You are strange and the worst person.*

H. S.: *I don't know . . .* [sobbing]

THERAPIST: *Just stay with your emotion. What is happening to your body?*

H. S.: *It hurts. I just feel hurt.*

THERAPIST: *Yes, where do you feel the hurt in your body?*

H. S.: *Around here.* [She rubs her chest]

THERAPIST: *Yes, it hurts. It really hurts. What image do you have, what are you remembering? I see you thinking or remembering something. What scene do you have in your mind?*

H. S.: *I remember my mother often told me, "You are a fool and a bad girl." And, I remember the scene [of] my parents harshly arguing [with] each other.*

THERAPIST: *Then what emotion comes up? What are you feeling in your chest?*

H. S.: *Lonely, I just feel lonely . . .*

THERAPIST: *This seems to be an important emotion for you. Could you just stay with it? Be with it nonjudgmentally.*

H. S.: *Yes,* [sobbing] *. . . I guess I have been thinking I will be alone forever. It feels like I'm in a darkness, and I am separated from everything in this world.*

THERAPIST: *Yes, it must be so lonely and scary for you. These thoughts brought such a heavy feeling to your mind.*

H. S.: *Yes, I think so. Yes, it is . . . I often think I will be alone forever*

At the next session, she reported, "It was a relief to feel that emotion and recognize that I have been feeling so lonely. I feared the loneliness would continue forever, but I noticed that it comes and goes."

H. S. was also able to pinpoint her avoidance behaviors pretty well. She identified avoiding eye contact, suppressing showing emotions as much as possible, avoiding talking to others about herself, always being polite, and behaving timidly (Module 5). One of her emotion-driven behaviors (EDBs) was adding, "I'm sorry" very often during conversations, even when saying sorry was completely irrelevant to the situation. This tendency was observed during almost every session. For example, when the therapist asked H. S. about her feedback about the session, she responded "I'm so sorry to say this, but it was interesting for me to know my pattern of cognitive interpretation."

The therapist and patient observed this behavioral pattern, and the patient started to engage in alternative behaviors. Instead of saying "I'm sorry," she started to say "Thank you" in her daily life. Although it was difficult for her to engage in this alternative behavior, as positive interaction increased, she gradually felt self-efficacy and confidence in interacting with people. She also realized that her overly suppressive and polite behavior might have made people feel distant and sometimes even irritated.

For Module 6, however, she obstinately refused to engage in interoceptive exposures during the session. This refusal seemed to be idiosyncratic to H. S., given that most of the other participants in the trial did not object to these exposures. She insisted that she did not need to do the exercises in session because she had already tried symptom induction tests at home. Her therapist decided to stop discussing the exposures and instead demonstrated a hyperventilation exercise to her to reduce her feelings of shame about being observed. Then, the therapist left the room so that H. S. could practice hyperventilation in the room without the presence of the therapist. Later, the therapist sat with his back to her as she engaged in interoceptive exposures. Finally, patient and therapist practiced the exercises together.

H. S. was also able to do the remainder of the exercises during the session (i.e., breathe through a thin straw, spinning while standing, and running in place). H. S. reported that she initially could not engage in hyperventilation because she was so concerned about how her therapist would see her. She thought that she must conduct the exercises perfectly. However, if she performed the exercises perfectly, she feared that she would not be able to tolerate the physical feelings, and she would lose consciousness. She predicted that if she lost consciousness, this would cause great trouble for her therapist, and the whole scene would produce unbearable shame for her. Through gradual exposures, she slowly was able to feel comfortable in engaging in the exercises in front of her therapist.

In the emotion exposures (Module 7), H. S. engaged in various tasks to challenge her avoidance and test her cognitive appraisal. Her anxiety in social situations led her to avoid many situations. See Table 16.1 for a list of her emotional and situational exposures.

Through various situation-based emotion exposures, she realized that other people do not pay as much attention to her as she previously thought. Moreover, she was unable to find evidence for her self-appraisals (e.g., "I make trouble for other people"). Also, her expectations and feelings of *Taijin kyoufusho*, such as her high standards for her clothes, were also confronted via situational exposure to observe and look for evidence for her expectations. According to her, people in Tokyo change clothes every month in accordance with the gradual change of the four seasons. Although she always tried to follow these rules, she felt that

Table 16.1. EMOTION EXPOSURE HIERARCHY FOR H. S.

	Description	Avoid	Distress
1 Worst	Imagining a fight between her parents	7	8
2	Going to a popular department store	8	6
3	Entering and then exiting a taxi by pretending to have forgotten her purse	7	7
4	Giving a five-minute speech in front of a confederate	7	6
5	Voicing her opinion to her parents	7	6
6	Appearing in public with an incorrectly buttoned shirt	6	6
7	Inviting a friend to eat out at a restaurant	6	5
8	Going to a festival at a shrine	5	5
9	Texting friends	3	3

she could not satisfactorily meet appearance standards, and she thought, "I make other people feel negative emotions because of the clothes I wear." As she tested these expectations, she found no evidence for these thoughts either.

Utilizing imaginal exposure, she was able to feel intense primary fear and loneliness when she pictured fights between her parents. The task of "telling my opinions to my parents" helped her too. During this task, she stayed in the present and was able to distinguish between her past relationship and her current one with her parents. Finally, her avoidance of positive emotions was notable. She planned to see a musical with her friends, another of her treatment goals. By going to see a musical and focusing on the positive emotions during this experience, she reported that she was able to experience positive emotions and enjoyed the experience. She continued to engage in activities that brought her interest and pleasure throughout this last phase of treatment.

Her posttreatment assessment showed a score of 14 on the SIGH-A, 10 of GRID-Hamilton Depression Scale, 54 of LSAS, and 19 on the BDI-II. At the termination, she reported feeling less anxiety and irritability. She reported, "I feel that I had put on some heavy protective gear and I had run away from everything that I feared. In addition, I have tried to read my environment too much. Although I have some anxiety about my future, now I feel myself lighter. I will able to walk my own life by myself. I feel a bit sorry for taking your time and effort for my treatment, but I would like to say 'Thank you.'"

A Colombian Case

J. H. is a 29-year-old single, white, Hispanic male, who presented as part of the previously described study of the UP at Universidad de los Andes in Bogota, Colombia, following several close encounters where he nearly lost his life. The most recent traumatic event occurred when he came under attack by two armed men in his neighborhood four months prior to presenting to treatment. He was seeking psychological services for the first time. His main presenting concerns were difficulty leaving his house and engaging in activities, and worsening mood following the loss of his two cats. He devoted his energy and affection toward his two pets. Apparently, a neighbor poisoned the cats. Since that moment J. H. was feeling very irritable, anxious and depressed.

J. H. was raised as an only child by his mother and grandmother in a city in the northeast of Colombia. His father had passed away before he was born. The city where he lived for most of his life has been characterized by continuous conflict between paramilitary, guerrilla, and official military forces. The area's oil-based industry had led to frequent political and military disputes over control of the territory. J. H. reported that violent events were a common and daily part of his life while growing up. For example, he witnessed several local shootings when he was younger, and he and his friends found corpses with torture marks (from crucifixion, being shot, being burned, and being raped). He also witnessed kidnapping, forced recruitment, and bomb attacks. In addition, he had faced several violent situations where his life was at great risk.

Following high school, he enlisted in the army and faced active combat. Almost all his high school classmates had become "guerrilleros" or joined the paramilitary forces, and most of them were now dead or in prison by his report. Following his discharge from the army, he began a career as a security guard on an oil pipeline, one of the few legal employment opportunities in the area. During his years as a guard, J. H. was involved in and witnessed or experienced several more violent events. He was forced into doing odd jobs (e.g., delivering supplies to the guerrilla or paramilitary troops), threatened, and shot by accident by one of the armed groups. As a guard, he witnessed massacres, forced displacements, tortures, and shootings; found mutilated corpses in the oil pipeline fields; and saw many violent events. He remembers these events as distressing in the moment, but he did not view any of them as traumatic.

Despite witnessing or being involved in violent, life-threatening events, J. H. reportedly did not experience anxiety or depressive symptoms that interfered with his functionality. However, everything changed for him following three events that directly threatened his life between 2013 and 2014. In 2013, he was the lone survivor of an attack by guerilla troops who shot and killed his closest friends. His friends, members of the paramilitary, were ambushed and killed by another paramilitary squad that was fighting with them over control of the region. He was able to seek cover and hide as the other group was killing the rest of his squad. Two months later, the paramilitary squad ambushed him and shot him in his left leg, although he was able to escape a second time.

Due to these events, he, his mother, and his grandmother fled to Bogota. When he moved to Bogota, a local nongovernmental organization (NGO) where he sought counsel recommended that he increase his safety by wearing a bulletproof vest, leaving his house infrequently, and cutting all connections with his hometown and those affiliated with it. Unfortunately, in 2014, he was mugged and attacked by two armed men in his neighborhood in Bogota. He escaped a third time and was unharmed by this attack. However, the incident led him to cut out almost all relationships, and his anxiety symptoms significantly worsened.

An assessment of his symptoms was conducted by a graduate-level clinician, who applied the "Hechos Victimizantes" questionnaire developed by the Colombian research team. He was diagnosed with posttraumatic stress disorder (PTSD). Consistent with this diagnosis were his symptoms of sudden flashbacks, nightmares, difficulties with sleep, high levels of physiological activation when reminded of events, hypervigilance and excessive worries about his safety, and avoidance of almost all social situations. His hyperarousal symptoms to threat included shivering, chest pressure, increased heart rate, shaking, and an exaggerated startle response to noises (e.g., motorcycles, his front door opening).

He stated that he did not trust anyone except his mother, grandmother, and extended family. Most of his days were spent worrying about the possibility of being attacked again. As a result, he avoided leaving his house unless it was "absolutely necessary." When he left the house, he reported that he avoided crowded places, including public transportation. He especially noticed facial expressions that he interpreted as aggressive reactions and that occasionally led him to verbal arguments. Finally, he carried a gun at all times, including at the time of the assessment, to protect himself.

J. H. was most concerned by his depressive symptoms, which consisted of constant sadness and low mood, anhedonia, insomnia, loss of appetite, feeling slowed down, and persistent guilt over his past actions (in the army, his time as a guard, etc.). There was significant overlap between these symptoms and those of PTSD. They interfered with his motivation to leave his house or engage in any activities inside the house (e.g., exercise). In part due to his low mood, he could not relate to others or date, and he had lost his workers' compensation benefits, with the exception of a small pension from his physical disability that did not cover his basic needs.

J. H. was also assigned an alcohol use disorder, as he had intensified his use of alcohol to several drinks each day to cope with the symptoms that he was experiencing. He reported drinking especially in the evenings to aid him with sleep and reduce his nightmares. The drinking made him feel "groggy" and less motivated in the mornings. Moreover, the alcohol use was not advised by his physician due to his other medical conditions of high blood pressure and congenital heart disease. In the past 12 years, he had consumed alcohol several times each week but reported no interference or distress from it until recently. His drinking served to help him cope, as he said during the assessment.

As mentioned previously, an additional treatment session ("Session 0") was added to the beginning of the protocol to help build the therapeutic relationship and allow more space for J. H. to feel heard by telling his own story. During this session, the therapist focused on establishing trust and explored J. H.'s impairment and functioning in several life areas. He expressed that during his whole life, he was in contact with violent acts but not emotionally distressed by them because "it was a normal part" of his life. Now, he stated, everything had changed, and he was changed.

At the second introductory session, the therapist explained the importance of following an agenda and provided psychoeducation about the diagnoses and symptoms that J. H. experienced. The therapist also provided information about the number of sessions, session duration, practicing skills learned in treatment, completing practice assignments between sessions, and the like. At the end of the session, J. H. expressed high motivation for treatment and giving the process a chance, even if that meant having to compromise and to face his fears. He expressed his enthusiasm about starting to deal with his situation and putting his life back on track. He expressed that he was very excited about a few employment opportunities that had arisen recently, and he needed to be emotionally healthy to pursue them.

At session 2, J. H. set goals for treatment (Module 1). His primary goal was to "adjust to living in Bogota," which he made more concrete by stating that he would engage in meaningful activities, accept invitations from others, go on dates, and go to community activities. He also wanted to "stop being scared all the time," which he made more concrete by writing that he would learn to distinguish real from perceived danger, plan for real danger if someone from his past pursued him, and stay in situations that are safe, despite the urge to escape. His last goal was to manage his negative emotions, which he made more concrete by stating that he wished to live in accordance to his values and reduce his alcohol use to one or two drinks per week.

As for the pros and cons of change and staying the same (also Module 1), J. H. stated that he did not perceive any disadvantages to changing. After discussing this further, he came up with disadvantages that included possible distress from treatment activities, hesitation to reduce his alcohol consumption, and reluctance to feel vulnerable during treatment. His identified benefits associated with changing included that he would build new relationships, date, feel more relaxed in activities outside his home, and engage in daily life activities that he was now avoiding. He concluded that the advantages outweighed the disadvantages, and he would remind himself of this fact when facing distress during treatment.

At session 3, J. H. presented to session with complaints about low financial resources and few dating prospects. The therapist asked him to elaborate on his complaint and used this as an opportunity to explore the nature of emotions and the three-component model of his emotional response. He explored how each of the three components interacted and contributed to the intensity of his experience (Module 2).

J. H. explained that he worried constantly about finances and finding work, as well as ruminating about his past dating mistakes, blaming himself for not being in a relationship (this information was placed in the thoughts bubble of the three-component model of emotions). He identified his emotions accompanying these thoughts as anxiety, sadness, and guilt, and physical sensations as muscle tension and shallow breathing. He noted that the emotions and physical sensations were both brought on and intensified by these thoughts. He also described behaviors such as distracting himself, watching TV, drinking alcohol, leaving situations early, and changing his breathing to attempt to avoid physical sensations and thoughts. The rumination and worrying were also identified as behaviors, and he reported that they occurred most often while on public transport or lying in bed before sleeping. The therapist asked him where these behaviors happened most often so that he could increase his awareness of when they were happening and intervene on them later.

J. H. also explored the function of emotions like sadness (also Module 2). He stated that in the past, sadness led him to appreciate lost opportunities, relationships, his mother, etc. His sadness helped him to realize that he had not appreciated his hometown, his family, friends, or fun activities, and now he started to focus on enjoying the things that he had more. However, sadness was also currently interrupting his normal functioning by leading to excessive thinking about all that he had lost, and it in part drove many of his maladaptive behaviors, such as staying inside, missing out on new opportunities, and increasing his alcohol consumption. Similarly, J. H. recognized that when he experienced fear in the past, this emotion had led him to take precautions that worked to preserve his safety. In contrast, in present situations, he noted that fear was frequently driving him to restrict pursuing his goals, such as studying, dating, and socializing. By exploring the utility of these more recent responses, J. H. concluded that the behaviors were unhelpful.

J. H. began to understand that the utility of emotions depends on the reactions that we have to these emotions. The concept of real versus learned alarms was explored in this module (Module 2). J. H. was able to contrast his fight-or-flight reaction to fear based on real danger to his response to fear from a nightmare that awakened him. The emotions and EDBs were similar, but the presence of danger in these two scenarios differed. J. H. quickly recognized the importance of distinguishing real from learned (or false) alarms in order to act more in accordance with his long-term treatment and life goals. Finally, J. H. concluded that in situations where he witnessed violent events and his life was in danger, he did not have a stressful reaction because he had perceived control, dangerous as the experiences were. On the other hand, the three most recent attacks were unexpected, and he felt that he had no control.

In Module 3, J. H. practiced nonjudgmental, present-focused emotional awareness. Learning to describe and experience the present moment as it is unfolding, moment by moment, was especially important for J. H. The three-component model of emotions was revisited to help J. H. observe and describe what is happening in the here and now for each of the three components, especially following triggers from internal or external reminders of his traumas.

The nonjudgmental, present-focused exercise was modified to be more concrete and to aid with anchoring in the present. First, J. H. was asked to close his eyes and imagine a situation when he experiences strong emotions. He reported an incident on an evening in the previous week, in which he ran away when he heard the rustling of a tree. As he pictured this situation, he remembered what he was thinking, feeling, and doing in each moment. J. H. reported thinking that he was under attack, experiencing fear, and running away. He was then instructed to worry about this situation.

While J. H. was in the middle of worrying, the therapist then asked him to conduct a one-minute, nonjudgmental, present-focused exercise. In this exercise, he was asked to shift his attention to the sensations that he experienced when touching a table in the room (e.g., texture of the surface, temperature of the surface, pressure on his fingertips). He then turned his attention to other sensations, such as listening to the ticking of the clock in the therapist's office, feeling the chair on his back, and feeling his feet touch the ground. He was instructed to do this same mindfulness exercise each day in the places where he usually ruminates or worries. It is important to note that this exercise was not taught to him to distract from his strong emotions. Instead, J. H. utilized present-focused anchoring to reduce his avoidance of emotions through worry. In addition, he anchored in the present with mindful breathing and a three-point check. He did this second exercise at random times of the day, three or four times each day, to get in the habit of anchoring in the present.

At the next session, J. H. reported that the emotional awareness skills of focusing on the task at hand helped him to manage his emotions. He practiced nonjudgmental, present-focused awareness exercises in bed and on the subway (where he usually ruminated). He found that the exercise was useful to focus on the current context and notice how it was different from past situations (e.g., his attacks).

During the in-session exercise of mood induction (also Module 3), J. H. started to relive one of the attacks as he listened to a song that he picked out. He started to describe the scene as follows: "We were at the pickup in a rural roadway and this song began to play." He then heard shots, and in that very moment, he could smell gunpowder. He continued, "Two vans stopped in front of us and started to shoot us. One of my friends who was ex-paramilitary told me to run and hide behind a nearby small hill. When the shooting finally stopped, I saw my friends' bodies lying on the ground and the assailants driving off in the distance." J. H. described that his heart was beating quickly, he was sweating, and he was experiencing a similar reaction to the one that he experienced during the attack. After he was instructed to sit with his emotions nonjudgmentally, he noted a desire to get up and run from the room. The therapist then asked him to anchor his attention back to the present moment as he had done when he was worrying. Soon after, J. H. responded that he knew he was in a safe place now. He intuitively acknowledged that his desire to run away meant that he was reacting to a past situation in the same way that he had when it occurred. Instead, by experiencing his strong emotions and staying in the room, he remained in the present.

At session 5, J. H. learned about the relationship between thoughts and emotions (Module 4). He noted the different interpretations that can be made from an ambiguous picture and how each one is like a story that we tell ourselves. J. H. identified that his thoughts and story following the traumas had become, "There is danger everywhere and I am never safe." For example, when he saw young men in his neighborhood, he immediately perceived them as a high potential threat and his thoughts jumped to "They are gang members and will rob me." He explored this thought using the downward arrow exercise and drilled down to "I have lost trust in people and myself" and the conclusion that he drew during the trauma of "I am weak and can't defend myself." He then connected how his thoughts influenced his emotions leading to fear and sadness. This process was tied back to behaviors by noting that his action during these thoughts was to quickly run away, missing out on opportunities to watch soccer matches on his neighborhood's outdoor screen with his young neighbors.

J. H. learned that these initial appraisals are automatic thoughts that strengthen his core beliefs that the world is a very dangerous and he is weak. He noticed that though he believed the initial appraisals easily, he could generate alternative appraisals. He stated, "I can take advantage of opportunities" and "I am strong enough to cope with difficult situations if they come up." He expressed that he wants to tell a new story, the current Bogota story, where he is able to do important things like look for work and connect with others.

Additional automatic thinking traps for J. H. included thinking that women would turn him down unless he purchased a drink for them when he went out (which he labeled a "jumping to conclusions" thinking trap). Also, J. H. thought that he would either have to take a woman on an expensive date that he could not afford or the rejection would be so painful that he would feel unable to date again (a "catastrophizing" thinking trap). He quickly restructured many of these thoughts on his own and said that he was exaggerating. He also responded to the therapist's questions by stating the true probability of being turned down was less than 10%, not the 90% that he felt was true. Also, he said, "It really is not that bad. I could just move on and find a more supportive girl. There are plenty of supportive girls, even in Bogota." He also said that a woman could ask him out, and that in Bogota, women tend to pay for themselves. Finding alternative "stories" helped J. H. slowly reduce his avoidance of social situations. He practiced being aware of his unhelpful automatic "stories" that kept him from pursuing his goals and changed them to increase the flexibility in his thinking. He reported that the "new stories" helped his emotions. Even the act of labeling the thoughts "stories" or "tales" increased his flexibility almost instantly.

J. H. continued to identify unhelpful behaviors (Module 5) that impeded his pursuit of long-term goals. Besides his more overt situational avoidance (EDBs) of leaving situations early or in response to a false alarm (e.g., a noise from the environment), he identified other important instances of emotion avoidances or EDBs. For example, he quickly recognized that carrying a gun around was a safety signal for him. When he left the gun at home, he realized that he was safe even without it. Previously, he had derived his safety from his gun and was unable to learn to trust that he was safe without it. Cognitive avoidances for him included rumination about the traumas or trying to avoid memories of the events. Subtle behavioral avoidances included delaying leaving his house.

J. H. recognized that though all these behaviors helped in the short term to relieve his anxiety, they hurt him in the long run. Leaving the house, for one, had become harder and harder for him over time prior to starting treatment. He also procrastinated following up on job opportunities, making plans with acquaintances, and the like. He identified that procrastinating similarly reduced his anxiety that he would not find work or that something dangerous would occur but kept him from "living his life."

For EDBs, J. H. noted that he keeps reacting to things that reminded him of his traumatic attacks. He concluded that running in response to these reminders is not useful, and that by responding to the false alarm, he was strengthening the reaction. J. H. reported that he had been using emotional awareness strategies to distinguish between real and learned dangers.

When he noted no real danger, he attended and stayed in social gatherings, such as organized victims' meetings. In addition, he started to approach neighbors whom he perceived as being safe about the dynamics of the neighborhood, and thus, confronted overgeneralized fears that everyone in the neighborhood was dangerous. He did not throw caution to the wind, given that there were many gang members in his neighborhood; instead, he learned to assess potential danger. By noticing if his reactivity is alerting him to the real versus perceived threats, he made more accurate assessments of situations than before and stopped running away from pleasurable activities. He also stopped the use of alcohol and reported focusing his attention on finding solutions to his concerns.

Interoceptive exposures helped J. H. to tolerate the physical aspect of his strong emotions and to increase his ability to view these physical symptoms nonjudgmentally without thinking that they are indicative of imminent danger (Module 6). He completed all the in-session exercises (e.g., straw breathing, running in place). However, he experienced a flashback during the hyperventilating and remembered the instance when he ran away from the paramilitary troops that killed his friends. The therapist asked J. H. to remind himself that he was reexperiencing a memory and asked him to focus his attention on one point in the room and listen to the ticking of the clock on the wall. He reported that his physical sensations were signals to him that something was wrong and he should escape. These exercises helped him to separate his physical sensations from his urges to run away. He reported that with practice, he was now able to sit with unpleasant sensations.

Finally, J. H. put together all the skills that he had practiced over the course of treatment to face emotionally provoking situations (Module 7). He had already started practicing changing his behaviors over the course of treatment as he had learned about his emotions and true versus false alarms. Nonetheless, he created a hierarchy that included attending community activities at the bottom, asking a woman on a date in the middle of the list, and staying in anxiety-provoking situations and taking steps to start his own small business at the top. Over the course of four sessions, he reported that he was easily attending community situations and enjoyed them quite a bit. He even asked a woman whom he met at a dancing event out for coffee. He reported that they did not have much in common, but he was still very proud of taking the initiative again to date.

Staying in situations proved to be trickier for J. H. Sometimes he stayed and white-knuckled the situation with great distress, and other times he left. After discussing this process further with the therapist, J. H. uncovered that he was utilizing the exposures as efforts to reassure himself that he was better and to prove to himself that he was "over" the traumas. At the first sign of anxiety, he was judging the experience as negative and proof that he was not over the traumas. The therapist encouraged him to refocus on nonjudgmental, present-focused awareness and gauging false alarm versus true alarm. J. H. also engaged in some more flexible thinking about the meaning of the anxiety. These steps seemed to help, and he reported staying in situations more and more. J. H. created smaller more manageable steps toward creating his small business and was able to tackle the steps easily.

Overall, J. H. made great strides forward in a brief period of time; see Table 16.2 for his scores on the Overall Depression Severity and Interference Scale (ODSIS) and Overall Anxiety Symptoms and Interference Scale (OASIS) over the course of treatment. He reduced his drinking, increased his involvement in activities, and showed a significant reduction in his symptoms. J. H. thus reached his treatment goals. At the end of treatment, he continued to attempt to face uncomfortable emotions in several areas of his life, and he was very thankful to the therapist for helping "give my life back."

CONCLUSION

This chapter presents applications of the UP with patients in international settings and from two different cultures. Although cultural presentations of symptoms may vary, the UP's focus on emotions, thoughts, and behaviors helps patients from varying cultures to become aware of their emotions, the ways that emotions are helping them in their daily lives, and the ways in which their relationship with their emotions may be less than useful to them in their cultural setting. The UP was developed to target negative reactions to emotions that are thought to maintain and increase unhelpful emotions, thoughts, and behaviors. As such, the UP may target a core universal human experience of emotions.

However, the application of the UP in any given culture should be carefully considered. The protocol is based on cognitive-behavioral models of interventions that have cultural assumptions and values (e.g., independence, assertiveness, and individualism) that may be counter to other cultures. Patients are adept at recognizing adaptive responses and the ways in which their emotions are impeding their functioning. Therefore, the UP can be modified to aid them with their relationship to their emotions while staying within the frame of the patients' values and culture.

Table 16.2. Anxiety and Depression Symptom Scores Throughout Treatment for J. H.

	S1	S2	S3	S4	S5	S6	S7	S8	S9	S10	S11	S12
OASIS	15	17	14	16	12	15	12	10	10	8	7	5
ODSIS	12	13	10	14	10	5	5	6	5	4	5	4

NOTES: OASIS = Overall Anxiety Symptoms and Interference Scale; ODSIS = Overall Depression Severity and Interference Scale

Overall, patients treated with the UP internationally saw meaningful reductions in their symptoms of depression and anxiety (de Ornelas Maia, Nardi, & Cardoso, 2015; Ito et al., 2016; Osma, Castellano, Crespo, & García-Palacios, 2015). More research in varied settings (both internationally and in the United States) will further determine the UP's applicability to these settings. Future research is needed to clarify what types of adaptation would be most useful, and for whom.

Depending on the setting, it is possible that patients may experience significant life stressors while undergoing psychological interventions (e.g., J. H., the Colombian patient, faced many stressors, including unemployment and active threats from his past). These stressors can be addressed within the context of the UP skills to aid patients to manage challenging life situations.

In summary, treatment with the UP seems to be adaptable to different cultures with promising initial results. The cases reviewed here, in addition to the preliminary results from the trials in Japan and Colombia, suggest that the UP is both feasible and acceptable to use with those from different cultures.

17

The Unified Protocol

Future Directions

CLAIR CASSIELLO-ROBBINS, HEATHER MURRAY LATIN,
AND SHANNON SAUER-ZAVALA ■

INTRODUCTION

Previous chapters in this book have been dedicated to describing applications of the Unified Protocol for Transdiagnostic Treatment of Emotional Disorders (UP; Barlow, Farchione et al., 2018; Barlow, Sauer-Zavala et al., 2018), an emotion-focused, cognitive-behavioral therapy (CBT), to the range of emotional disorders. These disorders are characterized by the experience of frequent and intense negative emotion, strong aversive reactions to these emotions (neuroticism), and efforts to escape or avoid these emotional experiences (Barlow, 1991; Watson & Naragon-Gainey, 2014). This conceptualization of emotional disorders, particularly its focus on neuroticism as a higher-order temperamental factor contributing to the development and maintenance of these disorders, is distinct from prior efforts to categorize psychological disorders (see Chapter 1).

This approach to understanding these disorders is an innovative development stemming from years of nosological research establishing commonalities across them and identifying core affective processes that contribute to the presentation of emotional disorders (Ellard, Fairholme, Boisseau, Farchione, & Barlow, 2010). Indeed, this conceptualization of emotional disorders was an important step in the development of the UP and its applicability to the range of emotional disorders.

Emotional disorders previously described in this book include anxiety, obsessive-compulsive disorder (OCD) and related disorders, major depressive disorder (MDD), bipolar disorder, posttraumatic stress disorder (PTSD), borderline personality disorder (BPD), and trauma-related, alcohol use, eating, and insomnia disorders. Further, cases have been presented showing that the UP is applicable to a wide range of presenting problems that utilize similar processes to emotional disorders (i.e., aversive reactions to negative emotions, efforts to escape or avoid emotional experiences), even though they are not classified as disorders in the *Diagnostic and Statistical Manual of Mental Disorders* (5th ed; DSM-5; American Psychiatric Association, 2013). These problems include nonsuicidal and suicidal self-injury, as well as chronic pain. Indeed, the cases presented in these chapters provide support for the transdiagnostic conceptualization of emotional disorders, as well as compelling examples of the creative ways in which the UP can be employed to target symptoms across the range of emotional disorders and their varying presentations.

The initial success of the UP across case studies, case series, and randomized controlled trials in no way implies that efforts to further understand and refine this protocol are complete. Data supporting the efficacy of this treatment have now inspired further research efforts to better understand the specific effects of individual treatment components, refine new methods of delivery, and promote effective dissemination to community clinicians. The purpose of this chapter is to describe future directions and projects related to the UP, how these endeavors will enhance our understanding of this protocol, and how this understanding will lead to more efficacious, efficient, and disseminable care.

FUTURE DIRECTIONS

Dismantling

The UP is an evidence-based treatment that is typically delivered over 12 to 16 sessions, and is hypothesized to target core mechanisms that contribute to the development and maintenance of emotional disorders, thus helping a patient improve his/her functioning. While the core framework of the UP is fixed, the way in which treatment content is delivered can be revised, and research efforts are underway to identify alterations to ensure that the UP is delivered in the most effective and disseminable ways possible. One particular modification to the delivery of the UP is of interest for future research: changing the order in which treatment modules are delivered.

Currently, the UP is designed as a treatment consisting of eight modules: motivation, psychoeducation, mindfulness, cognitive flexibility, emotion-driven behavior (EDB) and emotional avoidance, interoceptive exposure (IE), in vivo exposure, and relapse prevention (see Chapter 1 for a detailed description of the modules). The following modules are considered "core" modules; that is, each of them teaches emotion regulation skills that address a core affective process contributing to the experience of negative affect in these disorders: emotion awareness, cognitive flexibility, countering emotional behaviors, IEs, and in vivo exposures (Ellard et al., 2010). One question pertinent to future directions of the UP is to determine the degree to which the UP is a modular treatment and, if it is, how best to maximize the benefits of this treatment structure. Modular treatments are importantly different from traditional manualized treatments, and thus the designation of the UP as modular requires further substantiation from research.

The key difference between traditional manualized and modular treatments is the extent to which the skills in the protocol are interdependent or self-contained. In a traditional manualized treatment, skills are interdependent, and thus the order in which the treatment skills are delivered is key. However, in modular treatments, skills are not interdependent and the order in which they are delivered is flexible. The study by Chorpita, Daleiden, and Weisz (2005) suggests that a treatment can be considered modular if it meets the following criteria:

First, it must have partial decomposability (i.e., it can be divided into functional units). Second, the modules must have proper functioning (i.e., each module produces the intended results). Third, the modules must have a standardized interface (i.e., the modules connect in a structured fashion). Fourth, each module must be encapsulated, or self-contained — that is, the module must contain unique information that can be delivered independent of any other modules (known as *information hiding*). Importantly, modularity is not an all-or-nothing endeavor; there are degrees of modularity (Chorpita et al., 2005).

The UP clearly meets the first and third criteria. With regard to the first criteria, each module can be considered a functional unit. With regard to the third criteria, the UP modules are clearly integrated with one another; the UP framework connects them. However, the second and fourth criteria have yet to be evaluated. It is unknown if each module produces the intended results (i.e., change in the relevant skills) and whether each module is self-contained.

A modular treatment offers several advantages. From a research standpoint, modules provide a way to evaluate and understand specific treatment mechanisms that drive improvement in symptoms (Nakamura, Pestle, & Chorpita, 2009). Demonstrating a higher degree of modularity in the UP would allow researchers to examine the unique and specific effects of individual treatment components on a patient's symptoms. This mechanism-based understanding allows for future treatment refinement aimed at increasing treatment efficacy and disseminablility.

From a clinical standpoint, modular treatments are more flexible and allow for greater treatment personalization than traditional manualized treatments. That is, modules can be reordered as needed in order to address pronounced deficits earlier in treatment. Alternatively, a module could be skipped if its topic doesn't represent a skill that would benefit the patient. Further, the amount of time spent in each module could be lengthened or shortened as needed to ensure that the patient adequately learns the information related to the module. In fact, it is likely that modular treatments more closely approximate clinical practice, as research suggests that community clinicians are unlikely to follow a manual sequentially, preferring a more eclectic treatment that allows them to teach the skills most relevant to their case conceptualization of each patient (Park, Chorpita, Regan, Weisz, & Research Network on Youth Mental Health, 2014; Persons, 2005).

Modules can also increase the efficiency of treatment. Instead of progressing through a manual at a standard pace, a modular treatment can change pace to meet the needs of the patient. The combination of targeting areas of greatest need early in treatment and changing pace as deemed appropriate makes it possible that the length of treatment could be shortened, allowing therapists to treatment more patients in less time.

Finally, the flexibility of modular treatments could aid not only in sequencing treatment components, but also in determining when a patient has received an adequate "dose" of a treatment component (Murray et al., 2014). An assessment at the beginning of treatment could provide information about an individual patient's strengths and weaknesses and suggest an order in which to provide treatment modules so that they might be maximally beneficial. Throughout treatment, by providing clear criteria as to what constitutes an adequate dose of each component, potentially through the use of standardized measures, therapists will be able to tell when a patient has acquired the knowledge that a treatment module has to offer and whether the patient is using that knowledge adequately in a way that improves his/her functioning. Thus, therapists and patients will no longer be left wondering if a skill is adequately understood and whether it is time to move on to the next skill.

One well-known modular treatment effort is Project MATCH, a protocol based on the extant evidence-based treatments for anxiety, depression, and disruptive behaviors in children ages 8–13. In this protocol, the selection of modules is based on algorithms that represent conventional clinical applications of cognitive-behavioral principles to these problems. These algorithms allow problems to be targeted in order of importance, in addition to addressing treatment-interfering behaviors as they arise throughout the course of treatment (Chorpita et al., 2005). In a series of single-case experimental designs (SCEDs), Chorpita, Taylor, Francis, Moffitt, and Austin (2004) found that modular treatment via Project MATCH resulted in reductions in anxiety symptoms and improvements in life functioning for six out of the seven patients who participated. Further, in a randomized controlled trial comparing traditional manualized therapy, modular therapy, and usual care, Chorpita et al. (2013) found that modular treatment in Project MATCH afforded an advantage over usual care at two-year follow-up, whereas traditional manualized care did not. In this trial, the modular treatment also resulted in steeper trajectories of improvement than other conditions, suggesting that this treatment is more efficient than the comparison conditions (Weisz et al., 2012).

Another treatment utilizing a modular approach is the Common Elements Treatment Approach (CETA; Murray et al., 2014). Interestingly, CETA includes guidelines for sequencing treatment components and what constitutes an adequate dose of a given component. Both a pilot study and a randomized waitlist control trial suggest that CETA results in clinically meaningful improvements (Murray et al., 2014; Bolton et al., 2014). Taken together, findings from both CETA and MATCH suggest that there are substantial benefits associated with utilizing modular treatments.

Thus far, the UP modules have been applied in a fixed order, with some flexibility as to how much time is spent in each module, and all of its extant research support is for delivering treatment in this manner. Given the aforementioned benefits of, and the extant research supporting the efficacy of, modular treatments in other populations, it is relevant and beneficial to establish the extent to which the UP is a modular treatment. By establishing the properties of modularity within this treatment, we will encourage flexibility in the ways in which this protocol is delivered, with the intent of increasing its efficiency and disseminability, and be able to offer evidence-based guidelines for clinicians who would like to change the order in which skills are introduced.

Initial research efforts surrounding modularity are aimed at understanding the sensitivity and specificity of each module. That is, does a module produce change in a given domain when and only when it is introduced (sensitivity)? And does a given module effect more change in the targeted skill domain than in irrelevant skill domains (specificity)? The unique and specific effects of each module will be important to understand as we consider reordering modules based on treatment priorities.

Using multiple-baseline SCEDs, we have begun to examine the sensitivity and specificity of four of the five core modules (psychoeducation, mindfulness, cognitive flexibility, and countering emotional behaviors), in addition to identifying the measures that are the most sensitive to change in the domains relevant to these modules. These four modules were chosen because each teaches a specific skill, whereas exposures focus on the application of all these skills to feared situations. In a multiple-baseline SCED, the start of treatment is staggered across individuals in order to provide evidence that change occurs when and only when the treatment is introduced (Barlow, Nock, & Hersen, 2009).

In the initial evaluation of these four modules, patients were randomly assigned to receive a module immediately or to wait two weeks before receiving it. This design allows for an assessment of each module's sensitivity. In addition, patients were assigned to receive only one module, but they filled out measures relevant to all four modules in order to establish specificity. The results of this work provided preliminary support for the idea that each UP module leads to change in its associated domain (i.e., the cognitive module is associated with improved cognitive flexibility). Further, exploratory analyses suggested that both mindfulness and cognitive flexibility produced specific changes (i.e., changes only in the targeted domain), whereas psychoeducation and countering emotional behaviors led to more broad-based changes across skill domains (Sauer-Zavala et al., 2017). These results suggest that each module produces the intended results (i.e., change in the relevant domain) and is self-contained (i.e., it was able to be delivered in isolation), meeting the second and fourth criteria for modularity proposed by Chorpita et al. (2005).

With preliminary support suggesting that the UP is indeed a modular treatment, upcoming projects will examine whether modules can be reordered based on a patient's presenting problems and still result in efficacious treatment. In the next iteration of our work on modularity, we will assign participants to receive modules that target their deficits or their strengths in order to begin to understand whether treatment efficiency can be maximized by reducing deficits (i.e., beginning treatment with skills that address the domain where the patient has the most trouble, such as avoidance (EDBs) or negative automatic thoughts [cognitive flexibility]) or by enhancing strengths.

The long-term goal of the modularity work is to design efficient, flexible evidence-based treatments that closely approximate clinical practice and are thus easily disseminable. We hope that one day, the results of an assessment will note areas of an individual patient's strengths and weaknesses, allowing a clinician to order modules accordingly.

Dissemination

When considering strategies for disseminating the UP, evaluating the role of a transdiagnostic treatment within existing models and approaches, such as stepped care, and personalized medicine may maximize efforts to enhance access to quality mental healthcare. Stepped-care treatment strategies have become a necessary approach for treating a variety of disorders, given the discrepancy in the limited number of mental health providers and the high demand for such treatments (Clark, 2011; Layard & Clark, 2014; Haaga, 2000), the delay in treatment initiation (Wang, Berglund, et al., 2005), and the small proportion of providers administering evidence-based treatments (Weisz, Sandler, Durlak, & Anton, 2005; Comer, 2015). Studies estimate that fewer than half of those individuals in need of mental health services receive treatment, with even fewer (one-third of individuals receiving treatment) receiving services from a mental health professional (Wang, Berglund, et al., 2005).

In a stepped-care approach, costs of treatment are minimized while efficiency of care is maximized, as the patient's first line of treatment is an intervention with minimal intensity (Katon, Von Korff, Lin, Simon, & Walker, 2014). Patients are closely monitored, allowing for the identification of those patients requiring a more intensive dose of treatment. Once identified, they can quickly step up to a more intense treatment, often provided by trained specialists. Self-administered treatments (e.g., self-help books and computerized treatments; Haaga, 2000; Newman, 2000) are cost-efficient, low-dose, front-line treatment strategies. In addition, training community nonmental health providers increases the reach of those individuals in need of services while decreasing the cost burden associated with specialty care.

Stepped-care strategies have been implemented in the healthcare system of the United Kingdom (U.K.). For example, the Improving Access to Psychological Therapies (IAPT) program in Britain includes computerized CBT as a first-line treatment for depression and anxiety disorders. The IAPT initiative has increased access to care, with promising clinical outcomes. An initial evaluation of two of the U.K. sites in the first 13 months of the program found that 55% of patients attending at least two sessions met the "recovered" status. Treatment gains were maintained at the 10-month follow-up (Clark et al., 2009). Richards and Suckling (2009) reported results from another U.K. site, providing additional support for the effectiveness of the IAPT program. These researchers found very large effect sizes for patients completing the program, with recovery/remission rates around 75%. These findings are consistent with benchmark routine effectiveness studies (Stiles, Barkham, Mellor-Clark, & Connell, 2008). Given the aforementioned benefits of this approach, fitting the UP into a stepped-care model represents one viable way to disseminate this protocol.

In addition to stepped-care approaches, personalizing medicine has the potential to facilitate efficiency in the delivery of treatment, enhance treatment outcomes, and lower the costs associated with treatment. Personalized medicine has been a focus of many medically related treatments, relying on biological markers and neuroimaging techniques to identify accurate and reliable diagnostic variables associated with treatment response, and it is possible that these principles could be extended to psychological treatments as well. Moreover, customizing mental healthcare based on diagnostic tests or individual characteristics is a promising area of research.

DeRubeis and colleagues (2014) tested an approach to predict differential response to treatment with identified patient variables, using the Personalized Advantage Index (PAI) in a large randomized controlled trial for MDD. Patients randomized to the condition deemed "optimal" based on the PAI calculation demonstrated superior outcomes when compared to those assigned to the "nonoptimal" treatment. By identifying individual factors, such as demographic information, treatment history, and comorbidity, predicting optimal treatment response will not only improve treatment outcomes, but also reduce cost and time burdens associated with treatment nonresponse.

In the remainder of this section, two recent efforts of dissemination and implementation, particularly within the stepped-care model and personalized medicine approach, will be discussed. First, the aims of the Unified Protocol Institute (UPI), including training nonmental health specialists in the delivery of the UP, will be reviewed. Secondly, identifying innovative strategies using technology to expand the reach of the UP treatment will be discussed.

The UPI is a nonprofit organization initiated in response to numerous inquiries regarding training with the UP, and as a means to proactively disseminate the treatment. The UPI employs a stepwise approach to dissemination. The initial step in this process is an introductory workshop that provides information on the rationale for transdiagnostic CBT, as well as a detailed description of each UP skill module. Audio and video recordings of cases with complex, comorbid presentations are included to demonstrate how UP skills are applied. The introductory workshop provides a basic overview of the intervention and is meant to supplement the published UP Client Workbook and UP Therapist Guide.

More intensive training on the UP is offered in the form of two certification programs. While neither certification is required to deliver the UP competently, these processes are helpful in teaching therapists to deliver the treatment with fidelity. *Therapist Certification* entails supervision on a course of treatment with the UP. In order to accommodate national and international interest (the UP has been translated into seven languages), supervision is conducted over the phone or via videoconferencing (e.g., Skype). Successful completion of the program

indicates that a therapist has been deemed competent to deliver the UP to his/
her patients. The next step is *Trainer/Research Certification*, which indicates
that successful completers are competent to train others in their institution on
the UP (e.g., provide supervision) or to provide research-adherent treatment;
this approach is consistent with the train-the-trainer model for dissemination
(McHugh & Barlow, 2010).

Finally, the UPI offers consultation on program implementation for settings
that are interested in using the UP in a sitewide manner. This service usually
involves several planning meetings and then some combination of workshops
(for the majority of the staff) and trainer certification (for members of the organization's leadership team). In some cases, adaptations of the manual have been
developed for settings that deviate from the standard weekly outpatient care for
which the UP was originally created. For example, the UPI has provided program
implementation services for a multisite inpatient eating disorder program, and
the protocol was adapted to be delivered in groups dedicated to each module (e.g.,
psychoeducation groups, cognitive flexibility groups).

One interesting example of recent program implementation with the UP has
been in the context of the Visiting Nurses Association of Boston (VNA-B). Given
the established infrastructure of home-based medical care within the VNA-B system, this collaboration has the opportunity to fill a critical gap in service delivery, as the majority of patients who receive home-based health services are older
adults (Caffrey, Sengupta, Moss, Harris-Kojetin, & Valverde, 2011). Although
anxiety and depression are more common in older adults than the general population, with prevalence estimates ranging from 10% to 15% (Kessler et al., 2012),
these individuals are less likely to receive adequate treatment (Bartels et al., 2004;
Olfson & Pincus, 1996). These problems may be exacerbated in a homebound
population, where research suggests that depression is underdiagnosed and that
only one in five individuals with this disorder receives treatment, often at an inadequate dose (Bruce et al., 2002). When left untreated, mental health problems
have been shown to worsen medical outcomes in patients with comorbid general medical conditions by increasing risk for falls, complications, and rehospital-
ization (Cabin, 2010; Suter, Suter, & Johnston, 2008; Byers et al., 2008; Sheeran,
Brown, Nassisi, & Bruce, 2004; Sheeran, Byers, & Bruce, 2010), as well as increasing reliance on medical services (Friedman, Delavan, Sheeran, & Bruce, 2009).

Given the implications of untreated mental health problems within their patient
population, it is no surprise that the VNA-B expressed an interest in collaborating with mental health providers. The UP was an obvious choice for their organization because of this intervention's ability to extend beyond single diagnoses
(e.g., depression) to simultaneously address a wider range of presenting mental
health concerns. In addition, given the role of neuroticism in the development
and maintenance of medical conditions (Lahey, 2009), the UP may also exert a
direct effect on VNA-B's comorbid medical problems.

Program implementation with the VNA-B entailed training nonmental health
practitioners (in this case, medically trained nurses) to deliver the UP. The insurance reimbursement for VNA-B providers allowed only eight CBT sessions,

representing an additional challenge to deployment in this setting. Further, most of the VNA-B patients were homebound with limited mobility and could have mild cognitive decline. To adapt to these challenges, the UPI developed an eight-session version of the UP; care was taken to bring the reading level down to a sixth-grade level, and skills were modified to be practiced solely in the context of the patient's home (particularly for the exposure module). A three-day training workshop was conducted for nurses within the VNA-B organization who would be serving as UP therapists. The modified UP sessions were presented in a didactic manner, followed by extensive role-plays between VNA-B therapists and UPI staff.

To facilitate maintenance of the UP program within the VNA-B, it was also important to train a subset of their staff to fulfill a supervisory role. The VNA-B hired a licensed clinical social worker (LCSW) to oversee their mental health program, and this individual completed the UPI's Trainer Certification program. She received weekly supervision on a patient diagnosed with social anxiety disorder; explicit feedback on each session was possible, as all sessions were audio-recorded so that the UPI expert trainer could rate it for adherence and competence. The LCSW did not have a background in CBT; she approached the patient from a case management/problem-solving perspective. As such, early sessions required more feedback related to the UP philosophy of teaching patients to better tolerate their strong emotions rather than making structural life changes to reduce stressors. Despite this initial challenge, the LCSW was able to pass each session using established criteria and met 80% of the criteria on the adherence checklist, thus demonstrating satisfactory mastery of the protocol.

The UPI framework provides ample opportunity for future research. Our group collects outcome measures of satisfaction and knowledge acquisition following our workshops as standard practice. Feedback suggests that our workshops are generally well received and are effective in establishing new learning of UP treatment concepts. Within our program implementation model, other important questions related to dissemination and implementation have arisen. For instance, what is the minimum of level of training is necessary for clinicians for to successful deliver the UP? Further, are there training moderators [e.g., degree (Ph.D. versus MSW versus RN), familiarity with CBT] that influence the intensity of didactic and supervisory support necessary? Alternatively, are there personal characteristics of potential therapists (e.g., psychological mindedness, fear of exposure work) that also predict a clinician's ability to deliver this treatment?

Within the VNA-B project, for example, we are testing some of these questions by assessing the percentages of visiting nurses that reach our established levels of protocol adherence at increasingly supportive levels of supervision (e.g., weekly group supervision with a VNA-B LCSW, weekly individual supervision with an LCSW, and weekly supervision with a Ph.D.-level expert trainer). These efforts will allow us to establish best practices to ensure efficient dissemination of the UP.

In addition to the dissemination and implementation efforts, including efforts within the VNA-B, our group has focused on identifying innovative strategies to extend the reach of the UP and improve outcomes. Incorporating technology in the delivery of treatment has the potential to reduce many known barriers of seeking, providing, and receiving empirically supported treatment. As previously noted, there is a clear need to improve dissemination of effective treatments for mood and anxiety disorders, with fewer than half of individuals diagnosed with anxiety and mood disorders receiving psychological services and even fewer receiving empirically supported treatments (Wang, Lane, et al., 2005).

Given the call to bridge the science-to-service gap, there has been increased attention paid to advancing the application of new technologies, as well as understanding the potential limitations of integrating technology into mental healthcare. Kazdin (2015) identifies key characteristics to guide treatment development, specifically technology-based interventions, including reach, scalability, affordability, convenience, acceptability, flexibility and use of a nonspecialized workforce. The development of a web-based UP program is an idea currently under development. Such a platform would provide structured self-guided therapy sessions via a computer interface, which would meet the criteria that Kazdin proposes. For instance, given the expanding availability of Internet services (U.S. Census Bureau, 2011; Comer, 2015), many more individuals would have the ability to access a web-based UP than with traditional outpatient services for anxiety and mood disorders.

Delivering treatment through the Internet is also cost efficient, as the cost of training clinicians and paying for clinician time is completely removed. In addition, using the Internet is convenient and not restricted to typical work hours or a particular location. Consumers have already integrated technology into their daily lives and would likely find a web-based intervention acceptable. Moreover, receiving mental health services through the Internet may decrease the stigma associated with mental health treatment. The web-based UP will be designed to be flexible, in that individuals can move through the program at their desired pace, can review previous material covered, and opt out of modules. Finally, a web-based treatment program can increase treatment fidelity ensured by computerized delivery and decrease the need for specialized providers.

Considerable research to date provides support for the effectiveness of this form of treatment delivery when compared to control conditions (Andersson & Cuijpers, 2009; Andrews, Cuijpers, Craske, McEvoy, & Titov, 2010; Cuijpers et al., 2009), and also indicates that computerized CBT programs can result in outcomes comparable to those obtained in traditional face-to-face treatment for anxiety and depression (Titov et al., 2010, 2011). As previously discussed, computerized CBT programs have been integrated into the stepped-care approach in the mental healthcare system in the United Kingdom. The web-based UP would be an ideal first-line treatment for individuals with subclinical and clinical symptoms of anxiety and mood disorders, given the transdiagnostic approach and modular structure.

In addition to using technology as a vehicle for delivering the UP treatment, incorporating innovative strategies to enhance the uptake of treatment principles, facilitate generalization of the application of core treatment components, improve compliance, increase motivation, and decrease relapse warrants further investigation. Once the development of the web-based UP program has come to fruition, the "bells and whistles" of the program will be beta-tested to determine the impact of the technology. In addition, we intend to address the question "For whom are these innovative components most helpful?" By using technology, a web-based program will be able to personalize the delivery of the UP, maximizing efficiency and treatment response.

CONCLUSIONS

Given the accumulating evidence supporting the efficacy of the UP across a range of emotional disorders, our research group has increased efforts to enhance the efficiency and disseminability of the UP, as well as to implement the treatment across service delivery sectors. As discussed in this chapter, investigations are underway to better understand the specific effects of the individual treatment components. By using multiple-baseline SCEDs, the sensitivity and specificity of the core modules have been examined, providing preliminary support for the notion that the UP is a modular treatment. With this understanding, we hope to increase the flexibility of the treatment delivery, personalize the treatment components to the individual needs of the patient, and enhance the efficiency of the treatment.

In addition to increasing the efficiency of treatment, efforts are also underway to promote dissemination of the UP. The creation of the UPI was in response to training demands. Since the UPI's incubation, training has been delivered using a stepwise approach, expanding the ability of domestic and international mental health providers to receive varying degrees of training intensity. Also, the UPI provides consultation on program implementation across service delivery settings.

Recent program implementation efforts, including a multisite, inpatient eating disorder treatment facility and the VNA-B, have shown to be promising. Further, within the UPI, we collect outcome measures from training workshops in order to evaluate participant satisfaction with workshops, as well as knowledge acquisition of UP concepts. These efforts allow us to continuously monitor the efficacy of our dissemination efforts and make changes as needed to improve the effectiveness of our training.

Our group also has begun to develop strategies to extend the reach of the UP by building a web-based UP treatment program. We hope that this method of delivery will reduce barriers to seeking and receiving empirically supported treatment, including clinician availability, access to evidence-based treatments, and the stigma associated with seeking mental health treatment.

In conclusion, research efforts evaluating the UP across emotional disorders are proliferating and providing additional support, in a wide range of treatment settings, for the efficacy of the UP. Promising dissemination and implementation efforts are underway. With increased empirical support and excitement for this transdiagnostic modular approach, we are hoping to continue to develop collaborations with researchers and clinicians to further expand the protocol's reach.

REFERENCES

Abramowitz, J. S., Tolin, D. F., & Street, G. P. (2001). Paradoxical effects of thought suppression: A meta-analysis of controlled studies. *Clinical Psychology Review, 21*(5), 683–703. http://dx.doi.org/10.1016/S0272-7358(00)00057-X

Abramson, L. Y., Alloy, L. B., Hogan, M. E., Whitehouse, W. G., Gibb, B. E., Hankin, B. L., & Cornette, M. M. (2000). The hopelessness theory of suicidality. In T. E. Joiner & M. D. Rudd (Eds.), *Suicide science: Expanding the boundaries* (pp. 17–32). New York, NY: Kluwer Academic/Plenum Publishers.

Ahmed, M., & Westra, H. A. (2009). Impact of a treatment rationale on expectancy and engagement in cognitive behavioral therapy for social anxiety. *Cognitive Therapy and Research, 33*(3), 314–322. doi:10.1007/s10608-008-9182-1

Aldao, A., Nolen-Hoeksema, S., & Schweizer, S. (2010). Emotion-regulation strategies across psychopathology: A meta-analytic review. *Clinical Psychology Review, 30*(2), 217–237. doi:10.1016/j.cpr.2009.11.004.

Allen, L., McHugh, K., & Barlow, D. H. (2008). Emotional Disorders: A unified protocol. In D. H. Barlow (Ed.), *Clinical handbook of psychological disorders* (4th ed., pp. 216–249). New York, NY US.

Allen, L. B., Tsao, J. C. I., Seidman, L. C., Ehrenreich-May, J. T., & Zeltzer, L. K. (2012). A unified, transdiagnostic treatment for adolescents with chronic pain and comorbid anxiety and depression. *Cognitive and Behavioral Practice, 19*, 56–67.

Allen, L. B., Tsao, J. C. I., & Zeltzer, L. K. (2009). *Development and applications of a unified cognitive-behavioral therapy (CBT) for adolescents with chronic pain and comorbid anxiety/depression.* Paper presented at the Workshop conducted at the 8th International Symposium on Pediatric Pain, Acapulco, Mexico.

Allen, L. B., White, K. S., Barlow, D. H., Shear, M. K., Gorman, J. M., & Woods, S. W. (2010). Cognitive-behavior therapy (CBT) for panic disorder: Relationship of anxiety and depression comorbidity with treatment outcome. *Journal of Psychopathology and Behavioral Assessment, 32*(2), 185–192. doi:10.1007/s10862-009-9151-3

Allroggen, M., Kleinrahm, R., Rau, T. A. D., Weninger, L., Ludolph, A. G., & Plener, P. L. (2014). Nonsuicidal self-injury and its relation to personality traits in medical students. *The Journal of Nervous and Mental Disease, 202*(4), 300–304.

American Psychiatric Association. (1994). *Diagnostic and statistical manual of mental disorders* (4th. ed.). Washington, DC: Author.

American Psychiatric Association. (2000). *Diagnostic and statistical manual of mental disorders* (4th ed., text revision). Washington, DC: American Psychiatric Association.

American Psychiatric Association. (2013). *Diagnostic and statistical manual of mental disorders* (5th ed.). Washington, D.C.: American Psychiatric Association.

American Psychological Association Presidential Task Force Evidence-Based Practice. (2006). Evidence-based practice in psychology. *American Psychological Association*, *61*, 271–285.

Amir, N., Freshman, M., & Foa, E. B. (2000). Family distress and involvement in relatives of obsessive-compulsive disorder patients. *Journal of Anxiety Disorders*, 14(3), 209–217. http://doi.org/10.1016/S0887-6185(99)00032-8

Anderluh, M. B., Tchanturia, K., Rabe-Hesketh, S., & Treasure, J. (2003). Childhood obsessive-compulsive personality traits in adult women with eating disorders: Defining a broader eating disorder phenotype. *American Journal of Psychiatry*, *160*, 242–247. doi:10.1176/appi.ajp.160.2.242

Andersson, G., & Cuijpers, P. (2009). Internet-based and other computerized psychological treatments for adult depression: A meta-analysis. *Cognitive Behaviour Therapy*, *38*(4), 196–205. doi:10.1080/16506070903318960

Andrews, G. (1990). Classification of neurotic disorders. *Journal of the Royal Society of Medicine*, *83*, 606–607.

Andrews, G. (1996). Comorbidity in neurotic disorders: The similarities are more important than the differences. In R. M. Rapee (Ed.), *Current controversies in the anxiety disorders* (pp. 3–20). New York, NY: Guilford Press.

Andrews, G., Cuijpers, P., Craske, M. G., McEvoy, P., & Titov, N. (2010). Computer therapy for the anxiety and depressive disorders is effective, acceptable and practical health care: A meta-analysis. *PloS One*, *5*(10), e13196. doi:10.1371/journal.pone.0013196

Angst, J. (2009). Course and prognosis of mood disorders. In M. G. Gelder, N. C. Andreasen, J. J. Lopez-Ibor, Jr., & J. R. Geddes (Eds.), *New Oxford textbook of psychiatry* (2nd ed., Vol. 1, pp. 665–669). Oxford, UK: Oxford University Press.

Antony, M. M., Craske, M. G., & Barlow, D. H. (2006). *Mastering your fears and phobias: Workbook.* (2nd ed.). New York, NY: Oxford University Press.

Antypa, N., & Serretti, A. (2014). Family history of a mood disorder indicates a more severe bipolar disorder. *Journal of Affective Disorders*, *156*, 178–186. doi:10.1016/j.jad.2013.12.013

Arch, J. J., Twohig, M. P., Deacon, B. J., Landy, L. N., & Bluett, E. J. (2015). The credibility of exposure therapy: Does the theoretical rationale matter? *Behaviour Research and Therapy*, *72*, 81–92.

Arkowitz, H., & Burke, B. L. (2008). Motivational interviewing as an integrative framework for the treatment of depression. In H. Arkowitz, H. A. Westra, W. R. Miller, & S. Rollnick (Eds.), *Motivational interviewing in the treatment of psychological problems* (pp. 145–172). New York, NY: Guilford Press.

Asmundson, G. J., & Katz, J. (2009). Understanding the co-occurrence of anxiety disorders and chronic pain: state-of-the-art. *Depress Anxiety*, *26*(10), 888–901.

Asnaani, A., & Hofmann, S. G. (2012). Collaboration in multicultural therapy: Establishing a strong therapeutic alliance across cultural lines. *Journal of Clinical Psychology*, *68*(2), 187–197.

Baer, R. A., Smith, G. T., Hopkins, J., Kritemeyer, J., & Toney, L. (2006). Using self-report assessment methods to explore facets of mindfulness. *Assessment*, *13*, 27–45.

Baglioni, C., Battagliese, G., Feige, B., Spiegelhalder, K., Nissen, C., Voderholzer, U., . . ., Riemann, D. (2011). Insomnia as a predictor of depression: A meta-analytic evaluation of longitudinal epidemiological studies. *Journal of Affective Disorders*, *135*, 10–19.

Baker, R., Holloway, J., Thomas, P., Thomas, S., & Owens, M. (2004). Emotional process-ing and panic. *Behaviour Research and Therapy, 42,* 1271–1287.

Barlow, D. H. (1988). *Anxiety and its disorders: The nature and treatment of anxiety and panic.* New York, NY: Guilford Press.

Barlow, D. H. (1991). Disorders of emotion. *Psychological Inquiry, 2,* 58–71. doi:10.1207/s15327965pli0201_15.

Barlow, D. H. (2000). Unraveling the mysteries of anxiety and its disorders from the per-spective of emotion theory. *American Psychologist, 55,* 1247–1263.

Barlow, D. H. (2002). *Anxiety and its disorders: The nature and treatment of anxiety and panic.* 2d ed. New York, NY: Guilford Press.

Barlow, D. H., Allen, L. B., & Choate, M. L. (2004). Toward a unified treatment for emotional disorders. *Behavior Therapy, 35,* 205–230. doi:http://dx.doi.org/10.1016/S0005-7894(04)80036-4

Barlow, D. H., Bullis, J. R., Comer, J. S., & Ametaj, A. A. (2013). Evidence-based psy-chological treatments: An update and a way forward. *Annual Review of Clinical Psychology, 9,* 1–27.

Barlow, D. H., Cohen, A. S., Waddell, M. T., Vermilyea, B. B., Klosko, J. S., Blanchard, E. B., & Di Nardo, P. A. (1984). Panic and generalized anxiety disorders: Nature and treatment. *Behavior Therapy, 15*(5), 431–449. doi:http://dx.doi.org/10.1016/S0005-7894(84)80048-9

Barlow, D. H., & Craske, M. G. (1988). *Mastery of your anxiety and panic.* Albany, NY: Graywind Publications.

Barlow, D. H., Craske, M. G., & Cerny, J. (1989). Behavioral treatment of panic disorder. *Behavior Therapy, 20,* 261–282. doi:10.1016/S0005-7894(89)80073-5

Barlow, D. H., Ellard, K. K., Fairholme, C. P., Farchione, T. J., Boisseau, C. L., Allen, L. B., & Ehrenreich-May, J. (2011). *Unified Protocol for Transdiagnostic Treatment of Emotional Disorders: Client workbook* (1st ed.). New York, NY: Oxford University Press.

Barlow, D. H., Ellard, K. K., Sauer-Zavala, S., Bullis, J. R., & Carl, J. R. (2014). The ori-gins of neuroticism. *Perspectives on Psychological Science, 9*(5), 481–496. doi:10.1177/1745691614544528

Barlow, D. H., Farchione, T. J., Bullis, J. R., Gallagher, M. W., Latin, H., . . ., Cassiello-Robbins, C. (in press). Equivalence evaluation of the Unified Protocol for Transdiagnostic Treatment of Emotional Disorders compared to diagnosis-specific CBT for anxiety disorders. *JAMA Psychiatry.*

Barlow, D. H., Farchione, T. J., Fairholme, C. P., Ellard, K. K., Boisseau, C. L., Allen, L. B., & Ehrenreich-May, J. (2011). *Unified Protocol for Transdiagnostic Treatment of Emotional Disorders: Therapist guide.* New York, NY: Oxford University Press.

Barlow, D. H., Farchione, T. J., Sauer-Zavala, S., Latin, H., Ellard, K. K. . . ., Cassiello-Robbins, C. (2018). *Unified Protocol for Transdiagnostic Treatment of Emotional Disorders: Therapist guide.* 2nd ed. New York, NY: Oxford University Press.

Barlow, D. H., Gorman, J. M., Shear, M. K., & Woods, S. W. (2000). Cognitive-behavioral therapy, imipramine, or their combination for panic disorder: A randomized con-trolled trial. *JAMA, 283,* 2529–2536. doi:10.1001/jama.283.19.2529

Barlow, D. H., Nock, M. K., & Hersen, M. (2009). *Single-case experimental designs: Strategies for studying behavior change.* 3rd ed. Boston, MA: Allyn and Bacon.

Barlow, D. H., Sauer-Zavala, S., Carl, J. R., Bullis, J. R., & Ellard, K. K. (2014). The nature, diagnosis, and treatment of neuroticism: Back to the future. *Clinical Psychological Science, 2*(3), 344–365. doi:10.1177/2167702613505532

Barlow, D. H., Sauer-Zavala, S., Farchione, T. J., Latin, H., Ellard, K. K., ..., Cassiello-Robbins, C. (2018). *Unified Protocol for Transdiagnostic Treatment of Emotional Disorders: Patient workbook.* (2nd ed.). New York, NY: Oxford University Press.

Barnett, J. H., Huang, J., Perlis, R. H., Young, M. M., Rosenbaum, J. F., Nierenberg, A. A., ..., Smoller, J. W. (2011). Personality and bipolar disorder: Dissecting state and trait associations between mood and personality. *Psychological Medicine, 41*(8), 1593–1604. doi:10.1017/S0033291710002333

Barrera, M., Jr., & Castro, F. G. (2006). A heuristic framework for the cultural adaptation of interventions. *Clinical Psychology Science and Practice, 13,* 311–316.

Bartels, S. J., Coakley, E. H., Zubritsky, C., Ware, J. H., Miles, K. M., Areán, P. A., ..., Levkoff, S. E. (2004). Improving access to geriatric mental health services: A randomized trial comparing treatment engagement with integrated versus enhanced referral care for depression, anxiety, and at-risk alcohol use. *American Journal of Psychiatry, 161*(8), 1455–1462. doi:10.1176/appi.ajp.161.8.1455

Batemen, A. W., & Fonagy, P. (2004). Mentalization-based treatment of BPD. *Journal of Personality Disorders, 18,* 36–51. doi:10.1521/pedi.18.1.36.32772

Bauer, M., & Wisniewski, S. (2006). Are antidepressants associated with new-onset suicidality in bipolar disorder? A prospective study of participants in the Systematic Treatment Enhancement. *Journal of Clinical Psychiatry, 67*(1), 48–55.

Baumeister, R. (1990). Suicide as escape from self. *Psychological Review, 97,* 90–113.

Beattie, M. C., & Longabaugh, R. (1999). General and alcohol-specific social support following treatment. *Addictive Behaviors, 24*(5), 593–606. doi:10.1016/S0306-4603(98)00120-8

Beck, A. T. (1976). *Cognitive therapy and the emotional disorders.* Madison, CT: International Universities Press.

Beck, A. T. (1986). Hopelessness as a predictor of eventual suicide. *Annals of the New York Academy of Sciences, 487,* 90–96.

Beck, A., & Freeman, A. (1990). *Cognitive therapy of personality disorders.* New York, NY US: Guilford Press.

Beck, A. T., Rush, A. J., Shaw, B. F., & Emery, G. (1987). *Cognitive therapy of depression.* New York, NY: Guilford Press.

Beck, A. T., & Steer, R. A. (1988). *Manual for the Beck Hopelessness Scale.* San Antonio, TX: Psychological Corporation.

Beck, A. T., & Steer, R. A. (1990). *Manual for the Beck Anxiety Inventory.* San Antonio, TX: Psychological Corporation.

Beck, A. T., & Steer, R. A. (1991). *Manual for Beck Scale for Suicide Ideation.* San Antonio, TX: Psychological Corporation.

Beck, A., Steer, R., & Brown, G. (1996). *BDI-II: Beck depression inventory manual.* (2nd ed.). San Antonio, TX: The Psychological Corporation.

Begotka, A., Woods, D., & Wetterneck, C. (2004). The relationship between experiential avoidance and the severity of trichotillomania in a nonreferred sample. *Journal of Behavior Therapy and Experimental Psychiatry, 35,* 17–24.

Belanger, L., Morin, C. M., Gendron, L., & Blais, F. C. (2005). Presleep cognitive activity and thought control strategies in insomnia. *Journal of Cognitive Psychotherapy: An International Quarterly Journal, 19,* 17–27.

Belanger, L., Morin, C. M., Langlois, F., & Ladouceur, R. (2004). Insomnia and generalized anxiety disorder: Effects of cognitive behavior therapy for gad on insomnia symptoms. *Journal of Anxiety Disorders, 18,* 561–571.

Bentley, K. H., Cassiello-Robbins, C. F., Vittorio, L., Sauer-Zavala, S., & Barlow, D. H. (2015). The association between nonsuicidal self-injury and the emotional disorders: A meta-analytic review. *Clinical Psychology Review, 37,* 72–88.

Bentley, K. H., Gallagher, M. W., Carl, J. R., & Barlow, D. H. (2014). Development and validation of the Overall Depression Severity and Impairment Scale. *Psychological Assessment, 26*(3), 815–830. http://doi.org/10.1037/a0036216

Bentley, K. H., Nock, M. K., & Barlow, D. H. (2014). The four function model of nonsuicidal self-injury: Key directions for future research. *Clinical Psychological Science, 2,* 638–656.

Bentley, K. H., Nock, M. K., Sauer-Zavala, S., Gorman, B. S., & Barlow, D. H. (in press). A functional analysis of two transdiagnostic, emotion-focused interventions on nonsuicidal self-injury. *Journal of Consulting and Clinical Psychology.*

Berg, K. C., Crosby, R. D., Cao, L., Peterson, C. B., Engel, S. G., Mitchell, J. E., & Wonderlich, S. A. (2013). Facets of negative affect prior to and following binge-only, purge-only, and binge/purge events in women with bulimia nervosa. *Journal of Abnormal Psychology, 122*(1), 111. doi:10.1037/a0029703

Berking, M., Neacsiu, A., Comtois, K., & Linehan, M. (2009). The impact of experiential avoidance on the reduction of depression in treatment for borderline personality disorder. *Behaviour Research and Therapy, 47,* 663–670.

Betancourt, H., & Lopez, S. R. (1993). The study of culture, ethnicity, and race in American psychology. *American Psychologist, 48,* 629–637.

Bijur, P. E., Latimer, C. T., & Gallagher, E. J. (2003). Validation of a verbally administered numerical rating scale of acute pain for use in the emergency department. *Academic Emergency Medicine, 10*(4), 390–392.

Boettcher, H., Brake, C. A., & Barlow, D. H. (2016). Origins and outlook of interoceptive exposure. *Journal of Behavior Therapy and Experimental Psychiatry, 53,* 41–51. doi:10.1016/j.jbtep.2015.10.009

Bolton, P., Lee, C., Haroz, E. E., Murray, L., Dorsey, S., Robinson, C., …, Bass, J. (2014). A transdiagnostic community-based mental health treatment for comorbid disorders: Development and outcomes of a randomized controlled trial among Burmese refugees in Thailand. *PLoS Medicine, 11*(11), e1001757. doi:10.1371/journal. pmed.1001757

Bonnet, M. H., & Arand, D. L. (2010). Hyperarousal and insomnia: State of the science. *Sleep Medicine Reviews, 14,* 9–15.

Borges, G., Nock, M. K., Abad, J. M. H., Hwang, I., Sampson, N. A., Alonso, J., … Kessler, R. C. (2010). Twelve-month prevalence of and risk factors for suicide attempts in the World Health Organization World Mental Health Surveys. *Journal of Clinical Psychiatry, 71,* 1617–1628.

Borkovec, T. D. (1994). The nature, functions, and origins of worry. In G. C. L. Davey & F. Tallis (Eds.), *Worrying: Perspectives on theory, assessment, and treatment* (pp. 5–34). New York, NY: Wiley.

Borkovec, T. D., Abel, J. L., & Newman, H. (1995). Effects of psychotherapy on comorbid conditions in generalized anxiety disorder. *Journal of Consulting and Clinical Psychology, 63,* 479–483.

Borkovec, T. D., Alcaine, O. M., & Behar, E. (2004). Avoidance theory of worry and generalized anxiety disorder. In R. G. Heimberg, C. L. Turk, D. S. Mennin, R. G. Heimberg, C. L. Turk, & D. S. Mennin (Eds.), *Generalized anxiety disorder: Advances in research and practice* (pp. 77–108). New York, NY: Guilford Press.

Borkovec, T. D., Hazlett-Stevens, H., & Diaz, M. L. (1999). The role of positive beliefs about worry in generalized anxiety disorder and its treatment. *Clinical Psychology and Psychotherapy, 6*, 126–138.

Boswell, J. F. (2013). Intervention strategies and clinical process in transdiagnostic cognitive-behavioral therapy. *Psychotherapy, 50*, 381–386. doi:10.1037/a0032157

Boswell, J. F., Anderson, L. M., & Anderson, D. (2015). Integration of interoceptive exposure in eating disorder treatment. *Clinical Psychology: Science and Practice, 22*, 194–210. doi:10.1111/cpsp.12103

Boswell, J. F., Anderson, L. M., & Barlow, D. H. (2014). An idiographic analysis of change processes in the unified transdiagnostic treatment of depression. *Journal of Consulting and Clinical Psychology, 82*, 1060–1071. http://dx.doi.org/10.1037/a0037403

Boswell, J. F., & Bugatti, M. (2016). An exploratory analysis of the impact of specific interventions: Some clients reveal more than others. *Journal of Counseling Psychology, 63*(6), 710–720. http://dx.doi.org/10.1037/cou0000174

Boswell, J. F., Farchione, T. J., Ellard, K. K., & Barlow, D. H. (2012). *Treatment of depression with the Unified Protocol: Preliminary findings, clinical implications, and future directions.* Paper presented at the Association for Behavioral and Cognitive Therapies annual convention, November, National Harbor, MD.

Boswell, J. F., Farchione, T. J., Sauer-Zavala, S. E., Murray, H., Fortune, M., & Barlow, D. H. (2013). Anxiety sensitivity and interoceptive exposure: A transdiagnostic construct and change strategy. *Behavior Therapy, 44*, 417–431. http://dx.doi.org/10.1016/j.beth.2013.03.006

Bottlender, M., & Soyka, M. (2005). Outpatient alcoholism treatment: Predictors of outcome after 3 years. *Drug Alcohol Depend, 80*(1), 83–89. doi:10.1016/j.drugalcdep.2005.03.011

Bouton, M., Mineka, S., & Barlow, D. H. (2001). Modern learning theory perspective on the etiology of panic disorder. *Psychological Review, 108*, 4–32.

Bowen, R. C., D'Arcy, C., Keegan, D., & Senthilselvan, A. (2000). A controlled trial of cognitive behavioral treatment of panic in alcoholic inpatients with comorbid panic disorder. *Addictive Behaviors, 25*(4), 593–597. doi:10.1016/S0306-4603(99)00017-9

Brake, C. A., Sauer-Zavala, S., Boswell, J. F., Gallagher, M. W., Farchione, T. J., & Barlow, D. H. (2016). Mindfulness-based exposure strategies as a transdiagnostic mechanism of change: An exploratory alternating treatment design. *Behavior Therapy, 47*(2), 225–238.

Brieger, P., Röttig, S., Röttig, D., Marneros, A., & Priebe, S. (2007). Dimensions underlying outcome criteria in bipolar I disorder. *Journal of Affective Disorders, 99*(1–3), 1–7. doi:10.1016/j.jad.2006.08.012

Brockmeyer, T., Skunde, M., Wu, M., Bresslein, E., Rudofsky, G., Herzog, W., & Friederich, H. C. (2014). Difficulties in emotion regulation across the spectrum of eating disorders. *Comprehensive Psychiatry, 55*, 565 571. doi:10.1016/j.comppsych.2013

Brown, S. A. (2009). Personality and non-suicidal deliberate self-harm: Trait differences among a non-clinical population. *Psychiatry Research, 169*, 28–32.

Brown, A. J., Smith, L. T., & Craighead, L. W. (2010). Appetite awareness as a mediator in an eating disorders prevention program. *Eating Disorders: The Journal of Treatment and Prevention, 18*(4), 286–301. doi:10.1080/10640266.2010.490118

Brown, K., & Ryan, R. (2003). The benefits of being present: Mindfulness and its role in psychological well-being. *Journal of Personality and Social Psychology, 84*, 822–848.

Brown, K., Weinstein, N., & Creswell, D. (2011). Trait mindfulness modulates neuroendocrine and affective responses to social-evaluative threat. *Psychoneuroendocrinology*, 37, 2037–2041.

Brown, T. A., & Barlow, D. H. (2009). A proposal for a dimensional classification system based on the shared features of the DSM-IV anxiety and mood disorders: Implications for assessment and treatment. *Psychological Assessment*, 21(3), 256–271. doi:10.1037/a0016608

Brown, T. A. (2007). Temporal course and structural relationships among dimensions of temperament and DSM–IV anxiety and mood disorder constructs. *Journal of Abnormal Psychology*, 116, 313–328.

Brown, T. A., Di Nardo, P. A., Lehman, C. L., & Campbell, L. A. (2001). Reliability of DSM-IV anxiety and mood disorders: implications for the classification of emotional disorders. *Journal of Abnormal Psychology*, 110(1), 49.

Brown, T. A., Antony, M. M., & Barlow, D. H. (1995). Diagnostic comorbidity in panic disorder: Effect on treatment outcome and course of comorbid diagnoses following treatment. *Journal of Consulting and Clinical Psychology*, 63, 408–418.

Brown, T. A., & Barlow, D. H. (2014). *Anxiety and related disorders interview schedule for DSM-5 (ADIS-5): Patient interview schedule.* Oxford, UK: Oxford University Press.

Brown, T. A., Campbell, L. A., Lehman, C. L., Grisham, J. R., & Mancill, R. B. (2001). Current and lifetime comorbidity of the DSM-IV anxiety and mood disorders in a large clinical sample. *Journal of Abnormal Psychology*, 110, 49–58. doi:10.1037/0021-843X.110.4.585

Brown, T. A., Chorpita, B. F., & Barlow, D. H. (1998). Structural relationships among dimensions of the DSM-IV anxiety and mood disorders and dimensions of negative affect, positive affect, and autonomic arousal. *Journal of Abnormal Psychology*, 107, 179–192.

Brown, G. K., Have, T. T., Henriques, G. R., Xie, S. X., Hollander, J. E., & Beck, A. T. (2005). Cognitive therapy for the prevention of suicide attempts: A randomized controlled trial. *Journal of the American Medical Association*, 294, 563–570.

Bruce, M. L., McAvay, G. J., Raue, P. J., Brown, E. L., Meyers, B. S., Keohane, D. J., ..., Weber, C. (2002). Major depression in elderly home health care patients. *American Journal of Psychiatry*, 159(8), 1367–1374. doi:10.1176/appi.ajp.159.8.1367

Buckner, J. D., & Schmidt, N. B. (2009). A randomized pilot study of motivation enhancement therapy to increase utilization of cognitive–behavioral therapy for social anxiety. *Behaviour Research and Therapy*, 47(8), 710–715. doi:10.1016/j.brat.2009.04.009

Buckner, J. D., Timpano, K. R., Zvolensky, M. J., Sachs-Ericsson, N., & Schmidt, N. B. (2008). Implications of comorbid alcohol dependence among individuals with social anxiety disorder. *Depression and Anxiety*, 25(12), 1028–1037.

Bullis, J. R., Fortune, M. R., Farchione, T. J., & Barlow, D. H. (2014). A preliminary investigation of the long-term outcome of the Unified Protocol for Transdiagnostic Treatment of Emotional Disorders. *Comprehensive Psychiatry*, 55(8), 1920–1927. doi:http://dx.doi.org/10.1016/j.comppsych.2014.07.016

Bullis, J. R., Sauer-Zavala, S., Bentley, K. H., Thompson-Hollands, J., Carl, J. R., & Barlow, D. H. (2015). The Unified Protocol for Transdiagnostic Treatment of Emotional Disorders: Preliminary exploration of effectiveness for group delivery. *Behavior Modification*, 39(2), 295–321. doi:10.1177/0145445514553094

Burns, L., Teesson, M., & O'Neill, K. (2005). The impact of comorbid anxiety and depression on alcohol treatment outcomes. *Addiction*, 100(6), 787–796.

Butler, L., & Nolen-Hoeksema, S. (1994). Gender differences in responses to depressed mood in a college sample. *Sex Roles, 30*, 331–346.

Buysse, D. J., Thompson, W., Scott, J., Franzen, P. L., Germain, A., Hall, M., . . ., Kupfer, D. J. (2007). Daytime symptoms in primary insomnia: a prospective analysis using ecological momentary assessment. *Sleep Medicine, 8*, 198–208.

Bydlowski, S., Corcos, M., Jeammet, P., Paterniti, S., Berthoz, S., Laurier, C., . . ., Consoli, S. M. (2005). Emotion-processing deficits in eating disorders. *International Journal of Eating Disorders, 37*, 321–329. doi:10.1002/eat.20132

Byers, A. L., Sheeran, T., Mlodzianowski, A. E., Meyers, B. S., Nassisi, P., & Bruce, M. L. (2008). Depression and risk for adverse falls in older home health care patients. *Research in Gerontological Nursing, 1*(4), 245–251. doi:10.3928/19404921-20081001-03

Cabin, W. D. (2010). Lifting the home care veil from depression: OASIS-C and evidence-based practice. *Home Health Care Management & Practice, 22*(3), 171–177. doi:10.1177/1084822309348693

Caffrey, C., Sengupta, M., Moss, A., Harris-Kojetin, L., & Valverde, R. (2011). Home health care and discharged hospice care patients: United States, 2000 and 2007. *National Health Statistics Reports, 38*, 1–27.

Calmes, C., & Roberts, J. (2007). Repetitive thought and emotional distress: Rumination and worry as prospective predictors of depressive and anxious symptomatology. *Cognitive Therapy and Research, 31*, 343–356.

Calvocoressi, L., Lewis, B., Harris, M., Trufan, S. J., Goodman, W. K., McDougle, C. J., & Price, L. (1995). Family accommodation in obsessive-compulsive disorder. *American Journal of Psychiatry, 152*, 441–443.

Calvocoressi, L., Mazure, C., Stanislav, K., Skolnick, J., Fisk, D., Vegso, S., . . ., Price, L. H. (1999). Family accommodation of obsessive-compulsive symptoms: Instrument development and assessment of family behavior. *Journal of Nervous and Mental Disease, 187*(10), 636–642.

Cambanis, E. V. A. (2012). Treating borderline personality disorder as a trainee psychologist: Issues of resistance, inexperience and countertransference. *Journal of Child and Adolescent Mental Health, 24*(1), 99–109. doi:10.2989/17280583.2011.639075

Campbell-Sills, L., Barlow, D., Brown, T., & Hofman, S. (2006). Acceptability and suppression of negative emotion in anxiety and mood disorders. *Emotion, 6*, 587–595.

Campbell-Sills, L., Ellard, K. K., & Barlow, D. H. (2014). Emotion regulation in anxiety disorders. In J. J. Gross (Ed.), *Handbook of emotion regulation* (2nd ed., pp. 393–413). New York, NY: Guilford Press.

Campbell-Sills, L., Norman, S. B., Craske, M. G., Sullivan, G., Lang, A. J., Chavira, D. A., . . ., Stein, M. B. (2009). Validation of a brief measure of anxiety-related severity and impairment: The Overall Anxiety Severity and Impairment Scale (OASIS). *Journal of Affective Disorders, 112*(1–3), 92–101. http://doi.org/10.1016/j.jad.2008.03.014

Carl, J. R., & Barlow, D. H. (2015). *Enhancing positive emotions in anxiety disorders: A preliminary evaluation of a CBT module targeting disturbances in positive emotion regulation.* Unpublished doctoral dissertation, Boston University, Boston, MA.

Carl, J. R., Gallagher, M. W., Sauer-Zavala, S. E., Bentley, K. H., & Barlow, D. H. (2014). A preliminary investigation of the effects of the Unified Protocol on temperament. *Comprehensive Psychiatry, 55*(6), 1426–1434. doi:http://dx.doi.org/10.1016/j.comppsych.2014.04.015

Carney, C. E., Harris, A. L., Friedman, J., & Segal, Z. V. (2011). Residual sleep beliefs and sleep disturbance following cognitive behavioral therapy for major depression. *Depression and Anxiety, 28*, 464–470.

Carpenter, D., Clarkin, J. F., Isman, L., & Patten, M. (1999). The impact of neuroticism upon married bipolar patients. *Journal of Personality Disorders, 13*(1), 60–66.

Cash, M., & Whittingham, K. (2010). What facets of mindfulness contribute to psychological well-being and depressive, anxious, and stress-related symptomatology? *Mindfulness, 1*, 177–182.

Castro, F. G., Barrera, M., Jr., & Martinez, C. R. (2004). The cultural adaptation of prevention interventions: Resolving tensions between fidelity and fit. *Prevention Science, 5*, 41–45.

Castro, F. G., Barrera, M., Jr., & Steiker, L. K. H. (2010). Issues and challenges in the design of culturally adapted evidence-based interventions. *Annual Review of Clinical Psychology, 6*, 213–239.

Centers for Disease Control and Prevention. (2011). Web-based Injury Statistics Query and Reporting System (WISQARS) [online]. Retrieved from www.cdc.gov/injury/wisqars/index.html

Chadwick, P., Hember, M., Symes, J., Peters, E., Kuipers, E., & Dagnan, D. (2008). Responding mindfully to unpleasant thoughts and images: Reliability and validity of the Southampton Mindfulness Questionnaire (SMQ). *British Journal of Clinical Psychology, 47*, 451–455. doi:10.1348/014466508X314891

Chapman, L. K., DeLapp, R., & Williams, M. T. (2014). Impact of race, ethnicity, and culture on the expression and assessment of psychopathology. *Adult Psychopathology and Diagnosis*, 131.

Chapman, A. L., Gratz, K. L., & Brown, M. (2006). Solving the puzzle of deliberate self-injury: The experiential avoidance model. *Behaviour Research and Therapy, 44*, 371–394.

Charles, S. T., Gatz, M., Kato, K., & Pedersen, N. L. (2008). Physical health 25 years later: the predictive ability of neuroticism. *Health Psychology, 27*(3), 369–378.

Cheavens, J., & Heiy, J. (2011). The differential roles of affect and avoidance in major depressive and borderline personality disorder symptoms. *Journal of Social and Clinical Psychology, 30*, 441–457.

Cheavens, J., Rosenthal, M., Daughters, S., Novak, J., Kosson, D., & Lynch, T. (2005). An analogue investigation of the relationships among perceived parental criticism, negative affect, and borderline personality disorder features: The role of thought suppression. *Behaviour Research and Therapy, 43*, 257–268.

Chorpita, B. F., Albano, A. M., & Barlow, D. H. (1998). The structure of negative emotions in a clinical sample of children and adolescents. *Journal of Abnormal Psychology, 107*, 74–85.

Chorpita, B. F., Daleiden, E. L., & Weisz, J. R. (2005). Modularity in the design and application of therapeutic interventions. *Applied and Preventive Psychology, 11*(3), 141–156. doi:10.1016/j.appsy.2005.05.002

Chorpita, B. F., Taylor, A. A., Francis, S. E., Moffitt, C., & Austin, A. A. (2004). Efficacy of modular cognitive behavior therapy for childhood anxiety disorders. *Behavior Therapy, 35*(2), 263–287. doi:10.1016/S0005-7894(04)80039-X

Chorpita, B. F., Weisz, J. R., Daleiden, E. L., Schoenwald, S. K., Palinkas, L. A., Miranda, J., . . ., Gibbons, R. D. (2013). Long-term outcomes for the Child STEPs randomized effectiveness trial: A comparison of modular and standard treatment designs with usual care. *Journal of Consulting and Clinical Psychology, 81*(6), 999–1009. doi:10.1037/a0034200

Ciraulo, D. A., Barlow, D. H., Gulliver, S. B., Farchione, T., Morissette, S. B., Kamholz, B. W., . . ., Knapp, C. M. (2013). The effects of venlafaxine and cognitive behavioral therapy alone and combined in the treatment of co-morbid alcohol use–anxiety disorders. *Behaviour Research and Therapy, 51*(11), 729–735.

Cioffi, D., & Holloway, J. (1993). Delayed costs of suppressed pain. *Journal of Personality and Social Psychology, 64*(2), 274–282.

Claes, L., Muehlenkamp, J., Vandereycken, W., Hamelinck, L., Martens, H., & Claes, S. (2010). Comparison of nonsuicidal self-injurious behavior and suicide attempts in patients admitted to a psychiatric crisis unit. *Personality and Individual Differences, 48*(1), 83–87.

Claes, L., Vandereycken, W., & Vertommen, H. (2004). Personality traits in eating-disordered patients with and without self-injurious behaviors. *Journal of Personality Disorders, 18*, 399–404.

Clark, D. M. (1986). A cognitive approach to panic. *Behaviour Research and Therapy, 24*, 461–470.

Clark, D. M. (2011). Implementing NICE guidelines for the psychological treatment of depression and anxiety disorders: The IAPT experience. *International Review of Psychiatry (Abingdon, England), 23*(4), 318–327. doi:10.3109/09540261.2011.606803

Clark, D. M., Ehlers, A., Hackmann, A., McManus, F., Fennell, M., Grey, N., . . ., & Wild, J. (2006). Cognitive therapy versus exposure and applied relaxation in social phobia: A randomized controlled trial. *Journal of Consulting and Clinical Psychology, 74*, 568–578.

Clark, D. M., Layard, R., Smithies, R., Richards, D. A., Suckling, R., & Wright, B. (2009). Improving access to psychological therapy: Initial evaluation of two UK demonstration sites. *Behaviour Research and Therapy, 47*(11), 910–920. doi:10.1016/j.brat.2009.07.010

Clark, L. A. (2005). Temperament as a unifying basis for personality and psychopathology. *Journal of Abnormal Psychology, 114*, 505–521.

Clark, L. A., & Watson, D. (1991). Tripartite model of anxiety and depression: Psychometric evidence and taxonomic implications. *Journal of Abnormal Psychology, 103*, 103–116.

Clark, L. A., Watson, D., & Mineka, S. (1994). Temperament, personality, and the mood and anxiety disorders. *Journal of Abnormal Psychology, 103*, 103–116.

Clarkin, J. F., Foelsch, P. A., Levy, K. N., Hull, J. W., Delaney, J. C., & Kernberg, O. F. (2001). The development of a psychodynamic treatment for patients with borderline personality Disorder: A preliminary study of behavioral change. *Journal of Personality Disorders, 15*, 487–495. doi:10.1521/pedi.15.6.487.19190

Coen, S. J., Kano, M., Farmer, A. D., Kumari, V., Giampietro, V., Brammer, M., et al. (2011). Neuroticism influences brain activity during the experience of visceral pain. *Gastroenterology, 141*(3), 909–917 e901.

Coles, M. E., Mennin, D. S., & Heimberg, R. G. (2001). Distinguishing obsessive features and worries: the role of thought–action fusion. *Behaviour Research and Therapy, 39*(8), 947–959. http://doi.org/10.1016/S0005-7967(00)00072-3

Collimore, K., McCabe, R., Carelton, N., & Asmundson, G. (2008). Media exposure and dimensions of anxiety sensitivity: Differential associations with PTSD symptom clusters. *Journal of Anxiety Disorders, 22*, 1021–1028.

Comer, J. S. (2015). Introduction to the special series: Applying new technologies to extend the scope and accessibility of mental health care. *Cognitive and Behavioral Practice, 22*(3), 253–257. doi:10.1016/j.cbpra.2015.04.002

Comer, J. S., Kendall, P. C., Franklin, M. E., Hudson, J. L., & Pimentel, S. S. (2004). Obsessing/worrying about the overlap between obsessive-compulsive disorder and generalized anxiety disorder in youth. *Clinical Psychology Review, 24*, 663–683.

Compton, W. M., Thomas, Y. F., Stinson, F. S., & Grant, B. F. (2007). Prevalence, correlates, disability, and comorbidity of DSM-IV drug abuse and dependence in the United States: Results from the National Epidemiologic Survey on Alcohol and Related Conditions. *Archives of General Psychiatry Archives of General Psychiatry, 64*(5), 566–576. doi:10.1001/archpsyc.64.5.566

Corstorphine, E., Mountford, V., Tomlinson, S., Waller, G., & Meyer, C. (2007). Distress tolerance in the eating disorders. *Eating Behaviors, 8*(1), 91–91.

Costa, P. T., Jr., & McCrae, R. R. (1992). Four ways five factors are basic. *Personality and Individual Differences, 13*, 653–665.

Cox, B., Enns, M., Walker, J., Kjernisted, K., & Pidlubny, S. (2001). Psychological vulnerabilities in patients with major depression versus panic disorder. *Behaviour Research and Therapy, 39*, 567–573.

Craske, M. G., & Barlow, D. H. (2007). *Mastery of your anxiety and panic: Therapist guide.* New York, NY: Oxford University Press.

Craske, M. G., Treanor, M., Conway, C. C., Zbozinek, T., & Verliet, B. (2014). Maximizing exposure therapy: An inhibitory learning approach. *Behaviour Research and Therapy, 58*, 10–23.

Crawford, T. N., Cohen, P., Johnson, J. G., Kasen, S., First, M. B., Gordon, K., & Brook, J. S. (2005). Self-Reported Personality Disorder in the Children in the Community Sample: Convergent and Prospective Validity in Late Adolescence and Adulthood. *Journal of Personality Disorders, 19*(1), 30–52. doi:10.1521/pedi.19.1.30.62179

Crawford, J. R., & Henry, J. D. (2004). The positive and negative affect schedule (PANAS): construct validity, measurement properties and normative data in a large non-clinical sample. *British Journal of Clinical Psychology, 43*(Pt 3), 245–265.

Crowell, S. E, Derbidge, C. M., & Beauchaine, T. P. (2014). Developmental approaches to understanding suicidal and self-injurious behaviors. In M. K. Nock (Ed.), *The Oxford Handbook of Suicide and Self-Injury* (1st ed., pp. 183–205). New York, NY: Oxford University Press.

Cuijpers, P., Marks, I. M., van Straten, A., Cavanagh, K., Gega, L., & Andersson, G. (2009). Computer-aided psychotherapy for anxiety disorders: A meta-analytic review. *Cognitive Behaviour Therapy, 38*(2), 66–82. doi:10.1080/16506070802694776

Danner, U. N., Sternheim, L., & Evers, C. (2014). The importance of distinguishing between the different eating disorders (sub)types when assessing emotion regulation strategies. *Psychiatry Research, 215*, 727–732. doi:10.1016/j.psychres.2014.01.005

Davies, H., Schmidt, U., Stahl, D., & Tchanturia, K. (2011). Evoked facial emotional expression and emotional experience in people with anorexia nervosa. *International Journal of Eating Disorders, 44*, 531–539. doi:10.1002/eat.20852

Dawson, D. A., Goldstein, R. B., & Grant, B. F. (2013). Differences in the pro-files of DSM-IV and DSM-5 alcohol use disorders: Implications for clinicians. *Alcoholism: Clinical and Experimental Research, 37*(Suppl 1), E305–E313. doi:10.1111/j.1530-0277.2012.01930.x

de Graaf, R., Bijl, R. V., ten Have, M., Beekman, A. T., & Vollebergh, W. A. (2004). Pathways to comorbidity: The transition of pure mood, anxiety, and substance use disorders into comorbid conditions in a longitudinal population-based study. *Journal of Affective Disorders, 82*(3), 461–467.

Delinsky, S. S., & Wilson, G. T. (2006). Mirror exposure for the treatment of body image disturbance. *International Journal of Eating Disorders, 39,* 108–116. doi:10.1002/eat.20207.

de Ornelas Maia, A. C. C., Nardi, A. E., & Cardoso, A. (2015). The utilization of unified protocols in behavioral cognitive therapy in transdiagnostic group subjects: A clinical trial. *Journal of Affective Disorders, 172,* 179–183.

Derogatis, L. R. (2001). *Brief Symptom Inventory (BSI) 18: Administration, Scoring, and Procedures Manual.* Minneapolis, MN: NCS Pearson, Inc.

DeRubeis, R. J., Cohen, Z. D., Forand, N. R., Fournier, J. C., Gelfand, L. A., & Lorenzo-Luaces, L. (2014). The Personalized Advantage Index: Translating research prediction into individualized treatment recommendations. A demonstration. *PLoS One, 9*(1), e83875. doi:10.1371/journal.pone.0083875

Desrosiers, A., Klemanski, D. H., & Nolen-Hoeksema, S. (2013). Mapping mindfulness facets onto dimensions of anxiety and depression. *Behavior Therapy, 44,* 373–384. doi:10.1016/j.beth.2013.02.001

Di Nardo, P. A., Brown, T. A., & Barlow, D. H. (1994). *Anxiety Disorders Interview Schedule for DSM-IV:Lifetime Version (ADIS-IV-L).* New York, NY: Oxford University Press.

Dobkin, P. L., De Civita, M., Paraherakis, A., & Gill, K. (2002). The role of functional social support in treatment retention and outcomes among outpatient adult substance abusers. *Addiction, 97*(3), 347–356. doi:10.1046/j.1360-0443.2002.00083.x

Dolsen, M. R., Asarnow, L. D., & Harvey, A. G. (2014). Insomnia as a transdiagnostic process in psychiatric disorders. *Current Psychiatry Reports, 16,* 471.

Drake, C. L., Friedman, N. P., Wright, K. P., Jr., & Roth, T. (2011). Sleep reactivity and insomnia: genetic and environmental influences. *Sleep, 34,* 1179–1188.

Dugas, M. J., Ladouceur, R., Léger, E., Freeston, M. H., Langlois, F., Provencher, M. D., & Boisvert, J. M. (2003). Group cognitive-behavioral therapy for generalized anxi-ety disorder: Treatment outcome and long-term follow-up. *Journal of Consulting and Clinical Psychology, 71,* 821–825.

Duggan, K. A., Friedman, H. S., McDevitt, E. A., & Mednick, S. C. (2014). Personality and healthy sleep: The importance of conscientiousness and neuroticism. *PLoS One, 9,* e90628.

Eaton, N. R., Krueger, R. F., Keyes, K. M., Skodol, A. E., Markon, K. E., Grant, B. F., & Hasin, D. S. (2011). Borderline personality disorder co-morbidity: relationship to the internalizing-externalizing structure of common mental disorders. *Psychological medicine, 41*(5), 1041–1050. doi:10.1017/S0033291710001662

Edinger, J. D., & Carney, C. E. (2008). *Overcoming insomnia: A cognitive-behavioral ther-apy approach: Therapist guide.* New York, NY: Oxford University Press.

Edinger, J. D., Fins, A. I., Glenn, D. M., Sullivan, R. J., Jr, Bastian, L. A., Marsh, G. R., . . ., Vasilas, D. (2000). Insomnia and the eye of the beholder: Are there clinical markers of objective sleep disturbances among adults with and without insomnia complaints? *Journal of Consulting and Clinical Psychology, 68,* 586–593.

Edinger, J. D., Wohlgemuth, W. K., Radtke, R. A., Marsh, G. R., & Quillian, R. E. (2001). Does cognitive-behavioral insomnia therapy alter dysfunctional beliefs about sleep? *Sleep, 24,* 591–599.

Eftekhari, A., Ruzek, J. I., Crowley, J. J., Rosen, C. S., Greenbaum, M. A., & Karlin, B. E. (2013). Effectiveness of national implementation of prolonged exposure therapy in veterans affairs care. *JAMA Psychiatry, 70,* 949–955. doi:10.1001/jamapsychiatry.2013.36

Ekman, P., & Davidson, R. J. (Eds.) (1994). *The nature of emotion: Fundamental questions.* New York, NY: Oxford University Press.

Ellard, K. K., Bernstein, E. E., Hearing, C., Baek, J. H., Sylvia, L. G., Nierenberg, A. A., Barlow, D. H., & Deckersbach, T. (in press). Transdiagnostic treatment of bipolar disorder and comorbid anxiety using the Unified Protocol for Emotional Disorders: A pilot feasibility and acceptability trial. *Journal of Affective Disorders.*

Ellard, K. K., Fairholme, C. P., Boisseau, C. L., Farchione, T. J., & Barlow, D. H. (2010). Unified Protocol for the Transdiagnostic Treatment of Emotional Disorders: Protocol development and initial outcome data. *Cognitive and Behavioral Practice, 17,* 88–101. doi:10.1016/j.cbpra.2009.06.002

Ellis, A., Abroms, M., & Abroms, L. (2009). *Personality Theories: Critical Perspectives.* Thousand Oaks, CA: Sage.

El-Mallakh, R. S., & Hollifield, M. (2008). Comorbid anxiety in bipolar disorder alters treatment and prognosis. *Psychiatric Quarterly, 79*(2), 139–150. doi:10.1007/s11126-008-9071-5

Engel, S. G., Wonderlich, S. A., Crosby, R. D., Mitchell, J. E., Crow, S., Peterson, C. B., . . ., & Gordon, K. H. (2013). The role of affect in the maintenance of anorexia nervosa: evidence from a naturalistic assessment of momentary behaviors and emotion. *Journal of Abnormal Psychology, 122*(3), 709–719. doi:10.1037/a0034010.

Espie, C. A. (2002). Insomnia: conceptual issues in the development, persistence, and treatment of sleep disorder in adults. *Annual Review of Psychology, 53,* 215–243.

Etkin, A., Prater, K. E., Hoeft, F., Menon, V., & Schatzberg, A. F. (2010). Failure of anterior cingulate activation and connectivity with the amygdala during implicit regulation of emotional processing in generalized anxiety disorder. *American Journal of Psychiatry, 167,* 545–554. doi:10.1176/appi.ajp.2009.09070931

Etkin, A., & Wager, T. D. (2007). Functional neuroimaging of anxiety: A meta-analysis of emotional processing in PTSD, social anxiety disorder, and specific phobia. *American Journal of Psychiatry, 164,* 1476–1488. doi:10.1176/appi.ajp.2007.07030504

Evans, K., Tyrer, P., Catalan, J., Schmidt, U., Davidson, K., Dent, J., . . . Thompson, S. (1999). Manual-assisted cognitive-behaviour therapy (MACT): A randomized controlled trial of a brief intervention with bibliotherapy in the treatment of recurrent deliberate self-harm. *Psychological Medicine, 29,* 19–25.

Eysenck, H. J. (Ed.). (1967). *The biological basis of personality.* Springfield, IL: Charles C. Thomas.

Eysenck, H. J. (1981). A model for personality. New York, NY: Springer-Verlag.

Eysenck, H. J., & Eysenck, S. B. G. (1975). *Manual of the Eysenck Personality Questionnaire (adult and junior).* London, UK: Hodder & Stoughton.

Fairburn, C. G. (2008). *Cognitive behavior therapy and eating disorders.* New York, NY: Guilford Press.

Fairholme, C. P., Nosen, E. L., Nillni, Y. I., Schumacher, J. A., Tull, M. T., & Coffey, S. F. (2013). Sleep disturbance and emotion dysregulation as transdiagnostic processes in a comorbid sample. *Behaviour Research and Therapy, 51*(9), 540–546. doi:10.1016/j.brat.2013.05.014

Falicov, C. J. (2009). Commentary: On the wisdom and challenges of culturally attuned treatments for Latinos. *Family Process Journal, 48*, 292–309.

Fang, L., Heisel, M. J., Duberstein, P. R., & Zhang, J. (2012). Combined effects of neuroticism and extraversion: Findings from a matched case control study of suicide in rural China. *The Journal of Nervous and Mental Disease, 200*, 598–602.

Farchione, T. J., Fairholme, C. P., Ellard, K. K., Boisseau, C. L., Thompson-Hollands, J., Carl, J. R., ..., Barlow, D. H. (2012). The Unified Protocol for the Transdiagnostic Treatment of Emotional Disorders: A randomized control trial. *Behavior Therapy, 43*, 666–678. doi:10.1016/j.beth.2012.01.001

Fava, M., Rankin, M. A., Wright, E. C., Alpert, J. E., Nierenberg, A. A., Pava, J., & Rosenbaum, J. F. (2000). Anxiety disorders in major depression. *Comprehensive Psychiatry, 41*, 97–102.

Fernandez-Mendoza, J., Vela-Bueno, A., Vgontzas, A. N., Ramos-Platon, M. J., Olavarrieta-Bernardino, S., Bixler, E. O., & De la Cruz-Troca, J. J. (2010). Cognitive-emotional hyperarousal as a premorbid characteristic of individuals vulnerable to insomnia. *Psychosomatic Medecine, 72*(4), 397–403.

Ferster, C. B. (1973). A functional analysis of depression. *American Psychologist, 28*, 857–870.

First, M. B., Spitzer, R. L., Gibbon, M., & Williams, J. (1997). *Structural Clinical Interview for DSM-IV Axis I Disorders (SCID-IV).* New York, NY: Biometrics Research Department, New York State Psychiatric Institute.

Fisher, P. L., & Wells, A. (2005). How effective are cognitive and behavioral treatments for obsessive–compulsive disorder? A clinical significance analysis. *Behaviour Research and Therapy, 43*(12), 1543–1558. http://doi.org/10.1016/j.brat.2004.11.007

Fletcher, K., Parker, G. B., & Manicavasagar, V. (2013). Coping profiles in bipolar disorder. *Comprehensive Psychiatry, 54*(8), 1177–1184. doi:10.1016/j.comppsych.2013.05.011

Foa, E. B., Hembree, E. A., Cahill, S. P., Rauch, S. A. M., Riggs, D.S., Feeny, N. C., & Yadin, E. (2005). Randomized trial of prolonged exposure for posttraumatic stress disorder with and without cognitive restructuring: Outcome at academic and community clinics. *Journal of Consulting and Clinical Psychology, 73*, 953–964.

Fox, H. C., Hong, K. A., & Sinha, R. (2008). Difficulties in emotion regulation and impulse control in recently abstinent alcoholics compared with social drinkers. *Addictive Behaviors, 33*(2), 388–394. doi:10.1016/j.addbeh.2007.10.002

Freeston, M. H., Ladouceur, R., Thibodeau, N., & Gagnon, F. (1991). Cognitive intrusions in a non-clinical population. I. Response style, subjective experience, and appraisal. *Behaviour Research and Therapy, 29*(6), 585–597. http://doi.org/10.1016/0005-7967(91)90008-Q

Friedman, B., Delavan, R. L., Sheeran, T. H., & Bruce, M. L. (2009). The effect of major and minor depression on Medicare home healthcare services use. *Journal of the American Geriatrics Society, 57*(4), 669–675

Fullana, M. À., Mataix-Cols, D., Trujillo, J. L., Caseras, X., Serrano, F., Alonso, P., ..., Torrubia, R. (2004). Personality characteristics in obsessive-compulsive disorder and individuals with subclinical obsessive-compulsive problems. *British Journal of Clinical Psychology, 43*(4), 387–398. http://doi.org/10.1348/0144665042388937

Gallagher, M. W., & Brown, T. A. (2015). Bayesian analysis of current and lifetime comorbidity rates of mood and anxiety disorders in individuals with posttraumatic stress disorder. *Journal of Psychopathology and Behavioral Assessment. 37*, 60–66. doi:10.1007/s10862-014-9436-z

Gallagher, M. W., Payne, L. A., White, K. S., Shear, K. M., Woods, S. W., Gorman, J. M., & Barlow, D. H. (2013). Mechanisms of change in cognitive behavioral therapy for panic disorder: The unique effects of self-efficacy and anxiety sensitivity. *Behaviour Research and Therapy, 51*(11), 767–777. doi:http://dx.doi.org/10.1016/j.brat.2013.09.001

Gatchel, R. J., Peng, Y. B., Peters, M. L., Fuchs, P. N., & Turk, D. C. (2007). The bio-psychosocial approach to chronic pain: Scientific advances and future directions. *Psychological Bulletin, 133*, 581–624.

Gamez, W., Chmielewski, M., Kotov, R., Ruggero, C., & Watson, D. (2011). Development of a measure of experiential avoidance: The Multidimensional Experiential Avoidance Questionnaire. *Psychological Assessment, 23*, 692–713.

Gershuny, B. S., & Sher, K. J. (1998). The relation between personality and anxiety: Findings from a 3-year prospective study. *Journal of Abnormal Psychology, 107*, 252–262.

Gilbert, K. E., Nolen-Hoeksema, S., & Gruber, J. (2013). Positive emotion dysregulation across mood disorders: How amplifying versus dampening predicts emotional reactivity and illness course. *Behaviour Research and Therapy, 51*(11), 736–741. doi:10.1016/j.brat.2013.08.004

Gillihan, S. J., Farris, S. G., & Foa, E. B. (2011). The effect of anxiety sensitivity on alcohol consumption among individuals with comorbid alcohol dependence and posttraumatic stress disorder. *Psychology of Addictive Behaviors, 25*(4), 721–726. doi:10.1037/a0023799

Goldberg, D., & Fawcett, J. (2012). The importance of anxiety in both major depression and bipolar disorder. *Depression and Anxiety, 29*(6), 471–478. doi:10.1002/da.21939

Goldstein-Piekarski, A. N., Williams, L. M., & Humphreys, K. (2016). A trans-diagnostic review of anxiety disorder comorbidity and the impact of multiple exclusion criteria on studying clinical outcomes in anxiety disorders. *Translational Psychiatry, 6*, 1–9.

Gorman, J. M. (2007). *The essential guide to psychiatric drugs.* 4th ed. New York, NY: St. Martin's Griffin.

Gradus, J. L., Qin, P., Lincoln, A. K., Miller, M., Lawler, E., Sørensen, H. T., & Lash, T. L. (2010). Posttraumatic stress disorder and completed suicide. *American Journal of Epidemiology, 171*, 721–727. doi:10.1093/aje/kwp456

Grant, B. F., Chou, S. P., Goldstein, R. B., Huang, B., Stinson, F. S., Saha, T. D., . . . Ruan, W. J. (2008). Prevalence, correlates, disability, and comorbidity of DSM-IV borderline personality disorder: Results from the Wave 2 National Epidemiologic Survey on Alcohol and Related Conditions. *Journal of Clinical Psychiatry, 69*(4), 533–545. doi:10.4088/JCP.v69n0404

Gratz, K. L., & Gunderson, J. G. (2006). Preliminary data on an acceptance-based emotion regulation group intervention for deliberate self-harm among women with borderline personality disorder. *Behavior Therapy, 37*, 25–35.

Gratz, K. L., & Roemer, L. (2004). Multidimensional assessment of emotion regulation and dysregulation: Development, factor structure, and initial validation of the difficulties in emotion regulation scale. *Journal of Psychopathology and Behavioral Assessment, 26*(1), 41–54.

Gray, J. A. (1982). *The neuropsychology of anxiety.* New York, NY: Oxford University Press.

Green, M. J., Cahill, C. M., & Malhi, G. S. (2007). The cognitive and neurophysiological basis of emotion dysregulation in bipolar disorder. *Journal of Affective Disorders*, *103*(1–3), 29–42. doi:10.1016/j.jad.2007.01.024

Greenberg, L. S. (2008). Emotion and cognition in psychotherapy: The transforming power of affect. *Canadian Psychology*, *49*(1), 49–59. doi:10.1037/0708-5591.49.1.49

Greenberg, L. S., & Watson, J. C. (2005). *Emotion-focused therapy for depression*. Washington, DC: American Psychological Association.

Greenberg, R. P., Constantino, M. J., & Bruce, N. (2006). Are patient expectations still relevant for psychotherapy process and outcome? *Clinical Psychology Review*, *26*, 657–678.

Griffith, J. W., Zinbarg, R. E., Craske, M. G., Mineka, S., Rose, R. D., Waters, A. M., & Sutton, J. M. (2010). Neuroticism as a common dimension in the internalizing disorders. *Psychological Medicine*, *40*, 1125–1136.

Gross, J. J. (Ed.). (2014). *Handbook of emotion regulation*. 2d ed. New York, NY: Guilford.

Gross, J. J., & John, O. (2003). Individual differences in two emotion regulation processes: Implication for affect, relationships, and well-being. *Journal of Personality and Social Psychology*, *85*, 348–362.

Grosse Holtforth, M., Hayes, A. M., Sutter, M., Wilm, K., Schmied, E., Laurenceau, J. P., & Caspar, F. (2011). Fostering cognitive-emotional processing in the treatment of depression: A preliminary investigation in exposure-base cognitive therapy. *Psychotherapy and Psychosomatics*, *81*, 259–260. doi:10.1159/000336813

Gruber, J., Harvey, A. G., & Gross, J. J. (2012). When trying is not enough: Emotion regulation and the effort-success gap in bipolar disorder. *Emotion (Washington, DC)*, *12*(5), 997–1003. doi:10.1037/a0026822

Gruber, J., Hay, A., & Gross, J. (2014). Rethinking emotion: Cognitive reappraisal is an effective positive and negative emotion regulation strategy in bipolar disorder. *Emotion*, *14*(2), 388.

Gruber, J., Kogan, A., Mennin, D., & Murray, G. (2013). Real-world emotion? An experience-sampling approach to emotion experience and regulation in bipolar I disorder. *Journal of Abnormal Psychology*, *122*(4), 971–983.

Gruber, J., Purcell, A., Perna, M., & Mikels, J. (2013). Letting go of the bad: Deficit in maintaining negative, but not positive, emotion in bipolar disorder. *Emotion*, *13*(1), 168.

Gunter, R. W., & Whittal, M. L. (2010). Dissemination of cognitive-behavioral treatments for anxiety disorders: Overcoming barriers and improving patient access. *Clinical Psychology Review*, *30*(2), 194–202.

Gurtman, C. G., McNicol, R., & McGillivray, J. A. (2013). The role of neuroticism in insomnia. *Clinical Psychologist*, *18*, 116–124.

Gutner, C. A., Gallagher, M. W., Baker, A. S., Sloan, D. M., & Resick, P. A. (2016). Time course of treatment dropout in cognitive behavioral therapies for posttraumatic stress disorder. *Psychological Trauma: Theory, Research, Practice, & Policy*, *8*, 115–121. doi:10.1037/tra0000062

Haaga, D. A. F. (2000). Introduction to the special section on stepped care models in psychotherapy. *Journal of Consulting and Clinical Psychology*, *68*(4), 547–548. doi:10.1037/0022-006X.68.4.547

Hafeman, D. M., Bebko, G., Bertocci, M. A., Fournier, J. C., Bonar, L., Perlman, S. B., ..., Phillips, M. L. (2014). Abnormal deactivation of the inferior frontal gyrus during implicit emotion processing in youth with bipolar disorder: Attenuated by medication. *Journal of Psychiatric Research, 58*, 129–136. doi:10.1016/j.jpsychires.2014.07.023

Halmi, K. A., Agras, W. S., Crow, S., Mitchell, J., Wilson, G. T., Bryson, S. W., & Kraemer, H. C. (2005). Predictors of treatment acceptance and completion in anorexia nervosa: Implications for future study designs. *Archives of General Psychiatry, 62*, 776–781. doi:10.1001/archpsyc.62.7.776

Hamilton, M. (1959). The assessment of anxiety states by rating. *British Journal of Medical Psychology, 3250*–3255. doi:10.1111/j.2044-8341.1959.tb00467.x

Hamilton, M. (1960). A rating scale for depression. *Journal of Neurology, Neurosurgery, & Psychiatry, 23*(1), 56–62.

Hamilton, M. (1967). Development of a rating scale for primary depressive illness. *British Journal of Social & Clinical Psychology, 6*(4), 278–296. doi:10.1111/j.2044-8260.1967.tb00530.x

Handley, T. E., Inder, K. J., Kay-Lambkin, F. J., Stain, H. J., Fitzgerald, M., Lewin, T. J., & Kelly, B. J. (2012). Contributors to suicidality in rural communities: Beyond the effects of depression. *BMC Psychiatry, 12*, 105.

Harrison, A., Sullivan, S., Tchanturia, K., & Treasure, J. (2009). Emotion recognition and regulation in anorexia nervosa. *Clinical Psychology & Psychotherapy, 16*, 348–356. doi:10.1002/cpp.628

Harvey, A. G. (2001). Insomnia: symptom or diagnosis? *Clinical Psychology Review, 21*, 1037–1059.

Harvey, A. G. (2002a). A cognitive model of insomnia. *Behaviour Research and Therapy, 40*, 869–893.

Harvey, A. G. (2002b). Identifying safety behaviors in insomnia. *Journal of Nervous and Mental Disease, 190*, 16–21.

Harvey, A. G., Murray, G., Chandler, R. A., & Soehner, A. (2010). Sleep disturbance as transdiagnostic: Consideration of neurobiological mechanisms. *Clinical Psychology Review, 3*, 225–235.

Harvey, C. J., Gehrman, P., & Espie, C. A. (2014). Who is predisposed to insomnia: A review of familial aggregation, stress-reactivity, personality and coping style. *Sleep Medicine Reviews, 18*, 237–247.

Hayes, A. M., Beck, G., & Yasinski, C. (2012). A cognitive behavioral perspective on corrective experiences. In L. G. Castonguay & C. E. Hill (Eds.), *Transformation in psychotherapy: Corrective experiences across cognitive behavioral, humanistic, and psychodynamic approaches* (pp. 69–83). Washington, DC: American Psychological Association Press.

Hayes, A. M., Feldman, G. C., Beevers, C. G., Laurenceau, J. P., Cardaciotto, L., & Lewis-Smith, J. (2007). Discontinuities and cognitive changes in an exposure-based cognitive therapy for depression. *Journal of Consulting and Clinical Psychology, 75*, 409–421. doi:10.1037/0022-006X.75.3.409

Hays, P. A. (2009). Integrating evidence-based practice, cognitive-behavior therapy, and multicultural therapy: Ten steps for culturally competent practice. *Professional Psychology: Research and Practice, 40*(4), 354.

Hayes, S. C., Wilson, K. G., Gifford, E. V., Follette, V. M., & Strosahl, K. (1996). Experiential avoidance and behavioral disorders: A functional dimensional approach to diagnosis and treatment. *Journal of Consulting and Clinical Psychology, 64*, 1152–1168.

Heath, N. L., Carsley, D., De Riggi, M., Mills, D., & Mettler, J. (2016). The relationship between mindfulness, depressive symptoms and non-suicidal self-injury amongst adolescents. *Archives of Suicide Research, 20*(4), 635–649.

Hecht, H., Genzwürker, S., Helle, M., & van Calker, D. (2005). Social functioning and personality of subjects at familial risk for affective disorder. *Journal of Affective Disorders, 84*(1), 33–42. doi:10.1016/j.jad.2004.09.002

Heissler, J., Kanske, P., Schönfelder, S., & Wessa, M. (2014). Inefficiency of emotion regulation as vulnerability marker for bipolar disorder: evidence from healthy individuals with hypomanic personality. *Journal of Affective Disorders, 152–154*, 83–90. doi:10.1016/j.jad.2013.05.001

Herbert, B. M., Herbert, C., Pollatos, O., Weimer, K., Enck, P., Sauer, H., & Zipfel, S. (2012). Effects of short-term deprivation on interoceptive awareness, feelings, and autonomic cardiac activity. *Biological Psychology, 89*, 71–79. doi:10.1016/j.biopsycho.2011.09.004

Herbert, B. M., Muth, E. R., Pollatos, O., & Herbert, C. (2012). Interoception across modalities: On the relationship between cardiac awareness and sensitivity for gastric functions. *PLoS ONE, 7*, e36646. doi:10.1371/journal.pone.0036646

Hertenstein, E., Nissen, C., Riemann, D., Feige, B., Baglioni, C., & Spiegelhalder, K. (2015). The exploratory power of sleep effort, dysfunctional beliefs, and arousal for insomnia severity and polysomnography-determined sleep. *Journal of Sleep Research, 24*, 399–406.

Hilbert, A., & Tuschen-Caffier, B. (2004). Body image interventions in cognitive-behavioural therapy of binge-eating disorder: A component analysis. *Behaviour Research and Therapy, 42*, 1325–1339.

Hilbert, A., Tuschen-Caffier, B., & Vogele, C. (2002). Effects of prolonged and repeated body image exposure in binge-eating disorder. *Journal of Psychosomatic Research, 52*(3), 137–144. doi:10.1016/ S0022-3999(01)00314-2.

Hildebrandt, T., Loeb, K., Troupe, S., & Delinsky, S. (2012). Adjunctive mirror exposure for eating disorders: A randomized controlled pilot study. *Behaviour Research & Therapy, 50*, 797–804. doi:10.1016/j.brat.2012.09.004.

Hoehn-Saric, R., Schlund, M. W., & Wong, S. H. Y. (2004). Effects of citalopram on worry and brain activation in patients with generalized anxiety disorder. *Psychiatry Research, 131*, 11–21. doi:10.1016/j.pscychresns.2004.02.003

Hoertnagl, C. M., Muehlbacher, M., Biedermann, F., Yalcin, N., Baumgartner, S., Schwitzer, G., . . ., & Hofer, A. (2011). Facial emotion recognition and its relationship to subjective and functional outcomes in remitted patients with bipolar I disorder. *Bipolar Disorders, 13*(5–6), 537–544. doi:10.1111/j.1399-5618.2011.00947.x

Hofmann, S. G., Sawyer, A. T., Witt, A. A., & Oh, D. (2010). The effect of mindfulness-based therapy on anxiety and depression: A meta-analytic review. *Journal of Consulting and Clinical Psychology, 78*(2), 169–183. doi:10.1037/a0018555

Hollen, P. J., Gralla, R. J., Kris, M. G., McCoy, S., Donaldson, G. W., & Moinpour, C. M. (2005). A comparison of visual analogue and numerical rating scale formats for the Lung Cancer Symptom Scale (LCSS): does format affect patient ratings of symptoms and quality of life? *Quality of Life Research, 14*(3), 837–847.

Holma, K. M., Haukka, J., Suominen, K., Valtonen, H. M., Mantere, O., Melartin, T. K., Sokero, T. P., Oquendo, M. A., & Isometsä, E. T. (2014). Differences in incidence of suicide attempts between bipolar I and II disorders and major depressive disorder. *Bipolar Disorder, 16*, 652–661.

Holmes, A. J., Lee, P. H., Hollinshead, M. O., Bakst, L., Roffman, J. L., Smoller, J. W., & Buckner, R. I. (2012). Individual differences in amygdala-medial prefrontal anatomy link negative affect, impaired social functioning, and polygenetic depression link. *Journal of Neuroscience, 32*, 18087–18100.

Holowka, D. W., & Marx, B. P. (2011). Assessing PTSD-related functional impairment and quality of life. In G. J. Beck & D. M. Sloan (Eds.), *Oxford handbook of traumatic stress disorders* (pp. 315–332). New York, NY: Oxford University Press.

Hong, R. Y. (2007). Worry and rumination: Differential associations with anxious and depressive symptoms and coping behavior. *Behaviour Research and Therapy, 45*, 277–290.

Hopko, D. R., Lejuez, C. W., Ruggiero, K. J., & Eifert, G. H. (2003). Contemporary behavioral activation treatments for depression: Procedures, principles, and progress. *Clinical Psychology Review, 23*, 699–717. doi:10.1016/S0272-7358(03)00070-9

Horrell, S. C. V. (2008). Effectiveness of cognitive-behavioral therapy with adult ethnic minority clients: A review. *Professional Psychology: Research and Practice, 39*(2), 160.

Horwath, E., Johnson, J., Klerman, G. L., & Weissman, M. M. (1994). What are the public health implications of subclinical depressive symptoms? *Psychiatric Quarterly, 65*, 323–337. doi:10.1007/BF02354307

Hudson, J. L., Hiripi, E., Pope, H. G. Jr, & Kessler, R. C. (2007). The prevalence and correlates of eating disorders in the National Comorbidity Survey Replication. *Biological Psychiatry, 61*(3), 348–358.

Ilardi, S. S., & Craighead, W. E. (1994). The role of nonspecific factors in cognitive-behavior therapy for depression. *Clinical Psychology: Science and Practice, 1*, 138–156.

Institute of Medicine (US) Committee on Advancing Pain Research, C., and Education. (2011). Relieving Pain in America: A blueprint for transforming prevention, care, education, and research: National Academies Press (US).

International Association for the Study of Pain. (2012). IASP taxonomy, from www.iasp-pain.org/Taxonomy?navItemNumber=576

Ito, M., Horikoshi, M., Kato, N., Oe, Y., Fujisato, H., Nakajima, S., . . ., Usuki, M. (2016). Transdiagnostic and transcultural: Pilot study of Unified Protocol for depressive and anxiety disorders in Japan. *Behavior Therapy, 47*(3), 416–430.

Jabben, N., Arts, B., Jongen, E. M. M., Smulders, F. T. Y., van Os, J., & Krabbendam, L. (2012). Cognitive processes and attitudes in bipolar disorder: A study into personality, dysfunctional attitudes, and attention bias in patients with bipolar disorder and their relatives. *Journal of Affective Disorders, 143*(1–3), 265–268. doi:10.1016/j.jad.2012.04.022

Jackson, K. M., & Sher, K. J. (2003). Alcohol use disorders and psychological distress: A prospective state-trait analysis. *Journal of Abnormal Psychology, 112*(4), 599–613. doi:10.1037/0021-843X.112.4.599

Jackson, L. C., Schmutzer, P. A., Wenzel, A., & Tyler, J. D. (2006). Applicability of cognitive–behavior therapy with American Indian individuals. *Psychotherapy: Theory, Research, Practice, Training, 43*, 506–517.

Jacobson, N. S., & Truax, P. (1991). Clinical significance: A statistical approach to defining meaningful change in psychotherapy research. *Journal of Consulting and Clinical Psychology, 59*, 12–19. doi:10.1037/0022-006X.59.1.12

James, L., & Taylor, J. (2008). Revisiting the structure of mental disorders: Borderline personality disorder and the internalizing/externalizing spectra. *British Journal of Clinical Psychology, 47*, 361–380.

Jasper, F., Hiller, W., Rist, F., Bailer, J., & Witthöft, M. (2012). Somatic symptom reporting has a dimensional latent structure: Results from taxometric analyses. *Journal of Abnormal Psychology, 121*(3), 725.

Jensen, M. P., Karoly, P., & Braver, S. (1986). The measurement of clinical pain intensity: a comparison of six methods. *Pain, 27*(1), 117–126.

Johannes, C. B., Le, T. K., Zhou, X., Johnston, J. A., & Dworkin, R. H. (2010). The prevalence of chronic pain in United States adults: results of an Internet-based survey. *Journal of Pain, 11*(11), 1230–1239.

John, O. P., & Gross, J. J. (2004). Healthy and unhealthy emotion regulation: personality processes, individual differences, and life span development. *Journal of Personality, 72*(6), 1301–1333.

Johnson, C., Connors, M. E., & Tobin, D. L. (1987). Symptom management of bulimia. *Journal of Consulting and Clinical Psychiatry, 55*(5), 0022–006X.

Johnson, S. L., Gruber, J., & Eisner, L. R. (2007). Emotion and bipolar disorder. In J. Rottenberg & S. L. Johnson (Eds.), *Emotion and psychopathology: Bridging affective and clinical science* (pp. 123–150). Washington, DC: American Psychological Association. doi:10.1037/11562-000

Joiner, T. E. (2005). *Why people die by suicide.* Cambridge, MA: Harvard University Press.

Joyce, P. R., Mulder, R. T., Luty, S. E., McKenzie, J. M., Sullivan, P. F., & Cloninger, R. C. (2003). Borderline personality disorder in major depression: symptomatology, temperament, character, differential drug response, and 6-month outcome. *Comprehensive psychiatry, 44*(1), 35–43. doi:10.1053/comp.2003.50001

Judd, L. L. (2012). Dimensional paradigm of the long-term course of unipolar major depressive disorder. *Depression and Anxiety, 29*, 167–171.

Jylhä, P., Mantere, O., Melartin, T., Suominen, K., Vuorilehto, M., Arvilommi, P., . . ., Isometsä, E. (2010). Differences in neuroticism and extraversion between patients with bipolar I or II and general population subjects or major depressive disorder patients. *Journal of Affective Disorders, 125*(1–3), 42–52. doi:10.1016/j.jad.2010.01.068

Kabat-Zinn, J. (1982). An outpatient program in behavioral medicine for chronic pain patients based on the practice of mindfulness meditation: Theoretical considerations and preliminary results. *General Hospital Psychiatry, 4*, 33–47.

Kadimpati, S., Zale, E. L., Hooten, M. W., Ditre, J. W., & Warner, D. O. (2015). Associations between Neuroticism and Depression in Relation to Catastrophizing and Pain-Related Anxiety in Chronic Pain Patients. *PLoS One, 10*(4), e0126351.

Kagan, J. (1989). Temperamental contributions to social behavior. *Psychologist, 44*, 668–674.

Kagan, J. (1994). *Galen's prophecy: Temperament in human nature.* New York, NY: Basic Books.

Kanske, P., Heissler, J., Schönfelder, S., Forneck, J., & Wessa, M. (2013). Neural correlates of emotional distractibility in bipolar disorder patients, unaffected relatives, and individuals with hypomanic personality. *American Journal of Psychiatry, 170*(12), 1487–1496. doi:10.1176/appi.ajp.2013.12081044

Kanwar, A., Malik, S., Prokop, L. J., Sim, L. A., Feldstein, D., Wang, Z., & Murad, M. H. (2013). The association between anxiety disorders and suicidal behaviors: A systematic review and meta-analysis. *Depression and Anxiety, 30*(10), 917–929.

Kashdan, T. B., Breen, W. E., Afram, A., & Terhar, D. (2010). Experiential avoidance in idiographic, autobiographical memories: Construct validity and links to social anxiety, depressive, and anger symptoms. *Journal of Anxiety Disorders, 24*, 528–534.

Katon, W., Von Korff, M., Lin, E., Simon, G., & Walker, E. (2014). Stepped collaborative care for primary care patients with persistent symptoms of depression. *Journal of American Medical Association, 56*(12), 2581–2590. doi:10.1001/archpsyc.56.12.1109

Katz, D. A., & McHorney, C. A. (2002). The relationship between insomnia and health-related quality of life in patients with chronic illness. *Journal of Family Practice, 51*, 229–235.

Kaysen, D., Lindgren, K., Zangana, G. A. S., Murray, L., Bass, J., & Bolton, P. (2013). Adaptation of cognitive processing therapy for treatment of torture victims: Experience in Kurdistan, Iraq. *Psychological Trauma: Theory, Research, Practice, and Policy, 5*(2), 184–192.

Kazdin, A. E. (2015). Technology-based interventions and reducing the burdens of mental illness: Perspectives and comments on the special series. *Cognitive and Behavioral Practice, 22*(3), 359–366. doi:10.1016/j.cbpra.2015.04.004

Keightley, M. L., Seminowicz, D. A., Bagby, R. M., Costa, P. T., Fossati, P., & Mayberg, H. S. (2003). Personality influences limbic-cortical interactions during sad mood induction. *NeuroImage, 20*, 2031–2039.

Kerner, J., Rimer, B., & Emmons, K. (2005). Introduction to the special section on dissemination: dissemination research and research dissemination: How can we close the gap? *Health Psychology, 24*, 443–446.

Kessler, R. C., Avenevoli, S., Costello, J., Georgiades, K., Green, J. G., Gruber, M. J., . . ., Merikangas, K. R. (2012). Prevalence, persistence, and sociodemographic correlates of DSM-IV disorders in the National Comorbidity Survey Replication Adolescent Supplement. *Archives of General Psychiatry, 69*(4), 372–380. doi:10.1001/archgenpsychiatry.2011.160.

Kessler, R. C., Berglund, P., Demler, O., Jin, R., Merikangas, K. R., & Waltersm, E. E. (2005). Lifetime prevalence and age-of-onset distributions of DSM-IV disorders in the National Comorbidity Survey Replication. *Archives of General Psychiatry, 62*, 593–602.

Kessler, R. C., Chiu, W. T., Demler, O., & Walters, E. E. (2005). Prevalence, severity, and comorbidity of 12-month DSM-IV disorders in the National Comorbidity Survey Replication. *Archives of General Psychiatry, 62*, 617–627. doi:10.1001/archpsyc.62.6.617

Kessler, R. C., Cox, B. J., Green, J. G., Ormel, J., McLaughlin, K. A., Merikangas, K. R., . . ., Zaslavsky, A. M. (2011). The effects of latent variables in the development of comorbidity among common mental disorders. *Depression and Anxiety, 28*, 29–39.

Kessler, R. C., Nelson, C. B., McGonagle, K. A., Lui, J., Swartz, M., & Blazer, D. G. (1996). Comorbidity of DSM-III-R major depressive disorder in the general population: Results from the National Comorbidity Survey. *British Journal of Psychiatry, 168*, 17–30.

Kessler, R. C., & Wang, P. S. (2009). Epidemiology of depression. In I. H. Gotlib & C. L. Hammen (Eds.), *Handbook of depression* (2d ed., pp. 5–22). New York, NY: Guilford Press.

Kilpatrick, D., Resnick, H. S., Milanak, M. E., Miller, M. W., Keyes, K. M., & Friedman, M. J. (2013). National estimates of exposure to traumatic events and PTSD prevalence using DSM-IV and proposed DSM-5 criteria. *Journal of Traumatic Stress, 26*, 537–547. doi:10.1002/jts.21848

Klonsky, E. D. (2007). The functions of deliberate self-injury: A review of the evidence. *Clinical Psychology Review, 27*, 226–239.

Klosko, J., & Young, J. (2004). Cognitive therapy of borderline personality disorder. In Leahey (Ed.), *Contemporary Cognitive Therapy: Theory, Research, and Practice.* New York, NY US: Guilford.

Klosko, J. S., Barlow, D. H., Tassinari, R., & Cerny, J. A. (1990). A comparison of alprazolam and behavior therapy in treatment of panic disorder. *Journal of Consulting and Clinical Psychology, 58,* 77–84.

Kober, H. (2014). Emotion regulation in substance use disorders. In J. J. Gross & J. J. Gross (Eds.), *Handbook of emotion regulation* (2d ed., pp. 428–446). New York, NY: Guilford Press.

Koh, J. S., Ko, H. J., Wang, S. M., Cho, K. J., Kim, J. C., Lee, S. J., et al. (2014). The association of personality trait on treatment outcomes in patients with chronic prostatitis/chronic pelvic pain syndrome: an exploratory study. *Journal of Psychosomatic Research, 76*(2), 127–133.

Kollman, D. M., Brown, T. A., Liverant, G. I., & Hofmann, S. G. (2006). A taxometric investigation of the latent structure of social anxiety disorder in outpatients with anxiety and mood disorders. *Depression and Anxiety, 23*(4), 190–199.

Korte, K. J., & Schmidt, N. B. (2013). Motivational enhancement therapy reduces anxiety sensitivity. *Cognitive Therapy and Research, 37*(6), 1140–1150. doi:10.1007/s10608-013-9550-3

Kotov, R., Watson, D., Robles, J. P., & Schmidt, N. B. (2007). Personality traits and anxiety symptoms: The multilevel trait predictor model. *Behaviour Research and Therapy, 45,* 1485–1503.

Kraus, N., Lindenberg, J., Kosfelder, J., & Vocks, S. (2015). Immediate effects of body checking behaviour on negative and positive emotions in women with eating disorders: An ecological momentary assessment approach. *European Eating Disorders Review.* doi:10.1002/erv.2380

Krishnan, K. R. R. (2005). Psychiatric and medical comorbidities of bipolar disorder. *Psychosomatic Medicine, 67*(1), 1–8. doi:10.1097/01.psy.0000151489.36347.18

Kushner, M. G., Abrams, K., Thuras, P., Hanson, K. L., Brekke, M., & Sletten, S. (2005). Follow-up study of anxiety disorder and alcohol dependence in comorbid alcoholism treatment patients. *Alcoholism: Clinical and Experimental Research, 29*(8), 1432–1443. doi:10.1097/01.alc.0000175072.17623.f8

Kushner, M. G., Donahue, C., Sletten, S., Thuras, P., Abrams, K., Peterson, J., & Frye, B. (2006). Cognitive behavioral treatment of comorbid anxiety disorder in alcoholism treatment patients: Presentation of a prototype program and future directions. *Journal of Mental Health, 15*(6), 697–707. doi:10.1080/09638230600998946

Kushner, M. G., Sletten, S., Donahue, C., Thuras, P., Maurer, E., Schneider, A., ..., Van Demark, J. (2009). Cognitive-behavioral therapy for panic disorder in patients being treated for alcohol dependence: Moderating effects of alcohol outcome expectancies. *Addictive Behaviors, 34*(6), 554–560.

Lahey, B. B. (2009). Public health significance of neuroticism. *American Psychologist, 64*(4), 241–256. doi:10.1037/a0015309

La Roche, M. J. (2013). *Cultural psychotherapy: Theory, methods, and practice.* Washington, DC: Sage Publications.

La Roche, M., & Christopher, M. S. (2008). Culture and empirically supported treatments: On the road to a collision? *Culture & Psychology, 14*(3), 333–356.

Lavender, J. M., Wonderlich, S. A., Engel, S. G., Gordon, K. H., Kaye, W. H., & Mitchell, J. E. (2015). Dimensions of emotion dysregulation in anorexia nervosa and bulimia nervosa: A conceptual review of the empirical literature. *Clinical Psychology Review*, 6(40), 111–122. doi:10.1016/j.cpr.2015.05.010

Lawson, R., Waller, G., & Lockwood, R. (2007). Cognitive content and process in eating-disordered patients with obsessive-compulsive features. *Eating Behaviors*, 8(3), 305–310.

Layard, R., & Clark, D. M. (2014). *Thrive: The power of evidence-based psychological therapies*. London, UK: Penguin Publishers.

LeBlanc, M., Beaulieu-Bonneau, S., Merette, C., Savard, J., Ivers, H., & Morin, C. M. (2007). Psychological and health-related quality of life factors associated with insomnia in a population-based sample. *Journal of Psychosomatic Research*, 63, 157–166.

Lebowitz, E. R., Woolston, J., Bar-Haim, Y., Calvocoressi, L., Dauser, C., Warnick, E., …, Leckman, J. F. (2013). Family accommodation in pediatric anxiety disorders. *Depression and Anxiety*, 30(1), 47–54. http://doi.org/10.1002/da.21998

Lee, J. K., Orsillo, S. M., Roemer, L., & Allen, L. B. (2010). Distress and avoidance in generalized anxiety disorder: Exploring relationships with intolerance of uncertainty and worry. *Cognitive Behaviour Therapy*, 39, 126–136.

Lefebvre, J. C., & Keefe, F. J. (2013). The effect of neuroticism on the recall of persistent low-back pain and perceived activity interference. *Journal of Pain*, 14(9), 948–956.

Lejuez, C. W., Hopko, D. R., & Hopko, S. D. (2001). A brief behavioral activation treatment for depression: Treatment manual. *Behavior Modification*, 25, 255–286.

Lenzenweger, M. F., & Pastore, R. E. (2007). On determining sensitivity to pain in borderline personality disorder. *Archives of general psychiatry*, 64(6), 747–748; author reply 748–749. doi:10.1001/archpsyc.64.6.747

Leon, A. C., Solomon, D. A., Mueller, T. I., Turvey, C. L., Endicott, J., & Keller, M. B. (1999). The Range of Impaired Functioning Tool (LIFE–RIFT): A brief measure of functional impairment. *Psychological Medicine*, 29(4), 869–878.

Liebowitz, M. R. (1987). Social phobia. *Modern Problems of Psychopharmacology*, 22, 141–173.

Linehan, M. M. (1993). *Cogntive-behavioral treatment of borderline personality disorder.* New York, NY US: Guilford.

Lloyd, D., Nixon, R. D., Varker, T., Elliot, P., Perry, D., Bryant, R. A., …, Forbes, D. (2014). Comorbidity in the prediction of cognitive processing therapy treatment outcomes for combat-related posttraumatic stress disorder. *Journal of Anxiety Disorders*, 28, 237–240.

Lorberbaum, J. P., Kose, S., Johnson, M. R., Arana, G. W., Sullivan, L. K., Hamner, M. B., …, George, M. S. (2004). Neural correlates of speech anticipatory anxiety in generalized social phobia. *NeuroReport*, 15, 2701–2705.

Lovibond, S. H., & Lovibond, P. F. (1995). *Manual for the Depression Anxiety Stress Scales.* 2d ed. Sydney, Australia: Psychology Foundation of Australia.

Lozano, B. E., & Johnson, S. L. (2001). Can personality traits predict increases in manic and depressive symptoms? *Journal of Affective Disorders*, 63(1–3), 103–111. doi:10.1016/S0165-0327(00)00191-9

Lumley, M. A., Beyer, J., & Radcliffe, A. (2008). Alexithymia and physical health problems: A critique of potential pathways and a research agenda. In A. Vingerhoets, I. Nyklicek & J. Denollet (Eds.), *Emotion regulation: Conceptual and clinical issues* (pp. 43–68). New York: Springer.

Lynch, T. R., Trost, W. T., Salsman, N., & Linehan, M. M. (2007). Dialectical behavior therapy for borderline personality disorder. *Annual Review of Clinical Psychology*, 3, 181–205.

Lyubomirsky, S., & Nolen-Hoeksema, S. (1995). Effects of self-focused rumination on negative thinking and interpersonal problem solving. *Journal of Personality and Social Psychology, 69*, 176–190.

Lyubomirsky, S., Tucker, K., Caldwell, N., & Berg, K. (1999). Why ruminators are poor problem solvers: Clues from the phenomenology of dysphoric rumination. *Journal of Personality and Social Psychology, 77*, 1041–1060.

Maack, D. J., Tull, M. T., & Gratz, K. L. (2012). Experiential avoidance mediates the association between behavioral inhibition and posttraumatic stress disorder. *Cognitive Therapy and Research, 36*, 407–416.

MacLaren, V. V., & Best, L. A. (2010). Nonsuicidal self-injury, potentially addictive behaviors, and the Five Factor Model in undergraduates. *Personality and Individual Differences, 49*(5), 521–525.

Magidson, J. F., Liu, S.-M., Lejuez, C. W., & Blanco, C. (2012). Comparison of the course of substance use disorders among individuals with and without generalized anxiety disorder in a nationally representative sample. *Journal of Psychiatric Research, 46*(5), 659–666. doi:10.1016/j.jpsychires.2012.02.011

Maier, W., Minges, J., Lichtermann, D., Franke, P., & Gansicke, M. (1995). Personality patterns in subjects at risk for affective disorders. *Psychopathology, 28*(Suppl 1), 59–72.

Maller, R. G., & Reiss, S. (1992). Anxiety sensitivity in 1984 and panic attacks in 1987. *Journal of Anxiety Disorders, 6*, 214–247.

Marcus, M., Westra, H., Angus, L., & Kertes, A. (2011). Client experiences of motivational interviewing for generalized anxiety disorder: A qualitative analysis. *Psychotherapy Research, 21*(4), 447–461. doi:10.1080/10503307.2011.578265

Marks, I. M., Connolly, J., & Hallam, R. S. (1973). Psychiatric nurse as therapist. *British Medical Journal, 3*, 156–160.

Marlatt, G. A. (1994). Addiction, mindfulness, and acceptance. In S. C. Hayes, N. S. Jacobson, V. M. Follette, & M. J. Dougher (Eds.), *Acceptance and change: Content and context in psychotherapy* (pp. 175–197). Reno, NV: Context Press.

Marlatt, G. A., Larimer, M. E., Baer, J. S., & Quigley, L. A. (1993). Harm reduction for alcohol problems: Moving beyond the controlled drinking controversy. *Behavior Therapy, 24*(4), 461–503. doi:10.1016/S0005-7894(05)80314-4

Martin, C. S., Lynch, K. G., Pollock, N. K., & Clark, D. B. (2000). Gender differences and similarities in the personality correlates of adolescent alcohol problems. *Psychology of Addictive Behaviors, 14*(2), 121–133. doi:10.1037/0893-164X.14.2.121

Martinez-Mallen, E., Castro-Fornieles, J., Lazaro, L., Moreno, E., Morer, A., Font, E., . . ., Toro, J. (2007). Cue exposure in the treatment of resistant adolescent bulimia nervosa. *International Journal of Eating Disorders 40*, 596–601. doi:10.1002/eat.20423.

Maser, J. D., Norman, S. B., Zisook, S., Everall, I. P., Stein, M. B., Schettler, P. J., & Judd, L. L. (2009). Psychiatric nosology is ready for a paradigm shift in DSM-V. *Clinical Psychology: Science and Practice, 16*, 24–40.

Mata, J., Thompson, R. J., Jaeggi, S. M., Buschkuehl, M., Jonides, J., & Gotlib, I. (2012). Walk on the bright side: Physical activity and affect in major depressive disorder. *Journal of Abnormal Psychology, 121*, 297–308. doi:10.1037/a0023522

Matsumoto, R., Kitabayashi, Y., Narumoto, J., Wada, Y., Okamoto, A., Ushijima, Y., . . ., Fukui, K. (2006). Regional cerebral blood flow changes associated with interoceptive awareness in the recovery process of anorexia nervosa. *Progress in Neuro-Psychopharmacology and Biological Psychiatry, 30*, 1265–1270. doi:10.1016/j.pnpbp.2006.03.042

Mattila, A. K., Kronholm, E., Jula, A., Salminen, J. K., Koivisto, A. M., Mielonen, R. L., et al. (2008). Alexithymia and somatization in general population. *Psychosomatic Medicine, 70*(6), 716–722.

Mayberg, H. S., Liotti, B. M., Brannan, S. K., McGinnis, S., Mahurin, R. K., Jerabek, P. A., ..., Fox, P. T. (1999). Reciprocal limbic-cortical function and negative mood: Converging PET findings in depression and normal sadness. *American Journal of Psychiatry, 156,* 675–682.

McCormick, R. A., Dowd, E. T., Quirk, S., & Zegarra, J. H. (1998). The relationship of NEO-PI performance to coping styles, patterns of use, and triggers for use among substance abusers. *Addictive Behaviors, 23*(4), 497–507. doi:10.1016/S0306-4603(98)00005-7

McCracken, L. M., & Dhingra, L. (2002). A short version of the Pain Anxiety Symptoms Scale (PASS-20): preliminary development and validity. *Pain Research and Management, 7*(1), 45–50.

McCrae, R. R., & Costa, P. T. (1987). Validation of the five-factor model of personality across instruments and observers. *Journal of Personality and Social Psychology, 52,* 81–90.

McGue, M., Slutske, W., & Iacono, W. G. (1999). Personality and substance use disorders: II. Alcoholism versus drug use disorders. *Journal of Consulting and Clinical Psychology, 67*(3), 394–404. doi:10.1037/0022-006X.67.3.394

McHugh, R. K. & Barlow, D. H. (2010). The dissemination and implementation of evidence-based psychological treatments: A review of current efforts. *American Psychologist, 65*(2), 73–84. doi:10.1037/a0018121

McIntosh, V. V. W., Carter, F. A., Bulik, C. M., Frampton, C. M. A., & Joyce, P. R. (2011). Five-year outcome of cognitive behavioral therapy and exposure with response prevention for bulimia nervosa. *Psychological Medicine, 41,* 1061–1071. doi:10.1017/S0033291710001583

McKay, D., Kulchycky, S., & Danyko, S. (2000). Borderline Personality and Obsessive-Compulsive Symptoms. *Journal of Personality Disorders, 14*(1), 57–63. doi:10.1521/pedi.2000.14.1.57

McKinnon, M. C., Cusi, A. M., & MacQueen, G. M. (2013). Psychological factors that may confer risk for bipolar disorder. *Cognitive Neuropsychiatry, 18*(1–2), 115–128. doi:10.1080/13546805.2012.702505

McLaughlin, K. A., Mennin, D. S., & Farach, F. J. (2007). The contributory role of worry in emotion generation and dysregulation in generalized anxiety disorder. *Behaviour Research and Therapy, 45,* 1735–1752. doi:10.1016/j.brat.2006.12.004

McLaughlin, K. A., & Nolen-Hoeksema, S. (2011). Rumination as a transdiagnostic factor in depression and anxiety. *Behaviour Research and Therapy, 49,* 186–193. doi:10.1016/j.brat.2010.12.006

McMain, S. F., Links, P. S., Gnam, W. H., Guimond, T., Cardish, R. J., Korman, L., Streiner, D. L. (2009). A randomized trial of dialectical behavior therapy and general psychiatric management for borderline personality disorder. *The American Journal of Psychiatry, 166,* 1365–1374.

McManus, F., Shafran, R., & Cooper, Z. (2010). What does a transdiagnostic approach have to offer the treatment of anxiety disorders? *British Journal of Clinical Psychology, 49*(Pt 4), 491–505.

McNally, R. J. (2001). On the scientific status of cognitive appraisal models of anxiety disorder. *Behaviour Research and Therapy, 39,* 513–521. doi:10.1017/S0033291710001583

Mennin, D. S., Heimberg, R. G., Turk, C. L., & Fresco, D. M. (2005). Preliminary evidence for an emotion dysregulation model of generalized anxiety disorder. *Behaviour Research and Therapy, 43*, 1281–1310. doi:10.1016/j.brat.2004.08.008

Merikangas, K. R., Akiskal, H. S., Angst, J., Greenberg, P. E., Hirschfeld, R. M. A., Petukhova, M., & Kessler, R. C. (2007). Lifetime and 12-month prevalence of bipolar spectrum disorder in the National Comorbidity Survey Replication. *Archives of General Psychiatry, 64*(5), 543–552. doi:10.1001/archpsyc.64.5.543

Merikangas, K. R., Zhang, H., & Aveneoli, S. (2003). Longitudinal trajectories of depression and anxiety in a prospective community study. *Archives of General Psychiatry, 60*, 993–1000.

Merlo, L. J., Lehmkuhl, H. D., Geffken, G. R., & Storch, E. A. (2009). Decreased family accommodation associated with improved therapy outcome in pediatric obsessive-compulsive disorder. *Journal of Consulting and Clinical Psychology, 77*(2), 355–360. http://doi.org/10.1037/a0012652

Merwin, R. M., Zucker, N. L., Lacy, J. L., & Elliott, C. A. (2010). Interoceptive awareness in eating disorders: Distinguishing lack of clarity from non-acceptance of internal experience. *Cognition and Emotion, 24*, 892–902. doi:10.1080/02699930902985845

Michielsen, M., Comijs, H. C., Semeijn, E. J., Beekman, A. T., Deeg, D. J., & Kooij, J. S. (2013). The comorbidity of anxiety and depressive symptoms in older adults with attention-deficit/hyperactivity disorder: A longitudinal study. *Journal of Affective Disorders, 148*(2), 220–227.

Miller, M. W., Fogler, J. M., Wolf, E. J., Kaloupek, D. G., & Keane, T. M. (2008). The internalizing and externalizing structure of psychiatric comorbidity in combat veterans. *Journal of Traumatic Stress, 21*, 58–65. doi:10.1002/jts.20303

Miller, W. R., & Rollnick, S. (2002). *Motivational interviewing: Preparing people for change.* 2d ed. New York, NY: Guilford Press.

Miller, W. R., & Rollnick, S. (2012). Meeting in the middle: Motivational interviewing and self-determination theory. *The International Journal of Behavioral Nutrition and Physical Activity, 9.* doi:10.1186/1479-5868-9-25

Miller, W. R., & Rollnick, S. (2013). *Motivational interviewing: Preparing people for change.* 3d ed. New York, NY: Guilford Press.

Miranda, J., Bernal, G., Lau, A., Kohn, L., Hwang, W., & La Fromboise, T. (2005). State of the science on psychosocial interventions for ethnic minorities. *Annual Review of Clinical Psychology, 1*, 113–142.

Mizes, J. S., Christiano, B., Madison, J., Post, G., Seime, R., & Varnado, P. (2000). Development of the Mizes Anorectic Cognitions Questionnaire–Revised: Psychometric properties and factor structure in a large sample of eating disorder patients. *International Journal of Eating Disorders, 28*(4), 415–421.

Morin, C. M., & Benca, R. (2012). Chronic insomnia. *Lancet, 379*, 1129–1141.

Morin, C. M., Blais, F., & Savard, J. (2002). Are changes in beliefs and attitudes about sleep related to sleep improvements in the treatment of insomnia? *Behaviour Research and Therapy, 40*, 741–752.

Morin, C. M., Rodrigue, S., & Ivers, H. (2003). Role of stress, arousal, and coping skills in primary insomnia. *Psychosomatic Medicine, 65*, 259–267.

Morin, C. M., Vallieres, A., & Ivers, H. (2007). Dysfunctional beliefs and attitudes about sleep (DBAS): validation of a brief version (DBAS-16). *Sleep, 30*, 1547–1554.

Morley, K. C., Baillie, A., Sannibale, C., Teesson, M., & Haber, P. S. (2013). Integrated care for comorbid alcohol dependence and anxiety and/or depressive disorder: Study protocol for an assessor-blind, randomized controlled trial. *Addiction Science & Clinical Practice, 8*(1), 1.

Mountford, V., Haase, A., & Waller, G. (2006). Body checking in the eating disorders: Associations between cognitions and behaviors. *International Journal of Eating Disorders, 39,* 708–715.

Muehlenkamp, J. J. (2014). Distinguishing between suicidal and nonsuicidal self-injury. In M. K. Nock (Ed.), *The Oxford Handbook of Suicide and Self-Injury* (1st ed., pp. 23–46). New York, NY: Oxford University Press.

Mullins-Sweatt, S. N., Lengel, G. J., & Grant, D. M. (2013). Nonsuicidal self-injury: The contribution of general personality functioning. *Personality and Mental Health, 7,* 56–68.

Mundt, J. C., Marks, I. M., Shear, M. K., & Greist, J. H. (2002). The Work and Social Adjustment Scale: a simple measure of impairment in functioning. *British Journal of Psychiatry, 180,* 461–464.

Muñoz, R. F., & Mendelson, T. (2005). Toward evidence-based interventions for diverse populations: The San Francisco General Hospital prevention and treatment manuals. *Journal of Consulting and Clinical Psychology, 73,* 790–799.

Murray, G., Goldstone, E., & Cunningham, E. (2007). Personality and the predisposition(s) to bipolar disorder: heuristic benefits of a two-dimensional model. *Bipolar Disorders, 9*(5), 453–461. doi:10.1111/j.1399-5618.2007.00456.x

Murray, L. K., Dorsey, S., Haroz, E., Lee, C., Alsiary, M. M., Haydary, A., . . ., Bolton, P. (2014). A common elements treatment approach for adult mental health problems in low-and middle-income countries. *Cognitive and Behavioral Practice, 21*(2), 111–123. doi:10.1016/j.cbpra.2013.06.005

Nakamura, B. J., Pestle, S. L., & Chorpita, B. F. (2009). Differential sequencing of cognitive-behavioral techniques for reducing child and adolescent anxiety. *Journal of Cognitive Psychotherapy, 23*(2), 114–135. doi:10.1891/0889-8391.23.2.114

Naragon-Gainey, K. (2010). Meta-analysis of the relations of anxiety sensitivity to the depressive and anxiety disorders. *Psychological Bulletin, 136,* 128–150. doi:10.1037/a001805

Narasimhan, M., & Campbell, N. (2010). A tale of two comorbidities: Understanding the neurobiology of depression and pain. *Indian Journal of Psychiatry, 52*(2), 127–130.

National Institutes of Health (NIH). (2005). National Institutes of Health State of the Science Conference statement on manifestations and management of chronic insomnia in adults, June 13–15, 2005. *Sleep, 28,* 1049–1057.

Newby, J. M., McKinnon, A., Kuyken, W., Gilbody, S., & Dalgleish, T. (2015). Systematic review and meta-analysis of transdiagnostic psychological treatments for anxiety and depressive disorders in adulthood. *Clinical Psychology Review, 40,* 91–110.

Newman, M. (2000). Recommendations for a cost-offset model of psychotherapy allocation using generalized anxiety disorder as an example. *Journal of Consulting and Clinical Psychology, 68*(4), 549–555. doi:10.1037/0022-006X.68.4.549

Newman, M. G., & Fisher, A. J. (2010). Expectancy/credibility change as a mediator of cognitive behavioral therapy for generalized anxiety disorder: Mechanism of action or proxy for symptom change? *International Journal of Cognitive Therapy, 3,* 245–261.

Newman, M. G., & Llera, S. J. (2011). A novel theory of experiential avoidance in generalized anxiety disorder: A review and synthesis of research supporting a contrast avoidance model of worry. *Clinical Psychology Review, 31*(3), 371–382.

Nock, M. K. (2010). Self-injury. *Annual Review of Clinical Psychology, 6,* 339–363.

Nock, M. K., & Favazza, A. (2009). Non-suicidal self-injury: Definition and classification. In M. K. Nock (Ed.), *Understanding nonsuicidal self-injury* (pp. 9–18). Washington, DC: American Psychological Association.

Nock, M. K., & Prinstein, M. J. (2004). A functional approach to the assessment of self-mutilative behavior. *Journal of Consulting and Clinical Psychology, 72*, 885–890.

Nock, M. K., Cha, C. B., & Dour, H. J. (2011). Disorders of impulse control and self-harm. In D. H. Barlow (Ed.), *The Oxford Handbook of Clinical Psychology* (1st ed., pp. 504–529). New York, NY: Oxford University Press.

Nock, M. K., Guilherme, B., Bromet, E., Cha, C., Kessler, R., & Lee, S. (2008). Suicide and suicidal behavior. *Epidemiologic Reviews, 30*, 133–155. doi:10.1093/epirev/mxn002

Nock, M. K., Holmberg, E. B., Photos, V. I., & Michel, B. D. (2007). Self-Injurious Thoughts and Behaviors Interview: Development, reliability, and validity in an adolescent sample. *Psychological Assessment, 19*, 309–317.

Nolen-Hoeksema, S. (1991). Responses to depression and their effects on the duration of depressive episodes. *Journal of Abnormal Psychology, 100*, 569–582.

Nolen-Hoeksema, S. (2000). The role of rumination in depressive disorders and mixed anxiety/depressive symptoms. *Journal of Abnormal Psychology, 109*, 504–511.

Nolen-Hoeksema, S., Larson, J., & Grayson, C. (1999). Explaining the gender difference in depressive symptoms. *Journal of Personality and Social Psychology, 77*, 1061–1072.

Norman, S. B., Cissell, S. H., Means-Christensen, A. J., & Stein, M. B. (2006). Development and validation of an Overall Anxiety Severity and Impairment Scale (OASIS). *Depression and Anxiety, 23*, 245–249. doi:10.1002/da.20182

Norton, G. R., Rockman, G. E., Ediger, J., Pepe, C., Goldberg, S., Cox, B. J., & Asmundson, G. J. G. (1997). Anxiety sensitivity and drug choice in individuals seeking treatment for substance abuse. *Behaviour Research and Therapy, 35*, 859–862.

Norton, P. J., & Barrera, T. L. (2012). Transdiagnostic versus diagnosis-specific CBT for anxiety disorders: A preliminary randomized controlled noninferiority trial. *Depression and Anxiety, 29*(10), 874–882.

Norton, P. J., & Philipp, L. M. (2008). Transdiagnostic approaches to the treatment of anxiety disorders: A quantitative review. *Psychotherapy: Theory, Research, Practice, Training, 45*(2), 214–226. doi:10.1037/0033-3204.45.2.214

Nowakowski, M. E., McFarlane, T., & Cassin, S. (2013). Alexithymia and eating disorders: A critical review of the literature. *Journal of Eating Disorders, 1*, 21. doi:10.1186/2050-2974-1-21

Obsessive Compulsive Cognitions Working Group. (1997). Cognitive assessment of obsessive-compulsive disorder. *Behaviour Research and Therapy, 35*(7), 667–681. http://doi.org/10.1016/S0005-7967(97)00017-X

O'Connor, D. B., O'Connor, R. C., & Marshall, R. (2007). Perfectionism and psychological distress: Evidence of the mediating effects of rumination. *European Journal of Personality, 21*, 429–452.

Odlaug, B. L., Weinhandl, E., Mancebo, M. C., Mortensen, E. L., Eisen, J. L., Rasmussen, S. A., . . ., Grant, J. E. (2014). Excluding the typical patient: Thirty years of pharmacotherapy efficacy trials for obsessive-compulsive disorder. *Annals of Clinical Psychiatry, 26*, 39–46.

Oetting, E. R., & Beauvais, F. (1991). Orthogonal cultural identification theory: The cultural identification of minority adolescents. *International Journal of the Addictions, 25*(5a and 6a), 655–685.

Olfson, M., Marcus, S. C., Tedeschi, M., Wan, G. J. (2006). Continuity of antidepressant treatment for adults with depression in the United States. *American Journal of Psychiatry, 163*, 101–108.

Olfson, M., Mojtabai, R., Sampson, N. A., Hwang, I., Druss, B., Wang, P. S., . . ., Kessler, R. C. (2009). Dropout from outpatient mental health care in the United States. *Psychiatric Services, 60*(7), 898–907. doi:10.1176/appi.ps.60.7.898

Olfson, M., & Pincus, H. A. (1996). Outpatient mental health care in nonhospital settings Distribution of patients across provider groups. *American Journal of Psychiatry, 153*(10), 1353–1356.

Osma, J., Castellano, C., Crespo, E., & García-Palacios, A. (2015). The Unified Protocol for the Transdiagnostic Treatment of Emotional Disorders in group format in a Spanish public mental health setting. *Psicología Conductual, 23*(3), 447.

Otto, M. W., O'Cleirigh, C. M., & Pollack, M. H. (2007). Attending to emotional cues for drug abuse: Bridging the gap between clinic and home behaviors. *Science & Practice Perspectives, 3*(2), 48–55.

Otto, M. W., Simon, N. M., Wisniewski, S. R., Miklowitz, D. J., Kogan, J. N., Relly-Harrington, N. A., . . ., & Pollack, M. H. (2006). Prospective 12-month course of bipolar disorder in out-patients with and without comorbid anxiety disorders. *British Journal of Psychiatry, 189*, 20–25. doi:10.1192/bjp.bp.104.007773

Ozkan, M., & Altindag, A. (2005). Comorbid personality disorders in subjects with panic disorder: do personality disorders increase clinical severity? *Comprehensive Psychiatry, 46*(1), 20–26. doi:10.1016/j.comppsych.2004.07.015

Paquette, V., Levesque, J., Mensour, B., Leroux, J. M., Beaudoin, G., Bourgouin, P., & Beauregard, M. (2003). "Change the mind and you change the brain": Effects of cognitive-behavioral therapy on the neural correlates of spider phobia. *NeuroImage, 18*, 401–409.

Parham, T., White, J., & Ajumi, A. (1999). *The psychology of Blacks: An African-centered perspective.* Upper Saddle River, NJ: Prentice Hall.

Park, A. L., Chorpita, B. F., Regan, J., Weisz, J. R., & Research Network on Youth Mental Health. (2014). Integrity of evidence-based practice: Are providers modifying practice content or practice sequencing? *Administration and Policy in Mental Health and Mental Health Services Research,* 1–11.

Parthasarathy, S., Vasquez, M. M., Halonen, M., Bootzin, R., Quan, S. F., Martinez, F. D., & Guerra, S. (2015). Persistent insomnia is associated with mortality risk. *American Journal of Medicine, 128*, 268–275. e262.

Paulesu, E., Sambugaro, E., Torti, T., Danelli, L., Ferri, F., Scialfa, G., . . ., Sassaroli, S. (2010). Neural correlates of worry in generalized anxiety disorder and in normal controls: A functional MRI study. *Psychological Medicine, 40*, 117–124. doi:10.1017/S0033291709005649

Payne, L., Ellard, K. K., Farchione, T. J., Fairholme, C. P., & Barlow, D. H. (In press). Emotional disorders: A unified protocol. In David H. Barlow (Ed.), *Clinical handbook of psychological disorders: A step-by-step treatment manual* (5th ed.). New York, NY US: The Guilford Press.

Payne, L. A., Tsao, J. C. I., & Zeltzer, L. K. (2014). Unified protocol for youth with chronic pain in pediatric medical settings. In J. T. Ehrenreich-May & B. C. Chu (Eds.), *Transdiagnostic Treatments for Children and Adolescents: Principles and Practice* (pp. 385–401). New York: The Guilford Press.

Persons, J. B. (2005). Empiricism, mechanism, and the practice of cognitive-behavior therapy. *Behavior Therapy, 36*(2), 107–118. doi:10.1016/S0005-7894(05)80059-0

Peterson, M. J., & Benca, R. M. (2006). Sleep in mood disorders. *Psychiatric Clinics of North America, 29,* 1009–1032; abstract, ix.

Peterson, R. A., & Reiss, S. (1993). *Anxiety sensitivity index revised test manual.* Worthington, OH: International Diagnostic Systems Publishing.

Petit, G., Luminet, O., Maurage, F., Tecco, J., Lechantre, S., Ferauge, M., . . . & Timary, P. (2015). Emotion Regulation in Alcohol Dependence. *Alcoholism: Clinical and Experimental Research, 39*(12), 2471–2479. doi:10.1111/acer.12914

Phan, K. L., Fitzgerald, D. A., Nathan, P. J., & Tancer, M. E. (2006). Association between amygdala hyperactivity to harsh faces and severity of social anxiety in generalized social phobia. *Biological Psychiatry, 59,* 424–429. doi:10.1016/j.biopsych.2005.08.012

Phillips, K. A., Stein, D. J., Rauch, S., Hollander, E., Fallon, B. A., Barsky, A., . . ., Leckman, J. (2010). Should an obsessive compulsive spectrum grouping of disorders be included in DSM-V? *Depression and Anxiety, 27*(6), 528–555. http://doi.org/10.1002/da.20705

Phillips, M. L., & Vieta, E. (2007). Identifying functional neuroimaging biomarkers of bipolar disorder: toward DSM-V. *Schizophrenia Bulletin, 33*(4), 893–904. doi:10.1093/schbul/sbm060

Phinney, J. (1992). The Multigroup Ethnic Identity Measure: A new scale for use with adolescents and young adults from diverse groups. *Journal of Adolescent Research, 7,* 156–176.

Pickett, S. M., Lodis, C. S., Parkhill, M. R., & Orcutt, H. K. (2012). Personality and experiential avoidance: A model of anxiety sensitivity. *Personality and Individual Differences, 53,* 246–250. doi:10.1016/j.paid.2012.03.031

Plehn, K., & Peterson, R. A. (2002). Anxiety sensitivity as a predictor of the development of panic symptoms, panic attacks, and panic disorder: A prospective study. *Journal of Anxiety Disorders, 16,* 455–473. doi:10.1016/S0887-6185(02)00129-9

Pope, M., Dudley, R., & Scott, J. (2007), Determinants of social functioning in bipolar disorder. *Bipolar Disorders, 9,* 38–44. doi:10.1111/j.1399-5618.2007.00323.x

Porto, P. R., Oliveira, L., Mari, J., Volchan, E., Figueira, I., & Ventura, P. (2009). Does cognitive behavioral therapy change the brain? A systematic review of neuroimaging in anxiety disorders. *Journal of Neuropsychiatry and Clinical Neurosciences, 21,* 114–125. doi:10.1176/appi.neuropsych.21.2.114

Powers, M. B., Halpern, J. M., Ferenschak, M. P., Gillihan, S. J., Foa, E. B. (2010). A meta-analytic review of prolonged exposure for posttraumatic stress disorder. *Clinical Psychology Review, 30,* 635–641.

Prescott, C. A., Neale, M. C., Corey, L. A., & Kendler, K. S. (1997). Predictors of problem drinking and alcohol dependence in a population-based sample of female twins. *Journal of Studies on Alcohol, 58*(2), 167–181.

Purdon, C. (1999). Thought suppression and psychopathology. *Behaviour Research and Therapy, 37,* 1029–1054. doi:10.1016/S0005-7967(98)00200-9

Rachman, S., & de Silva, P. (1978). Abnormal and normal obsessions. *Behaviour Research and Therapy, 16*(4), 233–248. http://doi.org/10.1016/0005-7967(78)90022-0

Ramsawh, H. J., Ancoli-Israel, S., Sullivan, S. G., Hitchcock, C. A., & Stein, M. B. (2011). Neuroticism mediates the relationship between childhood adversity and adult sleep quality. *Behavioral Sleep Medicine, 9,* 130–143.

Randall, C. L., Thomas, S., & Thevos, A. K. (2001). Concurrent alcoholism and social anxiety disorder: A first step toward developing effective treatments. *Alcoholism: Clinical and Experimental Research, 25*(2), 210–220. doi:10.1111/j.1530-0277.2001.tb02201.x

Rasmussen, M. K., & Pidgeon, A. M. (2011). The direct and indirect benefits of dispositional mindfulness on self-esteem and social anxiety. *Anxiety, Stress, and Coping: An International Journal, 24,* 227–233. doi:10.1080/10615806.2010.515681

Rassin, E., Muris, P., Schmidt, H., & Merkelbach, H. (2000). Relationship between thought action fusion, thought suppression, and obsessive-compulsive symptoms: A structural equation model approach. *Behaviour Research and Therapy, 38,* 889–897. doi:10.1016/S0005-7967(99)00104-7

Rassovsky, Y., Kushner, M. G., Schwarze, N. J., & Wangensteen, O. D. (2000). Psychological and physiological predictors of response to carbon dioxide challenge in individuals with panic disorders. *Journal of Abnormal Psychology, 109,* 616–623. doi:10.1037//0021-843X.109.4.616

Reardon, J. M., & Williams, N. L. (2007). The specificity of cognitive vulnerabilities to emotional disorders: Anxiety sensitivity, looming vulnerability, and explanatory style. *Journal of Anxiety Disorders, 21,* 625–643. doi:10.1016/j.janxdis.2006.09.013

Reas, D. L., Whisenhunt, B. L., Netemeyer, R., & Williamson, D. A. (2002). Development of the body checking questionnaire: A self-report measure of body checking behaviours. *International Journal of Eating Disorders, 31,* 324–333. doi:10.1002/eat.10012

Rector, N. A., Hood, K., Richter, M. A., & Michael Bagby, R. (2002). Obsessive-compulsive disorder and the five-factor model of personality: Distinction and overlap with major depressive disorder. *Behaviour Research and Therapy, 40*(10), 1205–1219. http://doi.org/10.1016/S0005-7967(02)00024-4

Reiss, S. (1991). Expectancy model of fear, anxiety, and panic. *Clinical Psychology Review, 11,* 141–153. doi:10.1016/0272-7358(91)90092-9

Reiss, S., Peterson, R. A., Gursky, D. M., & McNally, R. J. (1986). Anxiety sensitivity, anxiety frequency and the prediction of fearfulness. *Behaviour Research and Therapy, 24,* 1–8.

Resick, P. A., Nishith, P., Weaver, T. L., Astin, M. C., & Feuer, C. A. (2002). A comparison of cognitive processing therapy with prolonged exposure and a writing condition for the treatment of chronic posttraumatic stress disorder in female rape victims. *Journal of Consulting and Clinical Psychology, 70,* 867–879. doi:10.1037/0022-006X.70.4.867

Resick, P. A., Wachen, J. S., Mintz, J., Young-McCaughan, S., Roache, J. D., Borah, A. M., . . ., & Peterson, A. L. (2015). A randomized clinical trial of group cognitive processing therapy compared with group present-centered therapy for PTSD among active duty military personnel. *Journal of consulting and clinical psychology, 83*(6), 1058–1068. doi:10.1037/ ccp0000016

Resick, P. A., Williams, L. F., Suvak, M. K., Monson, C. M., Gradus, J. L. (2012) Long-term outcomes of cognitivebehavioral treatments for posttraumatic stress disorder among female rape survivors. *Journal of Consulting and Clinical Psychology, 80,* 201–210.

Resnicow, K., Soler, R., Braithwait, R. L., Ahluwalia, J. S., Butler, J. (2000). Cultural sensitivity in substance abuse prevention. *Journal of Community Psychology, 28,* 271–290.

Reynolds, C. F., Redline, S., & The DSM-V Sleep-Wake Disorders Workgroup and Advisors. (2010). The DSM-V sleep-wake disorders nosology: An update and an invitation to the sleep community. *Journal of Clinical Sleep Medicine, 6,* 9–10.

Ribeiro, J. D., Bodell, L. P., Hames, J. L., Hagan, C. R., & Joiner, T. E. (2013). An empiri-cally based approach to the assessment and management of suicidal behavior, *Journal of Psychotherapy Integration, 23*, 207–221.

Ribeiro, S. C., Kennedy, S. E., Smith, Y. R., Stohler, C. S., & Zubieta, J. K. (2005). Interface of physical and emotional stress regulation through the endogenous opioid system and mu-opioid receptors. *Progress in Neuro-psychopharmacology and Biological Psychiatry, 29*(8), 1264–1280.

Richards, D. A., & Suckling, R. (2009). Improving access to psychological thera-pies: Phase IV prospective cohort study. *British Journal of Clinical Psychology, 48*(4), 377–396. doi:10.1348/014466509X405178

Riegel, B., Bruenahl, C. A., Ahyai, S., Bingel, U., Fisch, M., & Lowe, B. (2014). Assessing psychological factors, social aspects and psychiatric co-morbidity associated with Chronic Prostatitis/Chronic Pelvic Pain Syndrome (CP/CPPS) in men—a systematic review. *Journal of Psychosomatic Research, 77*(5), 333–350.

Roberts, M. E., Tchanturia, K., & Treasure, J. L. (2010). Exploring the neurocognitive signature of poor set-shifting in anorexia and bulimia nervosa. *Journal of Psychiatric Research, 44*, 964–970. doi:10.1016/j.jpsychires.2010.03.001

Roberts, R. E., Phinney, J. S., Masse, L. C., Chen, Y. R., Roberts, C. R., & Romero, A. (1999). The structure of ethnic identity of young adolescents from diverse ethnocul-tural groups. *Journal of Early Adolescence, 19*(3), 301–322.

Roemer, L., & Orsillo, S.M. (2009). *Mindfulness and acceptance-based behavioral thera-pies in practice.* New York, NY: Guilford Press.

Roemer, L., Salters, K., Raffa, S., & Orsillo, S. M. (2005). Fear and avoidance of internal experiences in GAD: Preliminary tests of a conceptual model. *Cognitive Therapy and Research, 29*, 71–88. doi:10.1007/s10608-005-1650-2

Rosellini, A. J. (2013). *Initial development and validation of a dimensional classifica-tion system for the emotional disorders.* Unpublished doctoral dissertation, Boston University, Boston, MA.

Rosellini, A. J., Boettcher, H., Brown, T. A., & Barlow, D. H. (2015). A transdiagnostic temperament-phenotype profile approach to emotional disorder classification: An update. *Psychopathology Review, 2*, 110–128. doi:10.5127/pr.00

Rosellini, A. J., & Brown, T. A. (2014). Initial interpretation and evaluation of a profile-based classification system for the anxiety and mood disorders: Incremental validity compared to DSM-IV categories. *Psychological Assessment, 26*(4), 1212.

Rosellini, A. J., Lawrence, A., Meyer, J., & Brown, T. A. (2010). The effects of extraverted temperament on agoraphobia in panic disorder. *Journal of Abnormal Psychology, 119*, 420–426. doi:10.1037/a0018614

Ross, H. E., Glaser, F. B., & Germanson, T. (1988). The prevalence of psychiatric disor-ders in patients with alcohol and other drug problems. *Archives of General Psychiatry, 45*(11), 1023–1031.

Rowland, J. E., Hamilton, M. K., Lino, B. J., Ly, P., Denny, K., Hwang, E. J., . . ., Green, M. J. (2013). Cognitive regulation of negative affect in schizophrenia and bipolar disor-der. *Psychiatry Research, 208*(1), 21–28. doi:10.1016/j.psychres.2013.02.021

Roy-Byrne, P. P., Craske, M. G., & Stein, M. B. (2006). Panic disorder. *Lancet, 368*(9540), 1023–1032. doi:http://dx.doi.org/10.1016/S0140-6736(06)69418-X

Rudd, M. D., Bryan, C. J., Wertenberger, E. G., Peterson, A. L., Young-McCaughan, S., Mintz, J., . . . Bruce, T. O. (2015). Brief cognitive behavioral therapy effects on post-treatment suicide attempts in a military sample: Results of a randomized clinical trial with 2-year follow-up. *American Journal of Psychiatry, 172*, 441–449.

Ruscio, A. M., Borkovec, T. D., & Ruscio, J. (2001). A taxometric investigation of the latent structure of worry. *Journal of Abnormal Psychology, 110*(3), 413.

Ruscio, A. M., & Ruscio, J. (2002). The latent structure of analogue depression: Should the Beck Depression Inventory be used to classify groups? *Psychological Assessment, 14*(2), 135.

Ruscio, A. M., Ruscio, J., & Keane, T. M. (2002). The latent structure of posttraumatic stress disorder: A taxometric investigation of reactions to extreme stress. *Journal of Abnormal Psychology, 111*(2), 290.

Sadock, B. J., & Sadock, V. A. (2000). *Kaplan & Sadock's comprehensive textbook of psychiatry, Vols. 1 & 2 (7th ed.).* (B. J. Sadock & V. A. Sadock, Eds.). Philadelphia, PA US: Lippincott Williams & Wilkins Publishers.

Salkovskis, P. M., & Harrison, J. (1984). Abnormal and normal obsessions—A replication. *Behaviour Research and Therapy, 22*(5), 549–552. http://doi.org/10.1016/0005-7967(84)90057-3

Samuels, J., Eaton, W. W., Bienvenu, O. J., 3rd, Brown, C. H., Costa, P. T., Jr, & Nestadt, G. (2002). Prevalence and correlates of personality disorders in a community sample. *The British journal of psychiatry: the journal of mental science, 180*, 536–542.

Samuels, J., Nestadt, G., Bienvenu, O. J., Costa, P. T., Riddle, M. A., Liang, K.-Y., . . ., Cullen, B. A. M. (2000). Personality disorders and normal personality dimensions in obsessive—compulsive disorder. *British Journal of Psychiatry, 177*(5), 457–462. http://doi.org/10.1192/bjp.177.5.457

Sanchez-Craig, M., Annis, H. M., Bronet, A. R., & MacDonald, K. R. (1984). Random assignment to abstinence and controlled drinking: Evaluation of a cognitive-behavioral program for problem drinkers. *Journal of Consulting and Clinical Psychology, 52*(3), 390–403. doi:10.1037/0022-006X.52.3.390

Sarin, S., Abela, J., & Auerbach, R. (2005). Response styles theory of depression: A test of specificity and causal mediation. *Cognition & Emotion, 19*, 751–761. doi:10.1080/02699930441000463

Sauer, S. E., & Baer, R. A. (2009). Responding to negative internal experience: Relationships between acceptance and change-based approaches and psychological adjustment. *Journal of Psychopathology and Behavioral Assessment, 31*, 378–386. doi:10.1007/s10862-009-9127-3

Sauer-Zavala, S., & Barlow, D. H. (2014). The case for borderline personality disorder as an emotional disorder. *Clinical Psychology: Science and Practice, 21*(2), 118–138.

Sauer-Zavala, S. E., Bentley, K. H., & Wilner, J. G. (2015). Transdiagnostic treatment of borderline personality disorder and comorbid disorders: A clinical replication series. *Journal of Personality Disorders, 29*, 179.

Sauer-Zavala, S., Bentley, K. H., & Wilner, J. G. (2016). Transdiagnostic treatment of borderline personality disorder and comorbid disorders: A clinical replication series. *Journal of Personality Disorders, 30*, 35–51.

Sauer-Zavala, S., Boswell, J. F., Gallagher, M. W., Bentley, K. H., Ametaj, A., & Barlow, D. H. (2012). The role of negative affectivity and negative reactivity to emotions in predicting outcomes in the Unified Protocol for the Transdiagnostic Treatment of Emotional Disorders. *Behaviour Research and Therapy, 50*, 551–557. doi:10.1016/j.brat.2012.05.005

Sauer-Zavala, S., Cassiello-Robbins, C., Conklin, L. R., Bullis, J. R., Thompson-Hollands, J., & Kennedy, K. (2017). Isolating the unique effects of the Unified Protocol treatment modules using single case experimental design. *Behavior Modification, 41*(2), 286–307.

Saunders, E. (2013). Sleep quality during euthymia in bipolar disorder: The role of clinical features, personality traits, and stressful life events. *International Journal of Bipolar Disorders, 1*(1), 16.

Scarrabelotti, M. B., Duck, J. M., & Dickerson, M. M. (1995). Individual differences in Obsessive-Compulsive behaviour: The role of the Eysenckian dimensions and appraisals of responsibility. *Personality and Individual Differences, 18*(3), 413–421. http://doi.org/10.1016/0191-8869(94)00122-9

Schmidt, N. B., Keough, M. E., Timpano, K. R., & Richey, J. A. (2008). Anxiety sensitivity profile: Predictive and incremental validity. *Journal of Anxiety Disorders, 22,* 1180–1189. doi:10.1016/j.janxdis.2007.12.003

Schneier, F. R., Foose, T. E., Hasin, D. S., Heimberg, R. G., Liu, S. M., Grant, B. F., & Blanco, C. (2010). Social anxiety disorder and alcohol use disorder co-morbidity in the National Epidemiologic Survey on alcohol and related conditions. *Psychological Medicine, 40*(6), 977–988. doi:10.1017/S0033291709991231

Schnurr, P. P., Lunney, C. A., Bovin, M. J., & Marx, B. P. (2009). Posttraumatic stress disorder and quality of life: Extension of findings to veterans of the wars in Iraq and Afghanistan. *Clinical Psychology Review, 29,* 727–735. doi:10.1016/j.cpr.2009.08.006

Segal, Z. V., Williams, J. M. G., & Teasdale, J. D. (2002). *Mindfulness-based cognitive therapy for depression: A new approach to preventing relapse.* New York, NY: Guilford Press.

Segerstrom, S. C., Tsao, J. C. I., Alden, L. E., & Craske, M. G. (2000). Worry and rumination: Repetitive thought as a concomitant and predictor of negative mood. *Cognitive Therapy and Research, 24,* 671–688. doi:10.1023/A:1005587311498

Selby, E. A., Anestis, M. D., & Joiner, T. E. (2008). Understanding the relationship between emotional and behavioral dysregulation: Emotional cascades. *Behaviour Research and Therapy, 46,* 593–611. doi:10.1016/j.brat.2008.02.002

Selby, E. A., Bender, T. W., Gordon, K. H., Nock, M. K., & Joiner, T. E., Jr. (2012). Non-suicidal self-injury (NSSI) disorder: A preliminary study. *Personality Disorders: Theory, Research, and Treatment, 3*(2), 167.

Selby, E. A., Joiner, T. E., Jr., & Ribeiro, J. D. (2014). Comprehensive theoretical models of suicidal behaviors. In M. K. Nock (Ed.), *The Oxford Handbook of Suicide and Self-Injury* (1st ed., pp. 286–307). New York, NY: Oxford University Press.

Semple, C. J., Dunwoody, L., Sullivan, K., & Kernohan, W. G. (2006). Patients with head and neck cancer prefer individualized cognitive behavioural therapy. *European Journal of Cancer Care (English Language Edition), 15,* 220–227.

Serpell, L., Livingstone, A., Neiderman, M., & Lask, B. (2002). Anorexia nervosa: Obsessive-compulsive disorder, obsessive-compulsive personality disorder, or neither? *Clinical Psychology Review, 22,* 647–669. doi:10.1016/S0272-7358(01)00112-X

Shafran, R., Fairburn, C. G., Robinson, P., & Lask, B. (2004). Body checking and its avoidance in eating disorders. *International Journal of Eating Disorders, 35,* 93–101. doi:10.1002/eat.10228

Shafran, R., & Rachman, S. (2004). Thought-action fusion: A review. *Journal of Behavior Therapy and Experimental Psychiatry, 35*(2), 87–107.

Shahar, B., & Herr, N. R. (2011). Depressive symptoms predict inflexibly high levels of experiential avoidance in response to daily negative affect: A daily diary study. *Behaviour Research and Therapy, 49*, 676–681. doi:10.1016/j.brat.2011.07.006

Shapiro, D. A., Cavanagh, K., & Lomas, H. (2003). Geographic inequity in the availability of cognitive behavioral therapy in England and Wales. *Behavioural and Cognitive Psychotherapy, 31*, 185–192.

Sharp, D. M., Power, K. G., & Swanson, V. (2004). A comparision of the efficacy and acceptability of group versus individual cognitive behaviour therapy in the treatment of panic disorder and agoraphobia in primary care. *Clinical Psychology and Psychotherapy, 11*, 73–82.

Sheeran, T., Brown, E. L., Nassisi, P., & Bruce, M. L. (2004). Does depression predict falls among home health patients? Using a clinical-research partnership to improve the quality of geriatric care. *Home Healthcare Nurse, 22*(6), 384–389.

Sheeran, T., Byers, A. L., & Bruce, M. L. (2010). Depression and increased short-term hospitalization risk among geriatric patients receiving home health care services. *Psychiatric Services, 61*(1), 78–80. doi:10.1097/00004045-200406000-00007

Shear, M. K., Vander Bilt, J., Rucci, P., Endicott, J., Lydiard, B., Otto, M. W., . . . , Frank, D. M. (2001). Reliability and validity of a structured interview guide for the Hamilton Anxiety Rating Scale (SIGH-A). *Depression and Anxiety, 13*(4), 166–178.

Sher, K. J., & Grekin, E. R. (2007). Alcohol and affect regulation. In J. J. Gross & J. J. Gross (Eds.), *Handbook of emotion regulation* (pp. 560–580). New York, NY: Guilford Press.

Shin, L. M., & Liberzon, I. (2010). The neurocircuitry of fear, stress, and anxiety disorders. *Neuropsychopharmacology, 35*, 169–191. doi:10.1038/npp.2009.83

Shin, L. M., Wright, C. I., Cannistraro, P. A., Wedig, M. M., McMullin, K., Martis, B., . . ., Rauch, S. L. (2005). A functional magnetic resonance imaging study of amygdala and medial prefrontal cortex responses to overtly presented fearful faces in posttraumatic stress disorder. *Archives of General Psychiatry, 62*, 273–281. doi:10.1001/archpsyc.62.3.273

Shivarathre, D. G., Howard, N., Krishna, S., Cowan, C., & Platt, S. R. (2014). Psychological factors and personality traits associated with patients in chronic foot and ankle pain. *Foot & Ankle International, 35*(11), 1103–1107.

Shneidman, E. S. (1993). Suicide as psychache. *Journal of Nervous and Mental Disease, 181*, 147–149.

Short, N. A., Allan, N. P., Raines, A. M., & Schmidt, N. B. (2015). The effects of an anxiety sensitivity intervention on insomnia symptoms. *Sleep Medicine, 16*, 152–159.

Simon, N. M., Otto, M. W., Wisniewski, S. R., Fossey, M., Sagduyu, K., Frank, E., . . ., Pollack, M. H. (2004). Anxiety disorder comorbidity in bipolar disorder patients: Data from the first 500 participants in the Systematic Treatment Enhancement Program for Bipolar Disorder (STEP-BD). *American Journal of Psychiatry, 161*, 2222–2229. doi:10.1176/appi.ajp.161.12.2222

Skinner, H. A., & Horn, J. L. (1984). *Alcohol Dependence Scale: Users guide.* Toronto, Canada: Addiction Research Foundation.

Sloan, D. M., Marx, B. P., Bovin, M. J., Feinstein, B. A., & Gallagher, M. W. (2012). Written exposure as an Intervention for PTSD: A randomized clinical trial with motor vehicle accident survivors. *Behaviour Research and Therapy, 50*, 627–635. doi:10.1016/j.brat.2012.07.001

Speisman, R. B., Kumar, A., Rani, A., Foster, T. C., & Omerod, B. K. (2012). Daily exercise improves memory, stimulates hippocampal neurogenesis and modulates immune and neuroimmune cytokines in aging rats. *Brain, Behavior, and Immunity, 28*, 25–43.

Steinglass, J., Albano, A. M., Simpson, H. B., Carpenter, K., Schebendach, J., & Attia, E. (2012). Fear of food as a treatment target: Exposure and response prevention for anorexia nervosa in an open series. *International Journal of Eating Disorders, 45*, 615–621. doi:10.1002/eat.20936.

Steinglass, J., Sysco, R., Glasofer, D., Albano, A. M., Simpson, H. B., & Walsh, B. T. (2011). Rationale for the application of exposure and response prevention to the treatment of anorexia nervosa. *International Journal of Eating Disorders, 44*, 134–141. doi:10.1002/eat.20784.

Steinglass, J. E., Albano, A. M., Simpson, H. B., Wang, Y., Zou, J., Attia, E., & Walsh, B. T. (2014). Confronting fear using exposure and response prevention for anorexia nervosa: A randomized controlled pilot study. *International Journal of Eating Disorders, 47*, 174–180. doi:10.1002/eat.22214

Stepanski, E. J., & Rybarczyk, B. (2006). Emerging research on the treatment and etiology of secondary or comorbid insomnia. *Sleep Medicine Reviews, 10*, 7–18.

Stephenson, M. (2000). Development and validation of the Stephenson Multigroup Acculturation Scale (SMAS). *Psychological Assessment, 12*(1), 77.

Stewart, S. E., Beresin, C., Haddad, S., Stack, D. E., Fama, J., & Jenike, M. (2008). Predictors of family accommodation in obsessive-compulsive disorder. *Annals of Clinical Psychiatry, 20*, 65–70.

Stice, E., Agras, W. S., Telch, C. F., Halmi, K. A., Mitchell, J. E., & Wilson, T. (2001). Subtyping binge eating-disordered women along dieting and negative affect dimensions. *International Journal of Eating Disorders, 30*(1), 11–27 doi:10.1002/eat.1050.

Stiles, W. B., Barkham, M., Mellor-Clark, J., & Connell, J. (2008). Effectiveness of cognitive-behavioural, person-centered, and psychodynamic therapies in UK primary-care routine practice: Replication in a larger sample. *Psychological Medicine, 38*(5), 677–688.

Storch, E. A., Rasmussen, S. A., Price, L. H., Larson, M. J., Murphy, T. K., & Goodman, W. K. (2010). Development and psychometric evaluation of the Yale–Brown Obsessive-Compulsive Scale—Second Edition. *Psychological Assessment, 22*(2), 223–232. http://doi.org/10.1037/a0018492

Straube, T., Mentzel, H. J., & Miltner, W. H. (2006). Neural mechanisms of automatic and direct processing of phobogenic stimuli in specific phobia. *Biological Psychiatry, 59*, 162–170. doi:10.1016/j.biopsych.2005.06.013

Strigo, I. A., Simmons, A. N., Matthews, S. C., Craig, A. D., & Paulus, M. P. (2008). Major depressive disorder is associated with altered functional brain response during anticipation and processing of heat pain. *Archives of General Psychiatry, 65*(11), 1275–1284.

Stringer, D., Marshall, D., Pester, B., Baker, A., Langenecker, S. A., Angers, K., . . ., Ryan, K. A. (2014). Openness predicts cognitive functioning in bipolar disorder. *Journal of Affective Disorders, 168*, 51–57. doi:10.1016/j.jad.2014.06.038

Strupp, H. (1973). The future of research in psychotherapy. In H. Strupp (Ed.), *Psychotherapy: Clinical, research, and theoretical issues* (pp. 733–756). Lanham, MD: Jason Aronson. doi:10.1037/11523-027

Swannell, S. V., Martin, G. E., Page, A., Hasking, P., & St. John, N. J. (2014). Prevalence of nonsuicidal self-injury in nonclinical samples: Systematic review, meta-analysis and meta-regression. *Suicide and Life-Threatening Behavior, 44*(3), 273–303. doi:10.1111/sltb.12070

Swartz, M., Blazer, D., George, L., & Winfield, I. (1990). Estimating the prevalence of borderline personality disorder in the community. *Journal of Personality Disorders, 4*(3), 257–272. doi:10.1521/pedi.1990.4.3.257

Sue, D. W., Gallardo, M. E., & Neville, H. A. (2013). *Case studies in multicultural counseling and therapy.* Hoboken, NJ: John Wiley & Sons.

Sullivan, M. J. L., Rouse, D., Bishop, S., & Johnston, S. (1997). Thought suppression, catastrophizing, and pain. *Cognitive Therapy and Research, 21*, 555–568.

Sunday, S. R., Halmi, K. A., & Einhorn, A. (1995). Yale-Brown-Cornell Eating Disorder Scale: A new scale to assess eating disorder symptomatology. *International Journal of Eating Disorders, 18*(3), 237–245. doi:10.1002/1098-108X(199511)18:3<237:AID-EAT2260180305>3.0.CO;2-1

Suter, P., Suter, W. N., & Johnston, D. (2008). Depression revealed: The need for screening, treatment, and monitoring. *Home Healthcare Nurse, 26*(9), 543–550. doi:10.1097/01.NHH.0000338514.85323.35

Svaldi, J., Griepenstroh, J., Tuschen-Caffier, B., & Ehring, T. (2012). Emotion regulation deficits in eating disorders: A marker of eating pathology or general psychopathology? *Psychiatry Research, 197*, 103–111. doi:10.1016/j.psychres.2011.11.009

Swendsen, J. D., Conway, K. P., Rounsaville, B. J., & Merikangas, K. R. (2002). Are personality traits familial risk factors for substance use disorders?: Results of a controlled family study. *American Journal of Psychiatry, 159*(10), 1760–1766. doi:10.1176/appi.ajp.159.10.1760

Tanji, F., Kakizaki, M., Sugawara, Y., Watanabe, I., Nakaya, N., Minami, Y., Fukao, A., & Tsuji, I. (2014). Personality and suicide risk: The impact of economic crisis in Japan. *Psychological Medicine, 45*(03), 559–573.

Tarrier, N., Taylor, K., & Gooding, P. (2008). Cognitive-behavioral interventions to reduce suicide behavior a systematic review and meta-analysis. *Behavior Modification, 32*(1), 77–108.

Taylor, S. (1999). *Anxiety sensitivity: Theory, research and treatment of the fear of anxiety.* Mahwah, NJ: Erlbaum.

Tchanturia, K., Anderluh, M. B., Morris, R. G., Rabe-Hesketh, S., Collier, D. A., Sanchez, P., & Treasure, J. L. (2004). Cognitive flexibility in anorexia nervosa and bulimia nervosa. *Journal of the International Neuropsychological Society, 10*, 513–520. doi:10.1017/S1355617704104086

Tchanturia, K., Davies, H., Roberts, M., Harrison, A., Nakazato, M., Schmidt, U., . . ., Morris, R. (2012). Poor cognitive flexibility in eating disorders: Examining the evidence using the Wisconsin Card Sorting Task. *PLoS ONE, 7*(1): e28331. doi:10.1371/journal.pone.0028331

Teasdale, J.D., & Barnard, P. J. (1993). *Affect, cognition, and change: Re-modeling depressive thought.* Hillsdale, NJ: Erlbaum.

Teesson, M., Hall, W., Slade, T., Mills, K., Grove, R., Mewton, L., . . ., Haber, P. (2010). Prevalence and correlates of DSM-IV alcohol abuse and dependence in Australia: Findings of the 2007 National Survey of Mental Health and Wellbeing. *Addiction, 105*(12), 2085–2094. doi:10.1111/j.1360-0443.2010.03096.x

Teesson, M., Hodder, T., & Buhrich, N. (2003). Alcohol and other drug use disorders among homeless people in Australia. *Substance Use & Misuse, 38*(3–6), 463–474.

Tegethoff, M., Belardi, A., Stalujanis, E., & Meinlschmidt, G. (2015). Comorbidity of mental disorders and chronic pain: chronology of onset in adolescents of a national representative cohort. *Journal of Pain, 16*(10), 1054–1064.

Tellegen, A. (1985). Structures of mood and personality and their relevance to assessing anxiety, with an emphasis on self-report. In A. H. Tuma & J. D. Maser (Eds.), *Anxiety and the anxiety disorders* (pp. 681–706). Hillsdale, NJ: Erlbaum.

Thielke, S., Vannoy, S., & Unutzer, J. (2007). Integrating mental health and primary care. *Primary Care: Clinics in Office Practice, 34*, 571–592.

Thomas, J., Knowles, R., Tai, S., & Bentall, R. P. (2007). Response styles to depressed mood in bipolar affective disorder. *Journal of Affective Disorders, 100*(1–3), 249–252. doi:10.1016/j.jad.2006.10.017

Thompson-Brenner, H., & Ice, S. (2014). *Integrating behavioral and emotional interventions.* Paper presented at the Annual Renfrew Center Foundation Conference, November, Philadelphia, PA.

Thompson-Hollands, J., Abramovitch, A., Tompson, M. C., & Barlow, D. H. (2015). A randomized clinical trial of a brief family intervention to reduce accommodation in obsessive-compulsive disorder: A preliminary study. *Behavior Therapy, 46*(2), 218–229. http://doi.org/10.1016/j.beth.2014.11.001

Thompson-Hollands, J., Bentley, K. H., Gallagher, M. W., Boswell, J. F., & Barlow, D. H. (2014). Credibility and outcome expectancy in the Unified Protocol: Relationship to outcomes. *Journal of Experimental Psychopathology, 5*, 72–82. doi:10.5127/jep.033712

Thompson-Hollands, J., Edson, A., Tompson, M. C., & Comer, J. S. (2014). Family involvement in the psychological treatment of obsessive–compulsive disorder: A meta-analysis. *Journal of Family Psychology, 28*(3), 287–298. http://doi.org/10.1037/a0036709

Thompson-Hollands, J., Kerns, C. E., Pincus, D. B., & Comer, J. S. (2014). Parental accommodation of child anxiety and related symptoms: Range, impact, and correlates. *Journal of Anxiety Disorders, 28*(8), 765–773. http://doi.org/10.1016/j.janxdis.2014.09.007

Tillfors, M., Furmark, T., Marteinsdottir, I., & Fredrikson, M. (2002). Cerebral blood flow during anticipation of public speaking in social phobia: A PET study. *Biological Psychiatry, 52*, 1113–1119. doi:10.1016/S0006-3223(02)01396-3

Titov, N., Andrews, G., Davies, M., McIntyre, K., Robinson, E., & Solley, K. (2010). Internet treatment for depression: A randomized controlled trial comparing clinician vs. technician assistance. *PLoS ONE, 5*(6), e10939. doi:10.1371/journal.pone.0010939

Titov, N., Dear, B. F., Schwencke, G., Andrews, G., Johnston, L., Craske, M., McEvoy, P. (2011). Transdiagnostic Internet treatment of anxiety and depression: A randomized controlled trial. *Behaviour Research and Therapy, 49*(8), 441–452. doi:10.1016/j.brat.2011.03.007

Tryer, P. (1989). *Classification of neurosis.* Oxford, England: John Wiley and Sons.

Tryon, W. W. (2008). Whatever happened to symptom substitution? *Clinical Psychology Review, 28*(6), 963–968. http://doi.org/10.1016/j.cpr.2008.02.003

Tsao, J. C. I., Lewin, M. R., & Craske, M. G. (1998). The effects of cognitive-behavior therapy for panic disorders on comorbid conditions. *Journal of Anxiety Disorders, 12*, 357–371. doi:10.1016/S0887-6185(98)00020-6

Tsao, J. C. I., Mystkowski, J. L., Zucker, B. G., & Craske, M. G. (2002). Effects of cognitive-behavioral therapy for panic disorder on comorbid conditions: Replication and extension. *Behavior Therapy, 33*(4), 493–509. doi:http://dx.doi.org/10.1016/S0005-7894(02)80013-2

Tsao, J. C. I., Mystkowski, J. L., Zucker, B. G., & Craske, M. G. (2005). Impact of cognitive-behavioral therapy for panic disorder on comorbidity: A controlled investigation. *Behaviour Research and Therapy, 43*(7), 959–970. doi:http://dx.doi.org/10.1016/j.brat.2004.11.013

Tull, M. T., & Roemer, L. (2007). Emotion regulation difficulties associated with the experience of uncued panic attacks: Evidence of experiential avoidance, emotional nonacceptance, and decreased emotional clarity. *Behavior Therapy, 38*, 378–391. doi:10.1016/j.beth.2006.10.006

Turner, B. J., Austin, S. B., & Chapman, A. L. (2014). Treating nonsuicidal self-injury: A systematic review of psychological and pharmacological interventions. *Canadian Journal of Psychiatry, 59*(11), 576–585.

Tuzer, V., Dogan Bulut, S., Bastug, B., Kayalar, G., Göka, E., & Bestepe, E. (2010). Causal attributions and alexithymia in female patients with fibromyalgia or chronic low back pain. *Nordic Journal of Psychiatry, Early Online*, 1–7.

Tyrer, P. J. (1989). *Classification of neurosis.* Chichester, UK: Wiley.

Urosević, S., Abramson, L. Y., Alloy, L. B., Nusslock, R., Harmon-Jones, E., Bender, R., & Hogan, M. E. (2010). Increased rates of events that activate or deactivate the behavioral approach system, but not events related to goal attainment, in bipolar spectrum disorders. *Journal of Abnormal Psychology, 119*(3), 610–615. doi:10.1037/a0019533

U.S. Census Bureau (2011). *Statistical abstract of the United States: 2011.* Retrieved April 4, 2013, from http://www.census.gov/compendia/statab

Van der Gucht, E., Morriss, R., Lancaster, G., Kinderman, P., & Bentall, R. P. (2009). Psychological processes in bipolar affective disorder: Negative cognitive style and reward processing. *British Journal of Psychiatry: The Journal of Mental Science, 194*(2), 146–151. doi:10.1192/bjp.bp.107.047894

Van Dijke, A., Ford, J. D., van der Hart, O., van Son, M., van der Heijden, P., & Buhring, M. (2012). Complex posttraumatic stress disorder in patients with borderline personality disorder and somatoform disorders. *Psychological Trauma: Theory, Research, Practice, and Policy, 4*(2), 162–168. doi:10.1037/a0025732

van Hecke, O., Torrance, N., & Smith, B. H. (2013). Chronic pain epidemiology and its clinical relevance. *British Journal of Anaesthesia, 111*(1), 13–18.

van Middendorp, H., Lumley, M. A., Jacobs, J. W., van Doornen, L. J., Bijlsma, J. W., & Geenen, R. (2008). Emotions and emotional approach and avoidance strategies in fibromyalgia. *Journal of Psychosomatic Research, 64*(2), 159–167.

Van Rheenen, T. E., Murray, G., & Rossell, S. L. (2015). Emotion regulation in bipolar disorder: profile and utility in predicting trait mania and depression propensity. *Psychiatry Research, 225*(3), 425–432. doi:10.1016/j.psychres.2014.12.001

Van Rheenen, T. E., & Rossell, S. (2013). Phenomenological predictors of psychosocial function in bipolar disorder: Is there evidence that social cognitive and emotion regulation abnormalities contribute? *Australian and New Zealand Journal of Psychiatry.* doi:10.1177/0004867413508452

Varela, R. E., Vernberg, E. M., Sanchez-Sosa, J. J., Riveros, A., Mitchell, M., & Mashunkashey, J. (2004). Anxiety reporting and culturally associated interpretation biases and cognitive schemas: A comparison of Mexican, Mexican American, and European American families. *Journal of Clinical Child and Adolescent Psychology, 33*(2), 237–247.

Vignarajah, B., & Links, P. S. (2009). The clinical significance of co-morbid post-traumatic stress disorder and borderline personality disorder: Case study and literature review. *Personality and Mental Health, 3*(3), 217–224. doi:10.1002/pmh.89

Vincent, N., Cox, B., & Clara, I. (2009). Are personality dimensions associated with sleep length in a large nationally representative sample? *Comprehensive Psychiatry, 50,* 158–163.

Vincent, N., & Walker, J. (2001). Anxiety sensitivity: Predictor of sleep-related impairment and medication use in chronic insomnia. *Depression and Anxiety, 14,* 238–243.

Vocks, S., Schulte, D., Busch, M., Gronemeyer, D., Herpertz, S., & Suchan, B. (2011). Changes in neuronal correlates of body image processing by means of cognitive-behavioural body image therapy for eating disorders: A randomized controlled fMRI study. *Psychological Medicine, 41,* 1651–1663. doi:10.1017/S0033291710002382

Waller, G., Ohanian, V., Meyer, C., & Osman, S. (2000). Cognitive content among bulimic women: The role of core beliefs. *International Journal of Eating Disorders, 28,* 235–241. doi:10.1002/1098-108X(200009)28:2<235::AID-EAT15>3.0.CO;2-1

Walsh, J. K. (2004). Clinical and socioeconomic correlates of insomnia. *Journal of Clinical Psychiatry, 65*(Suppl 8), 13–19.

Wang, P. S., Berglund, P., Olfson, M., Pincus, H. A., Wells, K. B., & Kessler, R. C. (2005). Failure and delay in initial treatment contact after first onset of mental disorders in the National Comorbidity Survey Replication. *Archives of General Psychiatry, 62*(6), 603–613. doi:10.1001/archpsyc.62.6.60

Wang, P. S., Lane, M., Olfson, M., Pincus, H. A., Wells, K. B., & Kessler, R. C. (2005). Twelve-month use of mental health services in the United States: Results from the National Comorbidity Survey Replication. *Archives of General Psychiatry, 62*(6), 629–640. doi:10.1001/archpsyc.62.6.629

Watson, D. (2005). Rethinking mood and anxiety disorders: A quantitative hierarchical model for DSM-V. *Journal of Abnormal Psychology, 114,* 522–536. doi:10.1037/0021-843X.114.4.522

Watson, D., & Clark, L. A. (1993). Behavioral disinhibition versus constraint: A dispositional perspective. In D. M. Wegner & J. W. Pennebaker (Eds.), *Handbook of mental control* (pp. 506–527). New York, NY: Prentice Hall.

Watson, D., & Clark, L. A. (1994). *The PANAS-X: Manual for the Positive and Negative Affect Schedule—Expanded Form.* Iowa City, IA: Iowa Research Online.

Watson, D., Clark, L. A., & Tellegen, A. (1988). Development and validation of brief measures of positive and negative affect: the PANAS scales. *Journal of Personality and Social Psychology, 54,* 1063–1070.

Watson, D., & Naragon-Gainey, K. (2014). Personality, emotions, and the emotional disorders. *Clinical Psychological Science, 2,* 422–442. doi:10.1177/2167702614536162.

Watts, B. V., Schnurr, P. P., Mayo, L., Young-Xu, Y., Weeks, W. B., & Friedman, M. J. (2013). Meta-analysis of the efficacy of treatments for posttraumatic stress disorder. *Journal of Clinical Psychiatry,74,* 541–550. doi:10.4088/JCP.12r08225.

Weathers, F. W., Litz, B. T., Herman, D. S., Huska, J. A., & Keane, T. M. (1993). *The PTSD Checklist (PCL): Reliability, validity, and diagnostic utility.* Paper presented at the annual meeting of the International Society for Traumatic Stress Studies, October, San Antonio, TX.

Wedig, M. M., Silverman, M. H., Frankenburg, F. R., Bradford Reich, D., Fitzmaurice, G., & Zanarini, M. C. (2012). Predictors of suicide attempts in patients with borderline personality disorder over 16 years of prospective follow-up. *Psychological Medicine*, *42*, 2395–2404.

Wegner, D. M., Schneider, D. J., Carter, S. R., & White, T. L. (1987). The paradoxical effects of thought suppression. *Journal of Personality and Social Psychology, 53*, 5–13. doi:10.1037//0022-3514.53.1.5

Weiler, M. A., Val, E. R., Gaviria, M., Prasad, R. B., Lahmeyer, H. W., & Rodgers, P. (1988). Panic disorder is borderline personality disorder. *Psychiatric journal of the University of Ottawa: Revue de psychiatrie de l'Université d'Ottawa, 13*(3), 140–143.

Weiss, N., Sullivan, T. P., & Tull, M. (2015). Explicating the role of emotion dysregulation in risky behaviors: A review and synthesis of the literature with directions for future research and clinical practice. *Current Opinion in Psychology, 3*, 22–29.

Weiss, N. H., Tull, M. T., Davis, L. T., Dehon, E. E., Fulton, J. J., & Gratz, K. L. (2012). Examining the association between emotion regulation difficulties and probable post-traumatic stress disorder within a sample of African Americans. *Cognitive Behaviour Therapy, 41*, 5–14. doi:10.1080/16506073.2011.621970

Weisz, J. R., Chorpita, B. F., Palinkas, L. A., Schoenwald, S. K., Miranda, J., Bearman, S. K., …, & Gray, J. (2012). Testing standard and modular designs for psychotherapy treating depression, anxiety, and conduct problems in youth: A randomized effectiveness trial. *Archives of General Psychiatry, 69*(3), 274–282. doi:10.1001/archgenpsychiatry.2011.147

Weisz, J. R., Sandler, I. N., Durlak, J. A., & Anton, B. S. (2005). Promoting and protecting youth mental health through evidence-based prevention and treatment. *American Psychology, 60*(6), 628–648. doi:10.1037/0003-066X.60.6.628

Westra, H., & Dozois, D. A. (2006). Preparing clients for cognitive behavioral therapy: A randomized pilot study of motivational interviewing for anxiety. *Cognitive Therapy and Research, 30*(4), 481–498. doi:10.1007/s10608-006-9016-y

Westra, H., Constantino, M. J., & Antony, M. M. (2015). *Motivational interviewing and cognitive behavioral therapy for severe generalized anxiety: Symptom outcomes.* Paper presented at the annual Society for Psychotherapy Research Conference, June, Philadelphia, PA.

Westra, H. A., Arkowitz, H., & Dozois, D. J. A. (2009). Adding a motivational interviewing pretreatment to cognitive behavioral therapy for generalized anxiety disorder: A preliminary randomized controlled trial. *Journal of Anxiety Disorders, 23*(8), 1106–1117. doi:http://dx.doi.org/10.1016/j.janxdis.2009.07.014

Whitfield, G. (2010). Group cognitive-behavioural therapy for anxiety and depression. *Advances in Psychiatric Treatment, 16*, 219–227.

Wicklow, A., & Espie, C. A. (2000). Intrusive thoughts and their relationship to actigraphic measurement of sleep: Towards a cognitive model of insomnia. *Behaviour Research and Therapy, 38*, 679–693.

Wilamowska, Z. A., Thompson-Hollands, J., Fairholme, C. P., Ellard, K. K., Farchione, T. J., & Barlow, D. H. (2010). Conceptual background, development, and preliminary data from the unified protocol for transdiagnostic treatment of emotional disorders. *Depression and Anxiety, 27*(10), 882–890.

Wildes, J. E., Ringham, R. M., & Marcus, M. D. (2010). Emotion avoidance in patients with anorexia nervosa: Initial test of a functional model. *International Journal of Eating Disorders, 43*, 398–404. doi:10.1002/eat.20730.

Williams, J. B., Kobak, K. A., Bech, P., Engelhardt, N., Evans, K., Lipsitz, J., . . ., Kalali, A. (2008). The GRID-HAMD: standardization of the Hamilton depression rating scale. *International Clinical Psychopharmacology, 23*(3), 120–129.

Williams, K. E., Chambless, D. L., & Ahrens, A. H. (1997). Are emotions frightening? An extension of the fear of fear concept. *Behaviour Research and Therapy, 35*, 239–248.

Williams, P. G., & Moroz, T. L. (2009). Personality vulnerability to stress-related sleep disruption: Pathways to adverse mental and physical health outcomes. *Personality and Individual Differences, 46*, 598–603.

Williams, A. C., Eccleston, C., & Morley, S. (2012). Psychological therapies for the management of chronic pain (excluding headache) in adults. *Cochrane Database of Systematic Reviews, 11*, CD007407.

Williamson, A., & Hoggart, B. (2005). Pain: a review of three commonly used pain rating scales. *Journal of Clinical Nursing, 14*(7), 798–804.

Wilner, J. G., Vranceanu, A. M., & Blashill, A. J. (2014). Neuroticism prospectively predicts pain among adolescents: results from a nationally representative sample. *Journal of Psychosomatic Research, 77*(6), 474–476.

Wolkenstein, L., Zwick, J. C., Hautzinger, M., & Joormann, J. (2014). Cognitive emotion regulation in euthymic bipolar disorder. *Journal of Affective Disorders, 160*, 92–97. doi:10.1016/j.jad.2013.12.022

Wood, P. S., & Mallinckrodt, B. (1990). Culturally sensitive assertiveness training for ethnic minority clients. *Professional Psychology: Research and Practice, 21*, 5–11.

World Health Organization. (2012). *Public health action for the prevention of suicide: A framework*. Geneva, Switzerland: WHO Press.

Wu, K. D., Clark, L. A., & Watson, D. (2006). Relations between obsessive-compulsive disorder and personality: Beyond Axis I–Axis II comorbidity. *Journal of Anxiety Disorders, 20*(6), 695–717. http://doi.org/10.1016/j.janxdis.2005.11.001

Wupperman, P., Neumann, C., & Axelrod, S. (2008). Do deficits in mindfulness underlie borderline personality disorder features and core difficulties? *Journal of Personality Disorders, 22*, 466–482.

Wupperman, P., Neumann, C., Whitman, J., & Axelrod, S. (2009). The role of mindfulness in borderline personality disorder features. *Journal of Nervous and Mental Disease, 197*, 766–771.

Yadollahi, P., Khalaginia, Z., Vedadhir, A., Ariashekouh, A., Taghizadeh, Z., & Khormaei, F. (2014). The study of predicting role of personality traits in the perception of labor pain. *Iranian Journal of Nursing and Midwifery Research, 19*(7 Suppl 1), S97–S102.

Young, R. C., Biggs, J. T., Ziegler, V. E., & Meyer, D. A. (1978). A rating scale for mania: Reliability, validity and sensitivity. *British Journal of Psychiatry, 133*(5), 429–435.

Young, J. E., Klosko, J. S., & Weishaar, M. E. (2003). *Schema therapy: A practitioner's guide*. New York: Guilford Press.

Yunus, M. B. (2012). The prevalence of fibromyalgia in other chronic pain conditions. Pain *Research and Treatment, 2012*, 584573.

Zanarini, M. (2003). Zanarini Rating Scale for Borderline Personality Disorder (ZAN-BPD): A continuous measure of DSM-IV borderline psychopathology. *Journal of Personality Disorders, 17*, 233–242.

Zanarini, M. C., Frankenburg, F. R., Chauncey, D. L., & Gunderson, J. G. (1987). The Diagnostic Interview for Personality Disorders: Interrater and test-retest reliability. *Comprehensive Psychiatry, 28*(6), 467–480. doi:10.1016/0010-440X(87)90012-5

Zanarini, M. C., Frankenburg, F. R., Dubo, E. D., Sickel, A. E., Trikha, A., Levin, A., & Reynolds, V. (1998). Axis II comorbidity of borderline personality disorder. *Comprehensive Psychiatry, 39*(5), 296–302.

Zanarini, M., Frankenberg, F., Reich, D., Silk, K., Judson, J., & McSweeney, L. (2007). The subsyndromal phenomenology of borderline personality disorder: A 10 year follow-up study. *American Journal of Psychiatry, 164*, 929–935. doi:10.1176/appi.ajp.164.6.929

Zayfert, C., & DeViva, J. C. (2004). Residual insomnia following cognitive behavioral therapy for PTSD. *Journal of Traumatic Stress, 17*, 69–73.

Zimmerman, M., & Mattia, J. I. (1999). Axis I diagnostic comorbidity and borderline personality disorder. *Comprehensive Psychiatry, 40*(4), 245–252.

Zucker, N. L., Merwin, R. M., Bulik, C.M., Moskovich, A., Wildes, J.E., & Groh, J. (2013). Subjective experience of sensation in anorexia nervosa. *Behaviour Research and Therapy, 51*, 256–265. doi:10.1016/j.brat.2013.01.010

Page numbers followed by *f* indicate figures; page numbers followed by *t* indicate tables; page numbers followed by *b* indicate boxes.

Unified Protocol for Transdiagnostic Treatment of Emotional Disorders: Client Workbook (Barlow et al.). *See* UP Client Workbook

Unified Protocol for Transdiagnostic Treatment of Emotional Disorders: Therapist Guide (Barlow et al.). *See* Therapist Guide to the UP

UP (Unified Protocol for Transdiagnostic Treatment of Emotional Disorders), ix. *See also specific topics*
  assessment and case conceptualization using, 22–24, 25t–28t, 26, 28–29, 30b
    case example of conceptualization with UP, 36–37
  certification programs, 297–298
  development, 9–16
  early results and current clinical trial, 14–15
  future directions, 291–92, 301
    dismantling, 292–96
    dissemination, 296–301
  Module 1: Setting Goals and Maintaining Motivation, 10, 41
    case material, 41–43, 92–93, 132–33, 219–20, 235–36
  Module 2: Understanding Emotions, 10–11
    case material, 93–97, 134–36, 220–21, 237–39
  Module 3: Mindful Emotion Awareness, 11–12, 221–22

    case material, 97, 99, 137–39, 221–22, 239–40
  Module 4: Cognitive Flexibility, 12
    case material, 99–101, 139–41, 222–223, 240–41
  Module 5: Countering Emotional Behaviors, 12–13
    case material, 102–4, 141–42, 225–26, 244
  Module 6: Understanding and Confronting Physical Sensations, 13–14. *See also* interoceptive exposure
    case material, 104–5, 142–43, 225
  Module 7: Emotion Exposures, 14.
    case material, 105–8, 143–46, 225–27, 245–48
  Module 8: Recognizing Accomplishments and Looking to the Future, 14. *See also* relapse prevention
    case material, 146–47, 227, 248–49
  origins, 1
  suggested session lengths for each module, 10b
UP Client Workbook (Barlow et al.), 222, 256, 274, 277, 277f, 297

Visiting Nurses Association of Boston (VNA-B), 298–299

worry, 46–47

Printed in the USA
CPSIA information can be obtained
at www.ICGtesting.com
LVHW051233181123
763968LV00002B/4